Belfast Studies in Language, Culture and Politics

General Editors
John M. Kirk and Dónall P. Ó Baoill

1: *Language and Politics: Northern Ireland, the Republic of Ireland, and Scotland*
published 2000 ISBN 0 85389 791 3

2: *Language Links: the Languages of Scotland and Ireland*
published 2001 ISBN 0 85389 795 6

Other volumes in preparation

www.bslcp.com

Linguistic Politics
Language Policies for Northern Ireland, the Republic of Ireland, and Scotland

Edited by

John M. Kirk and Dónall P. Ó Baoill

Cló Ollscoil na Banríona
Belfast 2001

First published in 2001
Cló Ollscoil na Banríona
Queen's University Belfast
Belfast, BT7 1NN

Belfast Studies in Language, Culture and Politics 3
www.bslcp.com

This book has received support from the Cultural Diversity Programme of the
Community Relations Council, which aims to encourage acceptance and
understanding of cultural diversity.

British Library Cataloguing-in-Publication Data
A catalogue record for this book is available from the British Library.

ISBN 0 85389 815 4

Typeset by John Kirk in Times New Roman 10

Printed by The Universities Press (Belfast) Ltd., Castlereagh.

The papers in this volume were presented at the
Language and Politics Symposium
23-25 August 2001
Queen's University Belfast
An event of the AHRB Research Centre for Irish and Scottish Studies

---

Note on the cover illustration

The picture is one of a set of 12 contemporary illustrations in Ulster in the 1570s published in John Derricke's *The Image of Ireland* in 1581. This book depicts Irish society when Ireland was rebelling against English rule in the sixteenth century, and when Henry VIII and Elizabeth I were trying to destroy the strong cultural unity of Gaelic Ireland. In the situation depicted, the war-band were probably Highlanders or Hebrideans since the Gaelic lords of Ireland employed professional soldiers (*ceatharnaich* or *gallóglaich)* from Scotland.

CONTENTS

viii

CONTRIBUTORS

Mary Delargy was, until Autumn 2001, an Assistant Librarian at the Linen Hall Library, Belfast, where she directed the *Languages of Ulster Project*. She is now a Research Fellow at the Institute of Ulster-Scots Studies, Magee College, (London)Derry.

Robert Dunbar is a Lecturer in Law at the University of Glasgow who specialises in the rights of minorities. A Canadian of Scottish Gaelic descent, he is a fluent Gaelic speaker and is a prominent Gaelic-language activist. He is currently writing a state-of-the-art article on Scottish Gaelic for a new book on all six Celtic Languages.

Andy Eagle is a Web Programmer in Bielefeld, where he spends much of his leisure time researching and writing about Scots and translating. His work is available on his website: www.scots-online.org. His family comes from St. Andrews but now live in Arbroath. He was educated at Queen Victoria School, Dunblane and Napier Polytechnic, Edinburgh. He also spent some time at the Fachhochschule Bielefeld.

Gavin Falconer is an Unner-Editor (*Screivit Accoont*) at the Northern Ireland Assembly, with responsibility for Scots, and a free-lance translator. He spends much of his leisure time researching and writing on Scots. A native of Milngavie, he studied Germanic and Celtic languages at the Universities of Liverpool, Freiburg and Queen's University Belfast.

Dr. Andreas Fischer is Professor of English Linguistics and Medieval Studies at the University of Zürich. He was born and brought up in Basel. His publications include *Dialects in the South-West of England* (1976), *The History and the Dialects of English* (1989) and *An Index to Dialect Maps of Great Britain* (1991). He is currently a General Editor of the English-German *Studienausgabe* of Shakespeare's plays.

Dr. Manfred Görlach is Professor of English Linguistics and Medieval Studies at the University of Cologne. His latest books include *Eighteenth-century English* (Heidelberg: Winter, 2000) and *A Dictionary of European Anglicisms* (Oxford: OUP, 2001). *English in Europe* and *A Textual History of Scots* are forthcoming.

Dr. Dauvit Horsbroch is a Research Fellow at the Institute for Irish and Scottish Studies at the University of Aberdeen and a prominent Scots-language (academic-) activist. With Steve Murdoch, he has authored two Aiberdeen

Univairsitie Scots Leid Quorum discussion documents entitled *Daena Haud yer Wheisht, Haud Yer Ain!* (1996) and *Kennin yer Earse fae yer Alba: The Scottish Office, the Gaelic Lobby and the Scots Language* (1998), produced in Scots and in English.

Dr. John M. Kirk is a Lecturer in English at Queen's University Belfast. His recent edited books include *Corpora Galore: Analyses and Techniques in Describing English* (Amsterdam: Rodopi, 2000), *Language and Politics* (Belfast: Cló Ollscoil na Banríona, 2000), *Language Links* (Belfast: Cló Ollscoil na Banríona, 2001), and *Travellers and their Language* (Belfast: Institute of Irish Studies, forthcoming).

The Lord Laird of Artigarvan represents the Ulster Unionist Party in the House of Lords, where he sits as a Peer on the Cross Benches. As a Public Relations professional, he advises David Trimble, First Minister of the Northern Ireland Assembly. He is Chair of the *Tha Boord o Ulstèr-Scotch*.

Dr. Caroline Macafee is a former Reader in English at the University of Aberdeen. Her prolific output has addressed most issues to do with Scots, past, present and future. She is Editor of *A Concise Ulster Dictionary* and the author of *Varieties of English Around the World: Glasgow* (1983), *Traditional Dialect in the Modern World* (1994), several chapters in *The Edinburgh History of the Scots Language* (1997) and in *The Edinburgh Companion to the Scots Language* (forthcoming), and the Introduction to the *Dictionary of the Older Scottish Tongue* (to appear upon the dictionary's completion).

Brendán Mac Cormaic is a member of the Executive of *Gaelscoileanna* and the Republic of Ireland's Council for Irish-medium Education.

Dr. Kenneth MacKinnon is Visiting Professor and Emeritus Reader in the Sociology of Language at the University of Hertfordshire, Honorary Fellow in Celtic at the University of Edinburgh, and an Associate Lecturer in Social Sciences, Education and Language Studies of the Open University. He is also currently an appointed member of the Ministerial Advisory Group on Gaelic (MAGOG), for language planning and development.

Dr. Kevin McCafferty is a Research Fellow at the University of Tromsø, where he has lived for the past ten years. He was born and brought up in (London)Derry. His study of (London)Derry English entitled *Ethnicity and Language Change* was published in 2001 by John Benjamins, Amsterdam. He has recently completed a state-of-the-art article on Northern Ireland English for a new volume of studies entitled *Language in the British Isles*.

Dr. Gordon McCoy is a Development Officer with the ULTACH Trust and a member of the Board of *Foras na Gaeilge*. His edited book *Aithne na nGael / Gaelic Identities* was published in 2000 by the Institute of Irish Studies.

Irene McGugan is an MSP for North-East Scotland. She is an SNP spokesperson for Children and Education and Convenor of the *Cross-Pairtie Group i the Scots Pairliament on the Scots Leid*. She was born in Angus and by profession is a social worker specialising in child care, in which she graduated from the University of Dundee.

Dr. Dónall P. Ó Baoill is Professor of Irish at Queen's University Belfast. His recent edited books include *TEANGA 19* (IRAAL, Dublin 2000*), Integrating Theory and Practice in LSP and LAP* (ALC & IRAAL, Dublin 2000), *Language and Politics* (Belfast: Cló Ollscoil na Banríona, 2000), *Language Links* (Belfast: Cló Ollscoil na Banríona, 2001) and *Travellers and their Language* (Belfast: Institute of Irish Studies, forthcoming). He is also co-author of *The Irish Deaf Community* Volume 2*, The Structure of Irish Sign Language* (ITÉ, Dublin 2000)

Seán Ó Cofaigh is an Under-Secretary at the Department of Arts, Heritage, Gaeltacht and the Islands.

Bertie Ó hAinmhire is Secretary of the *Coimisiún na Gaeltachta* and has been seconded from the Department of Arts, Heritage, Gaeltacht and the Islands. Previously, he had served at the Department of Foreign Affairs.

Dónall Ó Riagáin is Special Adviser to the European Bureau for Lesser Used Languages and formerly served both as President and Secretary General of that organisation. He also works as an independent consultant.

Ian J. Parsley is Chairman of *Ultonia Solutions*, a professional language consultancy firm, with its own website at www.ultonia.co.uk, and a Director of *GCC Stormont Strategy*, a lobbying and PR company. He runs a website on Ulster Scots: www.geocities.com/parsleyij/ullans.html including the electronic discussion list *ullans-l*. A native of Groomsport, he was educated largely in England and studied Germanic Languages at the University of Newcastle-upon-Tyne.

Stephen Peover is an Under-Secretary at the Department of Education, Northern Ireland with responsibility for Irish-medium education.

Dr. Edward Rooney is an Under-Secretary at the Department of Culture, Arts and Leisure, with responsibility for implementing language policy through the Department's Linguistic Diversity Unit.

Michael Russell is an MSP for South Scotland. He is Shadow Minister for Children and Education, a member of the Parliament's Education, Culture and Sport Committee, SNP Spokesperson on Gaelic, and Vice-Convenor of the *Buidheann Eadar-Phàrtaidh Gàidhlig ann am Pàrlamaid na h-Alba*. Born in Kent, he was educated in Scotland and graduated in Scottish History and Scottish Literature from the University of Edinburgh. By profession, he is a film and television director.

ACKNOWLEDGEMENTS

The papers in this volume were originally presented at the Second Symposium on Language and Politics, which we organised at Queen's University Belfast from 23-25 August 2001. We are most grateful to Helen Ó Murchú for her support and advice when we were planning the symposium. We are also grateful for financial support to *Foras na Gaeilge* and *Tha Boord o Ulstèr-Scotch*. For all his efficient and good-humoured assistance during the Symposium, we are indebted to Nic Dunlop.

The event was the natural successor to a similar one-day symposium which we organised on 12 August 2000. At the same time, the present Symposium had become the first of a series of three annual symposia which form part of a research project within the AHRB Research Centre for Irish and Scottish Studies. This project, which began on 1 January 2001, is led by the University of Aberdeen, with Queen's University Belfast and Trinity College Dublin as partners. We wish to acknowledge the encouragement and support which we have received from the Research Centre's Director, Professor Tom Devine, and from the Queen's Representative on its Management Board, Professor Edna Longley.

These symposia are organised by us on behalf of the Forum for Research on the Languages of Scotland and Ulster. We wish to acknowledge the encouragement and support which we have received from the Forum's committee and, in particular, from its Chair, Derrick McClure. It was at the Forum's Annual Conference, held in Edinburgh on 8 September 2001 under the title of *Literary Scots 1975-2000*, that Dauvit Horsbroch presented his paper 'A Hairst for a Bit Screive: Writin Historie in Scots'. We are delighted to be able to include it among the Scots papers in this volume. On that occasion, Irene McGugan also presented her paper in this volume under the title 'New Opportunities for the Language'.

In preparing this volume, we are grateful for the general institutional help which we have received from the School of English and, in particular, from the Head of School, Ellen Douglas-Cowie. For assistance with maps and scanning, we are grateful to Anniken Telnes Iversen and John Devlin. For assistance with the cover illustration, we are grateful to Queen's Audio-Visual Services, Chrisella Ross of *Gaidheil Alba*, Kay Muhr and Brian Lambkin. And for assistance with proof-reading, we are grateful to Patricia Lynch.

John M. Kirk and Dónall P. Ó Baoill
Belfast, December 2001

Introduction:
Linguistic Politics in the Gaeltacht and the Scotstacht[1]

John M. Kirk and Dónall P. Ó Baoill[2]

Setting the Context

For the two symposia on *Language and Politics* which we have organised in August 2000 and in August 2001, of which this is the second volume of edited proceedings,[3] the starting-point was the language provision in the Belfast / Good Friday Agreement and the subsequent legislation. In the year 2000-2001, such legislation includes the UK government's ratification of the *European Charter on Regional or Minority Languages* on 27 March 2001, for implementation from 1 July 2001, and Republic of Ireland's launch of a *Language Equality Bill*. Other related documents generated within Northern Ireland include the *Corporate Plan* or *Heich Ploy* of the *Tha Boord o Ulstèr-Scotch*, and the language provision in the proposed Bill of Rights.[4] Language policy legislation and its likely implementation and impact in practice this lies at the centre of this volume of papers.[5]

A second stimulus arose from the fact that we are dealing with part of an archipelago where there are different jurisdictions or polities: Northern Ireland, the Republic of Ireland, and Scotland. European legislation, such as the Charter, should apply to the entire archipelago, but it does not, because of the separate nation-states involved: the United Kingdom and the Irish Republic. Within the UK, not all legislation applies equally to all territories, not least because of the new devolved

---

[1] The *Scotstacht*, by analogy with the *Gaeltacht*, is a label which we have come to use to refer to the areas in which Scots is to be found in Scotland, Northern Ireland, and the Republic of Ireland.
[2] We wish to thank Gavin Falconer, Colin Neilands and Ian Parsley for discussion and for commenting on earlier drafts.
[3] The first volume of proceedings appeared as John M. Kirk and Dónall P. Ó Baoill (eds.) *Language and Politics: Northern Ireland, the Republic of Ireland, and Scotland* (Belfast: Cló Ollscoil na Banríona, 2000) Belfast Studies in Language, Culture and Politics 1, to be referred to in footnotes below as *Language and Politics*
[4] A version of the language provision in the proposed Bill of Rights appeared as Tom Hadden, 'Should a Bill of Rights for Northern Ireland Protect Language Rights?' in *Language and Politics* 111-120.
[5] We regret that Brice Dickson and Fionnuala Ni Aoláin, who each presented a paper on language rights in the separate Bill of Rights in Northern Ireland and in the Republic of Ireland respectively, were unable to contribute to the present volume.

administrations in Scotland and in Northern Ireland. We had come to realise that separate language policies, heavily informed by European thinking, were being pursued at national as well as devolved administrative levels, and that these policies were evolving at rather different speeds and with rather different scopes and emphases in practice, and that the time had come for all the issues involved to be addressed collectively.

Our third stimulus was the languages themselves. Irish Gaelic and Scottish Gaelic have traditionally formed the single indivisible continuum of the *Gaeltacht,* and yet the status of each language in its respective jurisdiction and speaker-attitudes towards the language are nowadays quite different, with the not unsurprising result that separate policies are being pursued. Scots – whether as a dialect, language, or tongue – also forms an indivisible continuum – a *Scotstachd* or *Scotstacht,* in effect – to be found in all three jurisdictions: Scotland, Northern Ireland and the Irish Republic. In the article of ratification signed by the UK government, Scots whether in Scotland or Northern Ireland is rightly treated as a single whole (as all academic contributors in this volume would agree).

Whatever the reality of these languages per se, their status and value is being reappraised by the new legislation emanating from Northern Ireland because it comes with an inescapable equality agenda. Political activists thus urge that Scots should be treated with equality of recognition and of funding and with the same rights as Irish, as equality and rights belong to speakers/citizens, regardless of the linguistic status or weight of comparison between the two languages. Some progress towards such goals has already been made by the work of *Tha Boord o Ulstèr-Scotch,* as shown by **Lord Laird** in his paper, although there has been less progress, especially by government, in the Republic despite the *Boord*'s all-Ireland remit.

In Scotland, neither material nor legal equality between Scots and Gaelic has ever been a plank of language activism. Separate developments in each jurisdiction are also true of the Gaeltacht: activists urge that both Scottish Gaelic and Irish need secure or protected status rather than legislated status in their home jurisdictions (and that despite the status of Irish in the Republic of Ireland as the first official national language!), but each jurisdiction is pursuing things differently, as shown, on the one hand, by the papers by Ó hAinmhire and Mac Cormaic on the Irish Gaeltacht and all-Irish education and, on the other, and those by Dunbar and MacKinnon on Scottish Gaelic. At the same time, the erosion of Irish in the South, which provides the motivation for securing its status, is not mirrored by the seemingly relentless expansion and growth in the use of the language in West Belfast and the BreacGhaeltacht. The *European Charter for Regional or Minority Languages,* now ratified by the UK Government, differs with respect to Irish in Northern Ireland and Gaelic in Scotland, as a comparison of the papers just mentioned will show. Although the promotion of Scots might not be dissimilar for Scotland and Northern Ireland, the

Republic's failure to sign the Charter denies to speakers of Scots those benefits of recognition and rights they have already acquired – at least in theory - in the UK.[6]

Aims and Objectives

The Belfast / Good Friday Agreement and the establishment of a North/South Language Implementation Body (*An Bord Teanga / Tha Boord o Leid*),[7] and also of an East-West Council of the Isles, which is without precedent, irrevocably came to interfuse and entwine the two minority traditions in Northern Ireland. It also associated with them speakers of the province's lesser-used (or so-called ethnic minority) languages and people who sign or use braille, in all of whom we are interested. After last year's broad-ranging inclusivity,[8] we decided to focus this year very sharply on the Scots and Gaelic agendas. Our aim in publishing edited versions of the papers is to deepen understanding on the various complex, interwoven and inter-connected strands of language policy argumentation, to generate a basis for fresh review, comparisons and insights both *within* each language group as well as *between* them, and to provide a reflective and critical synthesis. In so doing, our objective is also to provide (so far as we can) an up-dated record of legislative and institutional developments in the three jurisdictions between August 2000 and August 2001.[9]

Politicians

The organisation of this volume has a certain rationale. We let the politicians speak first. **Michael Russell**, SNP Spokesperson on Gaelic, and a Shadow Minister in the Scottish Parliament, throws his full shadow-ministerial weight behind the campaign for secure status for Gaelic in Scotland by announcing his intention to introduce into the Scottish Parliament a Secure Status for Gaelic Bill. **Irene**

---

[6] This is an issue which is regularly raised by Lord Laird, for instance, in the correspondence columns of *The Irish Times* e.g. 16 August 2001.

[7] For critical views, see Helen Ó Murchu, 'Language, Discrimination and the Good Friday Agreement: The Case of Irish', in *Language and Politics* 81-88, and Gordon McCoy (in this volume).

[8] *Language and Politics* includes papers on speakers of Chinese by Anna Man-Wah Watson, speakers of ethnic minority languages by Nadette Foley, the language of gays by P.A. MagLochlainn, and people who sign by Bob McCullough.

[9] To this end, we are delighted that we are able include the contributions by key statutory officials who have government-institutional responsibility for implementing these new language policies: Edward Rooney and Stephen Peover for Northern Ireland, Seán Ó Cofaigh, Bertie Ó hAinmhire, and Brendán Mac Cormaic for the Republic of Ireland. We regret that their counterparts in the Scottish Executive had to decline our invitation.

McGugan, Chair of the *Cross-Pairtie group i the Scots Pairliament on the Scots Leid* stresses the importance of taking *political* action for Scots in Scotland. **Lord Laird of Artigarvan**, Chair of *Tha Boord o Ulstèr-Scotch*, outlines the Agency's language policy in broad-brush terms not dissimilar to those already presented in the Agency's *Heich Ploy* ('Corporate Plan').

Language Policy and Northern Ireland

Much of the stimulation for current language policy has arisen from the underlying philosophy of the *European Charter for Regional or Minority Languages*[10] which, although unifying in intention, tolerates and celebrates diversity especially in implementation. No-one is better qualified at introducing the European Charter than **Dónall Ó Riagáin**.[11] In its ratification of the Charter, the UK Government made known the specific provisions in Part III as well as the general provisions in Part II, in respect of which it would undertake 'resolute action'. In his paper, Ó Riagáin provides an edited version of Parts II and III in a way which highlights (*in italics*) those provisions which, in Ó Riagáin's view, most apply to Irish in Northern Ireland. Excerpts of the Charter's text are reproduced not only because the Charter is much referred to, although less often quoted, but because, according to Ó Riagáin, its ratification *will* 'necessitate a dramatic shift in public perception of linguistic diversity in Northern Ireland'. Ó Riagáin urges Irish-language activists to review the provisions carefully and to inform the trienniel expert review process in 2005 of any further provisions which would be of benefit but are currently still missing; at the same time, he urges Scots activists to pursue Part III ratification with respect to Scots. This challenge is immediately taken up in several of the Scots papers – especially by **Dauvit Horsbroch**, in his detailed *Pirlicue*: 'Whit Scots Wants Fae Govrenment'.

Edward Rooney gives a personal overall view of three specific areas relating to the successful implementation of language policy in Northern Ireland, the setting of policy, progress thus far in the implementation of that policy and the issues which impact on the extent and speed of application of these policies. His paper is set against the background of the commitments given in the Belfast / Good Friday Agreement, *The European Charter for Regional or Minority Languages,* and to Section 75 of the Northern Ireland equality legislation, all of which have specific relevance for ethnic minorities and the deaf and braille communities. Rooney finds

---

[10] The *European Charter for Regional or Minority Languages* is available as Document ETS148 from the Council of Europe website at http://conventions.coe.int/Treaty/en/Reports/Html/148.htm. The Charter has been translated into Irish and is available from the editors upon request.
[11] Cf. Dónall Ó Riagáin, 'Language Rights as Human Rights in Europe and in Northern Ireland', in *Language and Politics* 65-73.

that, as a result of the setting up of *An Foras Teanga / Tha Boord o Leid*, language policy implementation is progressing significantly through the development of an action plan and the provision of guidance and support services, including translation services, to help implement the recommendations relating to sections of the *European Charter for Regional or Minority Languages*. A tv and film pilot scheme has been initiated, which will include an extensive training dimension and support has been forthcoming for a range of research projects in Irish and Ulster Scots. He outlines his own *modus operandi* in relation to successful implementation of the new 'linguistic' policy: clarity of purpose, shared goals, clear strategies, evidence of success, and promoting attainable and realistic targets. While this may be the fastest-growing policy area across Government, it would be unrealistic to expect this rapid scale of growth to be maintained. The slow pace of implementation has created a certain amount of frustration. Building on the positive developments and setting firm foundations are key elements for the success of language policy in the future.

Whatever comes to happen, there will always be a need for public education about the outcomes and benefits. First among such initiatives is the *Linguistic Diversity Education Project*, one part of the multi-faceted *Languages of Ulster Project*, which originated in the Linen Hall Library, Belfast and toured from January 2000 until October 2001. The exhibition celebrated standard English, sign, braille, 'lesser-used' languages, such as Chinese and Urdu, as well as Irish and Scots, and is described by **Mary Delargy,** its chief organiser.

European Comparisons

There then follow three articles containing four case studies of the most common comparators with Scots: Frisian, Low German, Norwegian, and Swiss German.

Comparisons of Scots with **Frisian** date back a long time. Sir William Craigie, the pioneer historical lexicographer, reportedly admired the Frisian's language loyalty over that of the Scots whom he blamed for acquiescing in the demise of their own language. Despite this, comparisons have been drawn between Scots and Frisians as two West Germanic languages, as two former medieval 'nation-state' languages, as two languages overshadowed by the language of dominating neighbours, as two languages now reduced to largely spoken forms and functions resulting in precarious diglossia or variable stylistic merger, and with limited written uses, and as two languages revivable through support and nurturing and education. North Frisian and East Frisian in present-day Germany have virtually died out; the current focus is on the speakers of West Frisian (*Frysk*) in the Netherlands, where, as **Manfred Görlach** acknowledges, legislative measures have led constructively to its growing revitalisation as a language of education, the courts, the churches, the government and in administration as well as of its traditional role as a vehicle of literary expression. Frisian is now the second official language of the Netherlands and is an official minority language within the EU. To these ends, Görlach recognises that there has had to be standardisation of the language, not dissimilar to that being experimented with Scots, but wonders which model is likely to be successful. At the same time, West Frisian is being constantly Dutchified and abandoned, even in the home, under late-twentieth-century social and market forces. The comparison between (West-) Frisian and Scots remains justified.

For Görlach[12] and also, before him, Hans Meier and Dietrich Strauss,[13] *the comparison for Scots is with **Low German** (Niederdeutsch, but which is also known as Nedersaksisch or Sassisch or Platt(dütsch)).* Middle Low German was once the medieval international language of the Hanseatic League; thanks to the European Charter, present-day Low German is recognised as a minority language in both the Netherlands (in respect of the dialect found in the province of Groningen: *Grunnegers*) and in Germany, including seven Länder. Görlach shows that traditionally Low German has been maintained as a medium of education, in local parliaments, and in civil administration, far more than Scots, and that new speech-based written forms are emerging for news broadcasts, although he wonders about their quality and how far comparisons might be made with speech-based texts in Scots which still can sound funny, de-intellectualised, or artificial. On the other hand, for all the similarities with Scots, Low German has not been symbolised as part of a nationalist political movement.

Reformers of Scots have often looked to **Norway** for inspiration.[14] As **Kevin McCafferty** shows, the nineteenth-century nationalism of Norway, which urged on itself its own national language, led to not one but two models: the Norwegification of Danish leading originally to *Riksmål*, nowadays *Bokmål*, and homogenised standardisation based on rural dialects, known originally as *Landsmål*, later *Nynorsk*.

---

[12] See M. Görlach, 'Scots and Low German: The Social History of Two Minority Languages', in M. Görlach (ed.) *Focus on Scotland* (Amsterdam: John Benjamins, 1985) 19-36, and M. Görlach, 'Norddeutschland, Schottland und Jamaica: zweisprachige oder bidialektale Regionen?', in D. Möhn (ed.) *Niederdeutsch und Zweisprachigkeit: Befund – Vergleiche – Ausblicke* (Leer: Schuster, 1988) 49-69.

[13] Both articles deserve to be (re-)read in the present context. H.-H. Meier, 'Scots, Swiss and Low German', in A.J. Aitken, M.P. McDiarmid, and D.S. Thomson (eds.) *Bards and Makars: Scottish Language and Literature Medieval and Renaissance* (Glasgow: GUP, 1977) 201-213. D. Strauss, 'Scots is not Alone: Further Comparative Considerations', in J.-J. Blanchot and C. Graf (eds.) *Actes du 2e Colloque de Langue et de Litterature Écossaises (Moyen Age et Renaissance, Université de Strasbourg, 5-11 Juillet 1978*, 80-97.

[14] Cf. e.g. J.D. McClure, A.J. Aitken and J.T. Low, *The Scots Language: Planning for Modern Usage* (Edinburgh: The Ramsay Head Press, 1980); J.D. McClure, *Why Scots Matters* (Edinburgh: The Saltire Society, 1988, revised edition 1997); J.D. McClure, *Scots and its Literature* (Amsterdam: John Benjamins, 1995).

Both have equal official status, although the wranglings about the archaic spellings of Nynorsk seem to show no signs of abating.[15] No-one actually *speaks* these two languages (unless actors or news broadcasters) – Norwegians *speak* dialect and *write* *Bokmål* or *Nynorsk*. McCafferty shows that, throughout the country, *Bokmål* is the dominant and preferred form of education, the press and the private and commercial sectors, including the choice of spell-checkers, whereas *Nynorsk* is regionalised to the South-west. On the basis of the Norwegian experience, McCafferty feels that there are lessons to be learned for reformers of Scots if the goal is to be widespread interest, acceptability and support (and not some mythical notion of 'purity'): avoid archaisms, avoid regionally narrow definition of dialect as the norm, and include the speech of urban areas (such as Belfast and (London)Derry in Northern Ireland) where much traditional speech has developed. This happily echoes all the advice from the Scots papers in this volume.

The fourth European comparison is with **Switzerland**. In 1938, in addition to German, French and Italian, Switzerland acquired a fourth 'national language': Romansh. Later revisions of the Swiss Constitution declared Romansh not an official language of the Confederation but 'an official language for communicating with persons of Romansh language', and that the Canton of Graubunden/Grisons, where Romansh is only to be found, is to maintain and promote the language. The present overview by **Andreas Fischer** shows that, even without the European Charter, a modern democratic country like Switzerland can come up with good solutions to linguistic problems. Although the issues surrounding official recognition of Romansh provide an important comparison for our concerns for Scottish Gaelic in Scotland and Irish in Northern Ireland, it is the situation of German in Switzerland which we feel is most relevant to that of Scots.[16] As Fischer shows, in a diglossic situation, speakers use two varieties of a language in functional distributions: (the various dialects of) Swiss German is used for everyday oral communication, whereas the standard High German is used for nearly all written communication, and orally on formal occasions. There is no need for revival or standardisation. With Scots for speech, and English for writing, Scotland has been in effect in a state of diglossia ever since the loss of independence in 1603. With accent the striking marker of identity, and a growing acceptance of regional accents on the media, diglossia can only be further strengthened.[17] Fischer shows that neither dialect levelling nor the absorption of

---

[15] See, e.g., an issue of *Bergens Dagbladet*, during March 2001, which had, as the main front page article a report over apparent controversies over the spellings for 'milk'; *melk* or *mølk*.

[16] As Meier and Strauß have done before – see note 13.

[17] For many present-day Scottish speakers, after all, it is primarily their accent which they consider to mark them as *Scottish*. Accent alone, however, does not qualify anyone to be a speakers of *Scots*, where morphological inflections, Scots cognates of

English loanwords diminishes the extent or use of Swiss German, and that its functional load particularly on radio and television and informal (speech-based) written genres such as personal letters and now email (despite the lack of any standard form) is increasing.

Of all four present comparisons, the Swiss German situation strikes us as closest to a realisable as well as an acceptable solution to the situation of Scots in both Scotland and Northern Ireland. Just as Swiss German serves as a marker of local and national identity, so too could that symbolic function be served by Scots in Scotland and Scots in Northern Ireland. We see no need for revival or standardisation on the scale or of the type envisaged by Ullansista reformers; Fischer is right to raise the spectre of marginalisation.

We are most grateful to our colleagues for drawing comparisons with the situations especially in Northern Ireland and Scotland. We believe that their influence on local language policies will be felt for a long while to come.

Language Policies on Scots

A major theme of this volume is the undeniable politicisation of Scots. To this politicisation, there are many strands of interweaving development, only a few of which can be given prominence in this short introductory section.

The volume presents six studies not only of Scots, but each study is also *in* Scots. **Dauvit Horsbroch** and **Ian Parsley** continue their criticisms of the disjointed language policy for Scots in Scotland and Northern Ireland by sharply identifying and unravelling the many inherent contradictions.[18] **Gavin Falconer** adds his own criticisms by providing an invaluable analysis of the use of Scots and Gaelic in the Scottish Parliament and Northern Ireland Assembly. **Caroline Macafee** is concerned with two central policy issues: the many presuppositions and implications of establishing the number of speakers of Scots (57% of the Scottish population, she reports) and possible models of approach which might inform policies towards Scots; her preference is for preserving the best of the past, without revival: the 'glass-case model'. **Andy Eagle** is concerned with policies for the revival of Scots and the nature and quality of revived Scots, although this is discussed in other papers, too. **Dauvit Horsbroch** and **Ian Parsley**, in second papers, are also concerned with the nature and quality of revival. Horsbroch re-examines the practice in the 14 academic history

---

core English lexis, traditional vocabulary and certain syntactic constructions are all criterial(as Horsbroch also shows).

[18] See Dauvit Horsbroch, '*Mair as a Sheuch atween Scotland an Ulster*: Twa Policie for the Scots Leid', in *Language and Politics* 133-141; and Ian Parsley, 'Language, Discrimination and the Good Friday Agreement: The Case of Ulster-Scots', in *Language and Politics* 89-90.

papers in Scots in the journal *Cairn, the Historie Tidescrift in the Scots Leid*, which Horsbroch edited from 1997-1998; Parsley compares an Ullans translation of an English text with four new translations in Scots which he shows to be authentic.

The *European Charter for Regional or Minority Languages* has proved a mixed blessing. Its signing in March 2000 and its ratification in March 2001 by the UK Government, and its implementation in Scotland and Northern Ireland (as well as, of course, Wales) from 1 July 2001 has formalised and legitimised much welcome and unprecedented moral, practical and financial support for Scottish Gaelic and Scots in Scotland, and for Irish and Scots in Northern Ireland. The general feeling among academics and activists is that, by undertaking to let itself be appraised and held to account regularly over its record of implementation, the Government will live up to its undertakings, particularly in the areas of broadcasting and education for Scottish Gaelic and Irish as well as more generally in facilitation, promotion and support for both varieties of Gaelic and Scots. Whereas the UK legislation arising from the Charter acknowledges Scottish Gaelic and Irish as separate regional languages, it is also helpfully and unambiguously clear on the fact that there is only one regional language called *Scots* and, therefore, that which is found in Northern Ireland is merely 'a variety' of the bigger whole.

The creation of legislative support has proven, however, to be insufficient to ensure effective (or, indeed, any) implementation or to prevent division. Despite common provision for common languages, implementation and attitudes in government and its agencies in Scotland and in Northern Ireland have conspicuously diverged. Northern Ireland has taken the lead. The Scottish Executive neither has a policy nor has the will to have a policy. The absence of a policy on Scots is attributable to different perceptions. Donald Dewar is on record[19] as claiming that, as everyone knows what Scots is, there's no need to do anything about it. As already stated, we regret that the senior civil servant with policy responsibility for language in Scotland, Francis Bruwis, felt unable to accept our invitation to speak at the Symposium.[20] He needed little time to consider whether he or anybody in officialdom might talk about Scots. In a telephone conversation with John Kirk on 9 July 2001, Bruwis claimed that:

> *as far as Scots was concerned, there was not a lot happening ... there was not much to be said ... that it was really a matter of having the right*

---

[19] In a letter from Donald Dewar to Aiberdeen Scots Leid Quorum, quoted by Dauvit Horsbroch in a talk in Aberdeen in June 1999

[20] On Gaelic, he understandably deferred to the Executive's Ministerial Advisers, Professor Donald Meek and Professor Kenneth MacKinnon, whose participation he positively encouraged. In the event, Professor MacKinnon participated and a written version of his power-pointed presentation is in this volume.

educational guidelines ... and that there was no need to do anything under the European Charter, because it's not ratified for Scots ...[21]

We find it disappointing in the extreme that Government policy – the ratification of the European Charter, with its direct implications for policy on Scotland – could not be reported on accurately by a senior officer of the Scottish Executive.

The adoption of Scots as a political issue by the Scottish National Party has led to the second perception that it is a separatist issue which, therefore, other parties should best leave alone.

A third perception is that Scots is no more than a question of literary form and style and therefore a matter for writers 'to do their own thing with' rather than for the Westminster Government, the Scottish Executive, or the general population. As some writers in Scots has espoused democratic socialism and Marxism, pro-union Scots throughout much of the mid-to-late twentieth century tended to distrust and disassociate themselves from revivalist efforts.

Nothing could be more different for the Scots dialect or legislated 'variety' in Northern Ireland. Overnight, in the early 1990s, Scots had become a political cause championed by unionist politicians. As a result of their talking it up,[22] Scots became part of the legislative measures securing peace. The Government has created an Agency with an annual budget of well in excess of £1m per annum. The promotion of Scots and in particular the pro-active revival of Scots and the use of Scots translation in institutional, informational and entirely non-literary contexts is government policy and already government practice,[23] as if revival had already happened.

To the envy of the Scottish Gaels and the Scots, political activism in Northern Ireland has yielded substantial outcomes and progress for both Irish and Scots. Success is always to be admired.

But that success is also a poisoned chalice. UK Government policy, following the European Charter, has created a linguistic apartheid: both *between* the *stewartries* or 'jurisdictions' of Scotland and Northern Ireland, and *between* the varieties of Gaelic and Scots in each stewartry. UK Government policy has created serious discrimination in terms of funding: there is something wrong when the

---

[21] Part II of the Charter was ratified for Scots on 27 March 2001 and came into effect on 1 July 2001.

[22] For accounts of the inclusion of a North-South Implementation Body for Language in the Belfast / Good Friday Agreement, see Aodán Mac Póilin, 'Language, Identity and Politics in Northern Ireland', *Ulster Folklife*, 45, 1999: 106-132, and John O'Farrell, 'The Language Game' in *Fortnight*. March 2001: 15-16.

[23] Examples of Ullans which appeared during 2001 include the 2001 Census, the *Heich Ploy*, and *Fordèrin Inlats o Jonick, A Yae Jonick Bill, fur Norlin Airlann*, (Jimp Wittens, Forehannit apen discoorse frae tha Offis o tha Heid Männystèr an tha Heid Männystèr Depute).

national variety of Scots in Scotland (spoken allegedly by 57% of the Scottish population or c. 2.85 million people, according to Macafee, in this volume) should receive c. £100,000 annually, whereas the Northern Ireland / Ulster variety of Scots (spoken by no more than 100,000-150,000 people, according to estimates) should receive £1.4m.

Moreover, greater provision for Gaelic or Irish than for Scots in each jurisdiction creates further discrimination. Parity of esteem between Scots and Irish is therefore urged by Lord Laird in this volume, entailing an upgrading for Scots and not the opposite for Irish. In Scotland, there is no such drive, because the separate autonomy of Gaelic has long been recognised. Nevertheless, unionist activists advocate European Charter Part III recognition for Scots in Northern Ireland on the grounds that *not* to do so would be a denial of human rights. Behind the urging of Part III Recognition for Scots by **Dauvit Horsbroch** in this volume, by contrast, is a different aspiration: his is an urging for a co-operative and collaborative *pro-Scots* lobby in areas of recognition and use in education, broadcasting and media in a single unified way, connecting throughout the Scotstacht the reality of the language with the reality of its speakers, and for an agreed single written form. For Horsbroch, and also **Irene McGugan**, the Gaelic/Irish question is simply irrelevant.

UK government legislation has brought about serious but probably unimagined linguistic apartheid. In the case of Scots, it could not have been intended that the legislation and its implementation would create two 'Scotses' or such apartheid. Through the revivalist agenda in Northern Ireland and the creation of Ullans, however, it has. The very name *Ullans* was invented for the purpose of creating a separate Ulster language. It is as if there were two agendas, diametrically opposed to each other: a *Boord* in Northern Ireland *versus* no equivalent in Scotland, promotion in Northern Ireland *versus* 'nothing-to-promote' attitude in Scotland, maximum funding (and on a par with Irish if possible!) in Northern Ireland *versus* minimal funding in Scotland. Underlying these agendas are perceptions differently shared by government and people alike: in Northern Ireland, Scots is promoted by activists - and now the government agency as well - as something *other than*, and therefore *additional to*, English – a view just as strongly (if not so prominently exposed in the press and media) challenged by most of the province's native Scots speakers who consider their Scots to be part of their *English*; in Scotland, Scots is not promoted, as **Caroline Macafee** in this volume argues because, although government and people recognise its distinctiveness, their Scots is not other than or additional to their English but already part of it.

An alternative analysis of the apartheid between Scots in Scotland and Northern Ireland is proposed by **Gavin Falconer**, who identifies five key factors:

- The key political issue: in Northern Ireland, it is esteem through recognition, whereas in Scotland any progress on Scots has been limited to education

- The issue of literary tradition in Scots: in Northern Ireland, it is more disjointed, whereas in Scotland it is less disjointed
- The issue of continuity with urban English: in Northern Ireland, Scots is relatively less continuous with urban English (although Belfast English is one of the many ingredients making up the amalgam of Ullans), whereas in Scotland it is more continuous
- The issue of self-definition: in Northern Ireland, Scots is defined against Irish, whereas in Scotland it is defined against English
- The issue of activism: in Northern Ireland, it tends to be driven by unionism, whereas in Scotland, if driven at all, it tends to be by nationalism (although there may be other agendas such as ecology or democratic socialism).

Further apartheid is to be found in the results or outcomes of revival. In Scotland, contemporary literary attempts no longer appear to take their cue from MacDiarmid's highly abstracted 'synthetic Scots' lyrics, but rather from the everyday speech of ordinary Scottish people, whether rural or urban. Most of the 30 short stories in *A Tongue in Yer Heid*[24] or the stories for young people in *A Braw Brew*[25] (to take two examples almost at random) feel intuitively – at least to the first named author of this article – to be based on speech, however different the written representation might appear on the page, not least orthographically. Present-day Scots is an oral medium and, to be *authentic,* any written version has to take its cue from actual current speech – even for institutional registers which are entirely written in nature and function, and which have no spoken equivalents. This point is persuasively *demonstrated* by Ian Parsley as well as by all the papers *in* Scots in this volume.

Dauvit Horsbroch, among others, sensibly issues an appeal: *nae mair Ullans*! Ullans is neither in accord with spoken and written tradition, nor is it in line with a folk tradition, nor recognised or admired by native speakers, who feel insulted and offended. Ullans is the opposite of James Fenton's literary dialect which shapes authentic Antrim Scots into lyrical virtuosity, beautiful and poignant vignettes of traditional Scots-based culture, which show genuine states of mind and feeling which only the living dialect can reproduce and convey. If revival there is to be, its success can only be guaranteed if it is based on the *authentic* living speech. Revival also depends on the desire of the native speakers for revival (as many papers in this volume stress), their willingness to participate, and their acceptance and approval of the revival results. Like the mirror-on-the-wall test, people need to recognise themselves in it; nobody recognises Ullans as authentic. By being *in* Scots, the papers in this volume show revival in action, and we believe that their practice and

---

[24] James Robertson (ed.) *A Tongue in yer Heid: A Selection of the Best Contemporary Short Stories in Scots* (Edinburgh: B&W Publishing, 1994)
[25] Liz Niven and Pete Fortuine (eds.) *A Braw Brew: Stories in Scots for Young Folk* (Newtown Stewart: Watergaw, 1997)

conventions would be acceptable to the wider Scots-speaking community as their language is realistic and transparent and in accord with native-speaker intuition and usage.

Despite the stubbornness of the Scottish Executive, there are hopeful signs of development from the grass roots. If Mohammed won't come to the mountain, the *Cross-Pairtie group i the Scots Pairliament on the Scots Leid* might yet come to the Scottish Executive and, that way, bring to the Executive proposals for measures based on the European Charter, the *Barcelona Declaration of Human Rights* and other language and human rights documents (as Irene McGugan indicates in her paper).

The differences with Northern Ireland are striking. Although a political parliamentary group, the Scottish committee includes representatives of all interested parties, including academic, writers, teachers, journalists, media people, and so on, including academics and linguists of Scots. It is clear that the way forward will arise from consensus among all parties with professional contributions and vested interests. Although, in terms of initial funding and resources for building support, Ulster appears to have jumped well ahead of Scotland, we believe that the approach now being adopted in Scotland might have a greater chance of lasting success.

All these issues are admirably summed up by **Ian Parsley**. For him, the choice is clear and simple: *politicisation* or *survival*. Approaches to survival have to be inclusive and impartial. Approaches which are inclusive, cross-party, and involving native speakers as well as all those with a vested professional or academic interest, as in Scotland, are likely to succeed. Approaches which are party-political, negatively-focussed, antagonistic and dismissive, ignoring native speakers and professionals or academics with the necessary expertise, as in Northern Ireland, will not. Approaches to survival have to be united, otherwise divided we fall. Unity for Scots requires unity between Scotland and Northern Ireland, unity between politicians and speakers, and also unity between them and all those with a vested professional or academic interest. Nobody wants politicisation to be sound the death-knell.

Although Lord Laird asserts in his paper that 'Ulster Scots is part of the solution, not part of the problem', Parsley convincingly argues that Ullans has now made Ulster Scots *part of the problem*. With metaphors, inevitably, these are different problems and different solutions, but it is important that Lord Laird's rhetoric should not be accepted uncritically. As Stephen Peover rightly urges for Irish, Government should facilitate and encourage; a change to such a policy for Scots is urgently needed in both Scotland and Northern Ireland. In showing resolute action to promote and support Scots before 1 July 2002, the UK Government needs to create the single trans-national policy for Scots and the Scotstacht, as urged in this volume.

These papers show beyond doubt that, if revival of Scots there is to be, the way forward amounts to a unified approach involving all interested parties and most crucially the native speakers themselves (*the taakers*) as well as the experts *that ken*. Along with our contributors, we repeat that there is one Scots language, of which the overwhelming majority of speakers are in Scotland. If Scots is to be needed for signage, schools or official documents and reports, what is needed is one single pan-national or trans-national written dialect which has been standardised on actual spoken speech (and is for that reason authentic), which builds on its shared strengths and overlaps with English, particularly for written purposes, and which is used in Scotland and Northern Ireland alike. Unity of approach on development will involve Scotland and Ulster working together, in a balanced and even-handed partnership.

Language Policies for Irish

The papers dealing with the Irish Language cover a wide range of issues, some political, some educational, others sociolinguistic and psycholinguistic in nature. These issues include the role of the language in forthcoming legislation, the Government's commitment to its maintenance as a viable vehicle of cultural transmission and interpersonal communication within Gaeltacht areas, its expansion through all-Irish medium education and subsequent demands on language planning strategies. Furthermore, the setting up of *Comhairle na Gaelscolaíochta* in Northern Ireland as the promotional body for Irish-Medium education and subsequently of *Iontaobhas na Gaelscolaíochta* as a trust fund to support innovative projects relating to Irish-medium education, is discussed and hailed as significant and far-reaching developments. Under Section 31 of the Education Act 1999, a similar structure to *Comhairle na Gaelscolaíochta* is about to be set up by the Irish Government and will probably come into effect in 2002. The background to this development and subsequent political wrangling are outlined in clear chronological order and the consequences which are likely to arise are carefully considered.

Two papers by **Stephen Peover** and **Gordon McCoy** outline in some detail how the conception and perspective of the Irish Language Movement and its followers in Northern Ireland have changed radically over the past 20 years in regard to the civil service and the Department of Education. This is due particularly to the success of Irish-medium education, especially in the last decade. Civil servants have been viewed in the past as being reluctant and obstructive in their official dealings with Irish speakers. However, perusal of the available files shows a different picture. The major sticking point seems to have been the application of the viability criteria for Irish-medium schools, which proved enormously difficult for all new schools. Despite some progressive steps, starting with the granting of approval to the Steelstown unit in Derry, which took only six months, it did not help matters that the criteria were raised again in the mid-1990s, having been reduced earlier. A radical approach to the funding of Irish-medium schools emerged in the mid-1990s whereby the Department of Education showed a willingness to support projects, which fell far short of the extant viability criteria. It was hoped that such tangible encouragement would help all units/schools to become self-sustaining. Later political developments, leading to the Belfast / Good Friday Agreement, copperfastened these earlier changes and helped the Department respond to the shift envisaged by the Agreement, some of which was carried out through the Education (NI) Order 1998.[26] A closer reading of some of these sections provides an explanation for recent actions taken by the Department to support and consolidate the work of Irish-medium schools. They include the creation of *Comhairle* and *Iontaobhas na Gaelscolaíochta*, the separation of criteria for urban and rural primary schools and the repayment in appropriate circumstances to the trust of capital funding spent on schools. This has led to a great overall improvement of the relationship between the Irish-language movement and the Department. There exists at this time a real opportunity to create shared enterprises agreeable to all which can only be to the long-term advantage of the Irish language and its culture.

McCoy in his paper argues that, due to the failure of different attempts to devolve power to local assemblies (e.g. Northern Ireland) until 1998, the multiculturalism policies pursued in Britain were being slowly adapted. However, the 1980s brought a huge upsurge of interest in the language, moving the language away from academia and into the workplace. This in turn meant cultivating a relationship with the British Government, resulting in the foundation of local support groups willing to negotiate for better funding and status not only for the language but for their own areas. Comparisons were made with the situation in Scotland and Wales – they were given preferential treatment – which merely showed inconsistencies within the language policies being pursued at the time. This 'pro-rata' argument only succeeded in bringing the number of Irish speakers returned in the 1991 Census under detailed scrutiny and analysis, resulting in further conflict and polarisation. Meetings between the Irish-language lobby and civil servants were often tense, abrasive and oppositional in the extreme. It was the oppressor versus the oppressed attitude that held sway, but the Government's approach was seen by others as re-active and ad hoc. Civil servants, who were mostly middle class, viewed Irish language activists and their tactics as being driven by blind idealism. The policy in the early 1990s was to support Irish at community level, but there were no plans at institutional level for a 'bilingual society'. However, as the decade progressed, the confrontational and oppositional tactics of earlier years were put aside and a more consensual approach took their place, wherever it was felt that progress could be made. During the peace negotiations of the early nineties, Sinn Féin and to a lesser extent the SDLP, and the Irish Government became strong allies of the language movement. This resulted in *Meánscoil Feirste* being granted full recognition and funding in 1996. On the communal side, many institutions such as banks, building societies, supermarkets and the electricity board adopted 'bilingual policies' in order to improve relationships with the wider community, especially in areas such as West Belfast.

---

[26] Further recent discussion of the Department of Education's policy for Irish is to be found in Eugene McKendry, 'Modern Languages education Policies in Ireland and Britain', in John M. Kirk and Dónall P. Ó Baoill (eds.) *Language Links: The Languages of Scotland and Ireland* (Belfast: Cló Ollscoil na Banríona 2001) 211-222.

The promotion of the Irish language by the British Government was agreed under the Good Friday Agreement in 1998, which heralded a new era for the language in Northern Ireland. Funds were channelled through partnership boards, including European funding, and schools not meeting enrolment criteria were to benefit enormously from these new developments. The setting up of a cross-border body for language, with its equality agenda of non-discrimination, strengthened the Irish language movement and began to have a social impact on language circles in Northern Ireland.   Irish is now part of officialdom, and the ratification of the *European Charter for Regional or Minority Languages* for Irish has brought many other benefits.   Promotion of the language is now in the hands of the Linguistic Diversity Unit of the Department of Culture, Arts and Leisure, which has already commissioned research on the needs of the Irish-language community, and which is developing an overall policy for the implementation of the Charter by Government. Translation services have been stretched to the limit in meeting the huge demands made on them at the moment.

The Irish language has not developed its full potential; the entire community in Northern Ireland is divided on how this can be achieved; and the debate is likely to continue.   Public signage and the availability of a limited number of Government services in Irish on request are likely topics of debate.   The Irish-language activists' opposition to civil servants and their perceived policies and the ensuing hostilities from both sides have been greatly reduced.   A major change of approach is now evident among Irish language speakers in their dealings with officialdom.   Discourse now refers to language rights, economic development and regeneration and new networking.   This new era can be heralded as a pro-active one.   Cross-community approval is probably the next big hurdle to be overcome and will prove a challenge to us all.

Seán Ó Cofaigh's paper concentrates on the preparation of the forthcoming language legislation in order to give effect to the Constitutional Status of the Irish language in the Republic of Ireland.   There is overall agreement that the Republic needs to move from non-statutory guidelines to a formal statutory system, which should also help meet and give effect to the philosophy underlying the Government's (1994) Strategic Management Initiative – namely – achievement of excellence in the provision of service to the public.   It was felt that it would be imprudent to outline unrealistic goals or indeed undertake unworkable procedures.   Mutual understanding and compromise will be required from both sides, those seeking services in Irish and the providers.   The forthcoming Bill will not be all-encompassing but will focus initially on the feasibilities and through a carefully considered plan of action build upon these.   This is now an urgent matter since the recent Supreme Court decision which states clearly that the State has a constitutional duty to provide Irish language versions of every State Act as soon as it has been made available in English.   The judge in delivering his judgement makes a comparison with the situation within the European Union.   Goodwill for the language is widely evident and the *Official*

Languages Equality Bill, to give it its official title, will ensure the language rights of all citizens in their dealings with State. The objectives of the Bill are:

• To specify the language rights of citizens consistent with the constitutional status of both official languages;
• To specify the obligations of Departments of State and of the public sector to provide services for citizens in the official languages;
• To place a statutory obligation on Departments of State and public sector organisations to make specific provision for delivery of an agreed quantum of State services through Irish
• To assign general responsibility to the Minister for Arts, Heritage, Gaeltacht and the Islands in regard to the delivery of State services through Irish
• To provide for the overseeing, monitoring and enforcing of the Act by the establishment of the Office of the official Language Commissioner.

Minister of State, Mary Coghlan, TD, commented on 12 June 2001 that:

> [*t*]*he Bill will set out a legal basis for the official languages (Irish and English) and, in addition, it will ensure the language rights of the citizen in his dealings with the State. ... [T]his Bill demonstrates that the Government remains fully committed to the promotion of the Irish language both within the Gaeltacht and countrywide ...*

Bertie Ó hAinmhire outlines in very broad terms the setting up of *Coimisiún na Gaeltachta* and its Terms of Reference. It is a Government Commission and has been requested to draw up an extensive action plan to be implemented immediately in order to stabilise language usage and the transmission of Irish within Gaeltacht areas. The Coimisiún decided from the outset that an extensive consultation process should be initiated. Public meetings were held throughout the Gaeltacht – written submissions were requested, and some 150 were received. Further studies and analyses were subcontracted to various language advisors and researchers. They reported on the impact of State Bodies such as *Údarás na Gaeltachta*, the Department of Arts, Heritage, Gaeltacht and the Islands, *Raidió na Gaeltachta* and TG4 have had on language usage and maintenance within the Gaeltacht, the present state of Irish-medium education in the Gaeltacht, the use of language within various domains such as family, school, among peers outside school and at social events. There are vast areas of agreement between issues raised at the public meetings, those identified by the researchers and the results of detailed analyses of census returns and other data. All that remains now is for the Coimisiún to agree and draw up a plan of action and the people of the Gaeltachtaí are expecting radical and far-reaching measures and proposals to provide equality of service and status to the Irish language on a par with English.

Brendán Mac Cormaic's paper gives a succinct account of the background to the proposals made in Section 31 of the Education Act, which came into effect in the Republic in January 1999. The contribution of *Gaelscoileanna*, the co-ordinating body for all-Irish education in the Republic, in promoting the setting up of an independent body to oversee the planning and implementation of all-Irish medium education has been immense. The co-ordinating efforts of *Gaelscoileanna*, *Eagraíocht na Scoileanna Gaeltachta* and *Comhdháil Náisiúnta na Gaeilge* were instrumental in achieving a separate structure for all-Irish education, culminating in its becoming an integral part of the Education Bill published by the then Minister for Education, Micheál Martin, in December 1997, and subsequently in the Education Act. Section 31 of this Act outlines the setting up of a *Comhairle* ('Council') for all-Irish education to deal with the particular needs of that sector under four headings: research, teacher training, support services and teaching materials. The structure of this new Body is under consideration at present. Its members, 21 in all, will be democratically elected and will be representative of the all-Irish sector and schools; its terms of reference will cover all the appropriate needs of the sector and the institution itself will be an applied rather than a consultative one. *Gaelscoileanna*, the co-ordinating body, will continue as a pressure group and may agree some contractual arrangements with the new Body in order to supply some of the services needed. A new Chief executive is to be appointed soon, and it may take several years before an appropriate structure has been put in place and is operating satisfactorily. The new structure has come about from the 'grass roots', from the bottom up and not from an independent governmental decision. It is hoped that all-Irish education will at last begin to achieve its objectives under a well-documented and applied language policy. The implications are immense – the recommendations of *Coimisiún na Gaeltachta* are also likely to add further weight to the necessity of having definite and workable language policies and supporting planning structures. A new sociolinguistic philosophy, encompassing language planning and maintenance in a bilingual society, is needed and should be informed by clear and constructive debate.

At the symposium, the paper presented by Seán Ó Riain comprised for the largest part the text of his pamphlet entitled *The EU and the Irish Language*,[27] which received its northern launch on 23 August 2001 and, because of that, not reproduced here. In that paper, after considering the European league of languages, in which Irish does not rank among the highest, Ó Riain addresses the issue of ever-decreasing numbers of learners of Irish by urging the rather novel solution of the prior teaching

---

[27] Seán Ó Riain, *An tAontas Eorpach agus an Ghaeilge: Féiniúlacht agus Éagsúlacht Teanga / The EU and the Irish Language: Identity and Linguistic Diversity.* Baile Átha Cliath / Corcaigh: Clódhanna Teo. Do Scríbhneoirí Gaeilge Chiarraí, 2001. Copies are available directly from the publisher.

of Esperanto. We are reminded of the arguments just as evangelically advanced by those who urge the teaching of Indo-European as the solution to the issue of which European languages should be taught outside of Europe; by teaching their historical roots, all the obvious languages would be being taught, as it were, simultaneously.

Language Policies for Scottish Gaelic

The general issues of language policy and language rights are further developed by **Robert Dunbar.** He identifies six classes of policies which governments can offer to what he calls 'minority languages rights regimes' as follows:

- a policy of **assimilation,** which aims at ensuring speakers of minority languages become unilingual speakers of the majority language of the State
- a policy of **integration or tolerance** which provides the right to use the minority language in any kind of private (as opposed to public) domain or sector and thereby participate fully in the life of the society
- a policy of **non-discrimination** which provides the right to use the minority language in some kinds of public domain or sector (e.g. courts), which might accompany a policy of integration or tolerance
- a policy of **protection** which provides legislative support for the minority language from acts of violence and abuse, which might accompany a policy of integration or tolerance
- a policy of **support for the maintenance of minority language group** identity, which provides for a range of public services (e.g. health care, local council services, etc.) through the medium of the minority language and typically the creation of rights to such services
- a policy of **strong support for the maintenance of minority language group** identity, which includes an element of compulsion in the use of the minority language for public services, and an element of regulation in the use of the minority language in public services.

As far as Scottish Gaelic and Scots are concerned, Dunbar advocates that they qualify for a policy of support (but not strong support).

Dunbar goes on to show that neither legislation such as the ratification of the European Charter nor constructive lobbying by the Gaelic activist community – especially *Comunn na Gàidhlig* - has been successful in securing a policy from the previous Westminster Government or from the Scottish Executive. Dunbar finds an implicit policy of integration or tolerance (with some non-discrimination but without protection) but no coherent policy directed at the maintenance of group linguistic identity. His hopes are now placed on the reporting mechanism required by European Charter ratification by June 2002 which obliges the Government to demonstrate the resolute maintenance action for Scottish Gaelic (and likewise for Scots) it will have undertaken. As he sees it, the action most urgently needed is a set of measures intended to bring about a reversal of decline.

Dunbar discusses constructively five areas where such Gaelic-maintenance measures could be undertaken: in education (particularly with regard to Gaelic-medium education), in administrative settings, in the courts, by and within the Scottish Parliament and the Scottish executive; and in broadcasting. Some of these measures were sent to the Scottish Executive in *Comunn na Gàidhlig's* submission of proposals and recommendations in 1997 intended to bring about a legislatively protected and 'secure status for Gaelic', on which, no doubt, the Ministerial Advisory Group on Gaelic, appointed in early 2001, for the purpose on producing a strategy for Gaelic within the Scottish Executive, is also working. The article ends with a consideration of the issues of enforcement, planning, and the need for public bodies to inform the public of their rights on the use of the minority language.

Dunbar has produced a clear and far-reaching critical prognosis of the current situation pertaining to Scottish Gaelic both in legislative politics and on the ground. We recommend this paper as compulsive reading to all those concerned with Gaelic policy.[28]

The second paper on Scottish Gaelic, by MAGOG-member **Kenneth MacKinnon,** shows that the position of the language at the moment is a precarious one. The language has never been treated as normal in everyday life and administration within Scotland and consequently its speakers have adopted attitudes and modes of behaviour which have resulted in a drastic reduction in the domains in which the language flourishes. Transmission of the language to future generations has declined rapidly; use of Gaelic in public has changed considerably from the early 1990s with strong reductions in its use in shopping activities, in church life, at social events etc.; Gaelic-medium education has not been effective and at secondary level there is no real provision for Gaelic-language continuity. There is very little realistic prospect of maintaining language peer groups in such a volatile situation. The decline among Gaelic speakers has resulted from powerful social and economic forces and further research is necessary at both the macro-society level and at the micro-community and family level in order to put in place an effective language planning

---

[28] Another splendid article is Wilson McLeod, 'Gaelic in the New Scotland: Politics, Rhetoric and Public Discourse', *Journal on Ethnopolitics and Minority Issues in Europe*, July 2001. Available at www.ecmi.de/jemie/download/JEMIE02MacLeod10-07-01.pdf. We are grateful to Gordon McCoy for bringing this article to our attention.

policy for language maintenance and transmission. Above all, fresh policy initiatives are required and education must be developed and integrated at all levels. Government goodwill and co-operation must also be forthcoming if Gaelic is to be revitalised in a manner that will ensure its future. Let us hope that Michael Russell's Bill and, in due course, the MAGOG Report will be successful in bringing about by the Scottish Executive the necessary changes of attitude as well as action for the better.

Conclusion

Recognising the importance of respect, understanding and tolerance in relation to linguistic diversity, we offer the publication of all the edited versions of these new papers, with all their views, criticisms and numerous constructive suggestions, as a contribution to the current, pressing and unfolding debate on language policy in the Gaeltacht and in the Scotstacht, stretching from Scotland through Northern Ireland to the Republic of Ireland, for all our readers: civil servants, government advisers, politicians, educators, language-based professionals, journalists as well as native-speakers, dialect-lovers, as well as all those eager to cherish and promote language diversity as part of 'the cultural wealth of the island of Ireland' and, indeed, also of Scotland and the whole of the archipelago.

Language and Politics Symposium in 2002

We look forward to welcoming everyone interested to the next Symposium, which is to be held at Queen's University Belfast from **18-20 September 2002** as part of ISAI2002, the fourth Irish-Scottish Academic Initiative Conference, under the theme of *Concepts/Contexts/Comparisons: Ireland(Ulster)Scotland*. We are delighted that Robert Phillipson, Tove Skutnabb-Kangas and Terence Dolan have agreed to be invited speakers.

Language and Politics in Scotland

Michael Russell

Feasgair math leibh h-uile, agus taing dhuibh airson an cothrom seo airson biadh, deoch agus craic. Agus poileataics.

There is, I think, probably a rule that after dinner speeches should be light in character, an aid to digestion and steer well clear of politics. I hope you do not feel by the end of this evening that you asked the wrong man! However, the subject I have been asked to speak on is language in Scotland, so the injunction against politics is, I am afraid, one which I may have to discard.

I'm very glad to be joining you this evening – however briefly – John Kirk has managed skilfully, by means of a flight a couple of hours ago and another at 8.30 tomorrow morning to fit Belfast in between two engagements in Ayrshire.

Your conference is an important one for the minority languages in both of our countries. I know that my depute, Irene McGugan is also speaking to you about the Scots language. The responsibility in our party for the languages of Scotland lies in my Education and Culture brief, and Irene and I divide them, in the nicest possible way.

But, although I speak more often about Gaelic than about Scots, my own background, growing up in Burns' county of Ayrshire, meant that I was raised in one of the heart lands of Scots speech and Scots literature. I now represent the South of Scotland which includes Ayrshire, together with other Scots-speaking strongholds, like the Borders.

I started to learn Gaelic, not at school – that would have been impossible in all but a small part of the Highlands even thirty years ago – but as part of my studies in Scottish literature at Edinburgh University. I am still learning, but I have been fortunate enough to produce and direct television in Gaelic and I do regard the campaign for the language as one of my priorities within the Scottish Parliament.

It has been said of Ireland that 'phrases make history here' and for all of us our history is inevitably bound up with the way we express our vision of the world. It is therefore not surprising that in Scotland, as in Ireland, language has sometimes been a symptom of division rather than a means of communication. But here in Northern Ireland it is good to see that there are positive attempts to ensure that language can also have a role as instrument of reconciliation and understanding.

Would it were so in Scotland. One of the very unexpected features of the process of devolution – the process that I believe will lead to further change in Scotland and a completion of the powers of our Parliament – has been the utter failure of the first Scottish government in 300 years to address, let alone tackle, the central issues of culture in our nation.

As the Edinburgh Festivals come to an end, the vast throngs of people that have flocked to the city in the last three weeks bear testimony to a huge national and international interest in culture, and some form of interest in the way that Scots approach it. Certainly the level of indigenous art and culture in the various Festivals is lower than I would wish to see, but the whole event makes a vital contribution to our national life and allows us to open a window on the world, a window that the world also can use to glimpse something of us.

It is therefore a source of shame that the only visible involvement of the Scottish Government in this year's festival has been the front page stories of the gutting of Scottish Ballet with the connivance of the Scottish Arts Council, and the persecution of its Artistic Director. Oh, and the first meeting of the implementation group for the Scottish Government's so called *National Cultural Strategy* – the first meeting, a year after the publication of the strategy: a year in which not one of the 63 'outcomes' in the document has been achieved.

But if a government puts no priority on culture, then it is axiomatic that it will put no priority on the living expression of that culture: the languages of Scotland. And, just as there has been no political will expended on our culture, so there has been no political will expended on our languages.   Quite the reverse.

But they are good at spin and hype. I have no doubt that even as I speak the Scottish Government spin machine will be cranking out statements from obscure back benchers or even more obscure ministers, attacking me for "talking Scotland down", and "talking Gaelic down". I will be "playing politics with culture ". I will, I have little doubt, be called a "scaremonger", or will be told that I want a "blank cheque", and that I have "nothing constructive" to add to the debate about Scotland's languages.

Invective is no substitute for debate, and what I want to encourage here tonight is debate. Real debate about the plight of Gaelic, and about the near certainty that the Census figures to be revealed later this year will show that in Scotland today less than 50,000 speak that language.

Our new democracy in Scotland was accompanied by new thirst for consensus amongst Scotland's bickering politicians. I support that desire but just as there is false debate, full of hype and fury but signifying nothing, so there is false consensus – the acceptance of received wisdom and willingness to settle for second best. I believe that for the past few years there has been just such a false consensus about Gaelic and I want to break it tonight by arguing for some radical and urgent action to save Gaelic. The imperative is clear. We must either use the language, or lose it.

The consensus which the Government would like all political parties and all language bodies to stick to is that, though Gaelic has suffered terribly in the past, there is an enormous renaissance underway now, thanks to the new Government's commitment to the language. Such is the scale of this renaissance, the myth goes, that we can leave the Government to stick to its tried and tested path for Gaelic. No need for radical reform, no need for legislation to give the language any rights.

There is only one problem with all of this. The problem is that if Gaelic policy keeps down its present, predictable, tried and tested path for very much longer, then Scottish Gaelic will be effectively dead within the lifetime of some of the people in this room.

It grieves me to have to say that. I want Gaelic to survive. I would even love it to have a recovery plan which involved no difference of opinion between the Government and the Opposition. I have tried, up until now to maintain such a consensus. But that is proving to be a false consensus indeed. The time has come for a much more open debate. As we would say in Scotland's other national langage, *facks are chiels at winna ding, an downa be disputit.*

And the facts are these: Gaelic, which 100 years ago was the language of a quarter of a million people in Scotland, was in 1991 the language of less than 70,000 and, as I have said, is probably the language now of about 50,000.

Now, I give credit, where credit is due. Since the early 1990s, Gaelic broadcasting has taken off, and is now in receipt of £9 million pounds of public funding a year. There are good things happening there and in the Gaelic arts world – finally with Government assistance – and amongst those things are the developing partnerships with Ireland including the Columba initiative. There are now, finally, Gaelic road signs in the Highlands, and Sabhal Mòr Ostaig, the Gaelic College on Skye, has made an enormous contribution to raising the status and profile of the language.

The fact is, however, that Gaelic as a spoken language is not flourishing. Gaelic speakers are dying in bigger numbers than new Gaelic speakers are coming on stream. There are fewer than 7,000 Gaelic children in Scotland who can speak Gaelic, and only a minority of them have access to Gaelic medium education.

And it is on the question of education that I'd like to concentrate, as it is possibly the biggest area of relevance to Gaelic over which the Scottish Parliament has control: Gaelic Broadcasting - bizarrely being the prerogative of Westminster under the current constitutional position.

Many of you will know the background to the present position of Gaelic education. Unlike in Ireland, there were, until the last ten years or so, very few obvious means by which a non-native like myself could hope to learn the language. The stated anti-Gaelic aims of the Scottish Education Act of 1872 were enforced with the aid of corporal punishment with some zeal well into the 1950s. Except for a few secondary schools which have always taught Gaelic as a senior subject chosen by a small minority, Gaelic has only really been tolerated, let alone promoted in the last twenty years. Indeed, I can think of people still in their thirties who, at the age of five had not a word of English, but who were thrown into the deep end at primary school, where the teachers – who also spoke Gaelic outside school – refused to speak a word of Gaelic in the classroom.

All this has changed, and again, I give credit where credit is due. But not much has happened to move the process on in the two years since the Scottish Parliament was elected. When I proposed an amendment to the 2000 Education Act to enshrine a right to Gaelic Medium Education in law – an amendment supported by some of the coalition Liberal party – it was the Government that voted it down. We had the incredible spectacle of the Minister for Gaelic voting against Gaelic education.

A great substitute for action is, of course, studies and reviews. Ministers in Scotland and their civil servants are certainly undertaking plenty of studies on Gaelic. I should rephrase that to avoid sounding dismissive, because I am not – the MacPherson Report, for instance, is a major contribution towards understanding where we are. But on top of that, we now have a Gaelic task force, a review group, and I have no doubt, more reviews on the way. The Government might like to bear in mind that it is possible to study a language to death. It has been done before elsewhere.

Studies a-plenty – but not much action. For example the cross party commitment to secure status for Gaelic - for legal recognition of the existence of Scotland's most ancient language, which existed at the time of the 1999 election, has disappeared. Gaelic was not mentioned in the Labour 2001 election manifesto and there is to be no bill in the first four years of our Parliament.

Meanwhile, Gaelic medium education is not growing nearly fast enough to stem the fall in the number of speakers and, even if there was a will to create such growth, there has been such a failure to co-ordinate training courses for Gaelic medium teachers that there are nowhere near enough even to fill current posts.

The Gaidhealtachd, which has suffered some of the worst depopulation in Europe in the last 150 years, is still losing its most precious asset: its people. It remains economically fragile, with unemployment well above the Scottish average. Local councils struggle to support an ageing population spread over a vast, thinly populated area, where the main traditional industries of crafting, fishing and textiles appear to be in drastic decline, and where the tourist industry has had a rocky year. There is a real danger of the Gaelic speaking heartlands being even further emptied of their population.

There is a way forward, though. In a moment I will say something about the **Secure Status Bill** that I am trying to introduce into the Parliament, against rather difficult odds. But we should be creating a new generation of fluent Gaelic speakers by investing in the most modern and most effective means of teaching English speakers to fluency. I am something of a living example about how difficult it is to get the opportunity to take the language to fluency, for I am far from fluent. We need to open the door to the Gaelic world, and we would find many people – not just from Scotland – keen to come in.

There are also many who want to enter the world of the Scots language. Progress with Scots has also been painfully slow, as my colleague, Irene McGugan, discusses in her own contribution. When the Scots language was last debated at length in parliament last year, the Government refused to accede to a call from academics and others for a question on Scots to be put into the 2001 Census. The Government told us that though they were unwilling to provide a question in the census, they would come up with "something else" to show their commitment to the language. We are still waiting.

Curiously, a census question, had there been one, would almost certainly have provided the opposite problem for the Government to the one provided by Gaelic. From the Government's point of view, there are just too many speakers of Scots – over a million self-identifying speakers, according to preliminary surveys.

Obviously there are problems of definition with Scots, as so many people operate at various points on a varied continuum between full-blooded Scots and Scottish Standard English, and because, for most people, their education will have provided them with very little exposure to Scots literature. Scots language activists find their campaign to be ten years behind that of Gaelic, but I am glad that they are now looking to learn from Gaelic, rather than merely be envious of it.

There are some positive signs for Scots as well as for Gaelic, but they have little to do with Government action or initiative. Scottish literature, including literature in Scots, is making its way onto the school curriculum, and, officially at least, schools no longer equate spoken Scots with insolence or innate stupidity, which was certainly the attitude of most teachers 40 years ago.

However, here the Government draws the line. Scots policy, as far as the Government is concerned is about literature and social inclusion – both extremely important. But it is definitely *not* about saving or developing Scots as a language which people can speak in formal settings, encouraging the use of written Scots for non-literary purposes, or even finding out how many people in Scotland speak the language. And it is most certainly not about spending money. According to answers to parliamentary questions, Scots gets less than £150,000 a year – rather less than the much more contentious Ulster Scots gets over here!

Scots remains threatened with assimilation with Scottish Standard English, largely because of the influence of television, which often plays a part in ensuring that it is subject to fairly extreme social stigmatisation and ridicule. Much remains to be done for Scots.

And we are now into the third year of the Scottish Government's term of office. They have barely a year and a half to come up with something substantial for either of Scotland's languages before the next Scottish elections.

I am happy to help, but it gives me no pleasure to say that at present there is little with which to help. And co-operation is a two-way thing. If every idea for Gaelic and Scots which is proposed by the Opposition continues to be shot down in flames by the Government, then the onus is on Ministers to come up with something better.

If the Government in Scotland is serious about saving Gaelic, then they have to tell us how many Gaelic speakers they would like to see in Scotland in, say, thirty years time. On the basis of the present trends, that is a figure which does not bear happy contemplation. I have asked, in parliamentary questions, by how much the Government is trying to stem the decline, but the Government seems to have no view on this. **I now challenge the Scottish Government to tell me how many Gaelic speakers it would like there to be, and how it is going to achieve that figure.**

My party and I will certainly help the Government form a new consensus on Gaelic, but we're no longer prepared to prop up the old false consensus, the old complacency. Gaelic pressure groups need, frankly, to become less deferential to Government, although I realise that means invoking various metaphors about pipers, payment and tunes. Gaelic Scotland, and the Gaelic organisations must seek before they will find. If they wait patiently, they will not be rewarded. Being inoffensive, I am told, gets you nowhere.

Neither does, I have to say, yet another task force, or more reviews. We must have a policy, and the means to implement a policy, which radically increases the presently tiny number of young people who can speak Gaelic. **We must have a bill that even symbolically gives Gaelic parity of status with English and puts obligations on Scotland's public and private sector to use the language.**

I do not want our languages and our cultures to suffer at the hands of conventional politics. I still think that, with good will, the Scots Parliament could work together as a body to make huge changes to our national life and to the prospects for our languages and our cultures. It could lead the way in overcoming indifference and scepticism; but instead, the Scottish Government seems at present merely to re-enforce those prejudices.

And we cannot wait forever. To do so would be to fail both past and future generations.

And that is why some months ago, I announced that, if the Government failed to introduce the Gaelic Bill promised in its manifesto, then I would introduce such a bill as an individual member.

That, I must say, has proved to be a huge and complex task for one member to take on, without the aid of the Civil Service. I cannot do the Government's whole job for them on Gaelic.

That is why I am choosing tonight to announce that I will be re-submitting my proposal for a Bill. It will be simpler and more modest in scope. It is beyond the staffing and other resources available to me as an individual member to draft the Bill which we had all been led to assume, before the election, that teams of civil servants would be working on. However, I hope that my new proposal for a Gaelic Language Bill will provide a bridgehead into legislation for Gaelic for first time.

I am, believe it or not, a great optimist for Gaelic. I passionately want it to flourish and take its place at the centre of Scottish cultural life, as I believe it will – when young people speak it in drastically bigger numbers than they do at present, and when we regard the use of any of Scotland's languages in whatever setting as a sign of our rich and diverse culture, rather than as a sign of either division or depression.

Chairman, I am sorry I have been overly political in this contribution. I am sorry if I have not aided your digestion.

But some things are more important than post-prandial relaxation. The precious gift of speech, of expression and of imagination, are too exciting to be allowed to wither and die as we dumb down and homogenise our cultures.

We have to stand up for diversity and for vision. We have to – as this conference has shown – stand up for the right to speak of what we see in the words and language that comes most naturally to us.

And to be silent is, in this case, to lose it all.

Gaelic in Scotland is in real peril, and I am impatient to see the Scottish Government wake up to that fact. I hope it does.

Scots in the Twenty-first Century

Irene McGugan

Thank you for the warm welcome, and for the invitation to visit Belfast for the first time, to take part in this very important debate on our languages and the importance of political and legislative measures for their future.

I am a Scottish National Party Member of the Scottish Parliament, advocate of independence for our country, SNP Depute Minister for Children, Education, Culture and Sport, and part of the principal opposition to the Scottish Executive. I am speaking to you today on the Scots Language principally as the Convenor of the *Cross-Pairtie Group i the Scots Pairliament on the Scots Leid.* ('Cross-Party Group in the Scottish Parliament on the Scots Language'), and as *Preses* ('President') of the Scots Language Society.

You may not be aware that in the Scottish Parliament speaking contributions are restricted to four minutes – which makes a speech of nearly half an hour something of a marathon. No one would dispute that Governments do have a role to play in preserving and nurturing the languages of the peoples whom they govern. Not to do so is offensive to human rights and to international treaties imposing obligations - sometimes very specific obligations on their government signatories. Governments spend their peoples' money on education systems and in promoting the framework in which these are regulated. Through all its channels, direct and indirect, taxation funds arts and libraries and cultural life. Through law-making, appointments, administration and pervasive influence, governments also have a greater or lesser say in such matters as broadcasting and publishing and, crucially for languages, in making them seem to their citizens worthwhile or pointless to preserve. There is a vast body of international experience that can inform dealing in good faith with minority and threatened language communities, through the adoption of effective policies. There is equally a sad history of the destruction of languages by discouragement and neglect.

Let me give you a little bit of Scottish political history. Before the Union of the Crowns in 1603, virtually everybody in Scotland, who did not speak Gaelic, spoke Scots. Scots was the State Language. It was spoken at Court, it was the language of the Scottish Parliament and the State Records were in Scots. Oh happy days! After Scotland lost her parliament (temporarily) in 1707, Scots came to be represented in education and in public life as a corrupt form of English. Generations of Scots have had to come to terms with a situation where the way of speech natural to them was officially regarded as unacceptable and unsuitable for formal use. In an age of despotism at the end of the 18th century, even Robert Burns was advised by the anglicised elite at the head of Scottish society not to write in Scots, as it would be dead within a few generations. Thankfully for world literature, Burns kennt better and continued to express in his mither tongue, songs like the great radical hymn "Is There For Honest Poverty" which so movingly opened our Parliament and established a new democracy for Scotland in 1999.

Despite this establishment death wish, Scots is still alive and thriving. You can still find brilliant examples of the rich diversity of dialects within Scots, all of them essential to the true expression of their own locality. Scots survives, but whereas in the past it could survive on its own, like many fragile living things, it now needs support and help.

It is reckoned that up to 1.5 million Scots speak the language, yet few have access to knowledge of it, and most remain ignorant of its brilliant cultural legacy.

With the advent of the Scottish Parliament, new opportunities have arisen, and perhaps it should not be unreasonable to expect a radical change in public attitudes in Scotland to what was formerly the State Language. Surely, you would think, our new Scottish democracy must recognise the culture and speech of the mass of the people if it is to approach the ideal of inclusivity cherished by all those who have worked for the creation of the Parliament? Because, for many, their desire for a Scottish Parliament was always tied in closely with the assumption that it would naturally offer direct support and encouragement for the indigenous culture. As yet this has not happened. This core strand of Scottish culture is marginalized, and our new democracy, I would contend, will not be successful until Scots is brought in from the margins to play the crucial role it merits in the cultural life of the people and the nation.

I'll give you one example of this. A broad alliance of Scots language organisations supported the case to have a question on Scots included in the 2001 Census. This case was successively rejected by the Scottish Office and then by the Scottish Executive apparently on the grounds that definition of terms would be too difficult, and any research conclusions on Census figures obtained might therefore be unsound. It was one of the most depressing days of my life to take part in a debate where negative attitudes towards the language remained and prevailed.   No alternative research approach has yet been proposed by the Executive, although it would seem only logical that an effective policy for Scots should be soundly based on valid research.[1]

So how can we make progress? One of the tangible benefits of the re-establishment of a Parliament in Edinburgh is that is has created an accessible political focus for interest groups on a whole range of activities. The founding principles of the Scottish Parliament include in fact, accessibility. Among the mechanisms for translating ideas into long-term political strategies is the cross-party group, which works on the principle of involving outside bodies and individuals with MSPs of all parties interested in their activities.   For the first time in centuries, possibly ever, the status, condition and future of the Scots

---

[1] For discussion, see Ian Máté, *Scots Language GRO(S). A Report on the Scots Language Research carried out by the General Register Office For Scotland in 1996* (Edinburgh: The General Register Office For Scotland, 1996); Macafee, Caroline, "The demography of Scots: the lessons of the Census campaign", *Scottish Language* 19, 2000, pp. 1-44; and Caroline Macafee (in this volume).

language are being given serious consideration at parliamentary level. After a preliminary meeting in November 2000, the *Cross-Pairtie Group i the Scottish Pairliament on the Scots Leid* (CPG) was established in January 2001, its purpose being:

> *tae forder the cause o the Scots Leid, lat memmers ken aboot the cultur and heritage o the leid and shaw the need for action tae uphaud Scots.*

We have made an excellent start in gathering together a large and diverse range of individuals from all areas of Scots language activism, and a small number of MSPs from across the party spectrum. MSPs who can and do speak Scots in their everyday lives. That is very significant! Membership of this group includes those at the very forefront of the Scots language campaign with phenomenal expertise and talent. That being the case, it will come as no surprise to anyone in this room that when I said that we had a "diverse" range of individuals, that also applies to their views.

However, we have been busy. Four members of our group are reviewing the current status of Scots within the context of International and European statements on the language, such as the *Barcelona Universal Declaration of Linguistic Rights*, in order to summarise the purposes and identify the articles with most relevance to the unusual but not unique situation of Scots.

Success is likely to be measured in small and incremental steps, but with no doubt about what our ultimate goal should be. A highly useful paper on the state of educational policy and resources vis-à-vis Scots was presented, and we now have a standing sub-group on this important issue. A member of the group has been asked to compile a Regional Dossier for Scots for the European Union. This is good, because it cannot fail to highlight the vulnerability of the language (as few official statistics exist) and will certainly underline the current lack of political and educational support for the language. We are considering how to build on the growing interest in Scots from school students and teachers, against a background of disinterest in producing material in Scots from mainstream publishers. In terms of Cultural Tourism, having identified serious omissions on the web-site of Visitscotland[21], the group initiated a dialogue with the organisation, and offered to collate information which would promote cultural tourism.

A related campaign issue is the use of English terms for traditional Scots features, which threatens to dilute our distinctive culture, e.g. *the Forth Estuary*. As Convenor, I have to remember that we are not a literary group, though writers, poets, singers and broadcasters are very well represented in our membership. Nor are we an academic group, though again we have representatives from, I think, every institution in Scotland with an interest or involvement in the Scots language. We are a *political* group. I am very particular about stressing the need

---

[2] http://www.visitscotland.com

to be positive and forward looking and about avoiding getting hung up on the many details of policy and opinion that might divide the Group. The sort of thing I mean is reflected to some extent in every discussion about Scots:

- Do we in fact need to go right back to basics and make the case for Scots as a language in its own right?
- Should there be a Scots word for everything or can we allow the common root with English to be reflected in our spoken Scots?
- Should there be a standard form of spelling?
- How do we get more written Scots into the public domain?
- And especially, how do we make a case, when figureheads for the language such as myself to some extent, put forward the case in English?

The discussions within the CPG are lively and on target for being really productive. But I am also aware that we will only really be making progress when these discussions are taking place *outside* the Parliament and in the streets and houses and schools and pubs of every village and town in Scotland. There is much criticism by activists of the Scottish Parliament and its perceived lack of recognition of Scots. Only three Motions have ever been lodged in Scots – all by me – and an English translation also had to be submitted. Signage throughout the buildings is in English and Gaelic only. We have had whole debates in Gaelic with translators available, but not for Scots.[3] *A Gaelic Dictionary of Parliamentary Terms*[4] has just been introduced. Nae word of sic a thing for Scots. We have a Parliamentary Gaelic Officer, but not one for Scots.

Recognition by the Parliament is crucial for the languages' survival and for the status it will give to those who speak it. I quote:

> *The Scottish Executive considers the Scots language to be an important part of Scotland's distinctive linguistic and cultural heritage.*

Despite this, the Scottish Executive, it has to be said, has singularly failed to come up with any commitment to the language –never mind anything like the high level of state endorsement and funding which Gaelic has enjoyed. I take nothing away from the efforts of the Gaels, the very survival of whose language is threatened – the success of the Gaelic lobby in promoting its cause results in part from the fact that it has been able in recent years to present a united front, has a clear view of what it is seeking and has possessed the resolution and resource to pursue its goals. Also there can be no doubt that the popular image of the Scots

---

[3] For further discussion on the use of Gaelic and Scots in the Scottish Parliament, see Gavin Falconer (in this volume). All debates (in Gaelic or otherwise) are recorded in the Official Report and reproduced on the Scottish Parliament's website at www.scottish.parliament.gov.uk.
[4] *A Gaelic Dictionary of Parliamentary Terms* (Edinburgh: The Scottish Parliament, 1999)

language suffers in comparison with that of Gaelic. In many people's eyes Gaelic is indissolubly linked to the romantically attractive and enduring perception of a magical Highland landscape enveloped in mists and myths. In stark and unappealing contrast, the Scots language is frequently portrayed as firmly enmired in the cauld and clairie kailyard. So we need to be making sure that Scots has proper respect too.

But even the *National Cultural Strategy*[5] has failed us. The paragraph devoted to the Scots Language in the document is somewhat mealy-mouthed. First it declares that Scots has been disparaged as a language for many years. The fact that successive governments have been largely responsible for that disparagement is glossed over. It is also worth noting that the National Cultural Strategy is not only printed in English and Gaelic, but is also available I understand in Urdu, Cantonese, Punjabi, Hindi and Gujerati. While I have no difficulty whatsoever with that, Scots speakers although outnumbering these five groups put together, have to make do with the English version.

What reasons could there be for this lack of governmental support? Maybe consideration of the Scots language is inextricably bound up with considerations of national identity, which might fuel aspirations for separate nationhood and the consequent fragmentation of the UK. Maybe if the Scots language was to be accorded greater recognition by the Scottish Parliament, there might be increased political pressure for Scotland to become a signatory in its own right to the international treaties which are relevant – but foreign affairs is a matter reserved to Westminster. And perhaps the most compelling reason of all for the Government to resist pressures to recognise Scots as an official language is financial. If implemented, the Articles of the European Charter would incur a very heavy economic cost in the areas particularly of education, culture and economic and social life. These might sound insurmountable, but we should also remember the other initiatives currently helping to keep Scots to the forefront politically:

- the work that is being done for the European Year of Languages;
- the ratification of the *European Charter for Regional or Minority Languages* that took effect on 1st July this year. Under Part 11 the focus is basically one of anti-discrimination – there is no requirement which commits the UK Government to protecting and preserving Scots. However, the Government is obliged to report from time to time on progress.

These are all significant achievements, which prove we are at least going in the right direction, at last.

Another significant development recently is that the Education, Culture and Sport Committee of the Scottish Parliament decided to undertake and inquiry and report on the role of cultural and educational policy and provision in supporting and developing Scots, Gaelic and minority languages. I have been

---

[5] *National Cultural Strategy* (Edinburgh: The Scottish Executive, August 2000)

appointed by the committee to undertake this enquiry! Evidence has already been received from a range of organisations and individuals with an interest in and knowledge of cultural and educational policy with relevance to the remit.

There will be many in the audience today who have something to contribute and, with that in mind, I have some handouts giving information about how that can be submitted. We would be most appreciative of input from Ireland, Germany, Norway and Switzerland.

We know to some extent what needs to happen to improve the status of the Scots language. The twin elements of education and the media are crucially important for the future of Scots. In general, the media in Scotland behave as if the Scots language does not exist, although a majority of the population understand and employ some Scots every day. In radio there has been some limited devolution to local radio and to BBC Radio Scotland. However, television in Scotland is almost entirely London-centred, so that even the small number of dramatic productions originating here are expected to conform to a pattern set elsewhere. Broadcasting unfortunately remains a matter reserved to Westminster, and until the Scottish Parliament has some control in this area, Scots will never be given its proper place in radio and TV.

With regard to education, for many teachers, the Scots Language component of *English Language 5-14 Curriculum* did not cause them to change their provision of Scots Language. A Scot poem to be learned by heart around the start of term 3 with very little explanation of what the words mean and where they come from, is still in 2001 the only Scots Language provision offered by many primary schools. A teacher recently told me that he visited primary schools whose names were comprised of some basic Scots words. At Burnbrae, the P7 children knew neither the word *burn* nor *brae* and at Bonnyholm Primary, the P6/7 composite class did not recognise the word *bonny*. Even worse it has now been established that in lots of schools, many pupils are unable to pronounce the *ch* sound, using *k* as in *lock* for *loch*. But there is an appetite for Scots in schools from pupils, teachers and advisers; it is now time for the Government to participate more full in the development of this essential aspect of Scottish life.

There is a general feeling that at last the opportunity exists to effect significant changes in attitude and allocation of resources to Scots, through the political process. Wishful thinking may not yet be consigned to the midden of history, but requests for political action, particularly towards improving the treatment of Scots, can now be made with greater confidence that they will not fall entirely on deif lugs. We need amongst other things:

- recognition by the UK Government of Scots, in parity with Gaelic under Part III of the *European Charter for Regional or Minority Languages*;
- for the Scots Language to have official status and be recognised in public life, including the Courts and the Law, as a valuable part of our national heritage;
- for the Scots Language to be included as an essential and integral part of the school curriculum both at primary and secondary level;

- and in view of the fact that Scots can be understood to a varying degree by the great majority of the Scottish people, it should be given its rightful place in the media as a valuable aspect of linguistic heritage.

In this new Scotland, there is no doubt that Scots is still subject to the same tired old prejudices, but now, maybe, we have the wherewithall to embarrass the establishment into greater commitment to Scotland's neglected Lowland tongue.

Language Policy and the Ulster-Scots Agency[1]

Lord Laird of Artigarvan

Introduction

The Ulster-Scots language has only been given the international and political recognition it deserves within the past decade. Much politically-motivated prejudice against its future development, however, has still to be fully overcome. The prejudice may be because some believe that Ulster-Scots has only managed to get where it is today for political reasons. Others even believe that the government wanted to give the unionists something to balance concessions to Irish, and invented Ulster-Scots. Nothing could be further from the truth.

The major factors underpinning the position of Ulster-Scots today are:

- There is strong community demand and support – even before the Ulster-Scots Agency was unleashed, much interest had been shown including the creation of the Ulster-Scots Heritage Council, the Ulster-Scots Language Society, and an Ulster-Scots Academy.
- There is academic support.
- Language rights have been recognised as part of the legislation on human rights.
- The equality obligation under current legislation gives support to the position of Ulster-Scots in public life.
- The Ulster-Scots position is paralleled by other minority language communities in Europe.

All these measures have come to mean that Ulster-Scots could not be ignored or suppressed. Government had only one option, and that was to accommodate it. Nevertheless, the Ulster-Scots movement as a whole recognises that a major exercise has still to be carried out to balance the negative agenda of some people. The inclusion of Ulster-Scots in the Belfast Agreement has transformed the dynamic Ulster-Scots movement from being a possible part of the *problem* to certainly being part of the *solution*. We should not forget that the Romans and the Nazis and many other colonial races believed that, before you could dominate a people, their culture and language had to be smashed. It is important to point out that it is in Northern Ireland that most Ulster Scots live, and that, politically, they would be unionists.

---

[1] Parts of this article were pre-published in the *News Letter* on 13.10.01 and 20.10.01.

While the Agency pays no attention to religion or politics, the reality is that the issue of Ulster Scots development has a political side.

Moreover, with its signing and subsequent ratification of the *European Charter for Regional or Minority Languages*, the UK Government has recognised for the first time the equal status of the Irish and Ulster-Scots languages. Equal status in theory, perhaps, but not equal needs or equal levels of development. Ulster-Scots needs a massive "catch-up" programme of investment to ensure that the equality agenda of the Belfast Agreement is met, and to ensure that the European Charter requirements for Ulster-Scots are met on an equivalent basis to other European regional languages, including Irish.

In the Republic of Ireland, Ulster-Scots is not as yet recognised as a European regional language because the Irish Government has not yet signed the European Charter. Irish is, of course, also a national language in the Republic. In order for the logic, the sentiment and the real implication of the Belfast Agreement to work, Ulster-Scots must also be afforded status as the third national language in the Republic. An alternative would be that Irish must be relaxed in status from its constitutionally privileged position to that of a European regional or minority language. I would not advocate that move in the logic, but I am not part of the decision-making process. The remit of the North/South Language Body and the Ulster-Scots Agency is for the whole island. Discrepancies in status between Ulster-Scots and Irish must be harmonised, north and south. Let everyone be clear again and, if necessary, I will repeat it again and again: our objective is not to reduce the status of Irish. So the logic must be a massive 'catch-up' programme for Ulster-Scots on both sides of the border. There is a long road to be travelled. With all the legal, moral and political support currently in place, however, the movement travels with great expectations.

The Ulster-Scots Agency (*Tha Boord o Ulstèr-Scotch*)

At this point, it might be useful to refer to the Mission Statement of the Ulster-Scots Agency, with regard to language, which reflects not just our desire but also our legal requirements:

> *The aim of the Ulster-Scots Agency is to promote the study, conservation, development and use of Ulster-Scots as a living language.*

The Ulster-Scots language – or *Ullans* as it is referred to in the legislation establishing our remit – was defined for us as follows:

The Ulster-Scots language or Ullans is the variety of the Scots language traditionally used in parts of Northern Ireland and County Donegal.

The role of the Ulster-Scots Agency, in relation to Ulster-Scots language development, with the authority of the Belfast Agreement, is defined as follows:

- To support its development as a modern European regional language with the vision of parity of status, recognition, funding and representation with Irish, throughout the island of Ireland, north and south.
- To ensure the survival and encourage the use of Ulster-Scots in both writing and speech in the core areas where it is and has been traditionally used.
- To encourage the use of Ulster-Scots in the media, in education, and in public formal contexts, to be facilitated by the development of a standard, formal written form, as well as encouraging the traditional forms still used in the written and spoken language.

Language Planning

In the rest of this paper, I would like to look more closely at the role of the Agency in relation to Ulster-Scots language planning.

The objective is the establishment of Ulster-Scots as a modern European regional language. Language planning involves two kinds of measures: measures to conserve and revitalise a linguistic tradition under threat; and measures to re-equip a traditional and even under-valued language. These measures would be pursued under the guidelines of the *European Charter for Regional or Minority Languages*. The process is sometimes referred to as *normalisation*. All language-planning measures, regardless of the level of objective, involve the extension of use into formal, written contexts, and the development of consistent standardisation with regard to spellings, syntax, vocabulary, and the development of a 'learnt' spoken form.

Language planning features prominently in the Agency's Corporate Plan. Due to its newness as well as the overwhelming speed with which interest in the language and culture has been re-awakened, we have decided to look again at our Corporate Plan, taking into account a consultation process during the winter of 2000-2001. This will no doubt involve a scaling up with a more urgent and focussed approach in the light of a better understanding of the implications of the Belfast Agreement. Naturally, this move will require more resources. Out of our total small budget, we are currently required to fund cultural development as well.

One priority will be the recognition of Ulster-Scots as a national or official state language in the Republic of Ireland. Ulster-Scots needs to be accorded parity of esteem with Irish. Ordinary peoples' reactions in Dublin are very supportive. In the modern European context, diversity is the recognised norm in all of the regions, and so it has to be here. To this end, the Belfast Agreement and its spirit of inclusiveness provides a very important political context.

A further related priority will be the recognition of Ulster-Scots as a European Regional Language. This is provided by the UK's signing and ratification of the *European Charter for Regional or Minority Languages*, and the Republic of Ireland has to do so as well. In this connection, I would also wish to recognise the work and support of the European Bureau for Lesser-used Languages. In a 'Europe of the regions', an important medium-term aim will be the de-politicisation of Irish and Ulster-Scots. I feel strongly that the two language communities should work together towards this objective; in fact, I believe that this is the only way forward.

A third priority will be the accomplishment of the above-mentioned language planning measures, with the two objectives of standardisation and of status-building. Status-building is very important because of the political dimension. The Agency's cultural policy helps to build Ulster Scots status and, interestingly, to create a market. To this end, the Institute of Ulster-Scots Studies, based at Magee College, has been a vital element. The two processes of standardisation and status-building are interlocked.

To these goals, some first steps are essential. The language policy of the Agency is seeking to bring about the following:

- New dictionary programme. This is the first step which the Agency is about to undertake, over a timescale of the next four or so years.
- New Standard Grammar. There already exists a grammar, which has been a major support, but the time will soon arrive when this must be enhanced.
- Spelling standardisation
- Tape-recorded Survey of Ulster-Scots Speech
- Electronic text database of Ulster-Scots literature
- Deliberate expansion of written forms into official and formal situations
- Identification and recognition of native speakers and traditional Ulster-Scots speaking areas
- Education both in and about Ulster-Scots which would include the cultural and historic aspects
- In due course, the development of an Ulster-Scots encyclopaedia
- Production of an Ulster-Scots Bible

This language policy has implications for signage, for language rights (which are underpinned by the principle of parity of esteem), and education (Ulster-Scots medium education will need to become available, if requested), and multi-lingualism will need to be promoted, in education and also elsewhere. It has implications for everyone. All must be involved in the promotion of Ulster-Scots. This is part of the future – not just for those who are interested in language, but for political reasons. Moreover, Language policy should be government-driven: it could be a great opportunity for the Republic of Ireland government, if they have the vision.

The Ulster-Scots are a small group who have been marginalized, and we offer no threat to anyone. If only the Republic of Ireland could show a generosity of sprit to unionists, they could dumbfound them, but there has no sign to date. Language policy for Ulster-Scots provides a great opportunity to show who the real multi-culturalists on these islands are.

In closing, I would like to pay tribute to our Irish colleagues, without whose help and encouragement we could not have gone so far as quickly. Well over 95% of the Irish community hold us in high regard. It is only the negative political agenda people who seem to have problems. I must confess that, 25 years ago, I took the view that Irish was a method of getting at unionists. I now admit that I was wrong. There may still be an element of this, but I feel the community from which I come and I myself are more mature today. As a result, I have learnt a lot about Irish, am keen to learn more, and have developed respect for the language and culture. Inclusiveness leads to discussion and to understanding, which is all to the good. The majority of all people now accept that Ulster Scots is not there to give offence to anyone. I will not stand for any deliberate offence being offered from our culture, and I expect none in return.

Language Rights / Human Rights in Northern Ireland and the Role of the *European Charter for Regional or Minority Languages*

Dónall Ó Riagáin

The concept of human rights is a living and dynamic philosophical, political and legal concept, which continues to develop even as we speak. It has been articulated over at least three centuries and has been enshrined in international law since the middle of the twentieth century. Our understanding of human right has grown and the responsibilities of the state and of society as a whole have been set out and codified. A very good example of this evolution is the area of women's rights over the past few decades, and the standards regarding the equal rights of women and men in domains such as paid employment and property ownership. The fact that these rights are now almost universally accepted in the western world should not lead us to forget that some of them were quite controversial even thirty of forty years ago. Persons, charged with mass murder in places like Bosnia, may now face an international court in the Netherlands. Most of us accept this as being proper order but overlook the reality that such a court is a relatively new concept.

European countries today operate on the basis of shared, common values. These comprise the rule of law, democracy, human rights, including the rights of persons belonging to national minorities, tolerance and a pluralistic society. The observance of these values is no longer a matter of choice, but a political and - in the case of human and minority rights – legal imperative.

Language rights are an intrinsic part of human rights and are being recognised as such more and more. One of the first human rights texts to gain widespread acceptance in the last century is the *Universal Declaration of Human Rights*, adopted by the United Nations in December 1948. Article 2 of the *Declaration* states that everyone is entitled to the rights and freedoms set forth in the *Declaration*, without distinction of any kind, such as race, colour, sex, **language**, religion, political or other opinion, national or social origin, property, birth or other status. The *Council of Europe Convention for the Protection of Human Rights and Fundamental Freedoms*, adopted in September 1953 echoed the same ideas but interestingly adds "association with a national minority" to the grounds on which discrimination is banned. Only in November of last year the Council of Europe added a new Protocol to the *Human Rights Convention* – Protocol No. 12. Article 1.1 of this Protocol states that:

> *The enjoyment of any right set forth by law shall be secured without distinction on any grounds such as sex, race, colour, **language**, religion, political or other opinion, national or social origin, association with a national minority, property, birth or other status.*

Note the very profound difference! The *Universal Declaration* refers only to "the rights and freedoms set forth in the Declaration" and the Human Rights Convention to "the rights and freedoms set forth in this Convention". The Protocol goes a lot further. It refers to "any right set forth by law". It is far too early to say how many states will sign and ratify this Protocol but it is clear that the common understanding of human rights and language rights is constantly developing. The two are inseparable. An acceptance and clear understanding of this is imperative. Fernand de Varennes[1] states:

> *There is often the mistaken view that the rights of minorities, or language rights, are part of a new generation of rights, or are collective rights in nature. This perception is both unfortunate and erroneous: unfortunate because it tends to consider language rights as less deserving than "real" human rights, and wrong because it fails to understand the actual sources of these rights. To put it simply, most – if not all – of what are called today language rights derive from general human rights standards, especially non-discrimination, freedom of expression, right to private life, and the right of members of a linguistic minority to use their language with other members of their community. All of these are "authentic", individual human rights as generally recognised in international law.*

I had the privilege a few years ago of working on an expert committee, charged with preparing a set of recommendations for the OSCE High Commissioner on National Minorities on the linguistic rights of these groups. It was an interesting and challenging task. We were not at liberty to "invent" such rights, however, well founded we might feel they were. We had to base our document on existing international legal instruments. For me it was a revelation to discover just how many such instruments there were, which at least touched on, if not explicitly dealt with, language rights. These had emanated from the United Nations General Assembly, the International Labour Organisation, the OSCE and the Council of Europe. One such instrument, which had not yet come into force in February 1998, when what are now known as the *Oslo Recommendations on the Linguistic Rights of National Minorities*, were formally launched in Vienna, was the *European Charter for Regional or Minority Languages*.

The *European Charter for Regional or Minority Languages* is a unique document in a number of ways. It is, to the best of my knowledge, the only international convention of its kind, exclusively directed at conserving and promoting regional or minority languages. It is interesting also in that it does not seek to confer rights on minorities or ethnic groups. They are not even mentioned.

This is no oversight but a conscious decision on the part of its authors to side-step the thorny issue of defining what a "national minority" is, not to

---

[1] Fernand de Varennes, *Journal on Multicultural Societies*, Vol. 3 No. 1 (August 2001) available at www.unesco.org/most.

mention even more delicate issues, such as self-determination, autonomy, changes in frontiers etc. The existence of national minorities [i.e. citizens of a state who do not have the same sense of ethnic identity as the majority of the population] is a widely accepted concept in Central and Eastern Europe. I have been very impressed by the unquestioning acceptance of ethnic diversity among the citizens of the Russian Federation. This is not to say that the rights of national minorities are respected as much as they should be. But at least their existence is not called into question. In contrast, some Western democracies refuse to accept the existence of ethnic diversity among their citizenry. France is a classic example where the legal system is based on the concept of citizenship. All French citizens are not only equal but are also uniform. Official France could not envisage the existence of a Germanic ethnic minority in the east of the country. The inhabitants of Alsace and Lorraine are French citizens and are no different from their fellow citizens in any other part of the Republic. Greece is much more draconian. To suggest that Aroumains, Arvanites or Slav-Macedonians differ in ethnic identity from other Greek citizens can be construed as spreading misinformation and undermining the security of the state – offences punishable by imprisonment.

Language and culture are central to any community's sense of identity. Some farsighted people in the Council of Europe saw that if language rights could be secured without ruffling governmental feathers, a real breakthrough would have been made in securing the rights of small ethnic groups and in ensuring peace and stability.

The wording of the Charter is carefully crafted to achieve its aims. It does not even speak of linguistic communities. It is addressed at languages. But all living languages exist because people use them and if languages are accorded rights, those who use them will also become beneficiaries. The Charter reaches back to more general concepts of human rights. Therefore we should not be surprised to find the following phrase in the Preamble to the Charter:

> *Considering that the right to use a regional or minority language in private and public life is an inalienable right conforming to the principles embodied in the United Nations International Covenant on Civil and Political Rights, and according to the spirit of the Council of Europe Convention for the Protection of Human Rights and Fundamental Freedoms;*

Language, as we have observed, is at the core of communal identity and if a community can use its language without inhibition or undue difficulty in the various domains of everyday life, then that community will enjoy a sense of confidence, self-esteem and belonging. At the same time people may wish to enjoy a dual identity. For instance, a young person of mixed parentage may wish to switch from one language to another as the situation requires without having to opt for the identity of one parent to the exclusion of that of the other. And why not? Diversity should be a source of enrichment, not a source of division.

It is also worthwhile noting that the Charter cannot be misused to undermine the integrity of the state. Article 5 clearly states:

Nothing in this Charter may be interpreted as implying any right to engage in any activity or perform any action in contravention of the purposes of the Charter of the United Nations or other obligations under international law, including the principle of sovereignty and territorial integrity of States.

Maybe it is appropriate at this juncture to add a word about the issue of terminology. Those who drafted the Charter were only too aware that terms like "regional or minority" were not perfect. But they were the most acceptable at the time. I think we are all conscious that this terminology is not well suited to either Ireland or the United Kingdom. Indeed, it has been suggested that this terminology is a reason why the Republic has not signed or ratified the Charter. The United Kingdom, in the absence of a written constitution, has nevertheless implicitly accepted the existence of ethnic diversity. If the UK were in Central Europe, Scotland and Wales might be referred to as regions – Scotland being an autonomous region. But the sense of identity felt by most Scottish and Welsh people is one of national, rather than regional identity. Nobody denies the existence of a Scottish or Welsh nation. If one were to stop people on the street here in Belfast and ask them about their nationality, the replies would probably vary greatly. Some might simply say *British* or *Irish*. Others might say *Northern Irish* or *Ulster*, *Ulster-Scottish* or use various combinations of these labels.

But we would be very foolish to allow the terminology to get bogged down. I think we should simply refer to Article 1 of the Charter where the terminology is defined in a clear and unambiguous manner. There are five parts in the Charter:

Part I   General Provisions
This deals primarily with definitions, undertakings and practical arrangements.

Part II   Objectives and Principles
All contracting parties [i.e. ratifying states] are obliged to accept these objectives and principles.

Part III   Measures to promote the use of regional or minority languages in public life
This is where we find details of the practical measures required of states in the various domains of life where language is used – Education, Judicial authorities, Administrative authorities and public services, Media, Cultural activities and facilities, Economic and social life and trans-frontier exchanges.

Part IV   Application of the Charter
Here we find out about the furnishing of reports and the role of the Committee of experts.

Part V **Final Provisions**
The procedure for signing, ratifying and the coming into effect of the Charter is set out here.

All ratifying parties must accept the provisions of Part II. In the case of the UK, Part II applies, not only to Welsh, Scottish Gàidhlig and Irish, but also to Scots in Scotland and Ulster-Scots in Northern Ireland. I have *italicised* those parts, which seem to me to be of particular relevance in the case of Northern Ireland.

Part II – Objectives and principles pursued in accordance with Article 2, paragraph 1

Article 7 – Objectives and principles

1   In respect of regional or minority languages, within the territories in which such languages are used and according to the situation of each language, the Parties shall base their policies, legislation and practice on the following objectives and principles:

a   the recognition of the regional or minority languages as an expression of cultural wealth;

b   the respect of the geographical area of each regional or minority language in order to ensure that existing or new administrative divisions do not constitute an obstacle to the promotion of the regional or minority language in question;

c   the need for resolute action to promote regional or minority languages in order to safeguard them;

d   the facilitation and/or encouragement of the use of regional or minority languages, in speech and writing, in public and private life;

e   the maintenance and development of links, in the fields covered by this Charter, between groups using a regional or minority language and other groups in the State employing a language used in identical or similar form, as well as the establishment of cultural relations with other groups in the State using different languages;

f   the provision of appropriate forms and means for the teaching and study of regional or minority languages at all appropriate stages;

g   the provision of facilities enabling non-speakers of a regional or minority language living in the area where it is used to learn it if they so desire;

> h   the promotion of study and research on regional or minority languages at universities or equivalent institutions;
>
> i   *the promotion of appropriate types of transnational exchanges, in the fields covered by this Charter, for regional or minority languages used in identical or similar form in two or more States.*

So we see here a number of real and substantial commitments in respect of both Irish and Ulster-Scots – their recognition as expressions of cultural wealth, resolute action in order to promote and safeguard them, to facilitate their use, in speech and in writing, in both public and private life, the provision of appropriate forms and means of teaching them and the promotion of transnational exchanges.

This necessitates a dramatic shift in public perception of linguistic diversity in Northern Ireland. Its implications should be examined and reflected upon.

In addition, the UK Government agreed to apply Part III of the Charter [Measures to promote the use of regional or minority languages in public life] to Welsh, Scottish Gàidhlig and Irish. Each ratifying state is required to chose a minimum of 35 paragraphs of subparagraphs from the articles in Part III, to be applied to each language covered by Part III in its instrument of ratification.

It chose 52 paragraphs in the case of Welsh, 39 in the case of Scottish Gàidhlig but only 36 in the case of Irish. This is not surprising nor should it be considered to be a rebuff for Irish but rather a reflection of the actual situation obtaining in Northern Ireland at the present time. The instrument of ratification is not a language development plan, less still is it a wish list. It is a legally binding agreement and all of its provisions have to be in place from the day it comes into effect. Let us look at what the UK has agreed to in the case of Irish in Northern Ireland. The chosen paragraphs or subparagraphs are *in italics.*

> **ARTICLE 8 [EDUCATION]**
>
> 1   With regard to education and in respect of territories other than those in which the regional or minority languages are traditionally used, the Parties undertake, if the number of users of a regional or minority language justifies it, to allow, encourage or provide teaching in or of the regional or minority language at all the appropriate stages of education.
>
> a   i   to make available **pre-school education** in the relevant regional or minority languages; or
>   ii   to make available a substantial part of pre-school education in the relevant regional or minority languages; or
>   iii   *to apply one of the measures provided for under i and ii above at least to those pupils whose families so request and whose number is considered sufficient;*

b   i   to make available **primary education** in the relevant regional or minority languages; or

        ii   to make available a substantial part of primary education in the relevant regional or minority languages; or

        iii   to provide, within primary education, for the teaching of the relevant regional or minority languages as an integral part of the curriculum; or

        iv   to apply one of the measures provided for under i to iii above at least to those pupils whose families so request and whose number is considered sufficient;

c   i   to make available **secondary education** in the relevant regional or minority languages; or

        ii   to make available a substantial part of secondary education in the relevant regional or minority languages; or

        iii   to provide, within secondary education, for the teaching of the relevant regional or minority languages as an integral part of the curriculum; or

        iv   to apply one of the measures provided for under i to iii above at least to those pupils who, or where appropriate whose families, so wish in a number considered sufficient;

d   i   to make available **technical and vocational education** in the relevant regional or minority languages; or

        ii   to make available a substantial part of technical and vocational education in the relevant regional or minority languages; or

        iii   to provide, within technical and vocational education, for the teaching of the relevant regional or minority languages as an integral part of the curriculum; or

        iv   to apply one of the measures provided for under i to iii above at least to those pupils who, or where appropriate whose families, so wish in a number considered sufficient;

e   i   to make available **university and other higher education** in regional or minority languages; or

        ii   to provide facilities for the study of these languages as university and higher education subjects; or

        iii   if, by reason of the role of the State in relation to higher education institutions, sub-paragraphs i and ii cannot be applied, to encourage and/or allow the provision of university or other forms of higher education in regional or minority languages or of facilities for the study of these languages as university or higher education subjects;

f   *ii   to offer such languages as subjects of adult and continuing education* g   *to make arrangements to ensure the teaching of the history and the culture which is reflected by the regional or minority language;*

h   *to provide the basic and further training of the teachers required to implement those of paragraphs a to g accepted by the Party;*

With regard to education and in respect of territories other than those in which the regional or minority languages are traditionally used, the Parties undertake, if the number of users of a regional or minority language justifies it, to allow, encourage or provide teaching in or of the regional or minority language at all the appropriate stages of education.

ARTICLE 9 [JUDICIAL AUTHORITIES]

The Parties undertake to make available in the regional or minority languages the most important national statutory texts and those relating particularly to users of these languages, unless they are otherwise provided.

ARTICLE 10 [ADMINISTRATIVE AND PUBLIC AUTHORITIES]

1   Within the administrative districts of the State in which the number of residents who are users of regional or minority languages justifies the measures specified below and according to the situation of each language, the Parties undertake, as far as this is reasonably possible:

a   iv   *to ensure that users of regional or minority languages may submit oral or written applications in these languages*

c   *to allow the administrative authorities to draft documents in a regional or minority language.*

2   In respect of the local and regional authorities on whose territory the number of residents who are users of regional or minority languages is such as to justify the measures specified below, the Parties undertake to allow and/or encourage:

b   *the possibility for users of regional or minority languages to submit oral or written applications in these languages;*

e   *the use by regional authorities of regional or minority languages in debates in their assemblies, without excluding, however, the use of the official language(s) of the State;*

f   *the use by local authorities of regional or minority languages in debates in their assemblies, without excluding, however, the use of the official language(s) of the State;*

g   the use or adoption, if necessary in conjunction with the name in the official language(s), of traditional and correct forms of place-names in regional or minority languages.

With regard to public services provided by the administrative authorities or other persons acting on their behalf, the Parties undertake, within the territory in which regional or minority languages are used, in accordance with the situation of each language and as far as this is reasonably possible:

c   to allow users of regional or minority languages to submit a request in these languages.

4   With a view to putting into effect those provisions of paragraphs 1, 2 and 3 accepted by them, the Parties undertake to take one or more of the following measures:

a   translation or interpretation as may be required;

5   The Parties undertake to allow the use or adoption of family names in the regional or minority languages, at the request of those concerned.

ARTICLE 11 [MEDIA]

The Parties undertake, for the users of the regional or minority languages within the territories in which those languages are spoken, according to the situation of each language, to the extent that the public authorities, directly or indirectly, are competent, have power or play a role in this field, and respecting the principle of the independence and autonomy of the media:

a   to the extent that radio and television carry out a public service mission:

iii   to make adequate provision so that broadcasters offer programmes in the regional or minority languages;

b   ii   to encourage and/or facilitate the broadcasting of radio programmes in the regional or minority languages on a regular basis;

d   to encourage and/or facilitate the production and distribution of audio and audiovisual works in the regional or minority languages;

e   i   to encourage and/or facilitate the creation and/or maintenance of at least one newspaper in the regional or minority languages

f   ii   to apply existing measures for financial assistance also to audiovisual productions in the regional or minority languages;

g   to support the training of journalists and other staff for media, using regional or minority languages.

The Parties undertake to guarantee freedom of direct reception of radio and television broadcasts from neighbouring countries in a language used in identical or similar form to a regional or minority language, and not to oppose the retransmission of radio and television broadcasts from neighbouring countries in such a language. They further undertake to ensure that no restrictions will be placed on the freedom of expression and free circulation of information in the written press in a language used in identical or similar form to a regional or minority language. The exercise of the above-mentioned freedoms, since it carries with it duties and responsibilities, may be subject to such formalities, conditions, restrictions or penalties as are prescribed by law and are necessary in a democratic society, in the interests of national security, territorial integrity or public safety, for the prevention of disorder or crime, for the protection of health or morals, for the protection of the reputation or rights of others, for preventing disclosure of information received in confidence, or for maintaining the authority and impartiality of the judiciary.

ARTICLE 12 [CULTURAL ACTIVITIES AND FACILITIES]

1   With regard to cultural activities and facilities – especially libraries, video libraries, cultural centres, museums, archives, academies, theatres and cinemas, as well as literary work and film production, vernacular forms of cultural expression, festivals and the culture industries, including inter alia the use of new technologies – the Parties undertake, within the territory in which such languages are used and to the extent that the public authorities are competent, have power or play a role in this field:

a   to encourage types of expression and initiative specific to regional or minority languages and foster the different means of access to works produced in these languages;

d   to ensure that the bodies responsible for organising or supporting cultural activities of various kinds make appropriate allowance for incorporating the knowledge and use of regional or minority languages and cultures in the undertakings which they initiate or for which they provide backing;

e   to promote measures to ensure that the bodies responsible for organising or supporting cultural activities have at their disposal staff who have a full command of the regional or minority language concerned, as well as of the language(s) of the rest of the population;

f   to encourage direct participation by representatives of the users of a given regional or minority language in providing facilities and planning cultural activities;

h   *if necessary, to create and/or promote and finance translation and terminological research services, particularly with a view to maintaining and developing appropriate administrative, commercial, economic, social, technical or legal terminology in each regional or minority language.*
2   *In respect of territories other than those in which the regional or minority languages are traditionally used, the Parties undertake, if the number of users of a regional or minority language justifies it, to allow, encourage and/or provide appropriate cultural activities and facilities in accordance with the preceding paragraph.*
3   *The Parties undertake to make appropriate provision, in pursuing their cultural policy abroad, for regional or minority languages and the cultures they reflect.*

ARTICLE 13 [ECONOMIC AND SOCIAL LIFE]
1   With regard to economic and social activities, the Parties undertake, within the whole country:
d   *to facilitate and/or encourage the use of regional or minority languages by means other than those specified in the above sub-paragraphs.*

ARTICLE 14 [TRANS-FRONTIER EXCHANGES]
The Parties undertake:
a   *to apply existing bilateral and multilateral agreements which bind them with the States in which the same language is used in identical or similar form, or if necessary to seek to conclude such agreements, in such a way as to foster contacts between the users of the same language in the States concerned in the fields of culture, education, information, vocational training and permanent education;*
b   *for the benefit of regional or minority languages, to facilitate and/or promote co-operation across borders, in particular between regional or local authorities in whose territory the same language is used in identical or similar form.*

The Charter came into effect for the UK on 1 July 2001. Within a year, by 1 July 2002, the government will have to present a report on the policy pursued in accordance with Part II and on the measures taken in application of those Provisions of Part III, which they have accepted. It will henceforth have to provide a further report every three years. These reports will have to be made public. A Committee of Experts, chosen by the Council of Europe, the members of which would be drawn from the ratifying states, will examine the reports.

Any body or association, legally established in the UK, may draw the attention of the Committee of Experts to matters relating to the undertakings entered into by the Government under Part III. After consulting the Government the Committee of Experts may take this information into account when preparing their report for the Committee of Ministers. In other words, if an Irish language organisation, for instance, felt that the UK Government was not living up to its commitments, it could inform the Committee of Experts accordingly. The Committee would investigate the complaint and, if they felt it was well founded, could refer to it in their report. From what I know of the Committee of Experts, they take their work very seriously and have visited some states to examine the situation at first hand.

Another important point is that a ratifying state may upgrade its instrument of ratification at any time and cover additional languages or undertake additional measures in respect of languages, already covered. If I were living here in Northern Ireland , I would be trying to identify additional paragraphs or sub-paragraphs, that could be applied to Irish if the necessary measures were put in place. I would target those measures that could be implemented within a reasonable time frame – say, three to five years. If I were an Ulster-Scot, I would endeavour to have those measures put in place which would enable the Government to extend Part III coverage to Ulster-Scots.

One of the problems bedevilling reform in Northern Ireland is that any change in policy can be interpreted by one community as being a concession to the other. In this regard, the European Charter for Regional or Minority Languages is a godsend. It is not a concession to anyone. It is the application of European standards to all – standards of language rights, of human rights. It is a living tool, now in our hands. How we use it is for us to decide.

This is an excellent basis for developing a language policy. Of course, we all have emotional attachments to a particular language. There is nothing strange or wrong about this. Our language and its attendant culture are part of what we are. But we should protect and promote our languages in the context of respecting other peoples' rights. Language rights are for my community but not just only for my community. They are for all peoples. Because of my rather unusual career, I have had the privilege of being able to help small language communities throughout Europe to conserve and promote their linguistic heritages. When I got to know my friends in the Ulster-Scots movement and when they asked me to lend them a helping hand, I had no philosophical or psychological problems with acceding to their request. Working together with them has been an enriching experience for me and I think for other people in both language movements. Together we have done some very interesting things and hopefully will do many more.

Language Policy Implementation:
A DCAL Civil Servant's Perspective

Edward Rooney

1. Introduction

At the outset, it may be helpful to explain what I mean by a "civil servant's perspective". Later in the symposium programme there are civil servants from both the North and the South who not only work in the general area of language policy, but who also have a genuine expertise in – even a passion for – language. That is not typical of civil servants and does not reflect my own position. I do not speak Ulster Scots, Irish, any of the ethnic minority languages, and I do not understand either British or Irish Sign Language. My job, however, is to ensure the successful implementation of language policy. In this article, I intend to set language policy in its context, summarise progress made so far in the implementation of language policy, and provide a personal view of some of the issues which impact on the extent and speed of implementation of this policy.

2. Context

2.1 The Belfast/Good Friday Agreement

The Belfast / Good Friday Agreement sets out the Government's commitment to the promotion of linguistic diversity. This is to:

> *recognise the importance of respect, understanding and tolerance in relation to linguistic diversity, including in Northern Ireland, the Irish language, Ulster-Scots and the languages of the various ethnic minority communities, all of which are part of the cultural wealth of the island of Ireland.*

The Agreement identified the following further commitments in relation to Irish in particular:

- To take resolute action to promote the language
- To facilitate and encourage the use of the language in public and private life where there is appropriate demand
- To seek to remove, where possible, restrictions which would discourage or work against the maintenance or development of the language
- To make provision for liaising with the Irish language community, representing their views to public authorities and investigating complaints

- To place a statutory duty on the Department of Education to encourage and facilitate Irish medium education ...
- To explore urgently ... the scope for achieving more widespread availability of TnaG in Northern Ireland
- To seek more effective ways to encourage and provide financial support for Irish language film and TV production.

2.2 *The European Charter for Regional or Minority Languages*

The Agreement paragraphs were framed in anticipation of the UK ratifying the Council of Europe's *Charter for Regional or Minority Languages.* The Charter itself was ratified in 27 March 2001 and came into effect on 1 July 2001, providing an overarching commitment to preserve Irish and Ulster-Scots along with Welsh, Scots and Scottish Gaelic. Both Ulster-Scots and Irish were specified for Part II of the Charter and Irish was further specified for Part III which included articles on education, judicial authorities, administrative authorities and public services, media, cultural activities and facilities, economic and social life and trans-frontier exchanges.

2.3 Equality / Human Rights Legislation

While Section 75 of the Northern Ireland equality legislation does not mention directly linguistic diversity, the general requirement to pay due regard to the need to promote equality of opportunity specifically refers to race and disability and appears to have particular relevance for ethnic minority and sign language. The European Convention on Human Rights is more explicit, with Article 14 requiring rights to be secured without discrimination on any ground such as language. In sum, language policy is developing in the context of a highly supportive political environment underpinned by both Northern Ireland and European agreements and legislation.

3. Progress

Significant progress has been made in language policy implementation particularly in the following areas:

3.1 North-South Language Implementation Body

The North-South Language Implementation Body (*An Foras Teanga / Tha Boord o Leid*) is responsible for implementing the Agreement commitments through its two agencies, *Foras na Gaeilge* and *Tha Boord o Ulstèr-Scotch.* The functions of the Language Implementation Body include:

- Promoting the Irish language
- Facilitating its use

- Advising administrations, public bodies and private and voluntary sectors
- Providing grant aid
- Undertaking research and promotional campaigns
- Developing terminology and dictionaries
- Supporting Irish medium education and teaching
- Promoting awareness and use of Ullans and Ulster Scots cultural issues within Northern Ireland and throughout the island.

Both agencies are up and running. *Tha Boord o Ulstèr-Scotch* has established its headquarters in Belfast and is seeking to set up a regional office in Donegal. This year it has funding of £1.3m and it supports a wide range of cultural, language and research activities. It has published its first corporate plan which sets out the following priorities:

- Supporting Ulster Scots as a living language and promoting its use and development
- Acting as a key contributor to the development of Ulster Scots culture
- Establishing partnerships with education and community sectors
- Developing public understanding of Ulster Scots language and culture.

Foras na Gaeilge has a staff complement of 65 and a budget of over £10m. Its first strategic plan has been approved and the agency's activities have included the support of language groups, publication of books and textbooks and the English-Irish dictionary project. It has also sponsored a major TV and radio advertising campaign to promote learning Irish.

Both agencies anticipate recruiting permanent Chief Executives in the Autumn-Winter 2001-2002.

3.2 The European Charter for Regional or Minority Languages

Within the Northern Ireland Executive, an inter-departmental Standing Charter Group has been established to help with implementation of the Charter. Its functions include developing an action plan for implementation, monitoring progress and preparing guidance and support services. Interim guidance on the use of Irish in official business was issued in July 2001 and a working group on translation services has been established under the auspices of the inter-departmental group. The translations working group is reviewing the demand for Irish translation services across Departments and shortly will bring forward recommendations for establishing a quality assured service. *Tha Boord o Ulstèr-Scotch* handles Ulster Scots translations.

3.3 Broadcasting Film and TV Production

A two-year Irish language TV and film production pilot scheme, based upon an action plan produced by Don Anderson, is due to commence this autumn. There will be a strong training dimension, linked to NVQ, and it is intended that the scheme will include a support package for production of films and TV programmes.

3.4 Research

A range of research projects has been supported for Ulster Scots and Irish, including investigation of the demand for Irish in official business; attitudes to provision of services in Ulster Scots and Irish; and research to assist language planning.

3.5 Ethnic Minority Languages and Sign Language

These are the areas where we have made least progress, but realise that there is enormous potential to have a positive impact. Preliminary discussions have been held with interested groups and we hope to begin the process of developing policies in earnest before the end of this year.

4. Implementing Language Policy: Issues

The following are high on my personal list of conditions for the successful implementation of new policy:

- Clarity of purpose
- Shared vision and goals
- Clear strategies and action plans for achieving these
- Evidence of success and impact
- Realism

So how does language policy measure up?

4.1 Clarity of purpose

While the spirit of support for language policy development emerges strongly from the relevant paragraphs of the Agreement, virtually every sentence contains at least one ambiguous or qualifying term which could be the subject of debate as to its precise meaning. Consider the following instances:

- *Take **resolute action** to **promote** the language*
- ***Facilitate and encourage** the use of the language in public and private life where there is **appropriate demand***

- **Seek to** remove, **where possible,** *restrictions which would discourage or work against the maintenance or development of the language*
- **Make provision** *for liaising with the Irish language community, representing their views to public authorities and investigating complaints*

Lack of clarity is not confined to the Agreement clauses. The *European Charter for Regional or Minority Languages* also contains its fair share of such terms.

4.2 Shared vision and goals

It helps the process of policy development and implementation if there is at least a basic consensus around vision and goals. This is becoming a common feature of DCAL's policy initiatives, with the *Future Search* methodology being adopted or planned in developing common ground in diverse areas including arts and culture, sport and libraries.

It may be that I have missed something, but my impression is that it is the differences rather than consensus that are most evident in the area of language policy. This can be said both in relation to attitudes and approaches to language development across Government Departments as well as in the interaction between and within different language groups. The shared vision and goals may be there, but if they are, they struggle to surface.

4.3 Strategies and action plans

The agencies have taken the first step towards developing Corporate or Strategic plans. It must be appreciated that these are first attempts at high level plans and as such represent a highly significant step forward. However, successful policy implementation requires more detailed business plans and at this stage, we are still waiting to see how these develop.

4.4 Evidence of success and impact

It is difficult to overstate the importance of producing evidence of the effectiveness of action to promote language policy development. This will require the gathering of robust data, identification of good practice and evidence to support the contribution of language policy to the wider community. And while it is a term that many baulk at, it also involves establishing value for money for this action.

4.5 Realism

There is a need for realism about both resource availability and about the speed of implementation of language policy. With respect to resource availability, it is worth remembering that the honeymoon period for language funding is likely to be short-lived, especially in a situation where there is intense competition for scarce resources. It does no harm to reflect that a higher proportion of DCAL's budget now goes to language than to sport. This area has moved very rapidly from being a relatively minor to a major player. It would be unrealistic to expect this scale of growth to continue.

Regarding speed of implementation, while there is an understandable frustration at the slow pace of progress, arguably this is the fastest growing policy area across Government. It is important to be realistic about what can be achieved within particular timescales.

5. Conclusion

Language policy is probably the fastest growing policy area across Government. Very significant progress has been made in a relatively short period. However, we are in a strategic 'catch-up' position with a lot of weaknesses to be addressed. If we are to continue the progress that has been made so far, then it important to build on the positive developments and ensure that a firm foundation is provided for language policy of the future. There is an imperative for everyone concerned with developing and implementing language policy to get their collective act together. There is no room for complacency or for expecting others to place a high value on the contribution of language policy to the community. The reality is that we are operating in competitive policy environment where each step forward will be hard fought for and where the arguments for public funding will increasingly centre around evidence of value for money. Language policy needs to be in a position to fight its corner.

Linguistic Diversity Education Project

Mary Delargy

The *Linguistic Diversity Education Project* is one part of the *Languages of Ulster Project*, which ran in the Linen Hall Library from January 2000 until October 2001. Other parts of this project include provision of classes in Irish, Ulster Scots and Mandarin and a number of outreach events organised in conjunction with other language bodies. By Autumn 2001, these have included the launch of the European Year of Languages 2000, in conjunction with NICILT at Queen's University; a one-day languages fair involving the Ulster Scots Heritage Council, Iontaobhas Ultach, Chinese Welfare Association, Multi-Cultural Resource Centre and a number of other education-based language organisations. A key part of the project has been our involvement with Diversity 21 and a wide range of other organisations in the development of the language exhibition 'In Other Words'. The accompanying booklet, recently re-printed, gave ten key phrases such as 'Hello' and 'Goodbye' in almost thirty different languages including sign language.

The original project, which began officially in 1993, was focused on the Irish language and was aimed at bringing it to as wide an audience as possible. This was achieved through an annual language lecture series – given for the most part through the medium of English and aimed at a generalist audience. Among topics covered were 'The Media and the Irish Language', 'Contemporary Irish Drama' and 'Women of Ulster in '98' – our first bilingual lecture. In addition the Library, with its tradition of radicalism and equality, was more than willing to host cross-community Irish language classes. I hesitate to use the phrase "neutral venue" so often seen in politically correct articles, carrying as it does the suggestion that any venue not thus described must implicitly have a political agenda, but this is the perception of the Library. This meant that many people who would have been nervous about attending Irish classes in other locations were happy to do so in the Library. From a small group of half a dozen brave beginners, the class has now grown beyond all our expectations – there are currently three classes weekly, one each at beginners', improvers', and advanced level, many of those in the advanced class having worked their way up from the beginners' level. It is worth noting, also, for those who consider whether people belong to one community or the other, and for those who see Irish as belonging to members of the Catholic community, that there are actually more Protestants overall, including a significant number of clergy.

It became obvious, however, that whatever our policy of inclusion, there was a whole community for whom there was not adequate provision within our library service: the Ulster Scots speaking community. By 1998, the language lecture series was broadened to include Ulster Scots and some very stimulating debate took place over the language issues. Our first lecture concentrated on the whole issue of the

Ulster Scots language and once again the language/dialect debate came to the fore. It was, however, heartening to hear one prominent Irish language activist putting forward the idea that it was in the best interests of Ulster Scots speakers to work alongside the Irish language movement since they would be able to learn from the mistakes made by Irish language activists.

As the project grew, we became even more ambitious as to what we might be able to achieve, while at the same time becoming aware of the many groups who were still effectively excluded from our library service. Thus it was that, with a great deal of soul searching and a financial package from the E.U. Special Support Programme, the *Languages of Ulster Project* was born, just as the new millennium dawned. Our remit - for in those days there were two of us working on the project - was to provide library services for all speakers of minority languages within Northern Ireland. How to go about providing those services was a difficult task. The Irish language service had not really been a problem for me as I was able to speak the language and already knew many of the key players in the movement.

With the Ulster Scots movement too, I had become acquainted with various people involved in attempts to promote the language. Although I had not got past being able to say *fair faa ye* and *sae lang noo*, the very fact that I worked in the Linen Hall Library, with its scholarly reputation, helped give me a credence I might not otherwise have had, especially given that some people were automatically suspicious of the fact that my colleague and myself were both Irish speakers. But how can you presume to offer a service to a group when you cannot speak the other person's language and have only the most basic understanding of their culture?

There were, of course, groups such as the Chinese Welfare Association and the Multi-Cultural Resource Centre who were able to provide some background information. There were many lessons to be learnt, however. Like the civil servants who so eloquently addressed us earlier in the proceedings, I discovered that there are enormous gaps between people's perceptions of what is possible and the reality of the situation. Unlike those civil servants, who felt that language groups sometimes made unreasonable and unrealistic demands, I have to confess that the unrealistic demands were mine. There were two main reasons for this - and I offer them not so much as an excuse for what happened - but more so that anyone coming behind can learn from the mistakes. Firstly, when I began, I was full of boundless enthusiasm for the project – there were lots of things we could be doing and we were going to do them all – now! The fact that the project was grant funded was actually something of a double-edged sword. It was extremely useful to have proper resources to organise the project and it was very helpful that we were working on it on a full-time basis, rather than the part-time basis on which the Irish language project had been run. That it was full-time, combined with the fact that it was time-limited, meant that we had to produce a certain amount of work in a very short time. It is one thing telling somebody whom you know quite well and with whom you have a good working relationship that the two of you will be putting on an exhibition in a fortnight's time. It is rather more difficult if it is someone whom you barely know, and you put the pressure on to try to have them involved in the project only to discover that they have a much more hierarchical structure which means that everything they work on has to be discussed at management level before being agreed, rather than running a project past a boss whose enthusiasm for starting projects is matched only by your own. Different projects have different priorities. As Lord Laird mentions (see this volume), the Ulster Scots Agency is concerned not only with language but also with culture. The Chinese Welfare Association works not only with language issues but also on all issues relating to the Chinese population in Northern Ireland. The Multi-Cultural Resource Centre is concerned with welfare rights and healthcare issues as well as linguistic difficulties. Despite these difficulties, the various groups managed to work together on a number of different projects over the last eighteen months – including 'In Other Words', our languages exhibition designed with the assistance of Diversity 21 and the pilot of which was the first project on which all the language groups involved had ever worked together, which has toured throughout Ireland - and an accompanying booklet, also entitled *In Other Words*, to celebrate European Year of Languages 2001.

We also held a 'Language Taster Week' in May 2001 to allow people who had never before tried learning a language to experience it in a one-hour session. These sessions proved very popular, especially the sign language class where our initial embarrassment was soon overcome as our teacher had us in fits of laughter as we struggled to relate the pictures before us and his facility in reproducing them into something which actually made sense. During 2000 and 2001 we have also offered two lots of classes in Ulster Scots language and literature, held in March/April 2000 and again in April 2001, and a ten week series of Mandarin classes, beginning in October 2000 - in fact I think the Linen Hall is unique in offering all these classes at once. The classes attracted quite an amount of interest, as many people were fascinated to see the wide range of backgrounds from which the people attending the classes came – a range of backgrounds as diverse as their reasons for wanting to learn a particular language.

The events which we organised as part of the *Languages of Ulster* programme, however, were open to two different interpretations. On the one hand there were those who saw what we were trying to do as a very positive thing, an awareness-building exercise in the wider community and an attempt at inclusivity. The 'In Other Words' exhibition is extremely popular, and has been constantly on tour since its opening in October 2000, having been in Belfast, Larne, Derry and Donegal – in fact there is a waiting list of potential venues. Many people in Northern Ireland think only of two lesser-used languages, Irish and Ulster Scots, and forget that very many other people have made their homes here and have brought their language with them. Of particular interest also has been the section of the exhibition dealing with words borrowed into the English language from other tongues - people are amazed at the number of influences on English, particularly the variety which we speak here in Ireland, which includes words such as *seugh* and expressions such as *I'm in the middle of doing it*, which arc not found in standard English but come directly from Scots or Irish. As always, there were the detractors – the begrudgers beloved of Irish literature who saw what we were doing as mere tokenism, who felt that they were not being adequately represented. Similarly, there was often a feeling- even among those of us who were doing the work - that we were only scratching the surface, that there was more than could be done to help people who spoke only one language to understand what it felt like to be part of a linguistic minority. The idea behind the education project is to raise awareness of these diverse linguistic groups among a wider audience. Although much excellent work has been done on the ground already, there are many people whose attitudes are still rather narrow. This was forcibly brought home to me one day when someone mentioned that he felt threatened by what he described as a group huddled together in the Linen Hall library speaking Irish. Despite the fact that my ultimate aim is to have groups interspersed throughout the Library speaking Irish, Ulster Scots, Cantonese or any other language of their choice, I realised that we still had a long way to go in changing people's attitudes, particularly as the person in question is himself involved in cross community work.

I wish that I could take the credit for the idea of the *Linguistic Diversity Education Project* myself, as I feel that it is a very worthwhile undertaking, but it is actually the brainchild of Mark Adair of the Community Relations Council. The project in its final format will be aimed initially at community groups, both single identity and cross community groups and, if it proves successful, will be adapted for use in schools. Our aim is to raise awareness of the wide range of languages spoken in Northern Ireland and the problems and issues faced by those among us whose first or preferred language is not English. Initial interest in the project has come not only from the various linguistic groups, Chinese Welfare Association, Iontaobhas Ultach and Ulster Scots Heritage Council, but also from statutory bodies and other interested parties.

Of particular interest to anyone using the pack will be the experiences of speakers of lesser-used languages within Northern Ireland. With the production of this pack, I would like the cooperation of people from the different linguistic groups. We want to hear your experiences, both good and bad, of growing up in these communities - we have already heard about some of the experiences of those who helped to establish education in a medium other than English, but we would welcome all experiences. We want participants in the symposium as well as readers of this book to write to us – to put pen to paper and tell us how you feel[1]. Obviously any submissions will eventually have to appear in English, but we want them in the language of your choice; where necessary English translations will be provided. The

---

[1] *Linguistic Diversity Education Project*, Linen Hall Library, Belfast, BT1 5GB

pack will also contain background information about each of the languages, an estimated number of speakers, its distribution throughout the province and the influence of the languages on English, particularly as we speak it here, as well as putting forward some questions for consideration. But most of all, we need you and your story. We look forward to hearing from you.

Finally, I would like to thank everyone who has supported the various language programmes in the Linen Hall Library over the last number of years, whether financially or through their time and expertise. *Go raibh maith agaibh.*

Postscript.

Looking at this paper with the benefit of hindsight, I feel that the view I put forward may seem to some people to be an unduly pessimistic one. There are inevitably problems in trying to involve a number of groups with different priorities in working on a project. Over a period of time, however, these problems can generally be resolved and, while the original project may eventually be found to be over-ambitious, a way of working which suits the needs of all the groups taking part can usually be found. Overall, I have thoroughly enjoyed my involvement in the *Languages of Ulster Project.*

Frisian and Low German: Minority Languages in Hiding[1]

Manfred Görlach

1. Introduction

Endangered ethnic or cultural identity is almost always connected with linguistic differences – whether they concern a dialect or language: often the existence of independent languages is indeed denied by the authorities by declaring them to be dialects of the bigger, often national language. Newspapers are full of reports of revolts which are connected with the status of vernaculars. For instance, a rebellion, which has been going on for at least fifty years, is connected with the non-recognition of Berber in the Kabyle mountains in Algeria. Berbers were particular enflamed in May 2001 when government representatives addressed the populace not only in Arabic, but used the almost incomprehensible standard form rather than the widely divergent local Western Maghreb variety. In Macedonia, peace largely depends on the recognition of Albanian as a second national language (which now, in August 2001, seems at least to be partially conceded by the Slavic majority), and in Corsica the demands for cultural/linguistic autonomy seem to have at long last now been successful, with a reform bill accepted in the French parliament in May 2001 – which for France leaves the question of Flemish, Breton, Basque, Catalan, Occitan/Provençal and Alsatian still unsettled.

As a consequence of the increased awareness, a rich literature has grown up devoted to the linguistic rights of minorities (cf. Barbour and Carmichael 2000, Foster 1996, Gardt 2000, Haugen 1981, Hinderling and Eichinger 1996, Stephens 1976, Williams 1991, Wirrer 2000). which it is wise to take into account for all aspects of language planning.[2] Part of the oversight is possibly because the linguistic minorities here discussed have never been militant.

2. Language and dialect

The European Charter evaded proper definitions of 'minority language' and 'regional language' distinguishing the concepts from dialect, perhaps wisely so,

---

[1] This paper was written for the 2001 Belfast Symposium devoted to the status of minority languages in Europe, a continuation of the successful symposium of the previous year (cf. Görlach 2000). For help with the present version I would like to thank John Kirk, Ulf-Thomas Lesle, Horst Haider Munske, Hermann Niebaum, Thomas Steensen and Dieter Stellmacher. The usual disclaimers apply.

[2] Some of these publications are characterized by strange oversights: for instance, Williams (1991) does not even mention the two languages here treated, and he also fails to refer to Lusatian/Sorbisch; moreover, in 1991, he uses a pre-unification map for Germany on the cover and on p. 14.

Map 1: Present-day Frisian: West Frisian, East Frisian, North[3]

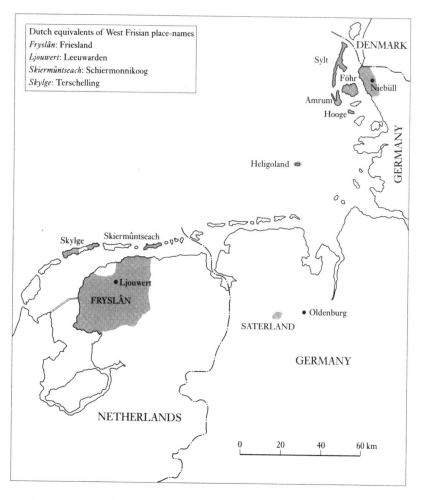

Dutch equivalents of West Frisian place-names
Fryslân: Friesland
Ljouwert: Leeuwarden
Skiermûntseach: Schiermonnikoog
Skylge: Terschelling

and also evaded the question of what makes a language indigenous and thereby eligible for inclusion. It is a strange fact that discussions, often heated, tend to arise about a few hundred speakers of Saterland Frisian, or even some ten remaining fluent speakers of Sette Commune Cimbrian close to Asiago in Northern Italy, whereas not even the numbers of Turkish or Kurdish speakers of some 2-3 million among the ethnic minority in Germany have been counted.

A starting-point for determining languageness can be Kloss's seminal definition ([2]1978) which I have modified in the form of the four A's: *abstand, ausbau*, attitude and acquisition (Görlach 2000). Although these parameters will

---

[3] Map 1 is reproduced from Salverda 1998, with permission from Blackwell Publishers Ltd.

prove to be too general for a description of the present-day status of the minority languages here discussed, I will have to take them up frequently and therefore repeat a short definition:

Abstand is, then, the structural distance between two varieties, most often measured against the nearest standard language; it has obviously to do with intelligibility, a less sophisticated criterion which is often adduced for decisions on whether a group of dialects can really be lumped together as one language, as in the case of Frisian.

Ausbau – the degree of standardization, and therefore also of homogeneity, and the range of functions of the variety.

Attitude – the perception of the variety as an independent language by its native speakers, and less so, by outsiders, and a whole battery of value judgments on whether it is felt to be 'clear, friendly, nice, useful, logical etc.'

Acquisition – whether it is learnt as a native variety for the whole period of language acquisition, or learnt as a second dialect, or possibly only remembered etc.

However, a second model will here be useful to describe the status of Frisian and Low German more closely; I would like to summarize the categorization suggested by White (1991) for minorities in Italy. He distinguishes ten types, viz. those which are unique to one state, either close-knit or diffuse; those which are contiguous to the speech of an adjacent state, either close-knit or diffuse; those which form minorities in two states, close-knit or diffuse; those which happen to be separated by a political border from the bulk of speakers; and other types of linguistic islands, most often the consequence of earlier migration.

It should be added, in order to avoid misunderstandings, that minority status is accepted for all branches of Frisian (part III, defined by ethnicity) whereas Low German/*Nedersaksisch* is a regional language (part II, defined by area).

3. The historical and present-day position of Frisian

3.1 The historical background

Alkmaaar and Jadebusen – but also been expanded by the emigration to the North Frisian islands and later the adjacent coastal strip in Schleswig. From the 13th century onwards the Frisians were politically devided: West Frisians lost their language becoming part of Holland, Central (= now called West) Frisians retaining their independence to the 16th century, but losing the province of Groningen, East Frisians being long independent but adopting Low German, and emigrant North Frisians constituting a small minority in the Duchy of Schleswig.

Map 2: West Frisian[4]

This division naturally enough hindered the creation of a common standard language.[5] The present-day distribution of Frisian is shown in Map 0.

3.2   West Frisian[6]

Some 400,000 speakers now make up some 60% to 70% of the total of 580,000 inhabitants of the province of Fryslân (Friesland), as shown in Map 2. The towns introduced Dutch as the H(igh) language, especially for written uses, from the 17th century onwards, and towndwellers increasingly used Frisian-coloured

---

[4] Map 2 is reproduced from Feitsma (n.d.).

[5] Frisians re-established contacts among each other especially from the Romantic period onwards, and have increased these in recent times. Important as these contacts were for Frisian identity, they had no substantial linguistic consequences (cf. Steensen 2001). Note that if a criterion for 'regional language' is its dominant use over a larger geographical area, West Frisian might well qualify for that status, its currency being similar to that of Low German.

[6] The following survey is largely based on the very informative summary by Feitsma (n.d.) complemented by data taken from chapters in Munske (forthcoming [2001?]).

Dutch for spoken communication; in addition, the mixed variety of urban Frisian developed which contrasted with both Dutch and rural Frisian. A new literary tradition of Frisian started in the late 17th century, when Gysbert Japicx created a tradition of impressive range and quality. From the 18th century onwards, there appears to have been a stable diglossia of written Dutch and spoken Frisian at least in the rural areas. A new literary revival was prompted by the Romantic movement in the early 19th century, which expanded the uses of Frisian and partly raised its prestige; another literary renaissance in the 20th century and political movements promoting the Frisian language re-established the language at least partially in a greater range of text types and of public domains. Drastic changes caused by in-migration into Fryslân after 1945 have recently changed the situation: colloquial forms of Dutch have in many families replaced the former diglossia. However, research undertaken in 1979 to 1982 still reported that 94% of the population understood Frisian quite well, 75% spoke it well, 65% read Frisian, but only 11% were able to write Frisian without problems. For 55% Frisian was the home language (against 35% for Dutch and 9% for the local dialect). 80% stated that reading Dutch was easier than reading Frisian, and the very limited writing competence makes the majority of Frisians practically illiterate in their mother tongue. There are now hardly any monolinguals left. The situation in the towns is quite different: of Ljouwert's (= Leeuwarden) 85,000 inhabitants, 25% reported Frisian, 15% (low-status, receding) urban Frisian and 60% Dutch as their mother tongue. (Feitsma, n.d. 28-9)

Official uses are even more restricted. The first Bible translation dates to 1943, but Frisian is practically not used in churches. Frisian has made some advance in schools; however, its use is normally restricted to 45 minutes per week, and it is hardly ever used as a medium. Bilingual education is frequently considered (by parents and authorities) as a stepping-stone to better Dutch. In secondary education, only 5% of the students attend the facultative Frisian lessons.[7] To promote literacy in the language, Frisian books and journals can be subsidized;[8] local administration has made some moves to introduce Frisian into official uses. However, the situation in (regional) radio and TV is deplorable, with hardly any Frisian employed.

---

[7] Bilingual programmes were started in Frisia in 1950s – before that time it had largely been considered a patriotic duty to speak Dutch (Zondag 2001). However, only from 1993 has Frisian been "a compulsory subject in the lower grades of secondary education", but it "remains in an extremely weak state of development". Even optimists are aware of the fact that "the linguistic map is changing dramatically and the threat of 'McDonaldization' is looming ahead." It is claimed that competence in Frisian is very high among elementary school teachers (96% can understand, 91% speak, 86% read, and 61% write Frisian).

[8] Meerburg (forthcoming [2001?]) states that there are today some 120 Frisian-writing authors of whom 25% write children's books; literature ranges from plays to literary journals. Academically, Frisian studies are represented at five universities, but clearly in a very marginal position; research is concentrated in the Fryske Akademy at Ljouwert.

Map 3: East Frisian[9]

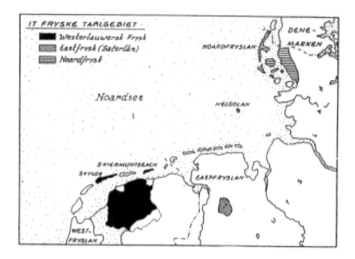

3.3   Saterland (East Frisian)

Of the extensive medieval language area only the name *Ostfriesland* survives. The 600 – 800 (?) remaining speakers of Seeltirsk outside the original Frisian area cultivated the fens in the 11th century, when they fled the disastrous floods of the coastal areas, especially of the Ems region; their language survived in three villages largely owing to their isolation, as shown in Map 3. Today, nothing can possibly save the language – the area is now easily accessible and part-industrialized and since East Frisian is without a written literature and taught for only a few hours in the local school,[10] the prospects are dire. Whether institutional support can be of any help where the speakers have largely come to think that St German is better for the educational and professional future of their children is open to doubt. European financial support may be welcome, but is unlikely to change the situation.

3.4   North Frisian

The language was transplanted to the islands of (present-day) Amrum, Föhr, Sylt and Heligoland in the seventh century, and to a coastal strip north of Eiderstedt in the tenth, which resulted in an early split between the two dialect groups – four varieties on the islands and the five dialects on the mainland, as shown clearly in

---

[9] Map 3 is reproduced from Feitsma (n.d.).
[10] A native-speaking kindergarten experiment has been tried, but it is too early to say anything about prospects.

Map 4: Distribution of German, Danish and Frisian in the Duchy of Schleswig c. 1850[11]

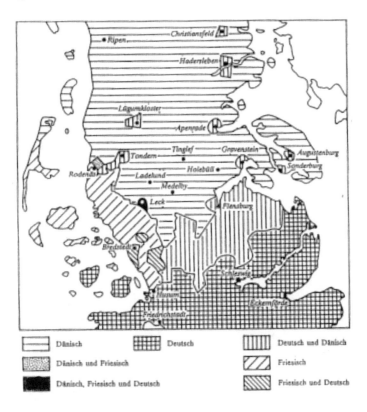

Dänisch	Deutsch	Deutsch und Dänisch
Dänisch und Friesisch		Friesisch
Dänisch, Friesisch und Deutsch		Friesisch und Deutsch

the map of North Frisian dialects at the beginning of the twentieth century in Århammar 1968, reproduced in Walker 1990 (not reproduced here) – all combined to form a virtual North Frisian, a decision based on historical reasons and their distance to the neighbouring Danish and (Low) German. Differences increased through Danish (respectively Low German) influence according to political domination up to the 19th century, and the fact that the disconnected linguistic islands were separated by fens and moors.[12] The present-day demographic situation is precarious: all the ten dialects put together number 8,000-10,000 speakers[13] which are a minority in most villages, and not even a

---

[11] Map 3 is reproduced from Dyhr 1990: 27.

[12] The North Frisian community was affected by drastic losses during its history: huge floods submerged major parts of the territory in 1362 and 1634; from the 19th century onwards, emigration was particularly high.

[13] Present-day figures are closer to 6000 – 7000: Föhr/Amrum 2000 – 2500, Sylt 500 – 700, Helgoland 500 – , Bökingharde 1500 – 2000, remaining mainland dialects 1000 – (Gorter and Walter 2001).

smaller town is left as predominantly Frisian-speaking. The survival of the dialects (which tend to differ one village to another) was made possible through their:

- isolation;
- diglossia (by which Frisian was not stigmatized vs. Danish, but (on the mainland) was felt to be inferior vis-à-vis (Low) German);
- the non-existence non-existence of a NF standard – which might then have had to compete with the languages of wider communication).

The linguistic situation is complicated by the fact that the traditional broad Danish dialect of Sønderjysk survives in a few villages and that Standard Danish mother-tongue is claimed by a some thirty (?) thousand speakers in the Flensburg area, all remnants of shifts of linguistic boundaries between the 16th and 19th centuries, as shown in Map 4. The presence of politically more relevant Danish speakers has possibly helped with the formal recognition of Frisian as a minority language.[14]

Modern developments (education, traffic, mobility, radio and TV[15]) have shrunk the domains in which Frisian has everyday uses; it survives best in a few areas where it can rely on high concentrations of speakers and high identificational value, as in the community of Risum-Lindholm on the mainland[16] and on western Föhr (a largely rural part, which has escaped excessive tourism). Whether the Martha's-Vineyard effect on Sylt, where islanders see their identity increasingly threatened by tourism, will have any lasting effects on the continuing (or even increasing) use of Sölring ('Sylt Frisian'), remains to be seen.

---

[14] Many parallels to this big sister effect come to mind: in Southern Tyrol, the Ladin community joined forces with the much larger and politically important German minority, and in Northern Ireland the recognition of Ullans is largely to compensate the status of Irish.

[15] Representation of North Frisian in the media is unbelievably low: the North German Radio broadcasts very few longer transmissions, but normally only three minutes in Frisian per week, and political moves to improve the situation have been unsuccessful. In churches, Frisian has long been thought not quite suitable, and services in Frisian are rare today; biblical translations into various dialects are of parts only, and some remain unpublished, but there is a recent hymn-book of 840 pages.

[16] Gorter and Walker (2001) find that owing to the leading role of Risum-Lindholm the local variety "is developing into the main mainland dialect, partly to the displeasure of the speakers of the surrounding dialects." Attitudes against such koinéization are strengthened by a new spelling system which does not agree with the German principles. Another danger, especially for Frisian acquired as a second dialect, is that it becomes relexified German.

4.   Low German

4.1   Definition

Map 5: The Dialects of German c. 1900 showing the regional distribution of High German (*Oberdeutsch*), Low German (*Niederdeutsch*) and Frisian c. 1900[17]

Low German (*Niederdeutsch* – see Map 5) is a linguistic construct; speakers name their own language *Platt(dütsch)*. The following exclusions are in order:

1. The term does not include the standard or dialect forms of Dutch in the Netherlands, Belgium and the Dunkirk area in France.
2. It does not cover mixed languages such as urban Missingsch in Hamburg, an inadequately acquired High German, forms of which are also used by the local Ohnsorg theatre for national TV productions.

---

[17] Map 5 is reproduced from Goossens 1977: 123

Map 6: Core Areas Determined by Dialect Lexis along the Dutch/German Border[18]

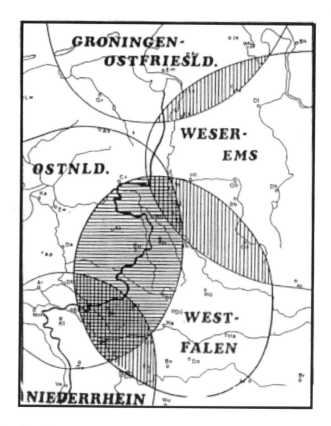

On the other hand it includes:

3. Low German outside Germany, most notably *Nedersaksisch*, such as in the Groningen province (Grunnegers) and Mennonite Plattdütsch (now mainly spoken in communities in Russia, Canada, Belize and Paraguay), as well as emigrant Pomerian in Brazil.

These definitions make the Low Franconian dialect of the German Lower Rhine (the Aachen-Düsseldorf-Cleve region) an only marginally Low German area However, the linguistic distinction becomes blurred because of overlapping focal areas in connection with a political boundary cutting right through traditional dialect distinctions (as shown in Map 6). Note that Grunnegers will have to be considered separately from, say, the neighbouring Low German dialect of

---

[18] Map 6 is reproduced from Kremer 1990: 96-97.

Ostfriesland, since the sociopolitical status differs according to national conditions, even where linguistic characteristics of the variety do not – it is commonly conceded (by e.g. Kremer 1990) that the political boundary (in fact for almost 400 years now) has had far fewer effects on the spoken dialects on either side than might have been expected.

4.2 Historical aspects

As I have repeatedly summarized (1985, 1988) the social history of Low German (*Niederdeutsch*) follows a pattern of dialectalization well-known from other European vernaculars which did not achieve full national standard in the Renaissance,[19] but were step by step replaced in their functions, by a neighbouring more powerful language – Occitan by French, Scots by English, Cashubian by Polish – and, almost, Catalan by Castilian Spanish. The loss of functions tends to affect the written and formal registers first (in administration and legal uses, church and education, books and newspapers), leaving the minority language deficient for many forms of communication – where often unperceived borrowing from the related H(igh) language is the obvious solution.

Diglossia can persist for centuries, but will ultimately be followed by a situation in which a continuum between H(igh) and L(ow) becomes stylistic, that is, where speakers no longer keep the two language systems apart – the typical dilemma of standard-dialect continua. The former independent language therefore becomes dialectalized.[20]

Note that historicity, the fact that a variety had respectable genres in prose and verse in earlier stages, does not stop this erosion – Low German had a translated Bible in the 16th century, by Bugenhagen, a pupil of Luther, and it boasts a rich literature, especially in the 19th century. Historicity can, however, be important for attitudes (speakers wanting to return to the linguistic independence of a glorious past) and for solutions in language planning where older forms can be revived to fill gaps in the modern envisaged standard.

4.3 Low German in Northern Germany

The geographical limits of Low German are clear-cut, as shown in Map 5. The dialects east of the Oder are now almost extinct after all German speakers were expelled after WWII. Berlin is no longer Low German speaking – the last speakers in suburbs were recorded about a hundred years ago. The division between *West-* and *Ostniederdeutsch* is based on a few isoglosses; in fact, regional forms like *Münsterländisch* and *Ostfriesisch Platt* diverge more from the common core than the two major dialects between each other.

---

[19] This did not stop Low German from being widely used as an international trade language of the Hansa, of course.

[20] The most recent book that includes Low German varieties under 'German dialects' without any comment is Niebaum and Macha (1999); this may come as a surprise since Niebaum holds a chair for Low German in Groningen.

Low German, then, never developed a full supraregional standard form – mainly because its use was not defined by a nation state, and because High German practically inherited the standard functions formerly filled by Latin, from the 16th century onwards. Attempts at creating at least a literary standard (such as the attempt by J.H. Voss) were not accepted. The major literary works were, in consequence, written in regional forms of Low German, such as by Reuter (Mecklenburg), Groth (Holstein) or Wibbelt (Münsterland). More recent attempts at creating standard orthographies and (partly) developing compromises in lexis and idiom (by Radio Bremen) and selecting a widely acceptable pronunciation have met with some hesitance or opposition among speakers of local dialects – the predicament of all language planning where code selection may endanger acceptability and where decisions *against* the native speakers are a risky basis for successful implementation.

Low German has retained a nominally strong demographic basis (of some 5 million claimed speakers), in spite of dramatic losses in certain, especially urban, areas and more recently among younger speakers even in the heartlands of the language (Schleswig-Holstein, Northern Lower Saxony, East Friesland) – the once very strong position in Mecklenburg was seriously affected by the educational policies of the GDR. However, investigations in 1984 found that Low German competence was claimed by as many as 71% in Schleswig-Holstein, but only 27% in North-Rhine/Westphalia (Stellmacher 1987) – but these figures are based on self-reports, and what was meant by 'knowledge of Low German' was left to the informants to define.[21] This still widespread competence means that it was possible to have Low German represented in the media (mainly spoken, on radio and TV) and, however experimentally, used in churches, local parliaments and in addressing civil servants, to an extent unheard of for Occitan/Provençal or Scots. It has also been used, marginally, in schools and extramural education, and has various universities and research institutes looking after scholarly research into its forms and functions.

One of the most notable experiments is the extensive use of Low German by Radio Bremen and NDR Hamburg-Welle. Compromises have been sought (and many people say, found) to bridge the established High German text types 'radio news' and the more narrative structures of Low German. A self-characterization summarizing twenty years of Low German news in Radio Bremen (translated from the quotation of 1997 in Möhn 1999: 71) claims:

> There is, on the one hand, the distanced, formulaic, technical language of news reports in High German, full of nouns and technical terms, and the intimate, concrete, uncomplicated, familiar diction of Low German on the other. Twenty years of experience have created an independent Low German news claiming the best of two worlds.[22]

---

[21] The most recent figures based on a poll are summarized in Stellmacher (1987: 93-5); The figures fulfil our expectations according to age, education, urban/rural and wider regional distribution – but not according to gender.

[22] This contrasts with Swiss German radio, where news are formulated in

This experience is of particular relevance for the expansion of other minority languages into new registers: using primarily spoken languages for formal written text types brings with it a twofold danger. The new register may sound totally artificial or even unintentionally funny (see Kirk 2000, Görlach 2000 for Ulster Scots) – or become de-intellectualized, and in consequence appear naive and childish.[23]

4.4 Low German (= *Nedersaksisch*) in the Netherlands

Low German, once an international language, has long since died out in Estonia/Latvia, Sweden or Denmark. The speech of the provinces of Groningen, Drenthe, Overijssel, etc. (formerly largely Frisian-speaking) has been 'Saxon' from the Middle Ages, but the position of the language is much weaker than that of West Frisian on the one hand, and of Low German in Germany.[24] There have been some experimental uses in literature (such as Shakespeare translations) but claims to language status vis-à-vis Dutch can be scarcely upheld – and are not frequently made. In fact, some 'proper' Dutch dialects seem to be as distant from the standard as Grunnegers is, and in fact the southernmost dialect Limburgish has been discussed as a possible candidate for the European Charter. Support from beyond the border, especially from the closely related Low German of Ostfriesland (as shown in Map 4) appeared to be largely lacking, and therefore the dialectalization of Nedersaksisch seemed to continue largely unnoticed and unheeded – before it came to be included in the Charter (see below). However, judgement is difficult – we do not even have estimates of numbers of speakers (and detailed descriptions of what it means to speak Nedersaksisch).

Schwyzerdütsch, news in Low German are translated – however freely (Möhn 1999: 71). See also Fischer (in this volume).

[23] For the methods of intervariational translation see the summary in Möhn (1999). The development has become possible by the creation of new dictionaries, including a High German into Low German one of 1986. From 1999 onwards, five translators each are responsible for Low German news in Bremen and Hamburg (Möhn 1999: 88). The large-scale identity of High and Low German culture means that encyclopedic equivalents can be assumed to exist. Lexical gaps can be filled, with due caution, by semantic extension of Low German items, by hybrids and paraphrases, or by leaving modern German lexis untranslated (= 14% of the nouns). This includes words from administration (*Finanzbehörde*) and youth language (*Punk, T-Shirt*). It would need more detailed tests to show whether new creations like *Versekerungskoopman* 'insurance broker' have a comic effect on some listeners. *Schadstoffausstoß* translated as *Schiet, de achtern ut den Utpuff rutflüggt* is certainly too narrow and smells of register misuse (catachresis).

[24] This is partly explained by *abstand*: Nedersaksisch is closer to standard Dutch – whereas Low Franconian on the German Lower Rhine (close to the basis of modern Dutch) is classified as a Low German dialect.

4.5   The Low German of the Mennonites

The history of the migrations of the religious minority – from Ostfriesland/ North Holland to Western Prussia / Dantzig to Russia and after 1917 largely dispersed to Canada, Belize and Paraguay – makes the retention of the dialect border on a miracle. However, structural, social and geographical criteria suggest that Mennonite *Plautdütsch* might well be classified as a language rather than as a dialect; at any rate, it does not come under the European Charter.[25]

5.   Consequences of the European Charter

5.1   Language planning for Frisian

The most welcome effect of the inclusion of Frisian in the Charter– in all its three regional varieties – is that an official recognition means a rise in prestige, and that it may give the speakers the reassurance that to hand on the language to future generations is worth the effort. However, the consequences are very different in practical application: For West Frisian any assistance can help stabilize existing efforts to expand the uses of Standard West Frisian into new domains, and in particular to secure for it more prominence in schools and the media – if the Frisians want this extension: this would be clearly opposite to the current tendencies which have seen an increasing expansion of the uses of Dutch. Experiences relating to other European minority languages can possibly help avoid exaggerated expectations on the basis of the Charter. A substantial support of the declining speech communities of Romansh, financially as well as legally, socially and attitudinally, has had only little effect for language maintenance. To keep up a language for the single reason of expressing ethnic identity is an idea foreign to most speakers, and whether European recognition can slow down, stop or even reverse trends that are evident all over Europe, is at least doubtful. For West Frisian the substantial numbers of speakers are possibly a factor in favour of retention – however, 'identity' can be, and often is, the stronger the more close-knit a community is – which in principle argues for a positive effect on small communities such as *Sater-Frisian*: all will depend here on establishing a link between local identity and the preservation of a language that has little additional use. My lack of knowledge of the community does not allow me to make any predictions.

North Frisian is different again. It was certainly a fortunate coincidence that Frisian was combined in the same Charter with Lusatian and Danish, because these other minorities had long achieved a greater degree of political and public awareness, and Low German brought in the weight of fifty times as many speakers. If recognition for North Frisian means extended representation in the media, improved teaching and a general raise of prestige, speakers may well

---

[25] If coverage of Frisian on the radio were to be increased would this be in the Mooring koiné of Risum? At present, at least the three major dialects are used.

decide to pass on the language to the next generation. I see a danger, however, in normative teaching (and all teaching is normative): if local standard forms (say a koiné based on Risum on the mainland) were introduced through the schools that are in conflict with the usage of the few remaining native speakers then the game is lost. On the other hand, if local dialects are used for teaching, all the materials must also be locally produced. Promotion of Frisian must therefore be strictly according to local usage: the identification of islanders with their native Sylt can only be through the local Sölring ('Sylt Frisian'), and not through a standard North Frisian[26]. Creating standard Romansh has not been a full success, since speakers did not recognize their individual dialect in the homogenized form, and school Lusatian (Sorbisch) has led to the bewildering situation that the native-speaking grandparents do not understand their grandchildren's Lusatian acquired in schools.

This concern has of course general implications: linguistic expansion as a consequence of necessary modernization as well as standardization tends to distance the new standard from 'unrefined' native usage – as does the fact that a language community comprises a greater number of second-language speakers. This will then be a greatly changed language, and the impact of these speakers will even be more consequential if they are taken as models for 'correctness' (a view that their better education may well produce).[27]

These doubts apart, we can say that everything that can be expected of institutions is apparently being done. Recent developments can be summarized from Walter (2001):

> *Following the ratification of the European Charter the Schleswig-Holstein Parliament organized a conference in Leck in February 1999 to discuss further developments. Similarly the Federal Ministry of the Interior organized two conferences on the implementation of the Charter in June 1999 and November 2000 in Bonn.* [...] *The Ministry produced a draft report which was sent to the various linguistic groups, asking for comment.* [The final version was published in 2000.]

However, whether these activities will help the Frisian language, it is too early to say.

---

[26] If coverage of Frisian on the radio were to be increased, would this be in the Mooring koiné of Risum? At present, at least the three major dialects are used.

[27] A distant relative of mine was admired by some villagers in the Upper Rhine area because of her 'fine' Romansh: she had learnt and used the 'proper' words for 'fridge' etc. for which the villagers used *Kühlschrank*. Although this 'evidence' is anecdotal, it has, I think, a more general meaning.

5.2   The European Charter and Low German

There has never been a nationalistic language-based movement in the Low German area:[28] speakers are Germans, they want to be, and they accept the existence and commonly the superiority of High German as a consequence of its range of functions, uses in written communication and its usefulness as an international language in Central Europe. That is, they have accepted, more or less, the dialect status of Low German. If Low German is, then, a language, it is, in spite of its increasing erosion, not a minority language – as Letzeburgsch is not in Luxemburg or Switzerdütsch is not in Switzerland. However, if I read the text of the Charter correctly, its regulations do apply to Low German in offering to restitute functions lost to the Big Brother:

> *The aim is to ensure, as far as reasonably possible, the use of regional or minority languages in education and the media and to permit their use in judicial and administrative settings, economic and social life and cultural activities. Only in this way can such languages be compensated, where necessary, for unfavourable conditions in the past and preserved and developed as a living facet of Europe's identity.* (Council, Report 9:4)

The fact that educational and cultural affairs are organized on a regional level in Germany helped with the recognition of Low German: five *Länder* agreed to "include Low German in Part III of the Charter, which requires that at least 35 separate provisions about its functions in public life be met", whereas two "propose to include Low German in Part II, which provides only a more general support" (Niebaum 1997:276). The results of these commitments are not yet visible, however.

Nedersaksisch provides a neat example of how decisions in one country can influence those in another (one is reminded of the fact that the status of Scots in Scotland and in Ulster cannot be decided independently of each other):

> Nedersaksisch [...] *was recognized as a regional language by the state in [...] 1995. [...] action committees were organized on the German mold [...] An important argument was the principle that one and the same regional language should not be treated differently in the Netherlands than it is in Germany.* (Niebaum 1997:276)

Steensen (forthcoming [2001?]) has a slightly different story to tell:

---

[28] T. Steensen reminds me of nationalistic tendencies in some 19th-century Low German thinkers. However, they never contemplated separate statehood.

> *During the parliamentary debate in the Netherlands the lobby wishing to include Low Saxon as a minority language was successful, although this 'language' will only be recognized under part III [...] Following this, further minority languages have been included in the Charter, to wit Limburgish, Yiddish and the Roma and Sinti languages. Still under consideration are sign language and the regional dialect of the province of Zealand.*

– the proliferation here evident indicates that political considerations are now clearly superseding purely linguistic definitions of (minority) language status based on *abstand* and *ausbau*.

5.3 Linguistic consequences

As has repeatedly been mentioned above, an extension of the functional range is a necessary consequence of the raise of the legal status and the prestige of both minority languages and regional languages – if, as linguists, we decide to use this largely meaningless distinction. As the discipline of language planning has long established, the first step in the creation of a standard language means code-selection. For West Frisian and Low German this decision has apparently been solved, at least to a certain extent, by concentrating on a common core – however much speakers of peripheral dialects may find uses in radio/TV or in written forms not representing their native dialect: this is bound to happen, and is a common experience, for instance documented for 'Dublin' as against 'Connemara' Irish. For the Saterland no problems arise because of the small, close-knit community of its speakers. However, a standardization of North Frisian is not wanted, and thereby an extension in schools, the media and other forms of visible presence very problematic.

For the next step of modernization, the experience gained from, e.g., radio uses for Low German should be helpful – the twofold danger of artificial or de-intellectualized language for new formal registers can be avoided with sufficient caution and *sprachgefühl* of the planners.

Which brings us to the final and crucial point of implementation. Even well prepared and lavishly financed programmes directed towards the retention, and more frequently revitalization if not revival, of minority languages are likely to fail unless there is a compelling motivation behind it. This, I am afraid to say, can only be in nationalistic, secessionist or otherwise ethnically divisive contexts. The recent history of the Balkans has seen the upsurge of linguistic segregation in tandem with political divisions: ethnic cleansing correlated with linguistic diversification and purist language planning. At the same time, minority languages that have no political support, nor even sufficient awareness of their speakers, are dying – Albanian in Greece and Croatia, and Aromunian/Vlak everywhere.

For the minority languages treated here there is now no background of ethnic or political nationalism and secession. In my view, the welcome measures envisaged by the European Charter are as well-meant as they will prove incfficient. However, predictions in linguistics are dangerous, as they are in all historical disciplines, and speakers may unpredictably come to feel more strongly about connections between their minority language and local (less likely: ethnic) identity than many do at present.

References

Århammar, Nils. 1968. "Friesische Dialektologie". In: L.E. Schmitt, ed. *Germanische Dialektologie. Festschrift Mitzka*. Vol. 2. Wiesbaden: Steiner. 264-317.

Århammar, Nils. 2000. "Nordfriesisch". In: Wirrer, 144-58.

Barbour, Stephen and Cathie Carmichael, eds. 2000. *Language and Nationalism in Europe*. Oxford: OUP.

Bichel, I., D. Herold and V. Holm, eds. 1989. *Niederdeutsch im Unterricht an Gymnasien. Anregungen und Arbeitshilfen*. Kiel.

Council of Europe, n. d. *European Charter for Regional or Minority Languages, Explanatory Report*, 9

Diercks, Willy. 1994. *Niederdeutsch in der Stadt Schleswig. Zu Attitüden und zur Sprachverwendung*. (ZDL-Beiheft 86) Stuttgart.

Dyhr, Mogens. 1990. "Hybridisiertes Südjütisch." In Kremer and Niebaum, 25-47.

Feitsma, A., et. al. n. d. *Die Friesen und ihre Sprache*. (Nachbarn, 32). Bonn: Niederl. Botschaft.

Fishman, Joshua A. 1961. *Reversing Language Shift. Theoretical and Empirical Foundations of Assistance to Threatened Language*. Clevedon: Multilingual Matters. ["The cases of Basque and Frisian", 149-86]

Fort, Marron. 2000. "Saterfriesisch". In: Wirrer, 159ff.

Foster, C. R., ed. 1980. *Nations Without a State: Ethnic Minorities in Western Europe*. New York: Praeger.

Gardt, Andreas, ed. 2000. *Nation und Sprache*. Berlin: de Gruyter.

Görlach, Manfred. 1985. "Scots and Low German: the social history of two minority languages." In Manfred Görlach, ed., *Focus on Scotland*. Amsterdam: Benjamins, 19-36.

Görlach, Manfred. 1988. "Norddeutschland, Schottland und Jamaica – zweisprachige oder bidialektale Regionen?" In Dieter Möhn, *et al.*, eds., *Niederdeutsch und Zweisprachigkeit. Befunde – Vergleiche – Ausblicke*. Leer: Schuster, 49-69.

Görlach, Manfred. 1990. "*Haw, the wickit things weans dae*. Max and Moritz in Scots." *Scottish Language* 9: 34-51.

Görlach, Manfred. 1995. "Sociolinguistic determinants for literature in dialects and minority languages." In M. G., *More Englishes*. Amsterdam: Benjamins, 220-45.

Görlach, Manfred. 2000. "Ulster Scots: a language?" In Kirk and Ó Baoill, 13-31.

Gorter, Durk and Alastair Walker. 2001. "Frisian as a European minority language." In Munske, Art. 79.

Haugen, Einar, ed. 1981. *Minority Languages Today.* Edinburgh: EUP.

Henkels, Walter. 1980. "'n bitten Bifall bi alle Parteien." *Deutsches Allgemeines Sonntagsblatt* Nr. 14, 6th April 1980 [on the attempt at talking Low German rather than High German in parliaments]

Hinderling, Robert and Ludwig M. Eichinger, eds. 1996. *Handbuch der mitteleuropäischen Sprachminderheiten.* Tübingen.

Kettner, Bernd-Ulrich. 1988. "Die norddeutsche Umgangssprache – eine neue Zweitsprache?" In *Niederdeutsch und Zweisprachigkeit. Befunde – Vergleiche – Ausblicke.* Leer: Schuster, 95-113.

Kirk, John M. 2000. "Two Ullans texts". In Kirk and Ó Baoill, 33-44.

Kirk, John M. and Dónall P. Ó Baoill, eds. 2000. *Language and Politics. Northern Ireland, the Republic of Ireland and Scotland.* Belfast: Clo Ollscoil na Banríona.

Kloss, Heinz. [2]1978. *Die Entwicklung neuer germanischer Kultursprachen seit 1800.* Düsseldorf: Schwann. ["'Friesisch'", 165-76, "'Niedersächsisch (Sassisch)'", 181-99]

König, Werner. 1978. *dtv-Atlas zur deutschen Sprache.* München: dtv.

Kööp, Karl-Peter. 1991. *Sprachentwicklung und Sprachsituation in der Norder-goesharde. Von der Mitte des 19. Jahrhunderts bis zur Gegenwart.* Bräist/ Bredstedt.

Kremer, Ludger and Hermann Niebaum, eds. 1990. *Grenzdialekte* (Germanistische Linguistik 101). Hildesheim: Olms.

Kremer, Ludger. 1990. "Zwischen Vechtegebiet und Niederrhein." In Kremer and Niebaum, 85-123.

Lesle, Ulf-Thomas. 1999. "Plattdeutsch unter dem Schutz der Europäischen Charta der Regional- oder Minderheitensprachen des Europarats".*Quickborn* 89:1, 2-20.

Mattheier, Klaus. J. 1980. *Pragmatik und Soziologie der Dialekte.* Heidelberg: Quelle and Meyer (UTB 994).

Meerburg, Babs Gezelle. Forthcoming [2001?]. "Die westfriesische Literatur des 20. Jahrhunderts." In Munske, (forthcoming [2001?])

Menge, Heinz H. 1995. "Rehabilitierung des Niederdeutschen. Erwartungen an die europäische Sprachpolitik." *ZGL* 23: 33-52.

Möhn, Dieter. 1999. "Norddeutsche Geräuschlexeme. Sprachschöpfungen für Comics." In Wagener, 137-46.

Möhn, Dieter and Reinhard Goltz. 1999. "Zur Aktualität des plattdeutschen Wortschatzes. Eine Vitalitätsprüfung am Beispiel von Nachrichtensendungen." *Niederdeutsches Jahrbuch* 122: 67-90.

Munske, Horst Haider, ed. Forthcoming [2001?]. *Handbuch Friesisch.* Tübingen: Niemeyer.

Newton, Gerald, ed. 1996. *Luxembourg and Lëtzebuergesch.* Oxford: Clarendon.

Niebaum, Hermann. 1997. "Low German and language politics. On the efforts to get Low German included in the *European Charter for Regional or Minority Languages.*" In B. Synak and T. Wicherkiewicz, eds., *Language Minorities and Minority Languages in the Changing Europe.*

Proceedings of the 6th International Conference on Minority Languages, Gda☐sk, 1 – 5 July, 1996. Gdansk: UP, 269-77.

Niebaum, Hermann and Jürgen Macha. 1999. *Einführung in die Dialektologie des Deutschen.* Tübingen: Niemeyer.

Salverda, Reinier. 1998. "Frisian." In Glanville Price ed. *Encyclopedia of the Languages of Europe.* Oxford: Blackwell. 177-184.

Speckmann, Rolf, ed. 1991. *Niederdeutsch morgen. Perspektiven in Europa. Beiträge zum Kongreß des Instituts für niederdeutsche Sprache. Lüneburg 19. – 21. 10. 1990.* Leer: Schuster.

Steensen, Thomas. 1986. *Die friesische Bewegung in Nordfriesland im 19. und 20. Jahrhundert (1879-1945).* Neumünster.

Steensen, Thomas. 1993. "Die Friesen in Schleswig-Holstein." In Rüdiger Wenzel, ed., *Minderheiten im deutsch-dänischen Grenzbereich.* Kiel: Landeszentrale für Politische Bildung, 159-95.

Steensen, Thomas. forthcoming. "Zur Entstehung interfriesischer Beziehungen." In Munske (forthcoming [2001?]).

Stellmacher, Dieter. 1987. *Wer spricht Platt? Zur Lage des Niederdeutschen heute. Eine kurzgefaßte Bestandsaufnahme.* Leer: Schuster.

Stellmacher, Dieter. 1997. "Sprachsituation in Norddeutschland." In Stickel, 88-108.

Stellmacher, Dieter. 1998. "Voraussetzungen für die soziolinguistische Erforschung des Saterfriesischen." In Peter Ernst and Franz Patocka, eds., *Deutsche Sprache in Raum und Zeit. Festschrift für Peter Wiesinger zum 60. Geburtstag.* Wien: Edition Praesens, 161-6.

Stellmacher, Dieter. 1998. *Das Saterland und das Saterländische.* Oldenburg.

Stellmacher, Dieter. [2]2000. *Niederdeutsche Sprache.* Berlin: Weidler.

Stellmacher, Dieter. and Ursula Föllner. 1995. *Die Mundarten in der DEUREGIO Ostfalen. Verbreitung, Wandel, Gebrauch.* (Veröffentlichungen des Ostfälischen Instituts der DEUREGIO Ostfalen, Band 1) Mannheim.

Stephens, Meic 1976. *Linguistic Minorities in Western Europe.* Llandysul, Dyfed: Gomer Press.

Stevenson, Patrick, ed. 1995. *The German Language and the Real World. Sociolinguistic, Cultural, and Pragmatic Perspectives on Contemporary German.* Oxford: Clarendon.

Stickel, Gerhard. 1997. *Varietäten des Deutschen. Regional- und Umgangssprachen.* Berlin: de Gruyter.

Ureland, P. Sture, ed. 1978. *Sprachkontakte im Nordseegebiet.* Tübingen: Niemeyer.

Van Leuvenstejn, J. and J. Berns, eds. 1992. *Dialect and Standard Language in the English, Dutch, German and Norwegian Language Areas.* Amsterdam: North Holland.

Wagener, Peter, ed. 1999. *Sprachformen. Deutsch und Niederdeutsch in europäischen Bezügen.* Stuttgart: Franz Steiner.

Walker, Alastair G. H. 1990. "Fisian." In Charles V.J. Russ ed. The Dialects of Modern German: A Linguistic Survey. London: Routledge. 1-30

Walker, Alastair G. H. 2001. "Extent and position of North Frisian." In Munske, Art. 28.
White, Paul. 1991. "Geographical aspects of minority language situations in Italy." In Williams, 44-65.
Williams, Colin H., ed. 1991. *Linguistic Minorities. Society and Territory.* Clevedon: Multilingual Matters.
Wirrer, Jan. 1993. "Die europäische Charta der Regional- und Minderheiten-sprachen und das Niederdeutsche." *Quickborn* 83, 3: 29-41.
Wirrer, Jan. 1998. "Zum Status des Niederdeutschen". *ZGL* 26: 308-40.
Wirrer, Jan. ed. 2000. *Minderheiten- und Regionalsprachen in Europa.* Wiesbaden: Westdeutscher Verlag.
Zondag, Koen. 2001. "Bilingual education in West Frisia." In Munske, Art. 27.

Norway: Consensus and Diversity[1]

Kevin McCafferty

Introduction

Norway differs from Northern Ireland in important ways. In cultural terms, it has always been an extremely homogeneous country. Even after the unprecedented immigration of recent decades, Norway remains more than 92% ethnically Norwegian and 86% Lutheran (Statistics Norway 2001a). And social democracy still rules to the extent that a Swedish minister called it the last remaining Soviet republic just a couple of years ago – in Norway, even the political Right can be heard defending the welfare state. Given high levels of cultural homogeneity, Norway has enjoyed a long-standing consensus in favour of a fairly successful project to build a single Norwegian nation. Norway, then, has conformed very closely to the nineteenth-century ideal of the single nation inhabiting a single state and *speaking* – though not necessarily *writing* – a single language.

And the resolution of language issues is another crucial difference between the two countries. Today there is a great deal of tolerance of linguistic diversity in Norway: the dialects of Norwegian, the languages of the Sami and Kven minorities of the north, and the languages of immigrants are now respected and protected to a degree that remains quite unusual in Europe.

Language has been at the heart of Norwegian nation-building, and the centrality of language in Norwegian nationalism has, naturally, had very different consequences in the past for Norwegian and the other languages spoken in the country. On the one hand, it ensured efforts to preserve and tolerate the total range of Norwegian dialects in the interests of creating a national language that was clearly distinct from Swedish and Danish. But on the other hand, the indigenous minority languages were actively suppressed with the explicit aim of eradicating them.

Issues arising from the treatment of immigrant languages and indigenous minority languages are also relevant to this forum, but I will concentrate on Norwegian and the development of the standard written language – or rather *languages* in the plural, since there are *two* written norms. The most widespread norm, *Bokmål* (lit. 'Book Language'), is the outcome of a process of reform aimed at making written Danish gradually more Norwegian. The other, *Nynorsk* (lit. 'New Norwegian' or 'New Norse'), was *the* major outcome of a nineteenth-century dialect survey, though it too has been through a process of reform that has

---

[1] The author would like to thank the organisers, Dónall Ó Baoill and John Kirk, for the invitation to give this paper, and Queen's University Belfast and the University of Tromsø for funding my trip to Belfast. Thanks are also due to Anniken Telnes Iversen for reading and commenting on the paper, and to her and Liam for letting me abandon my duties as a father on paternity leave to attend the Symposium.

rendered it less archaic than the original standard proposed in the mid-nineteenth century. It is worth stressing that no-one actually *speaks* these two languages – they are written forms that are only spoken (sometimes) by newscasters and actors. The general pattern in Norway is to speak dialect and write *Bokmål* or *Nynorsk*. Even in quite formal contexts, like parliamentary debates and academic lectures, dialect is used nowadays (Sandøy 1987:270).

What I have to say will be most relevant to the question of how to develop a written norm for Ulster-Scots, and in doing so, I assume that the ultimate aim of *Thà Boord o Ulster-Scotch* is to achieve the policy goals outlined by its chair, Lord Laird, at the Belfast symposium and elsewhere,[2] i.e., full parity with English and Irish Gaelic as an official language in both parts of Ireland. I begin with some historical background, then say something about the status of the written languages and rights, attitudes towards them, and attitudes towards dialects. And I round off by making some recommendations to those who would like to create a written norm for Ulster-Scots that might be used in schools, official contexts and literature.

Norwegian in Denmark-Norway

As with Scots, political union had dire consequences for the written language of Norway. The rich literary language known as Old Norse, which was fairly firmly standardised by the late-fourteenth century (Haugen 1976:329), fell into disuse following union with Denmark in 1380. From about 1500 onwards, the undisputed written language of Norway was Danish, after Norwegian had been abandoned by various state institutions. As in Scotland, the Reformation also helped speed the decline, with Christian III's Bible of 1550 serving to underscore the authority of Danish.

By the late-seventeenth century, grammarians regarded Norwegian as a Danish dialect (Haugen 1976:403; Seip 1921). Indeed, Danish was viewed as the common property of Denmark-Norway well into the nineteenth century. This belief was underpinned by the fact that Norwegian writers like Ludvig Holberg (1684-1754) had done much to shape and spread standard Danish. The perception of Danish as the common language of Denmark and Norway was even enshrined in the 1814 constitution of independent Norway, which referred to the common written language of Denmark and Norway simply as 'Norwegian'.

While they certainly *wrote* Danish, it would not be true to say that Norwegians ever *spoke* it, apart from students, writers and officials who had lived in Denmark. However, Danes dominated among the officials who ran Norway, and some Norwegians imitated their prestigious Danish speech. Some kind of supralocal Norwegian variety of Danish is attested from the late-seventeenth century. One eighteenth-century pastor went so far as to claim that: 'The most refined and letter-perfect pronunciation is that of Christiania [nowadays Oslo],

---

[2] For instance, in his recent dealings with the Irish government, whom he accuses of denying parity of esteem and equal rights to Ulster-Scots (*Irish Times*, 12.07.2001).

and there is spoken the prettiest Danish, except for the admixture of some provincial words' (J.N. Wilse, cited by Indrebø 1951:319). The pronunciation referred to was 'best' because it was closest to the spelling as a result of being learned in school and modelled on the written word. This kind of speech, associated with the upper classes in the towns, retained some prestige in Norway after 1814. It had native Norwegian phonology and prosody, and deviated from Danish by using many Norwegian forms of everyday words, Norwegian grammatical constructions, and vocabulary that was unknown in Denmark. But the association of this kind of speech with Danish was a handicap once that union had been dissolved.

Like a lot of other European countries, nationalism emerged as a real force in nineteenth-century Norway. And nationalism was at the time heavily influenced by Johann Gottfried von Herder's notion that every nation needed its own national language. In 1835, the national poet, Henrik Wergeland (1808-45) wrote a manifesto under the title 'On Norwegian Language Reformation', arguing that: 'It is no longer the *name* of a Norwegian written language and a Norwegian literature that the Norwegians wish to gain [...] but [...] the *reality* of an independent written language that challenges the spirits of Norway' (cited in Haugen 1976:405). His call-to-arms was taken up by many, and Norway has invested a lot in language planning in the intervening 175 years.

Reformers and revolutionaries

The current language situation is unusual in certain respects that set Norway apart from most other European countries:

- Language – i.e., the creation of a truly Norwegian national standard written language that would replace Danish – has had a central place in Norwegian nationalism since soon after the dissolution of the union of Denmark-Norway in 1814.
- It was understood from the beginning that the national language had to be based on the dialects actually spoken in Norway (and that understanding still dictates language policy today).
- Consequently, the dialects had to be respected and preserved if there was to be anything to build the national language on.
- And finally, this meant that tolerance of linguistic diversity was essential – the dialects had to be regarded as valid, correct varieties of Norwegian rather than substandard.

However, while nationalism awarded the dialects pride of place in the development of the national language, differences of opinion as to how to go about the task led to the development of not one but two written norms. These represent two different responses to the situation in which Norway found itself in 1814.

The lines in this conflict, which is still going on today, were drawn between reformers on the one hand and revolutionaries on the other. The reformers preferred to model a new written standard on the educated speech of the urban middle and upper classes. The revolutionaries regarded urban speech as tainted by Danish influence and preferred to give priority to rural dialects that were seen as more purely Norwegian.

The most notable figure in the early reformist camp was Knud Knudsen (1812-95), a teacher who was motivated by a desire to reduce pupils' problems in learning to read and write and believed that the difficulties could best be tackled by reshaping the written language to make it resemble their native speech more closely. But Knudsen also recognised that acquiring a more cultivated language was one of the main goals of education. Knudsen's line found support among some of the great national writers of the nineteenth century, notably Bjørnstjerne Bjørnson (an early Nobel literature laureate) and Henrik Ibsen. Their spelling might have been that of Danish, but their grammar and idiom were clearly Norwegian. A gradual process of spelling reforms has made the break with Danish and produced the modern *Bokmål* standard.[3]

The revolutionary side was dominated by Ivar Aasen (1813-96), who in 1836 proposed a plan for creating a new written form of Norwegian, which 'should not build on any specific dialect but on a sound linguistic comparison of the Norwegian dialects, to extract their common structure' (Haugen 1976:405). Aasen himself conducted the necessary fieldwork in 1843-46, travelling all over the south and west of Norway and as far north as Rana in Nordland. In his work, Aasen avoided towns and cities and sampled only rural dialects. This rural and western bias was perhaps the first big mistake he made – it meant that *Nynorsk* has always been associated with the west and is by many regarded as *bondsk*, a word that translates perfectly into Irish English as 'culchy'.

Aasen published a grammar in 1848 and a dictionary in 1850, and launched his first official norm in 1853, in which he and others wrote poetry, songs and novels. This early *Nynorsk* was quite archaic, because, where the dialects used very different forms, Aasen chose to solve the problem of what to include in his written norm by opting for those forms he knew to be oldest on the basis of comparison with Old Norse texts. For example, modern *Nynorsk* uses diphthongs, full vowels and –*r* endings even where many dialects have simplified the diphthongs, reduced unstressed vowels and dropped the –*r* in endings – in *Nynorsk*, the correct plural form of *stein* ('stone') is *steinar*, not *stener*, *steiner* or *steina*, which are the forms found in most dialects (Faarlund 1999:205). The motive for this archaicising tendency was in part to recreate written Norwegian as it might have developed if the union and the switch to Danish had never occurred. This might be regarded as Aasen's second mistake – giving priority to older forms meant that many people reading *Nynorsk* encountered very strange words, grammatical endings and constructions. And, of course, standardising the most conservative forms was also at odds with the principle of creating a written norm capable of representing all Norwegian dialects, which still remains the intention of Norwegian language planning (Faarlund 1999:205).

---

[3] Until 1929, *Bokmål* was known as *Riksmål*, while *Nynorsk* was called *Landsmål*.

The tendency to choose the oldest forms also further compounded the rural western bias, because it was in the west that the most conservative dialects were spoken. It therefore made subsequent reforms essential in order to increase the appeal of *Nynorsk* – efforts to make it more attractive to people in the southeast, where most of the population live, are still going on today (cf. many of the contributions in Kleiva et al. 1999). Nonetheless, a revised form of Aasen's standard *Nynorsk*, as established in his *Norsk Grammatik* [Norwegian Grammar] of 1864 and *Norsk Ordbog* [Norwegian Dictionary] of 1873, was recognised by the Norwegian parliament in 1885 as an official language equal to *Bokmål*. It was accepted for educational purposes in 1892.

The declared policy of the Norwegian parliament from 1938 to 1981 was ultimate unification of the two standards. This task was the objective of the Norwegian Language Commisson (*Norsk språknemnd*) established in 1951. This body opened up both standards to greater variation by increasing the range of acceptable alternative forms in *Nynorsk* and *Bokmål*. Today what are known as 'radical' *Bokmål* and 'moderate' *Nynorsk* may in fact be very similar, while very conservative *Bokmål* may still resemble Danish, and conservative *Nynorsk* is more similar to the archaic rural dialects and closer to the norm proposed by Aasen. The overlap is illustrated by the existence of optional forms like *soli/sola* ('the sun'; lit. sun-the) in *Nynorsk* and *solen/sola* in *Bokmål*, where *sola* was intended to become the agreed single norm (Faarlund 1999:206). But after the Language Commission got bogged down in endless controversy about spelling and what forms to permit, it was replaced in 1971 by a new Norwegian Language Council (*Norsk språkråd*) that had no remit to direct the process of unification. In 1981, the Language Council abandoned the aim of uniting the two norms into some kind of *Samnorsk* ('Unified Norwegian' or 'Common Norwegian'); coexistence between two partly overlapping norms is now the official policy, though the two norms are certainly closer to one another today than they were 100 years ago.

Status

Bokmål and *Nynorsk* have equal official status and have been equal since 1885. The Education Act 1969 (and its predecessors) requires all Norwegians to learn to read and write both. The Language Usage Act 1930 requires State agencies to use both languages. The most important provisions of the latter Act are as follows:

- Private individuals and other private legal persons shall receive responses in the language (Bokmål or Nynorsk) they use when addressing a State agency. Municipalities and counties may decide to require Bokmål or Nynorsk in the correspondence they receive from State agencies, or they may decide to remain linguistically neutral.
- The so-called civil service language of a lower administrative level in the State shall determine the form used at a higher level to handle correspondence between them, for example, and the civil

service language in turn is based on the municipality's choice of language.

• State agencies shall generally alternate between the two languages in the documents they produce for the public, i.e. everything from parliamentary documents, books and magazines to stamps and bank notes, so that neither language is ever used less than 25 per cent of the time. (Norwegian Language Council 2001)

However, *Bokmål* is clearly the dominant form. It is the language of most newspapers, textbooks, literature and other printed books – in most years, more books are published in foreign languages than in *Nynorsk*. An important current indicator of its dominance is that *Bokmål* is the language of almost all computer software. There are regulations aimed at supporting and promoting *Nynorsk*. For example, the Norwegian Broadcasting Corporation must try to fulfill a 25% quota for use of *Nynorsk* in speech and subtitling; for the last year or so, their main evening news has been read by pairs of newscasters, one using *Bokmål*, the other *Nynorsk*.

Education is perhaps the sphere that best shows the effects of the dichotomy between *Bokmål* and *Nynorsk*. All municipalities have had a referendum to choose an official first language of instruction in their schools, but everyone must learn the other written form as well. However, individual pupils (or their parents) may opt for the other standard as their main form – and if just 10 children in an age-group in any municipality opt for the other form, then the local education authority must provide parallel classes for them.

Table 1: *Nynorsk* as main language form (*hovedmål*) in schools (as percentage of all pupils) in selected years (after Johnsen 1987:122; Torp and Vikør 1996:209; Statistics Norway 2001c)

Year	Nynorsk (%)
1920	17.0
1930	19.5
1940	31.5
1944	34.1
1950	29.7
1960	22.7
1970	17.9
1980	16.4
1990	17.0
2000	15.0

The numbers of pupils receiving instruction through *Nynorsk* is taken to be the best indicator of the language's popularity. The rise and fall of *Nynorsk* is

Map 1: The Counties of Norway

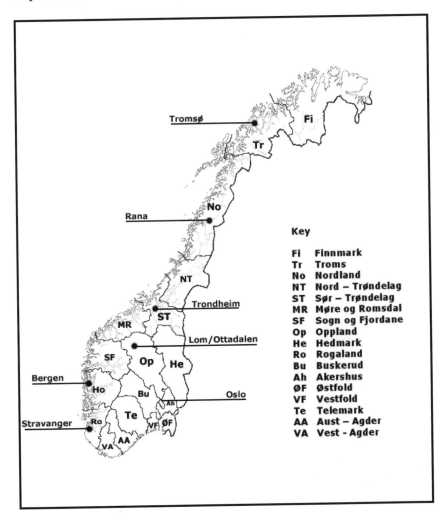

Key

Fi	Finnmark
Tr	Troms
No	Nordland
NT	Nord – Trøndelag
ST	Sør – Trøndelag
MR	Møre og Romsdal
SF	Sogn og Fjordane
Op	Oppland
He	Hedmark
Ro	Rogaland
Bu	Buskerud
Ah	Akershus
ØF	Østfold
VF	Vestfold
Te	Telemark
AA	Aust – Agder
VA	Vest - Agder

shown in Table 1, which gives the percentages of schoolchildren with each form as their main written language in selected years from 1920 to 2000. After official recognition, *Nynorsk* spread rapidly in school districts until the Second World War, reaching a peak of 34% in 1944 (Torp and Vikør 1996:209). However, it has never gained a foothold in the towns. After the war, it went into a steady decline that seems to have slowed slightly since 1970. Today, it is the preferred first written form of only 15% of schoolchildren (Statistics Norway 2001b), which is the lowest figure for at least 80 years, and it is the first written language of even fewer adults – estimates are that only 10-12% of adults use it.

Nynorsk also has a very clear regional profile (see Maps 1 and 2). While there are huge differences between counties in the core areas, it is strongest in the

Map 2: *Nynorsk* **Areas of Norway**[4]

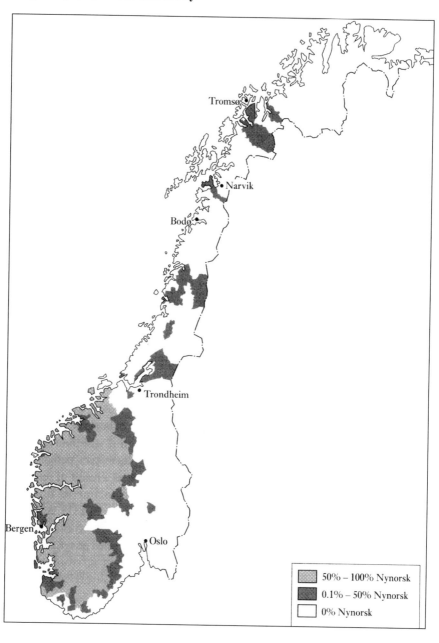

---

[4] Map 2 is reproduced from Walton 1998, with permission from Blackwell Publishers Ltd.

west, in the counties of Sogn og Fjordane (96.4% in 2000), Møre og Romsdal (54.9%), Hordaland (45.2%) and Rogaland (28.3%), and in the inland counties of Oppland (22.6%) and Telemark (17%). In no other county does use of *Nynorsk* exceed 7%; in fact, in ten out of 19 counties, less than 1% of schoolchildren use it as their main form. *Nynorsk* may nowadays be incorporating more and more eastern forms, in an effort to make it more acceptable in that part of the country (Jahr 1992:40), but it has so far made few inroads beyond the established core areas. And even there, it is actually losing ground, with the sole exception of Sogn og Fjordane.

Table 2: *Nynorsk* as main language form in schools, 1 September 2000 (%) (Statistics Norway 2001c)

County	Nynorsk (%)
Østfold	0
Akershus	0
Oslo	0.1
Hedmark	<0.001 (1/23 246 pupils)
Oppland	22.6
Buskerud	4.4
Vestfold	0
Telemark	17.0
Aust-Agder	6.9
Vest-Agder	3.0
Rogaland	28.3
Hordaland	45.2
Sogn og Fjordane	96.4
Møre og Romsdal	54.9
Sør-Trøndelag	0.3
Nord-Trøndelag	2.0
Nordland	0.2
Troms	0.6
Finnmark	<0.001 (1/10 204 pupils)
Svalbard	0

Attitudes to *Nynorsk*

No-one seems to go out asking whether people love or hate *Nynorsk*, though the decline in use indicated in Table 1 suggests less popularity – and perhaps less positive attitudes – today than 50 years ago. In a sense, there is a direct parallel with prejudices against Ulster-Scots, in that many regard *Nynorsk* as a kind of 'do-it-yourself language for culchies'. Broadly speaking, because of its concentration in the west and the inland mountain regions, *Nynorsk* has strong associations with old-fashioned rural life, non-conformist religion, temperance and strict moral values. It is also associated with strong nationalism – including opposition to the EU – and anti-urbanism (Haugen 1975:647-8). Conservative *Bokmål* is associated with political conservatism, the upper middle classes and the mainstream State Church, while more radical *Bokmål* correlates with anti-establishment views and politics in urban areas. These links are not hard and fast, or even proven in any sense, and I could find no firm statistics on language use and support for political parties, for instance. But concerns about the falling popularity of *Nynorsk* has led some researchers to try and locate the underlying causes.

It has been estimated that fully one-third of those who begin using *Nynorsk* in school later shift to *Bokmål* (Faarlund (1998:1). A study of shift from *Nynorsk* to *Bokmål* in a core *Nynorsk* area (Ottadalen in Oppland; see Map 1) actually finds that the shift away from *Nynorsk* might be much greater than that and sheds interesting light on the reasons why. Rødningen (1999, 2000) interviewed a large number of people in three municipalities in Ottadalen, where *Nynorsk* has always had a strong position in the schools and local dialect has been used in all social situations – shifting away from the local dialect has tended to be frowned upon and ridiculed in the area (Rødningen 1999:247). The shift in Ottadalen is more of the order of two-thirds; as shown in Table 3, use of *Nynorsk* drops from 94% to just 28% in one of the three municipalities, Lom, between primary school and starting work or third-level education. Rødningen records similar shifts in the other two municipalities.

Table 3: Shift from Nynorsk to Bokmål in Lom Municipality, Ottadalen, Oppland County (Rødningen 1999:248)

Lom Municipality, Oppland	NN%	BM%
Language of instruction in primary school	**94**	6
Main written form in 1st year secondary school	79	21
Main written form in final year secondary school	62	38
Language written privately while at school	55	45
Language written privately after leaving school	42	58
Language written at work/in third-level education	28	**70**

The reasons Rødningen's subjects gave for their decision to shift were:

a) *Bokmål* is the most commonly used form in Norwegian society (29%);
b) it is more difficult to write *Nynorsk* correctly and/or they had problems in understanding *Nynorsk* words (25%);
c) most textbooks were/are in *Bokmål* (19%).

Rødningen found this surprising, since the dialect in Ottadalen is one that should provide a good foundation for writing good *Nynorsk* (1999:249-250). Part of the problem seems to be frustration caused by the realisation that, in fact, the strategy of falling back on local dialect forms often led to errors, since the dialect forms of the area were not officially approved for use in written *Nynorsk*.

Other studies support the view that many people simply find *Nynorsk* more difficult. One survey of forms used by authors (Pettersen 1993) found that most *Bokmål* writers produced a fairly moderate form of *Bokmål*, while another study (Vikør 1995) found that the forms used by *Nynorsk* authors were not as focused. Faarlund (1998:1) thinks that the fact that *Bokmål* is relatively clear-cut is part of its attraction – *Nynorsk* users exploit their freedom of choice to a greater extent, so that people who read and write a lot of *Nynorsk* are much less likely to be exposed to a clear written norm. Some are arguing that the revised norm for *Nynorsk* that is currently in the pipeline should be much clearer in an attempt to turn the tide (Rødningen 1999:258; cf. also Faarlund 1999). I have interviewed a number of friends and colleagues recently about this – nearly all of them *Bokmål* users – and many of them have commented that what they find most striking about *Nynorsk* users is that they are always asking one another what is correct, whether they can use certain words, endings, spellings, etc. As one of them put it: 'You get the impression these people don't really know their own language'.

Attitudes to dialects

The effects of language planning and language conflict in Norway cannot simply be measured in terms of how many people use or shift away from *Nynorsk*. One of the major impacts has been on the status of and attitudes towards dialects. As Paul Kerswill puts it, echoing many Norwegian commentators:

> *It is fair to say that the presence of Nynorsk, and the large amount of officially sanctioned variation in both Nynorsk and Bokmål, has led to a greater acceptance of social and, particularly, regional variation in speech than in most other parts of Europe.* (Kerswill 1994:34)

In some respects, as Kerswill also notes (ibid.), greater acceptance of regional and social variation is partly a reflection of similar developments elsewhere in Europe, but it is also partly due to the absence of a firmly established supraregional standard speech in Norway. Even under the union with Denmark, the upper-class prestigious speech of Oslo, Bergen, Trondheim, Stavanger and other towns always reflected the phonology of the low-prestige local dialects of their areas, so that regional features have been less stigmatised than in many other countries. As for rural speech, the campaigns of Noregs Mållag (the Norwegian Language Movement) have long exploited identification of *Nynorsk* with local dialects in an effort to get people to 'speak dialect and write *Nynorsk*', and this too has contributed to reducing any stigma that might attach to any particular dialect. The increased acceptability of dialect since the 1970s, when this kind of campaigning reached particularly intense levels, is shown in survey findings that dialect seems to have strengthened its position and become even more acceptable – one study (Strømsodd 1979:83) reports that in Oslo 51.4% of interviewees under the age of 30 thought it acceptable for a lecturer to use dialect, while only 19% of people over 60 thought so (cited in Sandøy 1987:271).

But this openness towards and respect for dialect is also the result of the crucial role given to Norwegian dialects in the creation of both standard language forms. Although *Bokmål* was modelled originally on the upper-class speech of the towns and cities, the principle of emphasising the primacy of the spoken word has led to more and more 'broad' forms being permitted in *Bokmål* too. It is this that has created the overlap today between the two standard languages. Again, the strength of this principle is maybe most visible in the classroom. Norwegian education acts have for well over a century incorporated the 1878 parliamentary ruling that: '[...] instruction in primary schools, as far as possible, should take place in the spoken language of the children, i.e. in their dialects' (Vikør 1993:206). The current Act of 1969 states that:

> *I den munnlege opplæringa kan elevane bruke det mål dei talar heime, og læraren skal i ordtilfang og uttryksmåte ta omsyn til talemålet til elevane.* (Norwegian Education Act 1969 §41.1)

> *In oral instruction, pupils may use the dialect they speak at home, and the teacher must in his/her vocabulary and means of expression take full account of the spoken language of his/her pupils.*

This is actually a toned-down version of the 1878 rule – the earlier formulation required teachers to *adapt* their spoken language to the dialect of the children they were teaching. This official policy means that the preservation of the dialects is essential, because they are the basis of the written language. Many politicians saw preservation of dialects, and pride in them, as an essential part of nation-building (cf. Jahr 1992:42). Basing both standards on the spoken word also held out the hope of a long-term resolution of the language conflict between proponents of *Nynorsk* and *Bokmål*, since if both were based on the speech of ordinary Norwegians, they could eventually be unified (ibid.:42-3). In this way, the Norwegian parliament and policy-makers have often shown great psycholinguistic awareness, recognising that someone's first language is so integral a part of their personality that any attack on it is an attack on their human dignity (ibid.:45).

Conclusion: what can the Norwegian case teach Irish language planners?

The Norwegian experience of language planning, particularly the experience of developing a new standard written language on the basis of dialects, offers three major lessons that language planners involved in developing written Ulster-Scots might bear in mind.

First, Ivar Aasen's tendency to go for the most archaic forms he could find in the dialects erected a double barrier between *Nynorsk* and the majority of Norwegians – the archaic forms reinforced the western character of his norm, and even there, they were unfamiliar and incomprehensible to many people without a dictionary. Some Ulster-Scots activists have flirted with archaic spellings, notably

Philip Robinson in his (1997) grammar, and then shifted away from them. That is probably wise – as a rule, if a form's archaic, it should be avoided.

Second, recall that Aasen wanted a written standard based on existing dialects, but then made the mistake of defining the dialects very narrowly. The restriction of *Nynorsk* to the west and rural areas only is a lasting result of Aasen's narrow definition of what was acceptable or pure Norwegian. The Ulster-Scots movement might be in danger of making the same kind of mistake. It emphasises the rural nature of the dialects it finds acceptable; its policy statements seek to use a new norm in areas where Ulster-Scots has been the traditional dialect; and it defines these areas along the same lines as Robert J. Gregg (1972, 1985), who predefined his Ulster-Scots core areas, rather than finding the true extent of the Ulster-Scots core areas through his fieldwork. Following this line ignores the fact that the spoken English used all over the North of Ireland is influenced to some extent by Scots (cf. Kirk 1998, esp. Maps 5 and 6). Accepting this fact actually has the huge advantage for supporters of Ulster-Scots that they could stop claiming that Ulster-Scots is spoken by about 100 000 people in Ulster (but that these people are very shy about using it, very hard to find, and so forth) and instead claim that there are about 2m people in the nine counties of Ulster who speak Scots-influenced English.

Finally, Aasen and his followers deliberately ignored urban areas – their speech was not pure enough. This is a traditional belief among dialectologists, and Aasen was a very early dialectologist, but a lot of urban dialect surveys have been done in the last 40 years, and some of the most innovative of that work was done in Belfast by Jim and Lesley Milroy (J. Milroy 1981, 1992; L. Milroy 1987). We have ways today of studying and making sense of complex language variation, and these methods might be applied to a survey of the entire province that could then contribute a new written form of Ulster-Scots, Northern Irish English, or whatever we might want to call it. A written norm based on a survey of the entire province is bound to have a much wider appeal than a replication of Gregg's survey. And any new survey should include Belfast, Derry and all other urban centres – most people in Ulster live in towns today, and the urban dialects too still retain a lot of Scots forms.

Following recommendations like these certainly will not produce an Ulster-Scots that is as pure as it can possibly be – and it is probably about 300 years too late to get that anyway – but what emerges might be capable of attracting a broader spectrum of interest and support beyond the confines of the Ulster-Scots language movement and committed activists. The whole process might also contribute to improving the standing of *all* the non-standard varieties of English spoken in the north of Ireland and raising levels of awareness of the full range of dialect diversity in Ulster.

References

Faarlund, Jan Terje 1998. Ny læreboknormal for nynorsk. *Språknytt* 1:1-3.
Faarlund, Jan Terje 1999. Norma i nynorsk sedd i høve til austlandsmåla. In Turid Kleiva, Ingeborg Donau, Trygve Nesset and Helen Øygarden

(eds.), *Austlandsmål i endring. Dialektar, nynorsk, og språkhaldningar på indre Austlandet.* Oslo: Det Norske Samlaget. 205-219.

Gregg, Robert J. 1972. The Scotch-Irish dialect boundaries in Ulster. In Martyn F. Wakelin (ed.), *Patterns in th folk speech of the British Isles.* London: Athlone Press. 109-139.

Gregg, Robert J. 1985. *The Scotch-Irish dialect boundaries in the province of Ulster.* Port Credit, Ontario: Canadian Federation for the Humanities.

Haugen, Einar 1975. Språket: en sosiolingvistisk profil. In N. Rogoff Ramsøy and M. Vaa (eds.), *Det norske samfunn.* Bind II. Oslo: Gyldendal. 620-57.

Haugen, Einar 1976. *The Scandinavian languages. An introduction to their history.* London: Faber & Faber.

Indrebø, Gustav 1951. *Norsk målsoga.* Bergen: John Grieg.

Jahr, Ernst Håkon 1992. A rationale for language-planning policy in Norway. In Ernst Håkon Jahr, *Innhogg i nyare norsk språkhistorie.* Oslo: Novus. 38-46.

Johnsen, Egil Børre (ed.) 1987. *Vårt eget språk.* 3 Vols. Oslo: Aschehoug.

Kerswill, Paul 1994. *Dialects converging. Rural speech in urban Norway.* Oxford: Oxford University Press.

Kirk, John M. 1998. Ulster Scots: myths and realities. *Ulster folklife*, 44:69-93.

Milroy, James 1981. *Regional accents of English: Belfast.* Belfast: Blackstaff Press.

Milroy, James 1992. *Linguistic variation and change.* Oxford: Basil Blackwell.

Milroy, Lesley 1987. *Language and social networks.* (2nd. edition). Oxford: Basil Blackwell.

Norwegian Language Council 2001. Language usage in Norway's civil service. Oslo: The Norwegian Language Council (www.sprakrad.no).

Pettersen, Egil 1993. *Språknormering og forfatterne. Ortografi og morfembruk hos ti bokmålsforfattere fra hvert av årene 1937, 1957 og 1977.* Bergen: Universitetet i Bergen.

Rødningen, Dagfinn 1999. Ottadalen – ein utforbakke til bokmålet? In Turid Kleiva, Ingeborg Donau, Trygve Nesset and Helen Øygarden (eds.), *Austlandsmål i endring. Dialektar, nynorsk, og språkhaldningar på indre Austlandet.* Oslo: Det Norske Samlaget. 246-58.

Rødningen, Dagfinn 2000. Nærskylde skriftspråk i kontakt. Interferensproblem og normering i norsk, sett i lys av ei undersøking om språkskifte i Ottadalen. *Maal og minne* 1/2000: 65-84.

Sandøy, Helge 1987. *Norsk dialektkunnskap.* Oslo: Novus.

Seip, D.A. 1921. *Dansk og norsk i Norge i eldre tider.* Kristiania: Steenske Forlag.

Statistics Norway 2001a. Kulturstatistikk. Den norske kyrkja 1999, og trus- og livssamfunn utanfor Den norske kyrkja, per 1. januar 2000. Oslo: Statistisk Sentralbyrå (http:www.ssb.no).

Statistics Norway 2001b. Innvandring og innvandrere 2001. Oslo: Statistisk Sentralbyrå (http:www.ssb.no).

Statistics Norway 2001c. Utdanningsstatistikk. Elevar i grunnskolen. Endelege tal, 1. september 2000. Oslo: Statistisk Sentralbyrå (http:www.ssb.no).

Strømsodd, Svein Arne 1979. Dialektholdninger blant folk i to bydeler i Oslo. Unpublished MA thesis, University of Oslo.

Torp, Arne and Lars S. Vikør 1996. *Hovuddrag i norsk språkhistorie*. Olso: Ad Notam Gyldendal.

Vikør, Lars S. 1993. *The Nordic languages. Their status and interrelations*. Oslo: Novus.

Vikør, Lars S. 1995. *Rettskriving hos nynorskfrfattarar*. Norsk språkråds skrifter nr. 3. Oslo: Norsk Språkråd.

Walton, Stephen J. 1998. 'Norwegian'. In Glanville Price (ed.) *Encyclopedia of the Languages of Europe*. Oxford: Blackwell. 335-343.

Language and Politics in Switzerland

Andreas Fischer

1. Introduction: Switzerland as a multilingual country

Linguistically interested outside observers of Switzerland often quote Switzerland as a 'model' multilingual country and praise its positive features: Switzerland has four national languages, Switzerland has exemplary language policies, there are no serious language conflicts, the Swiss are all multilingual, and so on. Not all of this is true, of course, but a look at Switzerland certainly offers insights into a variety of (socio-)linguistic problems and ways of dealing with them. It is the aim of this paper to outline some basic features of the language situation in Switzerland, to update earlier surveys[1] and to pay special attention to those aspects which may throw some light on the language situation(s) in Scotland and Ireland.[2]

Switzerland has four traditional languages (German, French, Italian and Romansh), traditional meaning that they have been spoken in more or less the same areas of the country since the Middle Ages. One of these languages, Romansh,[3] is spoken in south-eastern Switzerland only. The other three are the languages of communication in regions of the country that form part of three large linguistic areas in Europe: German-speaking Switzerland is part of germanophone Europe consisting of Germany, Austria, Switzerland and areas in other countries such as France (Alsace) or Belgium. French-speaking Switzerland (the so-called *Romandie*) is part of francophone Europe consisting of France together with parts of Belgium and Switzerland, while Italian-speaking Switzerland (the Ticino and parts of the Canton of Graubünden) is immediately adjacent to Italy, as shown in Map 1. All four traditional languages have the status of national languages; German, French and Italian are also full official languages, whereas Romansh has been an official language to a limited degree since 1996 (a so-called *Teilamtssprache*, see section 2 below).

---

[1] Two instructive surveys are Pap (1990) and Dürmüller (1997), both written in English. The two volumes edited by Schläpfer (1982) and by Bickel and Schläpfer (1994) are in German.

[2] I should like to acknowledge the help I received from Anna-Alice Dazzi Gross (Lia Rumantscha, Chur) and Constantin Pitsch (Bundesamt für Kultur, Bern). Many thanks to Sarah Chevalier for corrections and suggestions. Tables and maps from *Rhaeto-Romansh: Facts & Figures* are reprinted by permission. The usual disclaimers apply.

[3] The English name for this language varies: in Dürmüller (1997), for example, we find Rhaeto Romanic, in Görlach (2000) Romaunsh and in Gross and Telli (2000) Romansch. In using the term Romansh I follow *Rhaeto-Romansh: Facts & Figures*.

Map 1: Switzerland's Four Languages

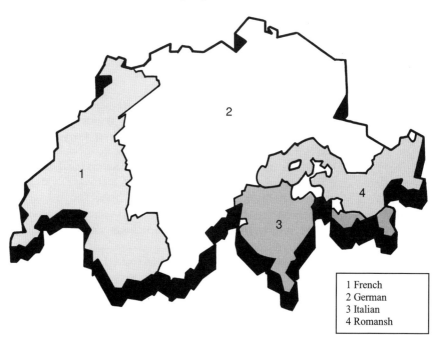

1 French
2 German
3 Italian
4 Romansh

Many more languages than the traditional four are present in Switzerland nowadays, but they have no official status and no territorial basis.

They were brought into the country in the years following World War II by guest workers, refugees and other immigrants. Hungarians (1956) and Czechs (1968) assimilated very quickly, but from the 1960s onwards guest workers, from – in roughly chronological order – Italy, the Iberian peninsula, Turkey and (former) Yugoslavia settled in such large numbers that Italian (outside of the traditional Italian-speaking regions of Switzerland), Spanish, Portuguese, Turkish, Serbo-Croatian and Albanian are now substantial minority languages. The number of speakers of the last three languages (plus Tamil) has further grown through the presence of temporary or permanent refugees from Turkey, the Balkans and Sri Lanka. Finally, English as a global language is present in Switzerland as it is throughout the world. It is used by the many native speakers of English who live in the country, it is the working language of many international organisations and businesses, and it is a very popular foreign language.

The national Censuses which are held every ten years usually include at least one language question. The figures for the years 1880, 1980 and 1990 in

Table 1 below[4] give an impression of the current state of affairs and of the development in the last hundred years. In a population of just under 7 million (in 1990), 63,6% identified themselves as speakers of German, 19,2% as speakers of French, 7,6% as speakers of Italian,[5] and 0,6% as speakers of Romansh. The number of speakers of Romansh is substantially lower than that of the speakers of the immigrant languages listed in Table 1.

Table 1: National Census for the whole of Switzerland, 1880, 1980, 1990

	1880		1980		1990	
	'Native Tongue'		'Native Tongue'		'Best Command'	
German	2,030,792	71.3%	4,140,901	65.0%	4,374,694	63.6%
French	608,007	21.4%	1,172,502	18.4%	1,321,695	19.2%
Italian	161,923	5.7%	622,226	9.8%	524,116	7.6%
Romansh	38,705	1.4%	51,128	0.8%	39,632	0.6%
Misc.	6,675	0.2%	379,203	6.0%	613,550	8.9%
Slavic					128,093	1.9%
Spanish					116,818	1.7%
Portuguese					93,753	1.4%
Turkish					61,320	0.9%
English					60,786	0.9%

One of the main characteristics of Switzerland's four traditional languages is their territorial character (with Romansh being a special case, see section 5 below). German, French and Italian are each spoken in well-defined areas, and the boundaries separating them are extremely stable. People growing up and living in the *Romandie* (the French-speaking part of Switzerland), for example, will normally have French as their mother-tongue, will speak French at home and will receive a French-medium education. They may learn German or Italian as a 'foreign language' at school (see section 3 below), but will not use these languages in their daily lives unless their job requires a degree of multilingualism. The direct contact between Italian and the other languages of Switzerland is limited because Italian is spoken in valleys south of the alps, the mountains forming a tangible physical barrier. There is some direct contact along the boundary between German-speaking Switzerland and the Romandie, notably in 'bilingual' towns such as Biel (German) / Bienne (French) or Freiburg /

---

[4] From *Rhaeto-Romansh: Facts & Figures*, p. 20 (slightly adapted). Between 1880 and 1980 the national Census inquired into the native tongue. In 1990 two questions were asked: 1. *Which is the language in which you think and over which you have the best command?*, and 2. *Which language(s) do you speak regularly? (a) at home, with relatives, (b) at school or at work* (not tabulated here). The results of the 2000 Census are not available yet. – Further Census figures for the years 1829 to 1980 are given in Pap (1990:118).

[5] Note that these figures include the guest workers and immigrants from Italy.

Fribourg. Most Swiss cantons are largely monolingual; only three are bilingual (Bern / Berne, Freiburg / Fribourg and Wallis / Valais; all German / French) and one (Graubünden) is trilingual (German / Romansh / Italian).

Thus, even though Switzerland is a multilingual state, territorial monolinguality is the rule. There are two groups for whom this is not true: speakers belonging to 'immigrant' minority groups and speakers of Romansh. The situation of the latter will be discussed in more detail in section 5 below.

In the main part of the paper I will address two general issues first, namely the legal situation at the federal level (section 2) and language policies in education (section 3), and then look at some special problems of German (section 4) and Romansh (section 5). In the conclusion (section 6) I shall examine whether the situation in Switzerland offers any lessons that may be useful for dealing with the language issues in Scotland and Ireland. References in the text are kept to a minimum, but in the notes there are a few suggestions for further reading (above all publications in English).

2. The legal situation: Languages in the Constitution of the Swiss Confederation

To assess the legal situation with regard to languages it is important to remember that Switzerland is a relatively non-centralised federal state (*Bundesstaat*) with a three-tiered system of government: below the federal or national level there are the cantonal or state and the municipal or community levels. By comparison with other European countries, cantonal and municipal sovereignty is more important, relatively speaking, than government at the federal level, and local autonomy (*Gemeindeautonomie*) is one of the cornerstones of the Swiss political system. The system of direct democracy practised in Switzerland (again functioning on all three levels) also means that the Swiss not only elect their legislative and their executive bodies at regular intervals, but that they decide a great many issues through ballots. This is also true with regard to language rights, where the cantonal and municipal levels are as important as the federal level. In the following, however, I will concentrate on the national level (i.e. the Constitution): cantonal rulings will be touched upon in connection with education and with Romansh.

Already the first Constitution of the Swiss Confederation, which dates from 1848 (and which was substantially revised in 1874), contained a so-called language article (*Sprachenartikel*) which named three national languages:[6]

---

[6] I quote the latest (1999) version of the Constitution in the 'unofficial translation' by Pierre A. Karrer, kindly made available to me by Constantin Pitsch (see note 2). This translation was commissioned by the federal government, but it is called 'unofficial' since the only 'official' versions of the Constitution are in German, French, Italian and Romansh. Translations of the earlier versions (1848, 1938, 1996) are mine, but I have followed Karrer's model as far as possible.

Article 109 (1848, retained as Article 116 in the revised Constitution of 1874)
The three main languages of Switzerland, German, French, and Italian, are the national languages of the Confederation.

Article 116 was revised in 1938, and in its new form it listed Romansh for the first time as one of the country's national languages:

Article 116 (1938)
1   The national languages of Switzerland are German, French, Italian, and Romansh.
2   The official languages of the Confederation are German, French, and Italian.

Concluding a lengthy debate about linguistic issues both in the national assembly and in the country at large, a substantially revised Article 116 was put to the ballot and was accepted in 1996 (with 76% of voters nationwide voting in favour):

Article 116 (revised version, 1996)
1   The national languages of Switzerland are German, French, Italian, and Romansh.
2   The Confederation and the Cantons shall encourage understanding and exchange between the linguistic communities.
3   The Confederation shall support measures taken by the Cantons of Grisons and Ticino to maintain and to promote Romansh and Italian.
4   The official languages of the Confederation are German, French, and Italian. Romansh shall be an official language for communicating with persons of Romansh language.

The revision of 1996 is characterized by two important changes. The new sections 2 and 3 make the maintenance and promotion of quadrilinguality a task of both the Confederation and the cantons; section 3 further states that the cantons of Graubünden (Grisons) und Ticino will receive federal support for dealing with their specific language problems. The second innovation, in section 4, means that Romansh now has the new status of a *Teilamtssprache* on the federal level.

When the whole Constitution was revised in the years immediately following, Article 116 was extended again and became Articles 4 and 70; Article 18 was added. The revised Constitution was accepted in a ballot in 1999.

Article 4, *National Languages* (1999)
The national languages are German, French, Italian, and Romansh. [previously 116, 1]

Article 18, *Freedom of Language* (1999)
The freedom of language is guaranteed. [new]

Article 70, *Languages* (1999)
1   The official languages of the Confederation are German, French, and Italian. Romansh shall be an official language for communicating with persons of Romansh language. [previously 116, 4]
2   The Cantons shall designate their official languages. In order to preserve harmony between linguistic communities, they shall respect the traditional territorial distribution of languages, and take into account the indigenous linguistic minorities. [new]
3   The Confederation and the Cantons shall encourage understanding and exchange between the linguistic communities. [previously 116, 2]
4   The Confederation shall support the plurilingual Cantons in the fulfilment of their particular tasks. [new]
5   The Confederation shall support measures taken by the Cantons of Grisons and Ticino to maintain and to promote Romansh and Italian. [previously 116, 3]

The new section 2 in Article 70 explicitly empowers the cantons to determine their official languages. Since fears had been voiced that the freedom of language (*Sprachenfreiheit*) enshrined in Article 18 together with shifts in population might endanger the traditional linguistic areas, section 2 explicitly protects the "traditional territorial distribution of languages" and the "indigenous linguistic minorities."

A new federal language (usage) act will specify how Article 70 is to be implemented. It is in preparation, but has not been discussed in parliament yet.

3 Educational issues

In Switzerland public education is largely a responsibility of the municipalities and cantons: the municipalities are responsible for what is called *Volksschule* ('primary and secondary schools'), the cantons for grammar schools and other forms of higher education including the universities. Coordination at the national level is ensured by certain federal regulations and also by decisions and recommendations made by a body called the Conference of Cantonal Ministers of Education (*Schweizerische Konferenz der Kantonalen Erziehungsdirektoren*, EDK).

'Foreign' language education has a central place in the Swiss education system, and according to a long-standing consensus, the first 'foreign' language taught in state schools (usually in the secondary schools) has always been another national language. In practice this has meant French for the German-speaking Swiss, German for the French-speaking Swiss, Italian for some of the inhabitants of the Cantons of Graubünden and Uri and French for the Italian-speaking Swiss. (Romansh will be discussed in section 5 below.) The second foreign language could be another national language,[7] a truly 'foreign' language like English or Spanish, or (in grammar schools) Latin. This consensus had symbolic as well as practical reasons: it was (and is) felt that any Swiss should be able to communicate in at least two of the national languages, and – from a practical point of view – there are many situations (in business or in politics, for example) where the Swiss do actually communicate across the language boundaries, not to mention the fact that (Standard) German, French and Italian are 'useful' languages in other parts of Europe.

Two recent developments are about to change this situation: one is that English (rather than a national language) is increasingly being taught as the first foreign language, the other is that foreign language education is beginning earlier, i.e. already in primary schools.[8] A few German-speaking cantons have already decided to introduce English as the first foreign language, and it is expected that the majority of the German-speaking cantons will follow suit in the very near future. The reasons for this change are that English is a necessary qualification in a great many jobs nowadays, that it is the most important and useful international language and that, being aware of this, parents want their children to learn English. The intention is to keep French as a second, obligatory foreign language so that children have a command of both English and French when they leave school. There will be more time for language teaching in general, of course, if 'foreign' language education in primary schools should become the rule.

The trend towards teaching English before another national language is a phenomenon of German-speaking Switzerland; the Romandie, on the other hand, continues to regard and to treat German as the most important 'foreign' language. It is foreseeable, therefore, that 'foreign' language teaching in the whole of Switzerland will be less balanced and reciprocal with regard to the national languages than in the past. This is one of several reasons why the trend towards more and earlier English is viewed with considerable scepticism and why some people feel that the traditional harmony with regard to languages (*Sprachenfrieden*) is in danger. Optimists and English-language enthusiasts, by contrast, maintain that English, because it is nobody's mother-tongue in Switzerland, may well become a kind of *lingua franca* for the different language-groups in the country to communicate with each other.

The situation is in flux. English will certainly gain more ground, especially in German-speaking Switzerland, but it is too early to say what influence this will have on individual language-competence and on Switzerland as a multilingual country.[9]

---

[7] Outside of the Canton of Graubünden, Romansh is not usually offered in schools, however.

[8] For details, see "Teil II: Englisch im öffentlichen Bildungssystem" in Watts and Murray (2001).

[9] English in Switzerland has been discussed in a substantial number of papers (listed in the bibliography). The volume edited by Watts and Murray (2001)

4 German: special problems

In a pioneering paper first published in 1959 Ferguson discussed German-speaking Switzerland as one of four case studies of diglossia, which he defined as follows (1959/1996:34f.): "*Diglossia* is a relatively stable language situation in which, in addition to the primary dialects of the language (which may include a standard or regional standards), there is a very divergent, highly codified (often grammatically more complex) superposed variety, the vehicle of a large and respected body of written literature, either of an earlier period or in another speech community, which is learned largely by formal education and is used for most written and formal spoken purposes but is not used by any sector of the community for ordinary conversation." In a diglossic sitation, in other words, speakers use two varieties of a language (L for Low for and H for High) in functional distribution:[10] in Switzerland, L is Swiss German (or rather: the various dialects of Swiss German), used for everyday oral communication, whereas H, Standard High German, is used for nearly all written communication and orally on formal occasions.

Diglossia in Switzerland has been studied and discussed in great detail and there is no need to repeat information here which is readily available.[11] Two remarks must suffice, one concerning recent developments within the diglossic situation, the other the role of L as a marker of identity.

In general terms German-speaking Switzerland is as diglossic as it was when Ferguson first described it, but two developments in the last few decades may be noted. Sharing the fate of many local varieties, the Swiss German dialects are undergoing a process of levelling, with regional and even supra-regional varieties replacing local ones (predominantly in urban and urbanised areas). The levelling happens between dialects (dialects influencing each other), but there is also a considerable influx of Standard German and of English lexis. As a second development one may note that Swiss German, the L, encroaches on the territory of Standard German, the H. Dialect is heard a great deal on local radio and television (even for news broadcasts), and young people increasingly use it in writing when they exchange personal letters or when they communicate electronically (via e-mail, SMS, etc.).[12] However, even though the domains of use of L have become somewhat more numerous, and even though the boundary

---

offers up-to-date information on all relevant aspects, but note that all contributions are in German. See also Murray, Wegmüller and Khan (2001), in French.

[10] The term *diglossia* is nowadays also used for two different languages (rather than two varieties of a language) used in functional distribution.

[11] See, for example, Ferguson (1959/1996), Keller (1982) and Siebenhaar and Wyler (1998).

[12] This is an interesting development, since there is no written standard of Swiss German and since written Swiss German is not taught anywhere. The only (other) domain where written Swiss German is found is dialect literature.

between L and H has shifted at the expense of H, the distinction as such is still there and is as clear as ever.

In the context of a conference on languages in Ireland and Scotland it seems appropriate to mention the symbolic function of Swiss German. For practically all speakers of Swiss-German, their dialect serves as a marker of local and national identity. The Swiss are not Germans or Austrians, and they show this by always using Swiss-German among themselves and by a marked disinclination to use Standard German in oral communication, even with Germans and with people who have learnt Standard German as a foreign language. (As a rule it can be said that when speaking to a foreigner the German-speaking Swiss would rather use a foreign language than Standard German.) This is not the place to explore the reasons for this interesting phenomenon, but it is worth pointing out that Swiss-German has this very marked symbolic function even though it is not written and even though it has no official status whatsoever.

5 Romansh: special problems

As mentioned above, the Canton of Graubünden is trilingual, and it is the only part of Switzerland where Romansh, the country's fourth national language, is spoken.[13] In terms of language-family relationships, the situation of Romansh is rather complicated. Most, but not all, linguists agree that there are between three to five different 'Rhaeto-Romance' languages: (Swiss) Romansh in Switzerland

Map 2: Where '(Rhaeto-)Romania' has survived

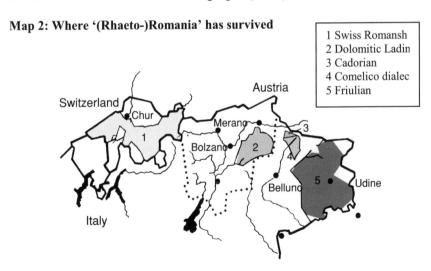

1 Swiss Romansh
2 Dolomitic Ladin
3 Cadorian
4 Comelico dialec
5 Friulian

---

[13] The best brief overview in English is *Rhaeto-Romansh: Facts & Figures* (1996). Billigmeyer (1979) is a comprehensive, but somewhat dated study. Liver (1999), in German, is an excellent introduction to linguistic aspects of Romansh, but treats sociolinguistic issues only very briefly.

plus Dolomitic Ladin, Cadorian, the Comelico dialect and Friulian in mountainous regions of north-eastern Italy, as shown in Map 2. (Swiss) Romansh, in turn, is by no means uniform, but is comprised of five substantially different regional varieties (idioms), called, respectively, Sursilvan, Sutsilvan, Surmeiran, Putèr and Vallader, as shown in Map 3. They are spoken in different parts of the canton, and they differ above all in phonology, but also in grammar and lexis. All five of them have been written since about the Renaissance.[14]

Map 3: The Romansh Language Territory

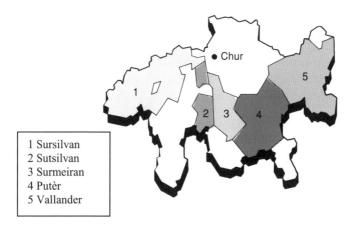

1 Sursilvan
2 Sutsilvan
3 Surmeiran
4 Putèr
5 Vallander

Romansh is a minority language not only in Switzerland as a whole, but also in the canton of Graubünden, as the Census figures in Table 2 show.[15]

Table 2: National Census for the Canton of Graubünden, 1880, 1980, 1990

	1880		1980		1990	
	'Native Tongue'		'Native Tongue'		'Best Command'	
German	43,664	46.0%	98,645	59.9%	113,611	65.3%
Romansh	37,794	39.8%	36,017	21.9%	29,679	17.0%
Italian	12,976	13.7%	22,199	13.5%	19,190	11.0%
Misc.	557	0.6%	7,780	4.7%	11,410	6.6%

---

[14] Strictly speaking, each of the five idioms is a group of local dialects united by a written standard. See text samples at the end.

[15] From *Rhaeto-Romansh: Facts & Figures*, p. 22 (slightly adapted). See note 4 for explanations.

Map 4: Romansh as the language of which respondents had the best command (source: 1990 nation-wide Census)

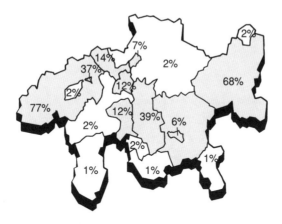

Map 5: Romansh as the language spoken at home, school and/or work (Source: 1990 nation-wide Census)

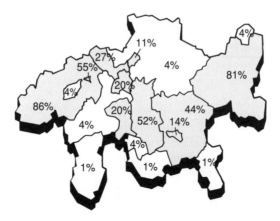

Within the canton the territorial principle mentioned above can also be observed in that German, (the five varieties of) Romansh and Italian are spoken in fairly well delimited areas. Practically all speakers of Romansh are Romansh-German bilinguals, and Romansh is not used with equal frequency in all five areas, as the survey results presented in Maps 4, 5 and 6 show. Of the five idioms, Sursilvan, Vallader and – to some extent – Surmeiran are well rooted in the respective communities, whereas the position of Sutsilvan and Putèr is shakier.

What support does Romansh receive? As mentioned in section 2 above, Romansh is now a *Teilamtssprache* or 'language accorded limited recognition' on the federal level; it is also – of course – one of the three official languages of the Canton of Graubünden. In the Romansh-speaking areas, Romansh is the

Map 6: The results of the 1992 SRG survey ('How well is Romansh understood?')

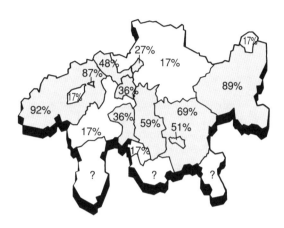

language of instruction in primary school; secondary school is taught in German, but Romansh remains a 'subject' throughout the curriculum. Experiments with bilingual education at the primary and secondary level are under way.

All five idioms are written, and there is a substantial body of literature and of teaching materials (language courses, readers, textbooks) for each of them. Nevertheless, the lack of a common written standard for Romansh was felt for a long time, since it would obviously be easier if texts could be written in or translated into, one form of Romansh rather than five. Several attempts in the last two centuries to develop a uniform written language failed, and it was only in the 1980s and early 1990s that Heinrich Schmid, a Romance scholar teaching at the University of Zurich, succeeded with a written standard called *Rumantsch Grischun* (RG).[16] RG is a so-called 'compromise language,' based to a large extent on three of the written idioms used in Romansh-speaking Graubünden: Sursilvan, Vallader and Surmeiran. It is meant purely as a written standard for communication within the whole canton and for use at the federal level.[17] From a political, legal and administrative point of view, RG has been a success so far: following the adoption of the new 'language article' 116 in the Federal Constitution in 1996, the Federation as well as the Canton now use RG for official publications. In a vote held in 2001, the people of the Canton of Graubünden also decided that instructions for balloting on the cantonal level should be published in RG only, thereby replacing an older ruling which

---

[16] Guidelines were published in 1982; a dictionary and an elementary grammar appeared in 1993. RG is also used in the first ever *Romansch-English / English-Romansch Dictionary and Phrasebook* (Gross and Telli 2000).

[17] See text samples at the end.

stipulated that these instructions should be printed in both Sursilvan and Ladin (Vallader). On the practical and psychological level, however, RG has not found full acceptance. People in the Romansh-speaking areas come across it in writing,[18] where it looks more foreign than when it is spoken with one of the regional or local accents. They (say that they) find it difficult to read, they fear that it may lead to confusion[19] and also that in the long run RG may endanger rather than support the survival of Romansh. Fears such as these are not unfounded, but it is too early to say what role RG will play in the struggle of Romansh to survive.

Romansh is relatively well represented in the media. A radio and television studio in Chur produces over eleven hours daily of radio broadcasts and a number of short television programmes (including news) in Romansh which are broadcast on the German-language channel. When earlier attempts to set up a daily Romansh newspaper failed, a state-supported news agency (*Agentura da Novidads Rumantscha*, ANR) was founded instead (in 1996). There used to be several weekly or bi-weekly newspapers in the various idioms, but these are now part of *La Quotidiana*, a Romansh-language daily that has been published since 1997.[20] The *Engadiner Post*, the German-language daily of the upper Engadin, now also has a daily section in Romansh.[21]

Measures to support and maintain Romansh at all levels are encouraged and coordinated by the 'Romansh League' (*Lia Rumantscha*), a private, but state-supported body that was founded in 1919 as an umbrella organisation for all Romansh organisations. The Universities of Freiburg / Fribourg and Zurich each have a Chair of Romansh language and / or literature, and Romansh also has a (naturally more limited) place in the departments of Romance languages of other universities.

What does the support of Romansh cost? It is impossible to give a complete answer to this question, since money is spent at different levels and within different budgets. The translation service of the Swiss Confederation, for example, now also produces translations into RG, but this activity is in essence no different from translations into the other three national languages. When, as a second example, primary school is taught in Romansh in a Romansh-speaking municipality, this will be funded through the regular budget for schools. Some information on this topic is given in *Romansh: Facts & Figures*:

---

[18] As a direct result of the 1996 revision of the 'language article', Romansh (as RG) is now used more frequently in writing, and in more text types.

[19] There are now six written forms of Romansh, all of which can be encountered in a single issue of the Romansh-language daily *La Quotidiana*, for example.

[20] Articles in *La Quotidiana* (published in Chur) are, variously, in one of the five traditional idioms or in RG.

[21] Articles in *Engadiner Post / Posta Ladina* (published in St. Moritz) are in Putèr or in Vallader, the two idioms spoken in the upper and lower Engadine, respectively.

> *Ever since it was set up in 1919, the Lia Rumantscha has been receiving grants from the federal and cantonal government, starting with 10 000 Swiss francs per year and growing in stages to a figure of 2,4 million (in 1995). [...] Annual federal subsidies paid to Graubünden for the maintenance and promotion of the Romansh and Italian languages and cultures were increased from 3,75 million Swiss francs to five million for 1996. Most of the increase in the federal grants is being used to promote the Romansh press. (p. 41)*

> *The LR's [Lia Rumantscha's] activities are financed with federal and cantonal grants [...], revenue from the sale of books, translation work, technical lexica, fees for attending courses and donations from a number of different private and public organisations and foundations. Currently [i.e. in 1996] the LR has some three million Swiss francs available to it every year for maintaining and promoting the Romansh language and culture. (p. 57)*

6. Conclusions: Switzerland compared to Ireland and Scotland

The historical, linguistic and political situations vary so much from country to country that one should be wary of facile comparisons regarding language and politics.[22] Nevertheless, the situation in Switzerland may offer a few lessons for both Ireland and Scotland:

1. Switzerland's bottom-up, three-level political organisation and its system of direct democracy help to defuse possible tensions by allowing the people (within limits) to decide on matters of local or regional importance. From this point of view, devolution and local governments are a good thing.
2. The so-called territorial principle (a multilingual nation consisting of largely monolingual regions) also helps to avoid tensions. Good fences make good neighbours, but the people separated by these fences should be encouraged to 'talk across' them.
3. Diglossia in German-speaking Switzerland and the important role of Swiss German both practically and symbolically show that a language or (in this case) a dialect does not need any official status to flourish and to serve as a marker of identity. To my knowledge there have been no significant attempts to make Swiss German a written, 'official' language in order to enhance its status. Doing so would raise the spectre of marginalisation or 'hollandisation', i.e. of ending up with a 'small' language which few people outside of

---

[22] Instructive comparisons, however, can be found in Meier (1997) and in Görlach (1985) and (1991).

the country in question will know. To the Swiss, Swiss German is a highly distinctive spoken dialect (or rather, a group of dialects) of German, no more and no less.[23] Knowledge of the status of Swiss German may be useful when dealing with the question of Ulster Scots / Ullans.[24]

4. The role of Romansh in Switzerland can be compared, to some extent, to that of Scottish Gaelic in Scotland or that of Irish Gaelic in the Republic of Ireland. Proportionally, there are about as many speakers of Romansh in Switzerland as there are speakers of Scots Gaelic in Scotland. Practically all speakers of Romansh and of Scottish Gaelic are bilingual, and many (most?) of them live in areas where the minority language is (still) the community language. Scots Gaelic has no official status in the United Kingdom, however, whereas Romansh is one of Switzerland's four national languages and to a limited extent also an official language; on the cantonal level it is even a 'full' official language. Nationally and regionally, a good deal more is done to maintain and promote Romansh in Switzerland than is done to maintain and promote Scots Gaelic in Scotland. The next few decades will show whether the measures taken in Switzerland are sufficient to halt the gradual decline of Romansh and whether Romansh stands a better chance of survival than Scottish Gaelic. Irish, of course, is the national language and one of the two official languages of the Republic of Ireland. While the number of native speakers of Irish, proportionally, is probably no greater than the number of native speakers of Romansh, all schoolchildren in the Republic learn Irish as part of their education. Nothing like this has ever been suggested in Switzerland, which has no language that could serve as the national language of all its inhabitants. Moreoover, Romansh is one of four (rather than two) traditional languages of the country, and the only one of these four which is not used outside of Switzerland.

5. The creation and implementation of *Rumantsch Grischun* is a unique experiment, and the future will tell how it affects Romansh.

---

[23] Görlach (2000:27) also makes this point, though with different emphasis:

> *For speakers who love their dialect and want to hand it on to the next generation(s), the question of dialect vs. language does not arise. And in fact, regional, national or ethnic identity can lead to a reversal of the tendency of dialect erosion, as the example of German-speaking Switzerland in the 20th century beautifully illustrates – and this development is happening under our eyes – without Swiss speakers claiming they speak Switzerlandish rather than German.*

[24] Scots is a different case, mainly because of its history.

There are hopes that it will strengthen the presence of Romansh as a supra-regional written language and also as a language that can be and is used for official communication, but there are fears that it may weaken the five traditional (spoken and written) idioms and thus speed rather than slow down or halt the decline of Romansh.

Appendix: Text Samples of Romansh[25]

English: The fox was once again hungry. Suddenly, it saw a crow sitting in a tree, holding a piece of cheese in its beak. I would find that really tasty, it thought to itself and called out to the crow: "What a pretty creature you are! If your song is as beautiful as your looks, then you must be the prettiest bird of all."

Sursilvan: L'uolp era puspei inagada fomentada. Cheu ha ella viu sin in pegn in tgaper che teneva in toc caschiel en siu bec. Quei gustass a mi, ha ella tertgau, ed ha clamau al tgaper: "Tgei bi che ti eis! Sche tiu cant ei aschi bials sco tia cumparsa, lu eis ti il pli bi utschi da tuts."

Sutsilvan: La vualp eara puspe egn'eada fumantada. Qua â ella vieu sen egn pegn egn corv ca taneva egn toc caschiel ainten sieus pecel. Quegl gustass a mei, â ella tartgieu, ed ha clamo agli corv: "Tge bel ca tei es! Scha tieus tgànt e aschi beal sco tia pareta, alura es tei igl ple beal utschi da tuts."

Surmiran: La golp era puspe eneda famantada. Co ò ella via sen en pegn en corv tgi tigniva en toc caschiel an sies pecal. Chegl am gustess, ò ella panso, ed ò clamo agl corv: "Tge bel tgi te ist! Schi ties cant è schi bel scu tia parentscha, alloura ist te igl pi bel utschel da tots."

Putèr: La vuolp d'eira darcho üna vouta famanteda. Co ho'la vis sün ün pin ün corv chi tgnaiva ün toc caschöl in seis pical. Quai am gustess, ha'la pensa, ed ha clomà al corv: "Che bel cha tü est! Scha teis chant es uschè bel sco tia apparentscha, lura est tü il pü bel utschè da tuots."

Vallader: La vuolp d'eira darcheu üna jada fomantada. Qua ha'la vis sün ün pin ün corv chi tgnaiva ün töch caschöl in sieu pical. Que am gustess, ho'la penso, ed ho clamo al corv: "Che bel cha tü est! Scha tieu chaunt es uschè bel scu tia apparentscha, alura est tü il plü bel utschè da tuots."

Rumantsch Grischun: La vulp era puspè ina giada fomentada. Qua ha ella vis sin in pign in corv che tegneva in toc chaschiel en ses pichel. Quai ma gustass, ha'la pensà, ed ha clamà al corv: "Tge bel che ti es! Sche tes chant è uschè bel sco tia parita, lur es ti il pli bel utschè da tuts."

---

25 From *Rhaeto-Romansh: Facts & Figures*, p. 23.

References

Andres, Franz. 1990. "Language relations in multilingual Switzerland." *Multilingua* 9.1:11-45.

Andres, Franz and Richard J. Watts. 1993. "English as a lingua franca in Switzerland: myth or reality?" *Bulletin CILA* 58:109-27.

Bickel, Hans and Robert Schläpfer, eds. 1994. *Mehrsprachigkeit – eine Herausforderung*. Basel: Helbing und Lichtenhahn.

Billigmeyer, Robert H. 1979. *A Crisis in Swiss Pluralism: The Romansh and their Relations with the German- and Italian-Swiss in the Perspective of a Millennium*. Contributions to the Sociology of Language 26. The Hague: Mouton.

Dingwall, Silvia and Heather Murray. 1999. "The future of English in Switzerland: a majority / minority problem?" *Bulletin suisse de linguistique appliquée* 69.2:189-206.

Dürmüller, Urs. 1986. "The status of English in multilingual Switzerland." *Bulletin CILA* 44:7-38.

Dürmüller, Urs. 1991. "Swiss multilingualism and international Communication." *Sociolinguistica, Internationales Jahrbuch für Europäische Soziolinguistik* 5:111-59.

Dürmüller, Urs. 1994. "Multilingual talk or English only? The Swiss experience." *Sociolinguistica, Internationales Jahrbuch für Europäische Soziolinguistik* 8:44-64.

Dürmüller, Urs. 1997. *Changing Patterns of Multilingualism: From Quadrilingual to Multilingual Switzerland*. Trans. Eileen Walliser-Schwarzbart. Zürich: Pro Helvetia, Arts Council of Switzerland.

Ferguson, C.A. 1959. "Diglossia." *Word* 15:325-40; reprinted 1996 in *Sociolinguistic Perspectives: Papers on Language in Society, 1959-1994*. Ed. Thom Huebner. Oxford Studies in Sociolinguistics. New York, Oxford: Oxford University Press, 25-39.

Görlach, Manfred. 1985. "Scots and Low German: the social history of two minority languages." *Focus on Scotland*. Ed. Manfred Görlach. Amsterdam, Philadelphia: John Benjamins, 19-36.

Görlach, Manfred. 1991. "Scotland and Jamaica – bidialectal or bilingual?" *Englishes: Studies in Varieties of English 1984-1988*. Amsterdam, Philadelphia: John Benjamins, 69-89.

Görlach, Manfred. 2000. "Ulster Scots: a language?" *Language and Politics: Northern Ireland, the Republic or Ireland and Scotland*. Ed. John M. Kirk and Dónall P. O Baoill. Belfast Studies in Language, Culture and Politics 1. Belfast: Cló Ollscoil na Banríona, 13-31.

Gross, Manfred and Daniel Telli. 2000. *Romansch-English / English-Romansch: Dictionary and Phrasebook*. New York: Hippocrene Books.

Keller, R.E. 1982. "Diglossia in German-speaking Switzerland." *Standard Languages: Spoken and Written*. Ed. W. Haas. Mont Follick Series 5. Manchester: Manchester University Press / Totowa, N.J.: Barnes and Noble, 70-93.

Liver, Ricarda. 1999. *Rätoromanisch: Eine Einführung in das Bündnerromanische.* Narr Studienbücher. Tübingen: Gunter Narr.

Meier, Hans H. 1977. "Scots is not alone: the Swiss and Low German analogues." *Bards and Makars: Scottish Language and Literature: Medieval and Renaissance.* Ed. Adam J. Aitken, Matthew P. McDiarmid and Derick S. Thomson. Glasgow: University of Glasgow Press, 201-13.

Murray, Heather, Ursula Wegmüller and Fayaz Ali Khan. 2001, *L'anglais en Suisse: Rapport de recherche.* Dossiers OFES [Office fédéral de l'éducation et de la science] 2001/1f.

Pap, Leo. 1990. "The language situation in Switzerland: An updated survey." *Lingua* 80:109-48.

Rhaeto-Romansh: Facts & Figures. 1996. Chur: Lia Rumantscha. Corrections and addenda (1996-2000).

Schläpfer, Robert (ed.). 1982. *Die viersprachige Schweiz.* Zürich, Köln: Benziger.

Siebenhaar, Beat and Alfred Wyler. 1998. *Dialect and High German in German-Speaking Switzerland.* Rev. ed. Trans. Maureen Oberli-Turner. Zürich: Pro Helvetia, Arts Council of Switzerland.

Watts, Richard J. and Heather Murray, eds. 2001. *Die fünfte Landessprache? Englisch in der Schweiz.* Zürich: vdf Hochschulverlag.

A Twalmonth An A Wee Tait Forder

Dauvit Horsbroch

Innin

Atween August fernyear an the day, the Scots leid haes seen chynges that wad a been unthocht o ten year syne. A year back Scots haedna muckle mair nor recognition fae Govrenment that it existit. A wad lyke for tae mak comment on a whein occurrents that haes taen place in the last twalmonth, bi wey o updatin ma last bit report, comprehendin the political staunin o Scots on baith sydes o the Sheuch, an a wee tait anent wrutten langage forby. Speakin in braid terms, the heidmaist twa occurents is the founin o the *Aw-Pairtie Curn on The Scots Leid in the Scots Pairlament*, and the ploys tae dae wi the *Boord O Ulstèr-Scotch*. Nane o thir ploys wad a haen onie chance o gettin aff the grun haed it no been for the UK Govrenment an the Republic o Irland comin thegither an disbursin fundin for the Scots leid in Ulster. An A wad lyke tae comment on this an the differ wi Scots in Scotland.

Ulster Is Kenspeckle

Apairt fae the tribbles, Ulster is nou kenspeckle in ither weys gettin. It seems tae this speaker that ower muckle ink haes been skailed anent the staunin o Scots in Ulster. As A unnerstaun it, the *European Chairter For Leids O The Curn* recognises whit we hae in Ulster as the furm the Scots leid taks in Ulster, but no as anither leid. Keepin mynd o this is gey important whan we conseider the wrutten langage in thir norlan coonties. Becis whit we ar seein is the ae leid bein wrutten twa gaits awthegither, allouin, o course, for a bittie differ atween local furms. Ane o ma maist important heids - sib tae wrutten Scots - is the furm it haes taen o recent years in Ulster. Athoot spennin ower lang, A maun say a puckle wurds becis it haes a bearin on whither or no fowk in public poseitions taks Scots serious.

In juist five or sax year a pucklie steerers - nane o thaim speakers o Scots (sae faur as A ken), lat alane versant in it - haes taen the wee tait tradeitional Scots spoken in the kintra an turnt it on its heid, at least in its wrutten furm. We hae a dictum in the wast o Scotland: *hot watter knocked stupit daesna mask tea.* For aw the unco wurds in the warld, the feck o texts makkit in Ulster read as Scottified Suddron; thay want eidiom, thay want tradeition ahin thaim, an abuin awthin, thay shuidna be sae divorced fae the speech o the fowk. It isna muckle wunner that monie fowk gies this leitratur a bye, sae tae speak.

As maist fowk ken, the Bodies set up tae cairrie-oot the *Belfast Guid Fryday Greement* comprehendit twa organisation for tae tak tae dae wi langage; ane for the

Earse leid an anither for the Scots leid in Ulster. The Depairtment o Cultur, Airts an Leisure (in the Executive o Norlan Irland) haes set up a Langage Diversitie Brainch forby. The organisation that taks tae dae wi Scots - *Tha Boord O Ulstèr-Scotch* - haes set furth a *Heich Ploy* for the years 2001 til 2004, an - orra for Scots - it leuks colourfae an glaizie tae.[1] Sae we walcome this eikin tae the staunin o Scots. On the ither haun, it is wrutten in a leid wanchancie awthgither an A haed tae warsle wi maist pairts tae lift the meanin. The remit o the *Boord O Ulstèr-Scotch*, waled fae its *Heich Ploy*, reads as follaes:

> *Tha Boord o Ulstèr-Scotch bis gart unnèr tha laa guide tha "forderin o mair forstannin an uise o tha Ulstèr-Scotch leid an o Ulstèr-Scotch fowkgate daeins, baith ben Norlin Airlann an athort tha islann."*

The tribble wi this an ither texts is the wey the semantics is tuimed oot the windae an a puckle wurds is made tae shouder ower monie meanins. It dings doun the ettles o the *Boord* awthegither. Whit ar we tae mak o the follaein bit screives:

> *The Noarth-Sooth Boord o Leid is cum aboot frae the Bilfawst Greeance as yin o tha Noarth-Sooth boords...Tha Boord maun gie answer til tha Noarth-Sooth Cooncil o Männystèrs, an maist o aa the twa Männystèrs, baith in tha Norlin Airlann Semmle an Dáil Eireann, as taks adae wi tha leid an tha heirskip o Ulstèr Scotch fowkgates.*

> *Fowkgates. Tae tak a muckle pairt in the graith o Ulstèr-Scotch fowkgates.*[2]

Whit *is* fowkgates? The ettle is tae hap the meanin o cultur but daes the 'weys o fowk' mean the ae thing as cultur? *Boord O Leid* wants comment tae; a leid is the parteiclar tongue o fowk whither it's the Scots leid, the Inglis leid, the Norn leid or the Frainch leid, but leid isna the ae thing as abstrack terms sic as langage or linguistic. Whit this shuid be cryed is the *Buird O Langage*.

Ane ither ensample gars me lowp up at it; on a veisit tae Derry a met in wi a buikie cryed *In Other Words: The Languages of Europe*, pitten thegither bi the *Linen Hall Library's Languages of Ulster Project*, Belfast, on behauf o the European Year o Leids. In this buikie the Suddron for staunart phrases in a whein leids is gien an we fin baith Scots an Ulster Scots on thair ain pages. Queer eneuch, the Ulster Scots is - A wad say - closer til ilka day langage nor the ane makin-on tae be Scots. Naebodie in

---

[1] This *Heich Ploy* wes approven bi the comatee o the North-Sooth Bodie in December 2000.

[2] Page 3 *Tha Boord o Ulstèr-Scotch Heich Ploy* 2000/1-2003/4. The Inglis version o this saecon quote reads "Culture. To be a key contributor to the development of Ulster-Scots culture.", see page 10.

Scotland says "be thankit" for *thankyou*; this shuid aether be juist *thanks* (or cheers), or, bein furmal, *monie thank*. The wurds "fair faw ye" daesna translate in Inglis as "hello"; in fact, fairfaw translatit fae modren Scots means "best or good wishes" - whit we wad say or wryte til a bodie on pairtin fae thaim. A'm dumfounert at "A'm geylies" for "I'm well"; whit ever is the maiter wi "A'm no bad"? An A'm no convinced o the want o makkin-up fause distinctions whan the ae leit for Scots as a hail wad dae. Whit maks this fleysome is that the fowk that pit the sae-cawed Scots thegither is nou daein it on behauf o Scots in Scotland tae.[3]

An this brings us tae ma verra dunt; A reckon it's tyme tae say nae mair, please. It daes the leid nae favours ava tae gang joco an DIY slingin its tradeitions the proverbial deifie. A bodie losses onie support fae the actual speakers, an we can tak it for grantit the ceivil servans an meinisters is lauchin up thair sleeves. The makkin an wrytin o Scots texts wants taen clean oot the hauns o stickit fowk an gien ower til ithers that is versant wi the leid, that haes a bittie trainin ahin thaim. Govrenment shuid be leukin the gait o feein text screivars that is skeilie in Scots an airmed wi qualifications. For ensample, ae companie is leukin intae steidin a college o IT Learnin in Donegal for fowk tae learn the Scots leid, whaurever thay byde. This cuid easy gang agley onless siller wes peyed oot tae bring in qualifeed fowk, an, whither we lyke it or no, it wad hae tae draw maistlie on fowk fae Scotland. This is affa important becis a bodie that bydes in Boston or Botanga wull jalouse that sic an IT college speaks for Scots on baith sydes o the Sheuch. An tae fowk in the *Boord O Ulstèr-Scotch*, an ither bodies, A say, daena misken ma remarks; it's in the intress o fowk in Scotland that ye dae weil, but sae faur it's fawin short o rael Scots. A wadna be an honest cheil gin A didna admit this.

Ane unleuked for affcome o hame raign leas the Scots leid ill-pit. Gin a bodie haes a scance at the *Cooncil O Europe Chairter*, Airticle 7 sets oot that the signatories (in oor case the Unitit Kinrik an the Republic O Irland) shuid foun thair ploys an polices on the follaein ettle;

> ...the respect of the geographical area of each regional or minority language in order to ensure that existing or new administrative divisions do not constitute an obstacle to the promotion of the regional or minority language in question.[4]

---

[3] Tae be fair, the ettles o the *Linen Hall Library* is weil meant, as Mary Delargy scrieves in this here buikie, but fowk shuidna run awa wi thairsels. Keek T. McBride (ed.) *In Other Words: The Languages of Europe Celebrating the Launch of the European Year of Languages in Northern Ireland,* (Belfast: The Linenhall Library 2001).

[4] Airticle 7b, *The Cooncil O Europe Chairter For Leids O the Curn*.

Houancver, this condeition haes been bruken becis the UK govrenment, keepin in mynd it haes recognised the ae Scots leid, funds an forders speakers o the leid differentlie in ane pairt o the UK an daes awmaist naethin for the lave o speakers in anither. Yet the speakers aw bydes in the ae state. An bi fundin an forderin anither wey o spellin, the Govrenment haes makkit a fause shed in the leid an caws apairt its identitie. This plain conters the *Chairter* awthegither. It wad be lyke the Republic O Irland giein siller an support tae mak a split-new Earse leid in Donegal alane, but nae-sayin it til onie ither pairt o the Republic.

In the year 2000-2001 Scots in Ulster wes fundit bi £1.3 million; £750,000 fae the UK Govrenment an £250,000 fae the Republic O Irland. This siller comprehends fundin o the *Boord O Ulstèr-Scotch* an an *Institute O Ulster Scots Studies* steidit at the Univairsitie O Ulster's Magee College. The *Boord O Ulstèr-Scotch* is etttlin tae open an office in Embro forby the twa it haes in Belfast an Donegal. The maist the UK haes spent on Scots in Scotland in onie year fae 1990 is £140,000 an this wes gien tae dictionar projecks an a datafoun. A'm sweirt tae soun lik A'm criticeizin the lyke o the *SNDA* at aw, but it haes tae be sayed that the Scots-speakin communitie wants mair nor dictionars tae express itsel fullie in this modren warld. The Govrenment can fin the siller for faur mair nor dictionars in Ulster, sae whit wey can it no fin it in Scotland?

Scotland Caws Ower Cannie

In Scotland we gang slaw an caw cannie. Atweil, we canna dae ocht else becis in Scotland awthin haes tae be duin wi consensus - tae lift a wurd faurben wi Ulster fowk - for in Scotland we hae the wecht o speakers. It is gey an intressin tae compare the twa gaits that Scots is gauin. In Scotland acteivitie is airtit at the pairlament itsel bi wey o owertures, an letters tae the Executive depairtments. In Ulster acteivitie is airtit bi wey o the *Boord O Ulstèr-Scotch*; its marra in Scotland, the *Scots Langauge Resource Centre*, isna warth a preen amang monie academics, an cairries sma wecht amang Scots speakers. In the run-up tae the Scots pairlament elections ane o the ideas pit forrit wes tae bring thegither a curn fowk in the pairlament tae support the leid. On 22 November 2000 a first gaitherin o intresstit fowk wes hauden in the pairlament o Scotland tae see whither sic an idea haed muckle support. It wes weil attendit, an maist important, fowk fae twa-three political pairties shawed an intress. The gaitherin haed afore it maiters sic as the *Universal Declaration O Langage Richts*, Scots signs in the pairlament, the scuils foraye, an fleitchin commissionars in the pairlament itsel. The affcome o this gaitherin wes the deceision taen tae gae aheid wi the idea an sae a curn cryed the *Cross-Pairtie Group in the Scottish Pairliament on the Scots Leid* wes institut alang wi a tocher o £250 fae the *Scots Leid Associe* [5] The official ettles o this *Curn* is gien as follaes:

> *Tae forder the cause o the Scots Leid, lat memmers (MSPs) ken aboot the cultur an heritage o the leid an shaw the need for action tae uphaud Scots.*

The first furmal gaitherin o the *Aw-Pairtie Curn* wes hauden on 31 Januar 2001 in a comatee chaumer o the pairlament biggins on George IV Brig, in Embro. Irene McGugan, a North-East Scotland commissioner, an the heidmaist supporter o Scots in the pairlament, haes pitten forrit a whein owertures tae the Executive o Scotland, on behauf o this *Aw-Pairtie Curn*. Ane owerture, for ensample, threapit that in Norroway the govrenment coffs the first thousan o ilka buik prentit in Norn an gies thaim tae librars an scuils an that the ae policie shuid be cairried oot in Scotland for Scots. But, as wi the census an ither speirs, the meinisters dang Scots doun. Aboot the ae tyme the *Scotsman* newspaper reportit:

> *... the general view among those anxious to promote Scots, in whatever form, is that the Scottish executive has singularly failed to come up with any commitment to the language - never mind anything like the funding it provides for Gaelic.*

an the report eikit

> *For while lobbyists fulminate at official indifference, they have also been gazing with disbelief at troubled Northern Ireland, where the terms of the Good Friday Agreement have seen Ulster Scots ... enjoying considerably enhanced fortunes.* [6]

Sae twa things, the cauldrif Executive, an the acteivitie in Ulster, haes steered up the Lawlan Scot. As a bodie that haes gane tae maist o the gaitherins hauden sae faur, A wad say the'r twa-three things tae tak tent o, albeit the *Aw-Pairtie Curn* isna lang stairtit. Ae thing is the laik o fowk fae pairties forby the SNP, tho ithers haed shawn an intress in the November. A canna say A'v seen onie ither pairtie coupon, but gin a bodie taks a swatch o the pairlament wabsteid the leit o memmers o the *Aw-Pairtie Curn* leuks rare. In theorie, Cathy Peattie, Labour pairtie Depute Convener for Equal Opportunities, an pairt o the Eddication, Cultur an Sport comatee, is a memmer, but

---

[5] Houanever, for this speaker, this name is a mixtur-maxtur, naether Inglis or Scots. The wurd *Scottish*, for ensample, is the Inglis wurd; it shuid richtlie be Scots Pairlament or even Pairlament o Scotland. Curn is a mair eidiomatic Scots forby. A bodie howps that this can be richtified.

[6] *Scotsman*, report bi Gil Gilchrist, 9t Januar, 2001.

an email tae her brocht furth nae repone ava, an she haesna been til onie but the first gaitherin. Ian Jenkins, Leibral Democrat forespeaker for Eddication, Culture an Sport, anither memmer, haesna taen onie mair intress aether. It micht be that thir fowk wants tae leuk unco politic bi pittin thair names forrit, but whan it comes tae the vote thay follae the pairtie whip. In fact, baith o the abuin fowk, alang wi aw the Leibral an Labour commissioners, votit agin haein Scots in the census in Februar 2000. The'r somethin faur wrang whan fowk sittin on thon comatees sees naethin wrang in supportin the richts o ane leid whyle dingin doun speakers o anither. An this is ane o the muckle problems for Scots the nou; whyle ither leids haes the remeid o law, the weird o Scots haes tae lippen on the shouglie fortunes o pairtie politics.

It wad be better for Scots, in ma opeinion, haed we less but mair commitit fowk in the pairlament. A maun gie a toot on the horn anent an auld norie that Scots is aboot makkin poyems an stories alane - whit in Inglis is cawed *creative writing* - an A div wunner whither the *Aw-Pairtie Curn* haes a whein fowk ower monie sut aroun the buird an uphaudin this narra, mercatorian intress. Tyme alane wull let dab.

The nou the *Aw-Pairtie Curn* is finnin its feet, A maun admit, an a richt programme haes yet tae be wirked oot. We want tae keep it shairp an on the pairlament, the European Chairter, the maiter o signs an Govrenment leitratur, an Scots as a scuils subjeck in its ain richt.

The UK Govrenment ratifeed the *Cooncil O Europe Chairter For Leids O The Curn* on 27 Mairch 2001 an it cam intil effect on 1st Julie this year. Houanever, it is the case yet that the'r nae beild for Scots becis it is unner Pairt II. The *Aw-Pairtie Curn*, forby finnin its feet, haes made pairt o its haunlin tae airt-oot chairters on human an langage richts that the UK haes signed up tae, an tae provide guidal on hou the thae chairters shuid affect Scots an Scots-speakin. This wull tak in ettles tae heize Scots up tae Pairt III staunin on the *Cooncil O Europe Chairter.*

The Executive aye threaps on makin a richt proveision for Scots in the scuils but, tae date, Scots haes aye been cuivered bi the guidal on Inglis. Whanever a bodie speirs at thaim aboot this proveision, the Executive wull say that the langage an leitratur o Scotland is weil cuivered an gies as ensamples owthors in Gaelic an Inglis tae. In a puckle cases, the'r nae Scots in the scuils ava. The readin o leitratur wrutten bi owthors o Scotland as a hail canna be coontit as a richt proveison for Scots in parteiclar whan we conseider that baith Scots Gaelic an Inglis exist as subjecks in thair ain richt. It wad be muckle the same as teachin Scots Gaelic as an orra pairt o the subjeck Earse. Onie Scots Gael wad be black affrontit, an richtlie sae. In Januar this year, the twa-three teachers amang the *Aw-Pairtie Curn* gaithered thegither whit infurmation thay cuid airt-oot anent the leid in the scuils an made the important pynt that, in Scotland, we haena a compulsor curriculum as thay div in Ingland. Insteid we hae Naitional Guidal that maks recommens but nae teacher is obleiged tae tak thaim on. Liz Niven, ane o the teachers in the *Aw-Pairtie Curn*, reportit in Januar this year:

> *In an already owercrowded curriculum the suggestion of a discrete Scots exam might seem unreasonable and, given its close relationship to English, unnecessary but, unless greater efforts are made to encourage teachers to include Scots in the langauge classes, little change will occur in most school classrooms."* [7]

For this bodie, the wey forrit is tae mak Scots an option in its ain richt, an tae offer teachers fundit trainin. This wad be seen as mair uisfae gin Scots wes brocht intae greater public uiss wi the blissin o official bodies. We howp that the *Aw-Pairtie Curn* can mak forder in this.

The Hinmaist Pech O The Census Fecht

Maist fowk wull be seik o hearin aboot the census bi nou - A ken this bodie is - but A shuid say somethin aboot occurents sib tae this, bi wey o a pirlicue on the subjeck. The notour census - as a whein fowk haes taen tae cawin it - wes hauden on 29t Aprile this year, an as promised in the press, a hantle protests war made agin the Executive deceision no tae comprehend the leid. An association cryed *Forgotten Folk* wes founit tae airt the protest an haes as its sluggorn *Mynd us an aa we byde here tae*.[8] The *Forgotten Folk* conveners declarit:

> *... this is a human richts issue, an ane that affects bairns tae, sae at aabodie shuid hae an interest, be thay Scots speakers or no."* [9]

In the run up tae the census itsel, the war a debate in Scotland as tae whither fowk spylin furms wad get liftit wi the polis an taen tae coort. The Office O Scotland an GRO, whan askit tae pit furth an intimation, wadna say eechie or ochie, but regairdit the protest as no warth a docken. Naebodie, sae faur as A ken, spyled a furm, but fowk gaed aff an wrate on their furms thay war Scots speakers whither the govrenment wantit tae ken or no. Haun blads, markin up memmers o the hoose as readers, speakers, an wryters o the leid, war pit in alang wi the census furms forby, tho A hear the GRO tellt its warkars tae juist awa an pit this geir stracht in the midden. Aw the same, A jalouse the GRO wes sweirt tae be drawn in a fecht that wad lea it thrawn leukin sib tae langage richts an Scots cultur as a hail. Sae nae martyrs haes been liftit. Hou monie fowk protestit is haurd tae say; the GRO isna lattin on. But, gauin bi comments fae aw the airts - an fae *Forgotten Fowk* - a puckle thousan

---

[7] Report bi Liz Niven tae the *Aw-Pairtie Curn*, Januar 2001.
[8] *Forgotten Folk* is heidit bi *Lallans* Editor an weil-kent Scots steerer, John Macphail Law.
[9] Staunart letter fae *Forgotten Folk*, Blackford Lodge, Perthshire, Aprile 2001.

bodies haed a shot at the hinneren. In a hunner year fae nou - whan awbodie here is lang plantit - historians wull can richtlie ken.[10]

Gauin Twa Gaits

A stuid here a year syne an sayed that A wes feart that the Scots leid wes shed bi mair as juist the Sheuch. Weil, we hae the makkins o a langage apairtheid in the Unitit Kinrik. An apairtheid that haes Inglis at the tap, Gaelic an Welsh in the mids, an Scots speakers at the bing-dowp. We hae it the nou in Scotland; awa intae the Pairlament an ye wull can fin yer wey aboot in the Scots Gaelic an Inglis leids but ye'll no get a swatch o ae sign in Scots, lat alane ocht ither proveision. An it's wrutten intae law; the *Cooncil O Europe Chairter*, nou in force, says that Earse, Scots Gaelic an Welsh speakers haes equal staunin, but that Scots speakers haes less staunin an less richts. It is the ettle o Scots groups in Scotland that this is nae mair nor a chairter atween hauns an that, at the hinneren, thay'r wantin Pairt III staunin for the leid. This is the threap o the *Aw-Pairtie Curn* in the Scots Pairlament.

Whit we want, an whit we daena hae the nou, is respeck atween the leids; the preen-heidit policies o Govrenment haes seen tae this. It is gey unfortunate that fower oot o the seiven memmers that war suin tae sit on the *Aw-Pairtie Curn On Scots Gaelic* votit agin haein Scots on the census; nae maiter whit thay thocht aboot the richts an wrangs o the quaistion, uphauders o ane leid o the curn shuidna be seen tae vote agin richts for anither. It's no politic, an it wad a been guid mainners tae abstein. Unner Pairt II o the *European Chairter*, the Pairties is yokit tae

> ... *undertake to promote, by appropriate measures, mutual understanding between all the linguistic groups of the country* ...

In baith Scotland an Ulster the ceivil servans in the UK govrenment hauds the ae braith o Scots speakers sib tae proveision for Earse an Scots Gaelic. In spite o general Govrenment intimations it is patent that Scots speakers is regairdit as haein less langage richts. Conform tae the *European Chairter*, the pairties o the *Belfast Greement* declarit that thay:

> ... *recognise the importance of respect, understanding and tolerance in relation to linguistic diversity, including in Northern Ireland, the Irish*

---

[10] O course, the GRO conductit a cognitive grunspeir o Scots-speakin the braid o Scotland in the simmer o 1996, an its owthors, Mr Ian Maté an Mrs Black, cam up wi an official feigur o 1.5 million speakers o Scots. See *Scots Language GR0(S) A Report on the Scots Language Research carried out by the General Register Office for Scotland in 1996,* (Edinburgh, 1996), p.16.

language, Ulster-Scots and the languages of the various ethnic minority communities ...[11]

It souns rare - an politic - on paper but it is weil seen that Scots speakers isna accordit respeck wi the ithers. Hou can we hae a richt unnerstaunin o ane an ithers leids, an feel at hame wi ane anithers leids, whan Govrenment is warm tae ane but cauldrif taewards caws fae the ither. An A'm speakin maistlie o Scotland nou. A bodie deasna hae tae gae faur tae hear Scots speakers girnin aboot the differ atween Gaelic an Scots. Nou, daena jalouse A'm awa doun a pettit gait; whit A'm sayin haes naethin tae dae wi the langage richts o Earse an Scots Gaelic speakers. It *is* patent thir leids wants the richts that thay hae. Whit *is* wrang is the gait the UK Govrenment an its brainches in Embro an Belfast is gauin. The Govrenment haesna a policie on Scots, an, in fact, nane o the fowk in Govrenment *seems* tae unnerstaun the issues tae dae wi Scots. But God kens, it isna for the want o fowk threapin on the subjeck. It isna muckle wunner the'r naebodie at this symposium fae Govrenment in Scotland tae speak on whit Govrenment is or isna daein. An the'r the patent differ atween Scotland an the islan o Irland whaur we'v haen ceivil servans fae baith sydes o the border.

An the laik o unnerstaunin comin oot o Embro haes reared its heid again. In August an September 2001 the GRO for Scotland intimatit that Govrenment policie:

... is not to create more Scots language speakers but rather to encourage more pupils to become aware of the Scots language and culture ... [bi wey o] ... the education system through the teaching of a proper awareness and appreciation of the language, rather than through any specific programmes.

Nou a bodie maun speir, hou *dae* ye makk a 'proper awareness' whan the'r nae "... specific programmes ...", an whan the policie o the Govrenment isna tae makk mair speakers o the leid.[12] No lang syne Irene McGugan pit forrit a puckle quaistion anent Scots policie an speirt at the Executive for answers as tae whit thay war daein. Mr Allan Wilson, on behauf o the Executive, reponed that the Executive didna conseider deil a haet shuid be duin tae conform tae the *European Chairter* anent Scots, that the Executive haedna nae policie anent nummers o speakers o Scots, an haedna set tairgets for nummers, aether for 2011 or 2021. An sae the Executive o Scotland gangs on, preen-heidit an thrawn tae the hinneren.[13]

---

[11] *Belfast Guid Fryday Greement*
[12] Letter fae W Reid, GRO Scotland, tae D Horsbroch, C01/E/12/051, 24t August, 2001.
[13] See *Scots Tung Wittins*, November 2001, p.2.

For the oncome A wad say tae steerers in Ulster think lang an haurd on this; can y'se afford tae breinge forrit makin fause distinctions atween Scots in Ulster an Scotland, an makkin sic orra-leukin texts whan ye haena eneuch speakers tae justifee it. Scots shuidna be traetit as twa leids becis it isna. Juist as Earse is the sister tae Scots Gaelic sae Inglis is the sister tae Scots, no Ulster Scots; Scots in Ulster is a *pairt* o Scots. It is the ae leid shed wi a bit watter wi maist o hits speakers in Scotland. But, becis o politics, Scots in Ulster is bein heized up abuin Scots as a hail tho the feck o steerers haesna a richt comman o the leid itsel, its historie, or tradeitions. The shuid be the ae bodie for forderin Scots as the ae leid wi brainches in Scotland an Ulster that haud regular trysts tae mak policie. The fowk that taks tae dae wi makkin an wrytin Scots shuid be fowk wi an academic backgrun that is trained in the leid no juist onie bodie aff the gait. The'r ower monie fowk makkin the wheel aw ower again, fowk that canna be fashed deekin intae the tradeitions o the leid wi the affcome that thay gie Scots an orra-leukin furm. This alane scunners ordnar speakers.

Manfred Görlach is richt tae scance wi haurd thocht, the occurents in Ulster, an in parteiclar, the wrutten furm o Scots. But, regairdless o aw the dykes that speakers haes tae lowp, it isna richt, A wad say, tae airgie that in the hinneren fowk wad maistlie be cantie speakin Inglis in thair ain tuin. Nae cheil, that isna a Scots speaker, can unnerstaun whit it means tae be a speaker. Ance reared up wi Scots as a mither tongue it isna eneuch tae forleit it an juist speak a regional Inglis. Regional Inglis alane isna eneuch tae tocher oor identitie. Speir at onie German wad *thay* gie up *thair* leid for Inglis wi a German tuin? A jalouse the repone wad be *nein*.[14]

Whit Scots Wants Fae Govrenment

Sae nou A come tae ma pirlicue an a short leit o whit the Scots leid wants fae Govrenment. A'm shair that the twalmonth bygane haes brocht supporters o Scots naur tae the things thay want for Scots; we can awreadie see some forderment in Ulster. But whit we want nou is for the leid as a hail tae get equal staunin an for the follaein tae tak place:

1. The Unitit Kinrik Govrenment - ower marked tyme - tae mak **Pairt III staunin** in the *European Chairter For Leids O The Curn* patent tae Scots.

2. The Executive O Scotland tae mak **Scots a subjeck in its ain richt in the scuils** alang wi siller for trainin teachers in the leid.

---

[14] At the *Dialect 2000* confeirance, hauden in Belfast in August 2000, Prof. Manfred Görlach conseidered that tuin alane is eneuch for tae identifee Scots identitie. See for ensample, Manfred Görlach, 'Ulster Scots: A language?', in John M Kirk an Dónall P Ó Baoill (eds), *Language and Politics Northern Ireland, The Republic of Ireland, and Scotland*, (Belfast, 2001), pp.13-31.

3. The Executive O Scotland tae makk **a meinister for Scots** that sees the leid fordered an weil-plenished in public lyfe.

4. The Executive O Scotland tae tak-on the follaein in Govrenment in Scotland:

a. Scots **signs in the Scots Pairlament biggin an admeinistration** that wad gie the leid a richt recognition in the daeins o govrenment.

b. Tae gie oot antrin **govrenment leitratur wrutten in Scots.**

c. Tae sponsor **a dictionar o Scots terms sib tae pairlament** for tae gie a lift tae the uiss o the leid in admeinistration an the political warld.

5. The Executive O Scotland tae foun a bodie for makkin **Scots-medium braidcastin** wi its heidmaist remit as programmes for younkers.

6. A jynt bodie for Scots in Scotland an Ulster for tae bring thegither the policies in the baith an mak siccar the wrutten leid is conform tae tradeition, tentie o spoken langage.

Heizin Scots tae Pairt III staunin in the *European Chairter* wad cuiver maist o thir heids, but Govrenment wad hae tae pit thaim in place first. It cuid dae nae waur the nou as pit a whein Scots signs up in the pairlament, alang wi Scots leitratur, an leuk again at the wey it deals wi the ae leid on baith sydes o the Sheuch. Sae athoot a sair fecht it cuid dae awa wi the warst discrimination an bring the leids til a guid accord.

The Scots Leid in the New Poleitical Institutions

Gavin Falconer

The retour o a pikkil hame ring ti Scotland an Norlin Airland haes been follaed bi the recogneition o Scots an its Ulster variant in the European Charter for Regional or Minority Languages, that cam intil effect in the Unitit Kingrik on 1t Julie 2001.

Westminster arreingements disnae allou for owertures ti be gien in ocht forby Inglish, tho, thank ti wantin laws, thon defineition comprehends the lyke o thon wrutten bi Chaucer, that isnae eith unnerstuiden. Wi mair leiberal rules — an, we can howp, mair apenness til thair ain cuiturs — the new forums at Holyrood in Embro an Stormont outby Belfast offers a byous inlat for the uiss o baith the twa stewartries' hamelt leids. Thir comprehends baith the Goidelic leids o *Éire* an *Alba* an Scots, that for the 150 yeir up ti 1603 wes the leid o state in Scotland an gaed on bein the ilkaday tung o aw Lawland clesses athout exception til efter the Act o Union wi Ingland in 1707.

The mair the Scots Pairlament in Embro haesnae but leimitit arreingements for the seimultaneous owersettin o Gaelic — warnishment maun be gien for ti uise the leid — it's haen a Gaelic officiar sin the simmer o 2000. Its report teuk the wird o redars for Gaelic text at the affset, but nou haes twa-thrie Gaelic speikars on the staff for ti dael wi skreids in the leid. For Scots, the'r nae seimultaneous owersettin; its editin at Holyrood wul be spoken anent later. In Norlin Airland the frequent uiss o the Erse leid bi Nationalists — an in parteiclar Republicans — made the feein o a redar an editor necessar on baith a prattical an poleitical level. Ranes for aiven-haunditness fae Unionist supporters o Ulster-Scots brocht about a seituation whaur, fae September 1999, the war an unner-editor for the variant an aw, an in Janwar 2001 his role wes raxt ti cuiver seimultaneous owersettin, for aw that the faceilitie is juist for the Heich Convener. The'r nae prior avisement nott for the uiss o leids ither nor Inglish in the Stormont Assemlie, an tho it's socht as gentiness, this isnae aye gaen alang wi. In baith the twa legislaturs, the'r ae ither hinner til the uiss o the leid. 'Scots owertures is alloued *sae lang as thay hae an Inglis version alang wi thaim.*'[1] Commeissioners wantin ti gie an owerture in Scots maun be guidwillie ti gie up hauf the tyme allocate til thaim til owersettin.

The Forder o Terminologie

It's axiomatic that, gin Scots is ti uise for poleitical ettils, it maun hae the lexical meins necessar. Houaniver, this is mebbe either sayed nor duin, for Seafield's observe that the dissolution o the auld Scots Pairlament wes 'ane end ti an auld

---

[1] Horsbroch 2000, p 135. The italics in the quotation haes been putten in for this paper.

sang' merkit ane o the hinmaist occasions Scots wes uised as a national medium o intellectual flyte. In the yeirs atwein 1707 an 1999, the leid o poleitical discourse an technological an social chynge wes Inglish. It's clair that, gin Scots is ti get redd o the *Halbsprache*[2] name, it maun recolonise siclyke specialist an heich-status fields. Ithers haes e'en putten forrit the notion that sicna project is vital gin the leid is ti pit ower ava:

> *If Scots is to continue, and to be worth continuing, then what is needed, to borrow a word from Derrick McClure, is a 'maximalist' position. The desire to be democratic and to imitate 'the people' is not the point on this issue, any more than it would have been for Ben Yehuda in 1882. The point, for those who want the distinctive note of Scots to be sounded, is first to re-invent the language.*[3]

Whan, on 16t Februar 2000, Brian Adam gied the langest Scots owerture yit haird at Holyrood (echt lynes), he made an unconscious admeission that it wes the leid o the ingil an no the *hustings*:

> *Fit's so wrang wi wantin ti speir as part o the census aboot ... fit wye we speik at hame?*[4]

A set o Ulster-Scots owersettins gien bi the *Ulster-Scotch Heirskip Cooncil* til the Editor o Flytes at the Norlin Airland Assemlie suin efter it wes setten up illustrates the pynt.[5] The Social Democratic and Labour Party (SDLP) is gien as *The Meedlin Fowk an Dargers' Pairtie*. The wale o *meedlin fowk* seems lyke ti hae cum fae the British experience o the SDP, the centrist curn that splet aff fae the Labour Pairtie in 1981. Houaniver, it can scantlins be taen as an equeivalent in ilka circumstance, sin Social Democrats is ex-Communists in a whein kintras. The mair thon's no true o the meidil-class Catholic SDLP, a fair fek wad cry the Alliance Pairtie thc centrists in Norlin Airland. In onie case, the SDP post-datit its Norlin Airland namesake bi a lok yeirs. The danger o ettlin at ower mukkil differentiation fae Inglish is apparand in the wird *dargers*. The Inglish wird *labour* cuivers aw wirkars, but it's no siccar ava that the Scots term haes thon brenth o meinin.[6]

The'r the problem an aw that, wi historical Scots no richt resairched yit, modren attempts at uiss can hae sum wirds gettin owergaen wi meinins — sumthin monie Scots wryters wul ken in the case o a wird the lyke o *ettil*. This is

---

[2] Görlach 2000 applies monie o the linguistic theories o leid defineition.
[3] Black 1985, p 14.
[4] The Scots Pairlament's wabsteid is at http://www.scottishparlament.uk. The italics in the quotation is mynes.
[5] A haenae been able ti airt out the author o the document, but in spellin an qualitie it's lik the fek o whit's produced in Norlin Airland at the meinit.
[6] *Darger* is gien in the CSD as 'a casual, unskilled labourer'.

eith seen in the owersettins gien for the Women's Coalition an the Unionist pairties. The noun *coalition* is gien as *cleek*, the mair *claught*, the parteiciple o the sib verb, is uised ti mein 'Unionist'.

Mairatower, the fu owersettin o the Women's Coalition, *Tha Weeminfowk's Cleek*,[7] brocht furth a bumbazed repone fae monie commentators, an twa-thrie o thaim uised it as a wapon for ti yoke on the fact that Scots wes nou thocht a form o speik wirth giein enhanced status til ava. Thae fowk no fameiliar wi Scots cuid mebbe be forgien for takkin *cleek* for a misspelt version o the Inglish wird *clique*; for ordnar the noun meins 'heuk' in Scots, tho in Ullans it haes the sense o 'jynin thegither'. The Democratic Unionists haes thair name gien as *Tha Claught Pairtie o tha Fowk*, whaur *fowk* is an owersettin o the Greek *demos*, tho a whein o thair enemies mebbe thinks o the German adjective *völkisch*. This brings us til the interestin pynt o gin it's better, for poleitical pragmatism, ti follae a policie o takkin tent o the unschuiled reaction o ae-leid Inglish speikars whan formulatin new terminologie. Or wad sicna course dae skaith til the ither valid ettil o differentiatin Scots for ti gie it a profile that micht cuid juistifie leid status? Sum fowk micht e'en ledge that reactin til aither conseideration wad amount ti giein ower the leid's autonomie. Houaniver, e'en whaur thon hinmaist concern is the heid ane, the'r in monie instances a flyte anent whit the *autonomous* Scots form wad be, an in parteiclar gin it suid be *tradeitional* — in monie cases meinin obsolete or obscure — or *organic*. Gin it's the saicont o thaim, than the Scots terms for monie ilkaday concepts micht be scantlins different fae the Inglish. Gin it's the first, ye find yeirsell facin the ae want o serious resairch as at the stairt.[8]

It seems fair ti assume that, wi thir owersettins, planned speciation haes steyed til the fore. This is eith seen in the equeivalent gien for Sinn Féin, *Oorsels Worlane*. Gin Sinn Féin haes fasht itsell wi whit in 1905 wes in sum circles at laest the ineitial haundicap o takkin on a haithen Gaelic name, whitfor owerset it intil Scots ava? Mairatower, the Scots haes juist cum back wi a wrang owersettin fae the Inglish, sin, for aw whit popular belief tells us, Sinn Féin disnae mein 'oursells wir lane' but juist 'oursells'.

---

[7] The motivation ahint spellin the definite airticle this wey is sayed ti be for ti evyte confusion wi the thrid person plural pronoun, that in the fek o Ulster-Scots skreivin is gien as *the*. Sic naïveté, for aw its lang heirskip, gies us evidence o Ulster's dislocate poseition forenent tradeitional Scots leitratur. A bodie micht mak compare wi the wey the Inglish verb *do* taks the steid o the saicont person singular pronoun *du* in a whein instances o Shetland leitratur fae the 19t centurie. An Ulster ensample o the lyke wad be the semi-leiterate Inglish slogan *Hands off are Province*.

[8] Dauvit Horsbroch haes produced a byous draucht o a pairlamentar haundbeuk, but a sicht mair comprehensive resairch is necessar for ti braiden an reaffirm the uteilitie o Scots.

Ae Scots or Twa?

Thon haes latten us hae a wee keek at the problems confrontin onie attempt ti uise Scots in the poleitical arena. Anither problem is mair general — is Scots ti forder on the basis o Ulster an Scotland cummin til a mids or as twa leids stairtin out different gaits?

The mair a bittie divergence atwein the twa varieties o Scots wes scantlins ti evyte, aw serious academic observers wad grie that thay represent the ae leid, no maiter whit thon leid's status micht be beis Inglish. Deed, as A'v pyntit out ithergaits, the'r mair differ atwein the Scots o the nor-aest an south-wast o Scotland nor atwein the south-wast an Antrim.[9] Sic thinkin mebbe disnae count for mukkil in a societie the lyke o Norlin Airland, whaur politics haes a wapon-gret role. Ae ensample o the pouer o politics ower linguistics can be seen in the wey Wast Belfast Republicans descrives thair imperfect ettils at lairnin Donegal Erse as a legeitimate byleid in itsell o aequal cultural wirth, e'en ledgin the status o *Breac-Ghaeltacht* for thair airt. A psychological explanation micht be that the feelin amang the local *Gaeilgeoiri* that thay'r as Erse as oniebodie in the Republic — mebbe mair Erse whan we mynd whit thay'r efter tholin on thon account — haes led thaim ti conclude that thair version o Erse is as organic as the ane in Gaoth Dobhair. A suid mebbe mouth here that thair form o the leid haes, in a pikkil cases, areddies been transmit athort thrie generations. Still an on, a bodie micht speir whit aw this meins for thae fowk that's lairnin o the leid haes been that successfu thay dinnae betray thair springheid in the anglophone aest o Ulster onie mair. Ar thay speikin the wrang byleid for whaur thay byde?

On the ither syde o Norlin Airland's cultural divide, Doc Phäap Roabysinn, the wryter o a kenspekkil gremmar o Ulster-Scots, haes cum out wi an e'en grandioser threip:

> *In simple terms, the relationship between Ulster-Scots an Lallans could be compared to the relative positions of Irish and Scottish Gaelic.*[10]

Yit oniebodie kennin a leid fae baith faimlies wul be awaur that, the mair aw varieties o Scots, wi the insular anes as an antrin exception, is eith unnerstuiden bi thaim as speiks the ither byleids, thon isnae the case, for prattical purposes, wi Erse an Scots Gaelic.[11] Deed, for a non-linguist, thon's ti wirk out fae the historical evidence. Efter aw, the Gaelic leid cam ti Scotland fae Airland aroun 1500 yeir syne, the mair mass Scots emigration ti Ulster haed its outgang as recent as the end o the 17t centurie (efterhin the war juist as monie fowk lowpin the kintra the ither gait, an ye micht cuid argie thon haed its ain linguistic affcum). Gin the leids in quaistin speciatit at oniethin lik the ae rate, it's obvious

---

[9] Falconer, furthcummin.

[10] Robinson 1997, p 1.

[11] Mac Póilin, furthcummin.

that the differs atwein Erse an Scots Gaelic is gauni be a sicht importanter nor the anes atwein the twa kins o Scots.

A bodie micht speir whitfor Doc Roabysinn haes uised the names *Ulster-Scots* an *Lallans*. Whitfor no juist speik o *Scots* in the twa stewartries, or at laest uise parallel terminologie? Thare seems ti be a bittie *wishful thinking* here, an it's mebbe adae wi the norie that haein a unique leid gies status ti uisers.

For aw the undoutit continuitie o spoken Scots, a nummer o factors, sum o thaim poleitical, ithers historical or sociolinguistic, is pouin the twa varieties different gaits. Thir can be tabulate as a series o opposeitions, shawn in Table 1:

Table 1: Scots in Northern Ireland vs. Scots in Scotland

Norlin Airland	Scotland
stress on poleitical recogneition (esteem)	stress on edication seistem (uteilitie)
disjyntit leiterarie tradeition	unbroken leiterarie tradeition
relative divide fae the urban Inglish	relative continuum wi the urban Inglish
sell-defineition agin the Erse leid	sell-defineition agin the Inglish leid
steirar tendencie ti Unionism	steirar tendencie ti Nationalism

A'm in course awaur o the mukkil — sum fowk micht say dangersum — degree o semplification that kythes in the table abuin, an the pynts made is nae dout wantin a bittie elucidation.

Aodán Mac Póilin haes gart us tak tent o the surprisin fact that the first recogneition gien ti Scots in Scotland on the pairt o the British Govrenment wes as an affcum o thair kennin Ulster-Scots as a variant.[12] This is e'en mair surprisin whan we mynd that the'r a sicht mair uisers in Scotland. Thon micht be explained bi the steirars shawin thair can ti capitalise on the huff gatten inti bi thae Unionists as sees the uphauld gien bi the British Govrenment for the Erse leid as buyin aff Nationalists wi nae parallel gestur til thair ain commontie.

Houaniver, wantin ti expedite recogneition cuid mebbe a chynged the orthographie o Scots in Norlin Airland an aw, sin thare maun siccar a been a temptation ti be as obscurantist as thay cuid in an ettil ti maximise differs wi Inglish. A jalouse the average bodie in Norlin Airland — deed, the average speikar o Ulster-Scots — wad find it aisier unnerstaundin a Scots text wrutten in Scotland nor ane wrutten in Ullans. It wad certes be interestin ti see a bittie resairch anent the quaistin. As Dauvit Horsbroch haes sayed,

> *Readin Scots wrutten in Ulster tae Scots wrutten in Scotland, it leuks lyke the'r faur mair o an ettle tae mak Ulster Scots leuk as different fae Inglis as can be.*[13]

---

[12] Ibid.

[13] Horsbroch 2000, p 140.

Lyke at the tyme o the growthe o the European vernaculars in the late Meidil Ages, wryters cuid mebbe be uisin wee mcrks ower the letters for ti gar whit wes a laich-status langage varietie seem intellectual. On the ither haund, bein jeilous o the fact that Erse haes thaim cuid mebbe be a factor an aw, an thon micht cuid explain sic prattics as the owersettin o proper names. The parallel — an conter — antiquarian element apparand in Ullans spellins cuid mebbe be relate til a desire ti gie Ulster-Scots, an the Protestant presence in Ulster, as lang a heirskip as possible.[14]

In Scotland the leid haed areddies wun ti sumthin gey neir staundardisation in the pages o 'Lallans' unner the editorship o David Purves, that did his best ti gie a heft til the uiss o the 1985 Recommendations for Writers in Scots. E'en in 2001, the arnae oniewhaur neir the level o spellin variation in Scotland a bodie finds in Norlin Airland. For aw that, the uiss o Scots in edication, that steyed devolved ti local authorities in the course o the centralisin premiership o Margaret Thatcher, haes brocht about chynge acause o the orthographic imperative no ti pit hinners in the wey o fowk no leiterate in ocht forby Inglish, parteiclar the vera yung. Naewhaur is this mair apparand nor in the drappin o tradeitional weys o representin Scots consonant souns in the recent recommends o the Scots Spellin Comatee an the pittin forrit o rules a sicht neirer til the anes Inglish haes.

A howp characterisin the leiterarie tradeition o Ulster-Scots as *disjyntit* haesnae affrontit ower monie fowk. Cryin the leiterarie tradeition in Scotland *unbroken* micht cuid be lichtit on whan we think o the wapon-gret chynges in orthographie thare efter the Union o the Crouns. *Mair disjyntit* an *less disjyntit* is mebbe better terms.

At the tyme o the Rhyming Weavers as wes wrytin wi ae ee on Burns, Scots leitratur in Ulster wes certes pairt o the *mainstream*. Houaniver, it's fair ti say that in the centurie up ti 1993 maist wrytin in Ulster-Scots wes o a naïve kin foundit on Inglish orthographie athout mukkil reference ti tradeitional precedents. Monie commentators blurs the border wi Norlin Hiberno-Inglish. Mairatower, the vital inpit fae universities that's been that apparand in Scotland in the course o the 20t centurie haes been wantin, for aw that this cuid mebbe chynge wi the upset o an Ulster-Scots centre at Magee College in Derry.

Jim Miller haes airtit out a divide regairdin competence in Scotland.

> *Putting it crudely but nonetheless with a very large grain of truth, working-class speakers have much of the syntax of Scots but the under-40s have lost the classic Scots vocabulary; middle-class speakers with a knowledge of the literature have the classic vocabulary but not the syntax; and many middle-class speakers have neither the syntax nor the vocabulary.*[15]

---

[14] Falconer, furthcummin.
[15] Miller 1998, p 55.

Juist as important whan producin leitratur is an awaurness o the gret wryters o the bygaen an an analeitical an, as faur as linguistics gaes, mensefu attitude til the historie an forder o the leid. In Norlin Airland sic knawledge is at a laich level in the general population. For aw the universalitie o the wirds *ay* an *wee* an the presence o sic linguistic merkars as *til* in Belfast Inglish, the'r faur less continuitie wi the leid o the landart Scots-speikin hertlands. Deed, knawledge o Scots itsell is mebbe a bittie leimitit; in the case o sum steirars a pikkil knawledge micht cuid be a dangersum thing. This cuid mebbe gae sum wey til explainin the fact that mukkil o the quaistinin o Ullans orthographie haes cum fae Scots an no fae thaim as bydes in Norlin Airland. It's mebbe true an aw that the relative strenth o Scots in Scotland ti see in urban byleids for ordnar clessified as Inglish cuid in an ironic wey mebbe a led til a sceptical attitude amang the Scots population regairdin recogneition.

The hinmaist problem in the forder o a common orthographie atwein Scotland an Ulster is gey an poleitical. Can the twa leid muivements wi thair respective tendencies ti Unionism an Nationalism wirk thegither? In Scotland, Scots haes aye haen a mair obvious poleitical nip nor Gaelic — lyke ti be acause it's, til a degree at laest, an apperceptional leid regairdit different dependin on a bodie's poleitical viewpynt.[16] 'Monie supporters oxter alang wi the SNP.'[17] The pragmatic deceision o Scots ti reclessifie the leid o the maist fek as an Inglish byleid efter 1603 wes a poleitical deceision itsell, an onie schame ti reverse its subsequent dwyne an win til a level o *Ausbau* an staundardisation conform ti leid status wul aye be hauden ti hae the ae motivation.

Onless the ither pairties comes up wi Scots policies thairsels, the leid is aye in danger o bein taen for anither SNP ploy.[18]

Nou that an aw-pairtie curn o MSPs haes been setten up for ti uphauld the leid we can howp onie pairtisan element can be setten asyde.

In the bipolar societie o Norlin Airland, Scots haes an e'en mair direct connection wi politics nor in Scotland. In pairt this haes been acause o a doutfu Catholic population *optin out* — as in the poleitical process up til the 1960s — an ambeivalence on the pairt o thae anes the Erse leid is a seimbol o identitie for. Juist as aften, the leid's Unionist advocates haes gien thaim cause ti believe it's nocht but a petulant reaction ti Erse or a *spoiler* ettilt at hinnerin its oncum.[19] The mair Nationalist politeicians speiks o *Irish culture*, Unionists speiks o *Unionist culture*. Giein Ulster-Scots sicna name, wi its impleicit equation o cultur an politics, micht cuid turn out ti be kittil, sin twa-thrie o the variant's maist kenspekkil makkars wes sympathisers o the United Irishmen.[20] Gin the accusation o sectarianism is ti jouk, steirars for the leid maun tak a radical new turn for ti

---

[16] McClure 1997, Chaipter 2.

[17] Horsbroch 2000, p 139.

[18] Horsbroch 2000, p 135.

[19] Mac Póilin, furthcummin.

[20] The maist vocal bein the best-kent o aw, James Orr.

attract Catholics, that's estimate ti mak up a thrid o native speikars.[21] Thay maun re-engage wi the aulder an braider muivement in Scotland an aw.

The Uiss o Scots in the New Legislaturs

For the follaein discussion A'm behauden til the editor o the Offeicial Report at the Scots Pairlament, that luit me hae instances o Scots uisage she'd collate thegither. The haillware o thaim is gien in Appendix 1. Efter commentin on thaim, A s'mak reference til the experience o Scots at the Norlin Airland Assemlie. The list gies details o 178 instances o Scots speik fae 12t Mey 1999 ti 25t Janwar 2001. Twintie o thaim wes obvious leiterarie quotation or pastiche, an a whein wes saws. For aw that a bodie mebbe disnae identifie thairsell as a Scots speikar wi siclyke fruizen items in the ae wey as thay wad wi the spontaneous uiss o Scots, A'v hauden thaim in the statistics. The Scots o the lave cuid mebbe be divid intil the follaein categories, that disnae exclude ilkither: langage that's lexis is Scots; langage that's phonologie is Scots; an langage that's grammar is Scots. Houaniver, scantlins onie o the instances reportit is in the thrid categorie, sin the grammar o Scots in Scotland haes been its laest durable kenmerk. In course, this depends on whit ye define as gremmatical variation. Whyles the fact that the quotations isnae ti get but in wrutten form maks a deceision kittil. Dis the *us* in the phrase 'Gie us the money'[22] refer til the first person singular or plural? Suid a bodie pit plural pronouns the lyke o *youse* or *yeez*[23] intil the categorie ava? Efter aw, thay'r uised in Inglish byleids an aw. Is forms the lyke o 'Ah telt ye'[24] Scots gremmar acause thay conjugate as raiglar a verb that's strang in Inglish, or ar the nae substantive differ, sin the form in quaistin is aye the semple past?

Gin we leimit oursells ti syntax, it's clair the'r no mukkil that cuidnae cum unner the braid heidin o Inglish nor o the Humber, be it staundard or byleid. This maun be true o sic kittil pynts as 'Aye, that'll be right'[25] or 'Ministers are like a bunch of peeries now, they are spinning that much.'[26] The'r nae instances o the Norlin Subject Rule, that disnae for ordnar form pairt o Scots Inglish, or o the construction *just after doing*, that dis, at laest in the wast. Forby morphologie, that's aye strang, the Scots naitur o the gremmar seems ti be a quaistin o degree an no absolute differ.

Scots lexical items seems ti hae a heicher status nor the native syntax o the leid than, an this wad fit in wi Miller's observe abuin. It's mebbe the case an aw that a whein Scots kenmerks haesnae been thocht important eneuch for inclusion in the list. The maun siccar hae been a case whaur the wird *outwith* wes

---

[21] Lee Reynolds, owerture ti McCracken Simmer Schuil, Belfast, 25.07.00.

[22] David McLetchie, 02.06.99.

[23] For ensample, Tommy Sheridan, 24.06.99.

[24] Kenny MacAskill, 02.06.99.

[25] Kenny McAskill, 23.03.00.

[26] Bruce Crawford, 03.02.00.

uised, for ensample. In the field o syntax, the uiss o the past parteiciple in the construction *needs done* wad mebbe no a been kent as different fae Staundard Inglish, nor wad the uiss o the relative *that* ti refer til a bodie. A richt leuk at whit Scots the speik o the Scots Pairlament is wad hae ti cuiver the haill corpus o transcripts, no juist the maist obvious uisses o Scots — an e'en than in uneditit form.

Ae interestin aspect o the uiss o Scots in the Scots Pairlament is that the'r nae instances whaur it gets uised as a medium for flyte. The general notion seems ti be a rhetorical luim; whyles it cuid mebbe represent an unintentional drap in register an aw. The exception is in course the owerture gien bi Brian Adam, but it suid be taen tent o that Scots wes uised ti speik anent Scots. The mair Tommy Sheridan haes been kent ti furthspeik at poleitical forgaitherins in an urban Scots byleid, he haesnae duin this in Pairlament, tho his personal contribution til the list is disproportionate mukkil.

Dis the discussion abuin mein that Scots as spoken in the Scots Pairlament — an, bi extension, Scotland as a haill — is integrate intil Inglish in a saemless an naitral wey? Gin thon wes the case, ye wadnae expect onie poleitical bias in the statistics for its uiss, sin it wad be a subconscious kenmerk o speik. Whan we mynd the ower-representation o speikars o Scots or urban byleids wi Scots elements amang the wirkin cless, thare micht cuid be grunds ti expect a wee tendencie awa fae Staundard Inglish amang Labour an SSP steirars, tho sum fowk haes mebbe cum ti hae their douts anent the first pairtie's proletarian credentials nouadays. On the ither haund, it micht cuid be the case that, sin a fair fek o the Scots uised wes quotation an lexical items, the'd be a bias ti pairties tradeition associates wi the meidil clesses, an thon micht cuid mein the Tories.

Wi the information in Table 2 ablo (but athout ocht fae fowk deponin afore the Comatees or fae *time for reflection*), we'r in a poseition ti prie our theories.

Table 2: Uiss o Scots in the Scots Pairlament

Political Party	n.
SNP	72
Labour	31
Conservative	24
Liberal Democrat	24
SSP	5
Independent	1
Green	0
Total	**157**

The kenmerk that lowps out first fae the table is the ower-representation o the Scots National Pairtie, that isnae for ordnar associate wi ae cless. The mair the pairtie haesnae but 35 out o 129 MSPs, thay'v uised mair Scots nor onie ither curn. This micht indicate a poleitical motivation for uisin the leid, or mebbe juist reflect the fact that Nationalists is in onie case lyker ti tak an interest in Scots cultur, comprehendin the leiterarie an linguistic. Nae dout thair argiement wad be that memmers o ither pairties unneruise the naitral Scots elements o thair eidiom acause o feelins o inferioritie (Labour, wi 56 Commeissioners, haes accountit for but 31 instances). Mebbe a fruitfu field for onie investigation intil the degree that sic uiss or non-uiss indicates whit wey MSPs is wantin ti be thocht o micht be the relative frequencie o Scots in the Chaumer an Comatees (the'r nae differ made atwein thaim in Table 2 abuin).

The mair sic accusations an rebuttals can eith becum circular, thare dis seem ti be a bittie evidence for the twa theories foundit on Jim Miller's observe. The Scots Socialist Pairtie, wi ae MSP, Tommy Sheridan, haes accountit for five instances, an ithers cuid mebbe a been redd out bi the editin process. The Scots Tories, wi but 18 MSPs, haes accountit for neir as mukkil Scots as Labour. This is mebbe no surprisin, sin thay'v tradeitional been keen on thae expressions o Scots identitie athout a separatist reflex. We aw mynds Nicholas Fairbairn's weirin o tartan trews in the Palace o Westminster an Michael Forsyth's Gaelic repone til a Commons quaistin, that provokit the Heich Convener, Bernard Wetherill, til a crabbit skraich o 'What does that mean?' Sae lang as Scots is uised as an enrichin element an no as a medium o flyte forenent Inglish, it can be appreciate as an aspect o Scots cultur — an mebbe ane ti mak repone til the accusation o bein an 'Inglish' pairtie.

> *Many people think of themselves as patriotic Scots and enjoy the atmosphere of Burns suppers, ceilidhs, folk concerts an the like — activities which I do not in the least mean to denigrate — and yet appear to be unable to recognise the fact, or to accept its implications, that in their everyday lives they are passively or actively supporting a socio-political system aimed at consigning all the grounds for this patriotism to the graveyard of history.* [27]

But dae the Scots Tories *uise* the leid different nor the fek o Labour an SNP memmers? Gin we tak a swatch at the list for ti see whit mukkil conseists o Scots wirds an whit mukkil o langage that's phonologie or morphologie is ither nor the

Table 3: Differ o uise o Scots i the Scottish Pairlament

Pairtie	Instances	Wi Differ		Lexical	Wi Phonological or Morphological Differ	
	n.	n.	%		n.	%
SNP	72	39	54.17		45	62.50
Labour	31	17	54.84		22	70.97
Leib-Dem	24	15	62.50		11	45.83
Tory	24	15	62.50		17	70.83
SSP	5	2	40.00		4	80.00

---

[27] McClure 1997, p 64.

Inglish, we can mak compare atwein the pairties, as shawn in Table 3 abuin.[28]
The'r hairdlie onie differ atwein the Tories an the SNP in the proportion o lexis ti
phonologie or morphologie. The orra-leukin result is for the Scots Leibral-
Democrats, the ae pairtie o the five tap anes for Scots wi mair lexis nor
phonologie or morphologie. The'r a whein different weys o explainin thon:

The Poleitical Discourse
> The SNP uises Scots acause it's Nationalist, an the Tories acause thay
> feel thay hae ti shaw thairsells ti be Scots. Wirkin-cless Labour
> Commeissioners or thaim as taks an interest in the socialist fowksang
> tradeition wul uise Scots; New Labour micht no.

The Geographical Discourse
> Sin it's a sair fecht for pairties ither nor Labour ti get waled inby the
> central belt, Tory an SNP Commeissioners is lyker ti represent kintra
> airts whaur Scots, comprehendin lexis, is aye strang — an as an affcum
> o thon ti uise the leid mair. In a whein cases, the'r strang local feelins
> (sumthin the Tories wes aye for), an the Scots uised cuid juist be relate ti
> fowk's affection for the *local* byleid. Fowk fae the central belt is less
> lyke ti ken the classic vocabular o the leid, an fowk fae the present or
> umwhyle *Gàidhealtachd* (representit bi a whein Leibrals) no lyke ava.

The Cless Discourse
> Uiss o Scots isnae sae mukkil the wale o the Commeissioners, but mair a
> case o whit thay feel aw richt wi. The *better-spoken* a Commeissioner,
> the less blyth thay ar ti uise the phonologie o the leid. At the ae tyme,
> the edication sic fowk is lyke ti hae cuid a acquent thaim wi the
> tradeitional lexis. Haes the Leibrals taen the place o patreician *one-
> nation* Tories the whyle the Conservative Pairtie haes been gien ower til
> the clessless bairns o Margaret Thatcher? Can sicna cless discourse be
> splet aff fae politics?

We cuid argie for iver anent the different theories. Leukin at the last ane
wad mein haein a deuk at the indiveidual eidiolects o the Commeissioners,
sumthin no athin the skowth o this airticle. Mebbe the best thing a bodie cuid say
anent the haill quaistin o Scots an politics is gie warnishment that we suid tak tent
til the fact that the'r but 129 MSPs. E'en ae bodie cuid chynge the results for his
or hir haill pairtie, an thon's parteiclar true o the smawer curns.

The editin o Scots at the Scots Pairlament seems indeicative o a view
that Scots is a pairt o Inglish. Deed, the instances listit — Brian Adams's
owerture is mebbe an exception — uphaulds thon notion, for aw that it micht be
juist as correct in linguistics ti say that Scots fowk nou speiks a mixtur-maxtur o
Scots an Inglish, sumthin that can hae nae effect on the status o 'pure' Scots.

---

[28] In this pairt A'm behauden til the rede o Dr Fiona Douglas, that made me
awaur o the wark o Prof A.J. Aitken in the field o analysin Scots speik.

Knawledge o the leid is certes gien mention as a plus in recruitment advertisements for the Offeicial Report at the Scots Pairlament.

In the absence o a staundard, the report's policie at Holyrood micht be the ae credible ane, tho Hansard at the Norlin Airland Assemlie ettils ti keep til the wird list furthsetten in *Lallans* eissues 39-43. Mair recent, the Scots Spellin Comatee haes brocht out new recommends, but takkin thaim on buird at this aerlie stage afore the'r been an inlat for braid flyte cuid mebbe turn out premature. Gin a bodie is ti traet Scots as a leid in the pages o Hansard, than the important thing is that the'r a staundard o sum kin — best wi an extensive list o ensamples — an no a flawless intellectual seistem. Mairatower, the war nae Norlin Airland inpit til the Comatee, an it's been evident in recent yeirs that Norlin Airland steirars is takkin anither gait awthegither wi thair spellin.

> *In Ulster, whaur the'r no monie speakers, an whaur the leitratur is, we can airgue, less, a bodie can get awa wi mair in the wey o language plannin.*[29]

The Erse-langage asseistant editor o Hansard haes the faceilitie o a computerised list o terms compluthert bi an umwhyle professor o the leid at Queen's Universitie an twa-thrie ithers fae UCD, as gaed throu the Offeicial Reports o Stormont an the Dáil for ti produce an aw-Airland staundard ti faw back on in cases o dout. A list cuiverin Scots Gaelic at Holyrood haes been produced bi the ae firm, but the'r been nae schame for Scots. Pairt o the raison for this micht be the mammoth amount o academic resairch that wad be necessar. On the ither haund, mebbe the totie amount o Scots spoken isnae felt ti merit the siller. Alang wi thon, the'r the problems associate wi thae steirars as wad prefer a sindert staundard for Ulster-Scots. Dr Ian Adamson, that's interests isnae leimitit ti Scots, haes e'en alloued he wad be blyth ti see the ae thing duin for Erse Gaelic in Norlin Airland.[30]

The seituation o Scots in the Norlin Airland Assemlie is baith sempler an complicater nor in Scotland. The'r mair o a claen brek wi Inglish, but baith the Inglish an Scots o Ulster — mair nor thair Scots equeivalents — haes a wapon-gret Gaelic substratum. Suid ye tak Rev Dr Ian Paisley's complete evyte o the wird *whether* — or *if* in the sense o *whether* — as a merk o Erse or Ulster-Scots?[31] Efter aw, he is a native o Ballymena, heid toun o the strangest Scots-

---

[29] Horsbroch 2000, p 135.

[30] Dr Adamson jalouses that Bairbre de Brún, the Sinn Féin Halth Meinister, that's a native o Dublin, speiks Suddron Erse. In fact she speiks Ulster Erse wi a Suddron accent.

[31] This is true o the frequent uiss o the condeitional in Ulster-Scots an aw, that's a general kenmerk o *Béarla na hÉireann*. Its springheid micht lig, in pairt at laest, in the generalisation o an echo o the Erse dependent form, that's uised in quaistins an negative sentences. The fact that Erse haes nae wirds for Inglish *yes* an *no*, meinin that fowk repeats the verb uised in a quaistin whan gien thair

speikin airt on the island. Alang wi thon, the'r the quaistin o whether a whein uisages represents organic Scots or juist Inglish byleid elements taen up bi the Ulster variant efter the Plantation.

Mebbe the maist salient disteinction ti mak is atwein whit a bodie micht cry *intentional* an *unintentional* uiss o Scots. Ae Forgaitherar fae Wast Tyrone uised the phrase 'The money wes teuk an divid' in Comatee, but it wes raiglarised. In onie case, the forms in quaistin micht juist as aisie been clessified as Hiberno-Inglish. A Belfast Forgaitherar uised the wird *til*, an the mair thon ane is athout a dout Scots, it gat snodden out an aw. Nae girns cam fae aither, an it seems fair ti think that thay war thankrif til — or at laest no ower affrontit bi — the Hansard staff that editit the transcripts.

Ulster-Scots lexical items is leimitit in the Inglish speik o the Assemlie, an e'en whan uised, thay tend ti invite an observe, as the follaein exchynge fae 20t November 2000 shaws.

Mr McMenamin:
Yes. Will the Minister assure me that his Department will check stations throughout the North of Ireland to make sure they will operate when needed? I represent a rural area and my office is constantly receiving calls from residents complaining of sheughs *being blocked throughout the constituency. Will funding be made available to upgrade these* sheughs *and small drains in and around rural constituencies?*

Mr Campbell:
I do not wish to make light of it, but it will be interesting to see how Hansard deals with the spelling of sheugh.

Eugene McMenamin later brocht up a pynt o order wi the Depute Heich Convener for ti inform hir o the Hansard spellin.

Tho Scots disnae mak mukkil heidwey in itherwyss Inglish owertures gien in the Assemlie, it siccar maks up for it in its uiss as a leid. Settin asyde extraneous factors the lyke o the oncum made bi Erse in poleitical lyfe — an the desire on the pairt o sum Unionists ti emulate thon success wi Ulster-Scots — the fact that Scots elements in urban Inglish byleids the lyke o Belfast's haes dwyned in recent yeirs haes mebbe gien an ironic heft til its acceptance as a leid.

Forby the antrin *sheugh*, *burn* or *thran*, the'r been awmaist nae Ulster-Scots in Stormont Comatees. Erse, for aw its ilkaday uiss in the Chaumer, haes been leimitit ti Barry McElduff's walcum for *Comhairle na Gaelscolaíochta*[32] an explanation o the phrase *dúirt bean liom gur 'úirt bean léithi*[33] bi the native speikar Bríd Rodgers.

---

repone (sumthin that happens in Hiberno-Inglish an aw) haes mebbe gien a heft ti siclyke.

[32] The council for Erse-medium edication.

[33] *A wuman telt me that a wuman telt her* — in reference til the haivers anent fit-and-mou.

In the Chaumer, the'r been severals occasions whaur Scots haes been uised on a susteined basis, an thir's ti see in Table 6 ablo. Whaur it isnae immidentlie clair, the topic spoken on follaes the teitle o the flyte in brackets.

Table 4: Uise o Scots in the Norlin Airland Assemlie

Date	MLA	Topic
09.11.98	Ian Adamson	Ulster-Scots Academy
09.03.99	Ian Adamson	Assembly Standing Orders (Ulster-Scots)
27.06.00	Jim Shannon	The Arts in Northern Ireland (Ulster-Scots)
18.12.00	Ian Adamson	Budget (2001-2) (Ulster-Scots)
18.12.00	Mr Speaker	Budget (2001-2) (Ulster-Scots)
18.12.00	Jim Shannon	Budget (2001-2) (Ulster-Scots)
19.12.00	Ian Adamson	Languages: North/South Ministerial Council Sectoral Meeting (Ulster-Scots)
06.03.01	Ian Adamson	Programme for Government (Ulster-Scots)
06.03.01	Jim Shannon	Programme for Government (Targeting Social Need)

Dr Adamson is a memmer o the Ulster Unionist Pairtie, an Mr Shannon o the Democratic Unionists, so the poleitical bias wi regaird ti uiss o Scots is e'en stairker in Norlin Airland, tho ti Unionism an no Nationalism. The fact that but ae Forgaitherar fae ilkane o the twa mukkil Unionist pairties haes uised the leid cuid mebbe indicate that it's a minoritie interest e'en athin thair bloc. A table o the kin produced wi the data fae the Scots Pairlament wadnae shaw us but the relative poseitions o thae twa heid feigurs. In fact, Dr Adamson haes spoken faur mair Scots nor Mr Shannon, that haesnae juist uised it less frequent but niver hauden on for langer nor a paragraph.

The stent o the Heich Convener's Scots wes the lyne:

This big heid-yin can uise the Ulster-Scotch no tae bad — as onie guid Ballymena man wad.

His contribution is mebbe the ae instance o Scots bein uised that micht be cryed spontaneous (for aw that it cuid mebbe a been lairnt for the occasion an aw). In the haill ither instances, owersettins wes skreidit aff. Deed, Dr Adamson uised twa o his owertures twyst: On 09.11.98 an 09.03.99; an on 19.12.00 an 06.03.01.

When it cums til the subject maiter o Scots owertures, it'l be obvious fae haein a swatch at the table that, in gey neir the haillware o instances, Scots haes been uised ti speik anent Scots. Mr Shannon's owerture on TSN maun be regairdit as a bittie o a brekthrou in the normalisation o the leid in the Assemlie.

Ae eissue that micht be relevant til the Norlin Airland Assemlie is *tokenism*, whaur a stock non-Inglish phrase is eikit ontil itherwyss Inglish speik. Sinn Féin Forgaitherars is uised wi thankin the Heich Convener bi sayin 'Go raibh maith agat, a Chathaoirligh', the hinmaist wird aften no richt in the nominative case. Thay wad repudiate the allegation bi ledgin thay war aw daein thair pairt for ti gie a heft til the profile o the Erse leid, sumthin wantin whan it cums til the moderate Nationalist SDLP. The Republicans div hae versant speikars, but. The mair thair Halth Meinister, Bairbre de Brún, that lairnt Erse, gies aw hir statements bilingual, the SDLP Agricultur Meinister Bríd Rodgers, that cums fae the Donegal Gaeltacht, disnae — for aw that she an a whein ither o hir pairtie's officehauldars teuk thair aiths in the leid. In Ulster-Scots, the'r no been mukkil ava o whit a bodie micht cry *tokenism*; Mr Shannon speired anent the Ulster-Scots for *no* whan votin an anent the term for *Member of the Legislative Assembly* but didnae uise thaim whan speikin Inglish. The quaistin maun arise gin the apparand want o *tokenism* on the pairt o pairlamentar uisers o Scots is adae wi the superior cultural mense o Unionists. It cuid juist cum fae the fact that eith ingang til Ulster-Scots for Inglish speikars — or at laest the perception o't — allous fowk ti lowp the *tokenist stage*.

Pirlicue

A'v putten forrit the notion ithergaits[34] that the connection atwein Scots an Norlin Airland constitutional eissues micht at the hinner-end be a haundicap acause o the kittil an thrawn-thegither combine o orthographies the leid's been langilt wi in its quest for status an the effect o negative poleitical connections amang neutral or hostile sections o the populace. On the ither haund, the'r nae doutin the ineitial impetus gien ti Scots in the stewartrie, that's nou owertaen its parent byleids in Scotland in poleitical recogneition an siller, tho no in uiss in schuils, quantitie an qualitie o leitratur or nummer an percentage o speikars amang the general population. It's e'en putten ower turnin factors the lyke o the leimitit knawledge o Scots amang the populace til its better, sin the resultin want o unnerstaundin haes faceilitate recogneition as a leid. Still an on, A feel the tap-hivvie naitur o Scots forder in Norlin Airland meins the edifice haes been biggit on a shouglie fundstane. The motivation ahint it maun be the premature rane for pairitie wi Erse, that haes a faur langer tradeition o steirin an a level o forder as a leid that's a sicht mair complete.

Scotland's Nationalists mebbe isnae lyke ti mak a mukkil eissue o Scots, sin monie fowk regairds it as juist pairt o Scots Inglish, an giein it a central steid in politics cuid eith cum aff in embarrassment, parteiclar whan we mynd its leimitit uteilitie in a whein spheres o lyfe. As A sayed areddies, the lykest raison for the feelin that Scots is Inglish is the leid's ubeiquitie, e'en in a wattert-doun form, in the hoachin Lawland pairts o Scotland. The aw-pairtie curn in the Scots Pairlament cuid mebbe help owercum a bittie o the reticence.

The fact that Scots haes been kent bi the European Bureau for Lesser Used Languages an in the European Charter for Regional or Minority Languages wul mebbe help keep flytes anent siller an recogneition meidlin free o pairtie politics, at laest in Scotland. It wul be gey an haird argiein that Gaelic haes a richt ti siller an Scots disnae, for aw that ye maun hae yeir douts about spendin on

---

[34] Falconer, furthcummin.

the saicont leid iver winnin til the samen levels. Ye can imagine a Scots *piggybacking* o Gaelic on siller eissues, than, but wi faur less o the reflexive bile seen athort the Sheuch, no laest acause the leids' supporters in Scotland wul aw be cultural nationalists, whitiver thair poleitical gaits.[35]

The mair the behaviour o Ulster-Scots steirars aften gars thair Scots conterpairts thraw up thair haunds at thair wanfortune, A jalouse thay'l be thankrif at the hinner-end, baith til the dochter byleid athort the Sheuch an til the Gaelic leids o Airland an Scotland. Gin a common staundard for Scots is taen on buird in the twa stewartries, a fair fek o the skaith thocht ti hae been duin bi tapthrawn Ulster-Scots steirin cuid mebbe be putten richt. The Scots leid itsell wul hae been geylies strenthened bi sicna cummin thegither. Wi wysslik forder, the Scots Pairlament curn micht weill gie us a haund daein thon.

---

[35] On the Conservative syde, John Buchan springs ti mynd. Amang aulder socialists, the'r a plethora enthusiasts for tradeitional sang.

Beibliographie

Black, David 1985 'Scots and English', *Chapman*, Vol. 41, 1985. pp. Nn-nn

Eagle, Andy 'Reinventing the Wheel? Or Maun Ulster Scots be Spelt Ither nor Mainland Scots?', no furthsetten, ti get fae *http://www.scots-online.org/airticles/index.htm*.

Falconer, Gavin furthcummin 'The Scots Dialect in Northern Ireland: A Rival for Irish?', In *A Festschrift for Hildegard L.C. Tristram* (Freiburg: privately published)

Görlach, Manfred 2000 'Ulster-Scots: a Language?' in Kirk, John M. and Ó Baoill, Dónall P. (eds.): *Language and Politics: Northern Ireland, the Republic of Ireland, and Scotland* (Queen's Univesity Belfast: Cló Ollscoil na Banríona) pp. 13-31.

Horsbroch, Dauvit 2000 '*Mair as a Sheuch Atween Scotland an Ulster*: Twa Policie for the Scots Leid?' in Kirk, John M. and Ó Baoill, Dónall P. (eds.): *Language and Politics: Northern Ireland, the Republic of Ireland, and Scotland* (Queen's Univesity Belfast: Cló Ollscoil na Banríona) pp. 133-141.

Kirk, John M. 1998 'Ulster Scots: Realities and Myths', *Ulster Folklife*, Vol. 44, 1998. pp. 69-93.

McClure, J. Derrick 1997: *Why Scots Matters* revised edition (Edinburgh: The Saltire Society).

Mac Póilin, Aodán 'Cross Border Language Developments: North-South, East-West', paper gien at the Centre for Cross-Border Studies, Queen's University, Belfast, 12.05.01.

Miller, Jim 1998 'Scots: a Sociological Perspective', in Jackson, Robin and Niven, Liz (eds.) *The Scots Language: Its Place in Education* (Newton Stewart andDumfries: Watergaw). Pp. 45-56.

Purves, David 1997: *A Scots Grammar* (Edinburgh: The Saltire Society).

Robinson, Philip 1997: *Ulster-Scots: A Grammar of the Traditional Written and Spoken Language* (Belfast: The Ullans Press).

Appendix: Scots spoken in the Scottish Parliament

1. 1707 was the end of an auld sang. (Winnie Ewing, 12.5.99, 6)
2. This is the start of a new sang. (Sir David Steel, 12.5.99, 9)
3. Ah telt ye. (Kenny MacAskill, 2.6.99, 187)
4. Facts are chiels [*cheels* {?} *in the original Burns quote*] [th]at winna ding. (Annabel Goldie, 2.6.99, 182; Kay Ullrich, 8.6.99, 303, 6.10.99 – David McLetchie)
5. Gie us the money. (David McLetchie, 2.6.99, 172)
6. werenae very impressed (Tavish Scott, 3.6.99, 239)
7. a bit of a pauchle (Colin Campbell, 3.6.99, 246)
8. a platform for ritual girning (John Home Robertson, 3.6.99, 251)
9. In the first referendum, we Scots were feart. (George Reid, 9.6.99, 372)
10. sold our fishermen doon the watters (David McLetchie, 9.6.99, 374)
11. I am sookin in with the boss. (Ian Jenkins, 16.06.99, 468)
12. fair drookit (Donald Dewar, 17.06.99, 524) ('drookit' also used by Lyndsay McIntosh, 17.06.99, 1/539; Fergus Ewing, 17.06.99, 542)
13. The people of Scotland did not vote for a mak-a-fool-o Parliament. (Cathie Craigie, 17.06.99, 549) (*the member preferred 'mak a fool aw', and it was reported in the daily version as such*)
14. mak do with (Cathie Craigie, 17.06.99, 549)
15. a complete boorach (Bruce Crawford, 17.06.99, 554) (*misreported in The Scotsman as 'Gourock'!*)
16. I didnae know that he was here, right enough. (Tommy Sheridan, 17.06.99, 627)
17. If the formula disnae work, do not use it. (Tommy Sheridan, 17.06.99, 628)
18. gave youse a gubbing (Tommy Sheridan, 24.06.99, 756)
19. for one who is hirpling around the city (Christine Grahame, 24.6.99, 771)
20. I see some well-kent faces. (Margaret Smith, 29.06.99, Health and Community Care Committee, 3)
21. We're no saying, 'reinvent the wheel'. (Tommy Sheridan, 23.08.99, Social Inclusion, Housing and Voluntary Sector Committee, 39)
22. Nae problem. (Margo MacDonald, 31.8.99, European Committee, 66)
23. trips doon the watter (Duncan Hamilton, 1.9.99, 63)
24. 'It wisnae me; I wisnae there.' (Roseanna Cunningham, 2.9.99, 79)
25. Everyone is wrang but our Jim. (Kenny MacAskill, 2.9.99, 96)
26. this douce city (Mike Russell, 2.9.99, 152)
27. 'He canna Scotland see wha yet / Canna see the Infinite'. (Mike Russell quoting Hugh MacDiarmid, 2.9.99, 153)
28. Masel, Ah cannae actually draw. (Trish Godman, 2.9.99, 161)
29. the gallus nature of Glasgow (Des McNulty, 2.9.99, 170)
30. 'We'll ken whaur we cam frae / an whaur we ur gan / We'll aw hae a say each / wumman an man.' (Cathie Peattie quoting Liz Niven, 2.9.99, 175)
31. gey thin soup (David Davidson, 2.9.99, 175)
32. getting nabbed by the polis (Alex Salmond, 9.9.99, 284)
33. 'It wisnae me.' (David McLetchie, 9.9.99, 291)
34. What is contained in the document is cauld kail het up. (Kenny MacAskill, 9.9.99, 306)
35. When I was young we used to go doon the coast in the summer. (Janis Hughes, 9.9.99, 314)

36. rummlin through his old cuttings (Donald Dewar, 9.9.99, 344)
37. get us into a fankle (John Swinney, Enterprise and Lifelong Learning, Committee, 15.9.99, 82)
38. Colin had a copy by Gil, and I didnae. (Kenny Gibson, Local Government Committee, 21.9.99, 64)
39. You shouldnae have gone into coalition, then. (Gil Paterson, Procedures Committee, 21.9.99, 65)
40. While in Bute House Donald Dewar has to dae withoot. (Alex Johnstone, 22.9.99, 637)
41. something that we put up with or thole (Fergus Ewing, 22.9.99, 652)
42. I do not intend to join the behoochie tendency. (Fergus Ewing, 22.9.99, 654)
43. our sheriffs are not all bampots (Christine Grahame, 23.9.99, 718)
44. gey cauld down there [in the Borders] (Christine Grahame, 29.9.99, 844)
45. ... even although the First Minister might feel tempted to bury the hatchet in John Reid's heid. (Dennis Canavan, 30.9.99, 954)
46. Away hame and think again. (Alex Neil, 7.10.99, 1118)
47. Tak tent of that phrase. (Margaret Ewing, 7.10.99, 1127)
48. Sit doon, keep quiet and dae whit ye're telt. (Bruce Crawford, 7.10.99, 1134)
49. It is nonsense to blame the farmers for the guddle. (Ross Finnie, 7.10.99, 1216)
50. I do not know why the council hasnae stepped in and done something about it. (McQueen, Justice and Home Affairs Committee, 26.10.99, 236)
51. You talk about people being scared — I cannae be any mair scared. (Thomas Hanratty, Justice and Home Affairs Committee, 26.10.99, 256)
52. Tony Blair, a big feartie (David McLetchie, 28.10.99, 148)
53. I am not, however, absolutely thirled to the figure. (Brian Adam, Finance Committee, 2.11.99, 103)
54. The figure of plus 15 will disappear like snaw aff the proverbial. (Kay Ullrich, 3.11.99, 263)
55. What difference does it make if we hear about confidential details today or three weeks later? It only causes a stushie. (Ian Jenkins, Education, Culture and Sport Committee, 9.11.99, 250)
56. During the election, there was a stushie — if I may use Ian's word — about Labour trying to attract votes by publicising investment in a sports academy. I remember glossy pictures of people playing keepie-uppie and so on. (Michael Russell, Education, Culture and Sport Committee, 9.11.99, 250)
57. hanging a good soundbite on a shoogly peg (Jamie Stone, 11.11.99, 535)
58. He said, 'Och, the millennium is rubbish.' (Jamie Stone, 11.11.99, 536)
59. tell you to away and bile yer heid (Brian Monteith, Procedures Committee, 16.11.99, 187)
60. what is wrang (Gil Paterson, Procedures Committee, 16.11.99, 187)
61. We have all got guid Scots tongues in wir heids. (Gil Paterson, Procedures Committee, 16.11.99, 188)
62. It disnae happen. (Gil Paterson, Procedures Committee, 16.11.99, 188)
63. It should no be hyped up. (Gil Paterson, Procedures Committee, 16.11.99, 188)
64. withoot putting barriers in its way (Gil Paterson, Procedures Committee, 16.11.99, 188)
65. Och, they would get used to it. (Gil Paterson, Procedures Committee, 16.11.99, 190)
66. just yin buddie (Murray Tosh, Procedures Committee, 16.11.99, 191-2)

67. the various rammies and stushies going on behind the scenes (Paul McManus (BECTU), Enterprise, Culture and Sport Committee, 23.11.99, 339)
68. I remember the word 'menadge' — I will not say that we would be able to run one in Parliament — which is another form of working-class saving. (Trish Godman, 1.12.99, 1105)
69. left in a complete guddle (Ross Finnie, Rural Affairs Committee, 3.12.99, 283)
70. rubbished by one of many Government sources as 'numpties' (Alex Salmond, 9.12.99, 1414)
71. I felt my head fair birling again. (Christine Grahame, 15.12.99, 1561)
72. Will the minister give way? I wouldnae mind getting a wee mention. (Tommy Sheridan, 13.1.00, 73)
73. The image springs to mind of the minister as an old wifie at a church social, carefully cutting the cake into slices and deciding upon which plate the crumbs will fall. (Nick Johnston, 26.1.00, 459)
74. not just the high heid yins, but ordinary back benchers such as myself (Jamie Stone, 2.2.00, 646)
75. What I am saying is that we have heard spin after spin. In fact, ministers are like a bunch of peeries now, they are spinning that much. (Bruce Crawford, 3.2.00, 704)
76. It does not matter a docken leaf. (Margo MacDonald, European Committee, 8.2.00, 424)
77. I did not have the pleasure of seeing that particular edition of 'Newsnight', which seems to have been a splendid intellectual version of a good-going stair-heid brawl. (Donald Dewar, 10.2.00, 1003)
78. the mither tongue of at least 1.5 million Scots (Irene McGugan, 16.2.00, 1085)
79. Burns kent better. (Irene McGugan, 16.2.00, 1085)
80. the Scots leid (Margaret Ewing, 16.2.00, 1091)
81. a few drams or pints (Brian Monteith, 16.2.00, 1091)
82. I dinna ken fit tae dee — heid or hert? (Nora Radcliffe, 16.2.00, 1095)
83. I canna see me changin ma wey o thinkin. (Alex Johnstone, 16.2.00, 1097)
84. Our bairns are speaking Scots. (Cathy Peattie, 16.2.00, 1097)
85. I am no even gaunae try. (Cathy Peattie, 16.2.00, 1098)
86. Naebody speaks like that any langer. (Cathy Peattie, 16.2.00, 1098)
87. Ur we no aw Jock Tamson's bairns, and should we no be treated like that? (Gil Paterson, 16.2.00, 1100)
88. herdsmen or orramen (Margaret Ewing, 16.2.00, 1101)
89. Fit is so wrang wi wantin to speir as part o the census aboot foo much money we mak and fit wye we speak at hame? I cannae see oniethin wrang wi that. I havenae heard onie argument today that persuades me itherwise. I am quite happy to speak in Scots, but I know that the Presiding Officer will rule me oot o order if I do much mair. (Brian Adam, 16.2.00, 1106)
90. It is the wye I wid speak at hame. I am quite happy to dae that. (Brian Adam, 16.2.00, 1106)
91. He says that it is okay to ask aboot language in the household survey, but it is nae okay to ask aboot it in the census. (Brian Adam, 16.2.00, 1106)
92. aw o us who are politicians (Brian Adam, 16.2.00, 1106)
93. I have grave doots aboot it. (Brian Adam, 16.2.00, 1106)
94. I understood automatically such phrases as 'sneck the yett'. (Margaret Ewing, 16.2.00, 1112)

95. Naebody spicks that language. (Margaret Ewing, 16.2.00, 1113)
96. I love the poetry of Burns and MacDiarmid and never go anywhere without my nickie-tams. (Jamie McGrigor, 16.2.00, 1116)
97. I think that the Executive is deaved by legal problems. (Annabel Goldie, 17.2.00, 1238)
98. to drap a hammer on wir foot (Alan Ritchie (Union of Construction, Allied Trades and Technicians), 21.2.00, Social Inclusion, Housing and Voluntary Sector Committee, 679)
99. At the moment, we cannae make those improvements. (John Wright, Social Inclusion, Housing and Voluntary Sector Committee, 21.2.00, 702)
100. Fae June last year, we had been trying to arrange a meeting with Wendy Alexander. (Willie Coleman, Social Inclusion, Housing and Voluntary Sector Committee, 21.2.00, 703)
101. We are concerned that everything is being put into the dark the noo. (Willie Coleman, Social Inclusion, Housing and Voluntary Sector Committee, 21.2.00, 703)
102. Bob Allan was brought fae Clackmannanshire, but he asked us more questions than he would let us ask him. We asked him 13 questions, but he couldnae answer them. (Willie Coleman, Social Inclusion, Housing and Voluntary Sector Committee, 21.2.00, 703)
103. Yeez can dae it nae bother. (Jim Lennox, Social Inclusion, Housing and Voluntary Sector Committee, 21.2.00, 707)
104. The city council will have to accept what we want or else we're no giein them the money. (Jim Lennox, Social Inclusion, Housing and Voluntary Sector Committee, 21.2.00, 709)
105. a considerable stramash among the crofting industry (Jamie Stone, 24.2.00, 147)
106. 'The best laid plans o' mice an' men / Gang aft a-gley.' (Alex Fergusson, 24.2.00, 216)
107. The staff went out chapping on doors. (Foster Evans (Employers in Voluntary Housing), Social Inclusion, Housing and Voluntary Sector Committee, 21.2.00, 718)
108. The motion is a wee bitty negative, a wee bitty moany. (Gordon Jackson, 2.3.00, 323)
109. a few old bodachs (Jamie Stone, 2.3.00, 416)
110. I think that we should ca cannie on that and rework what has been proposed. (Hugh Henry, European Committee, 21.03.00, 555)
111. We will bring a shortleet to the committee for discussion. (Hugh Henry, European Committee, 21.03.00, 557)
112. a toon of 'honest men and bonie lasses.' (John Scott, 23.3.00, 904)
113. Aye — that'll be right. (Kenny MacAskill, 23.3.00, 982)
114. 'Ah kent yer faither' — or, in Jack McConnell's case, 'Ah kent yer auntie in Bridge of Weir'. (Colin Campbell, 30.3.00, 1259)
115. honest enough to admit that they are agin Holyrood (Jamie Stone, 5.4.00, 1332)
116. [David McLetchie's] somewhat pawky manner occasionally suggests something from Trollope. (Donald Dewar, 6.4.00, 1457)
117. You've no got a daddy. (Karen Gillon, Education, Culture and Sport Committee, 9.5.00, 954)
118. Facts are chiels; he should face up to them. (David McLetchie, 11.5.00, 592)
119. his little bothan (John Munro, 11.5.00, 635)
120. The minister was all respice and nae prospice. (Alex Neil, 17.5.00, 673)
121. The minister can spin like a peerie. (Kay Ullrich, 18.5.00, 782)

122. The Labour party should be black affrontit. (Tricia Marwick, 18.5.00, 808)
123. Haud me back. (Gordon Jackson, Justice and Home Affairs Committee, 7.6.00, 1393)
124. "Sae come aa ye at hame wi freedom / Never heed whit the houdies croak for doom / In yer hous aa the bairns o Aidam / Will fin breid, barley-bree an paintit room." (Cathy Peattie, 21.6.00, 608)
125. for or agin (Anne Middleton (STUC), Local Government Committee, 26.6.00, 1069)
126. Och, well — on you go. (Allan Wilson, 29.6.00, 874)
127. Susan's coat is on a very shooglie nail. (Kay Ullrich, 6.7.00, 1175)
128. 'the hell o' a' diseases' (Dorothy-Grace Elder quoting Burns, 6.7.00, 1219)
129. the year that is awa (Jim Wallace, 6.7.00, 1236)
130. furth of Scotland's shores (Mike Russell, Education, Culture and Sport Committee, 6.9.00, 1320)
131. If I was going there, I wouldnae start from here. (Mike Watson, 20.9.00, 474)
132. When my grandmother burned her girdle scones, she would cut up the farls as usual for the tea table ... 'Aye turn the bonnie side tae London.' Today, I hope that the Scottish housewife in similar plight would say, 'Aye turn the bonnie side tae Embro'! (Father George Thompson (St Peter's Catholic Church, Dalbeattie), 27.9.00, 639)
133. well-kent faces (Gordon Jackson, Justice and Home Affairs Committee, 27.9.00, 1783)
134. Haud yer wheesht. (Fergus Ewing, 28.9.00, 721)
135. Haud on. (Christine Grahame, 28.9.00, 747)
136. You might as well be deid. (Margaret Ewing, 28.9.00, 847)
137. selected unopposed in a smoke-filled room by three men, or women, and a dug (Kenny Gibson, 5.10.00, 954)
138. I am sorry, but it wouldnae. (Kenny Gibson, 5.10.00, 985)
139. elected by a ba hair (Kenny Gibson, 5.10.00, 985)
140. Like a stalk o rock, I am Scottish through to the core. (Henry McLeish, 26.10.00, 1172)
141. furth of Edinburgh (Mike Watson, Finance Committee, 31.10.00, 815)
142. 'Here's tae us — wha's like us? Damned few and they're a deid.' (Reverend David Miller, 1.11.00, 1183)
143. the cauld kail that David McLetchie throws around in this place (Henry McLeish, 2.11.00, 1346)
144. The document ... is self-congratulatory, navel-gazing mince, which will mean heehaw to the general public and, worse still, heehaw to the people who are being discriminated against. (Fiona Hyslop, 8.11.00, 1426)
145. The Boundary Commission made a right sotter. (Nora Radcliffe, 9.11.00, 1540)
146. lack of urgency about the high heid yins' attitude (Donald Gorrie, 9.11.00, 1613)
147. the two new haudit-and-daudit members who are sitting on the SNP benches (Ben Wallace, 16.11.00, 105)
148. As one of them said to me, 'You cannae go on daeing that once you're merrit'; another expression that was used was, 'You've got tae screw the heid'. (David Colvin (Safeguarding Communities Reducing Offending), 20.11.00, 1899)
149. balances between hill farms and more inby farming (James Morris (SSPCA), Rural Affairs Committee, 21.11.00, 1381)
150. The word 'gardyloo' was well known in Edinburgh. (John Young, 22.11.00, 271)
151. Haud yer hand. (John Young, 22.11.00, 271)

152. I hate to correct John Young, but the saying was 'Haud yer haund'. Another old one is 'Haud yer wheesht'. (Gil Paterson, 22.11.00, 273)
153. I have always said that I am a Paisley buddie. (Kenny Gibson, Local Government Committee, 12.12.00 1330)
154. I was not asking him to clipe on the working group. (Alasdair Morgan, Justice and Home Affairs Committee, 12.12.00, 1994)
155. The thought of cliping never came into my head. (Christine Grahame, Justice and Home Affairs Committee, 12.12.00, 1994)
156. chapped on my door (Tommy Sheridan, 14.12.00, 987)
157. Undisclosed freemasonry ... should be consigned to the dustbin with the tawse. (Thomas Minogue (petitioner), Public Petitions Committee, 19.12.00, 821)
158. the way in which teachers feel hauden doon by over-regulation (Donald Gorrie, 10.1.01, 14)
159. **Euan Robson** rose —
    Gordon Jackson: Aw no, Euan. (Gordon Jackson, 10.1.01, 41)
160. the old adage that there are nae jobs in the Borders (Euan Robson, 10.1.01, 56)
161. **Kenneth Gibson:** I propose the convener, Trish Godman. / **Jamie Stone:** You big sook. / **Colin Campbell:** I second Gibson's proposal. / **The Convener:** I do not think that 'big sook' is parliamentary language. / **Gibson:** I was not being a big sook so much as launching a pre-emptive strike — the convener wanted me to be the reporter. (Jamie Stone, Trish Godman, Kenneth Gibson, 14.11.2000, Local Government Committee, 1297)
162. the cludgie stane of Scone (Robbie the Pict, Public Petitions Committee, 23.1.01, 867)
163. calcareous freestone, mair frae Methven than Mesopotamia (Robbie the Pict, Public Petitions Committee, 23.1.01, 868)
164. So, can we have oor Perthanon marble back, please mister? (Robbie the Pict, Public Petitions Committee, 23.1.01, 868)
165. someone who is cantankerous, thrawn or downright independent (Mary Scanlon, 25.1.01, 611)
166. 'It's coming yet for a' that. / That man to man, the world o'er / Shall brithers be for a' that.' and 'O wad some Pow'r the giftie gie us / To see oursels as others see us! / It wad frae monie a blunder free us / An' foolish notion.' (David Mundell, 25.1.01, 713)
167. 'In gath'rin votes you were na slack, / Now stand as tightly by your tack: / Ne'er claw your lug, an' your back, / An' hum an' haw, / But raise your arm, an' tell your crack / Before them a'.' (Fergus Ewing, 25.1.01, 717)
168. whether the dinners are formal or informal, posh or couthie (Fergus Ewing, 25.01.01, 717)
169. 'Fareweel to a' our Scottish fame, / Fareweel our ancient glory; / Fareweel even to the Scottish name, / Sae fam'd in martial story!' (Fergus Ewing, 25.01.01, 718)
170. David Mundell, with his 'honest, sonsie face' (Ian Jenkins, 25.01.01, 718)
171. 'Here lie Willie Michie's banes: / Oh Satan, when ye tak him, / Gie him the schulin o your weans, / For clever deils he'll mak them!' He always said to me, 'When you go to hell, you'll need to teach these weans.' (Ian Jenkins, 25.01.01, 719)
172. 'auld Ayr, wham ne'er a town surpasses / For honest men and bonnie lasses'. (John Scott, 25.01.01, 720)
173. The handsel disappeared. (John Scott, 25.01.01, 721)

174. Burns suppers are ... a reminder that we are all Jock Tamson's bairns. (Jamie Stone, 25.01.01, 723)
175. People say, 'Och, well, we know what Burns was like'. (Cathy Peattie, 25.01.01, 726)
176. a young woman who ... has been left with a thorn — a babbie. (Cathy Peattie, 25.01.01, 727)
177. 'Ye banks and braes o' bonie Doon, / How can ye bloom sae fresh and fair? / How can ye chant, ye little birds, / And I sae weary fu' o' care! / Thou'll break my heart, thou warbling bird, / That wantons thro' the flowering thorn: / Thou minds me o' departed joys, / Departed never to return.' (Cathy Peattie, 25.01.01, 727)
178. Then let us pray that come it may, / As come it will for a' that, / That Sense and Worth, o'er a' the earth / Shall bear the gree, and a' that / For a' that, and a' that, / It's comin yet for a' that, / That Man to Man the warld o'er, / Shall brothers be for a' that.' (Cathy Peattie, 25.01.01, 727)

Scots: Hauf Empty or Hauf Fu?

Caroline Macafee

Up tae the 1990s there naethin at could be cried a politics o Scots though there was nae want o activism. Earlier generations o activists were rappin at the windaes o the eddication system. Tae gie an instance, the Saltire Society published, in 1953, *Scotland in the Schools. A Report on the Scottish Content of our Education.* The champions o the leid – and o Scottish history an music as weel – were aye tirlin at the lock near fifty year later. In 1998, in guid hert at the prospeck o the new Pairlament in Embro, the Scottish Consultative Council on the Curriculum (SCCC) produced anither thorough review o the Scottishness o the schuil curriculum. But – waly waly – it was self-censort in anteecipation o the Labour victory – though it was leakt on the Internet.

Ither efforts 50 year syne were direckit at the braidcast media. David Abercrombie (supportit be ithers, includin Jack Aitken) was raxin for the preevilege o hearin Scottish *accents* on the radio, never min the Scots leid (Abercrombie, 1992). Ah lea it tae ithers, at hes been mair direckly involved, tae gang ower the poleeticisation o Scots in the last decade. In this screed, Ah wint tae explore the backgrun at the poleetical process hes tae be played oot fornenst – the nummers an regional distribution o the spickers, the beliefs o spickers aboot their leid, an the rival discoorses aboot Scots at guides the actions o the institutional players.

Table 1: Scots speakers (as indicated by percentages) ordered by region, based on Murdoch and Gordon (1995) and compared with GRO-commissioned Surveys 1 and 2 based on Máté (1996: Table 2)

Region	Murdoch	Máté Survey 1	Máté Survey 2
	%	%	%
Scotland	57	31	33
Grampian	90	60	58
Orkney	90	-	-
Shetland	77	-	-
Fife	73	48	36
Dumfries/Galloway	70	39	30
Tayside	60	30	54
Borders	57	2	33
Central	53	19	30
Lothian	53	23	34
Strathclyde	42	28	28
Western Isles	33	30	4
Highland	15	15	20

Table 2: Scots speakers resident and Scots speakers schooled by region, based on Murdoch and Gordon (1995)

Place of schooling/residence	Scots speakers schooled		Resident Scots speakers		
	n	*%*		*n*	*%*
Borders	13	16	*81*	17	30	*57*
Central	11	22	*50*	16	30	*53*
Dumfries & Galloway	17	21	*81*	21	30	*70*
Fife	18	19	*95*	22	30	*73*
Grampian	23	24	*96*	30	30	*100*
Aberdeen	33	34	*97*	24	30	*80*
Total Grampian	**56**	**58**	*97*	**54**	**60**	*90*
Highland	11	35	*31*	5	30	*17*
Skye	1	7	*14*	4	30	*13*
Total Highland	**12**	**42**	*31*	**9**	**60**	*15*
Lothian	12	21	*57*	-	-	-
Edinburgh	8	13	*62*	-	-	-
Total Lothian	**20**	**34**	*59*	**16**	**30**	*53*
Orkney	17	20	*85*	27	30	*90*
Shetland	26	27	*96*	23	30	*77*
Strathclyde	19	38	*50*	9	30	*30*
Glasgow	20	48	*42*	16	30	*53*
Total Strathclyde	**39**	**86**	*45*	**25**	**60**	*42*
Tayside	21	31	*68*	18	30	*60*
Western Isles	5	33	*15*	10	30	*33*
All	**255**	**409***	*63*	**258**	**450**	*57*

* The numbers do not add up to 450 as individuals educated outside Scotland have been omitted.

Table 1 gies the figgers for Scots spickers (in the auld admeenistrative regions) fae the research o Steve Murdoch (1995) an merkat research commeesioned be the General Register Office (Máté, 1996). This wes pairt o the testin o the rejeckit question on Scots for the 2001 Census. Forbye the mercat research there was cognitive research cairried oot in sma groups aroon the kintra. Ah've reanalysed thir sets o data (Macafee 2000a) an Ah'll be yaisin thir figgers in this screed.

Luckin at the tap line o Table 1, the figger for Scotlan oweraw, ye'll see at Murdoch's figger is muckler. His methodology was mair intensive an curcuddoch. Ah'm inclined tae believe at his figgers are mair liker the truith. But there muckle disparities in bouk amang the regions – Strathclyde especially was an enormous region an the proportion o Scots spickers wasnae sae heich there as ither, sae an adjustment bude tae be made. If we tak a wechtit average, it pulls Murdoch's total figger for Scots spickers doon tae 53%. An we hae tae

Table 3: Definition of 'Glaswegian' by region of origin (based on Máté, 1996: Table 2)

Region of Origin	Accent	Acent/Slang	Accent/Dialect	Dialect	Dialect/Slang	Slang	Accent/Dialect/Slang	Dialect/Language	Language	No Data	All
Borders				3	3						6
Central	3	5		3	1					1	13
Dumfries / Galloway	3			11	2		1				17
Fife				1							1
Grampian	1		1	20	2			1	2	1	28
Highlands	1									4	5
Lothian	5	1		6	3						15
Strathclyde	7	1	1	5	6					1	21
West. Isles	1										1
All	21	7	2	49	17					7	107

mind, at thir figgers is juist for grown-ups. The figgers for bairns an teenagers wad maistlike be laicher.

Lukkin at the regional distribution o spickers, we can see the nummer is sma i the Heilan region – e'en tho this taks in the NE neuk o Caithness, bit this wasnae includit in ony o the Hielan samples. Gin we ignore Heilan an the Western Isles, an concentrate on the regions at are athin – or maistly athin – the Scots-spickin area, we fun a wheen regional disparities, wi percentages reengin fae 42% in Strathclyde tae 90% in Orkney an in Grampian. The fowk walit in ilka survey were intendit for tae be a random sample o the population, sae they werenae necessarily local tae the area whaur they kythe in the figgers. Murdoch did a vera interestin recoont in terms o whaur fowk gat their schuilin. This is pitten furth in Table 2.

This shaws, for instance, at oot o saxteen fowk schuiled i the Borders, 13 (81%) sayed they could spick Scots, bit oot o thirty fowk *resident* in the Borders, seeventeen (57%) sayed they could spick Scots. The ilk doonward shift atween schuilin an residence kythes in a nummer o regions. It appears tae be attributable tae the muckle excess o fowk schuiled in Strathclyde (near hauf as mony again as the sample walit as Strathclyde residenters).

Whit we are seein here is nae doot a dispersal o population fae Strathclyde an especially the 'overspill' fae Glesca's rehoosing policies o the 1960s. It is no surprisin at this has a smoorin effeck on the figgers for Scots spickers, whan we conseeder the language attitudes aboot Gleswegian dialeck hauden baith be Gleswegians an be ithers aroon Scotlan.

Table 4:   Scots speaking and use of Scots words (based on Máté, 1996: Table 2).

"Can you speak Scots or a dialect of Scots"?	"Do you use Scots/dialect words?"					
	Never	*Rarely*	*Sometimes*	*Often*	*Normally*	*All*
No	0	7	9	1	0	17
Don't know	0	0	8	0	0	8
Yes	0	3	29	19	33	84
All	0	10	46	20	33	109

Table 3 shaws the language labels walit fer Gleswegian fae a leet o possible labels. For maist regions, the maist preferred label is 'Dialect', wi the possible addeetion o 'Slang', especially in Strathclyde itsel. But the label 'Accent' is tae the fore in Strathclyde an in Lothian. It's no at aw clear at the general public is able for tae mak a consistent an meaninfu disteenction atween 'Accent' an 'Dialect', but thir results is certainly consistent wi ither findins shawin at Gleswegian is perceived as gey thin Scots, or some wey atween Scots and Inglis (cf. Hardie, 1997).

The cognitive research interviews conduckit be the GRO confirmt the findins o earlier wark. There a tendency amang young Gleswegians tae perceive Scots as juist the passin slang o an aulder generation (cf. Menzies, 1991; Macafee, 1994). Sae it is on the same level as their ain neologisms an catchphrases an naethin special.

Anither findin fae the cognitive research confirmt Aitken's (1982) suggestion at there a model or 'ideal Scots', agin the which actual Scots speech is meesurt an seen tae fa short. The language o Robert Burns was whiles speceefically mentiont. Meesurt agin this ellwand the ilkaday spoken leid o the interviewees was, they felt, no the real thing, no Scots.

It is weel kent at there muckle mair positive attitudes tae Scots i the NE. Gaein back tae Table 3, we see at this gaes as faur as allooin Gleswegian the label 'Language'. But e'en i the NE, whaur Scots is mair likely tae be seen as a leid, an up tae 100% in some constituencies coontit thairsels spickers, there an obvious tension atween positive attitudes tae the mither tongue an instrumental beliefs i the utility o Inglis (Löw, 1997, 2001; McGarrity, 1998).

Tables 4 an 5 shaws the repone tae the question "Do you use Scots/dialect words?" i the cognitive research. There a five-pint scale fae 'never' tae 'normally'. Ye will observe at the modal value for 'All' in Table 4 is 'sometimes'. Luckin doon the columns, aw the fowk at say they 'normally' yaises Scots wirds says 'yes' they spick Scots, and the vast majority o thaim at 'aften' yaises Scots wirds says the like – they spick Scots. Howanever, thaim at says they 'sometimes' yaises Scots wirds is dividit – Ah haennae gien the percentages in the table – roonaboot 60% 'yes', 20% 'don't know' and 20% 'no'. Thaim at says they yaise Scots wirds 'rarely' is likely tae hae deeficulties wi the question forbye. Seiven oot o ten sayed 'no', bit the ither three sayed 'yes'. It

Table 5: Individuals who use Scots words 'sometimes' by Scots speaking and region of origin (based on Máté, 1996: Table 2).

Region of Origin	'Sometimes' use Scots words			"Can you speak Scots or a dialect of Scots?"					
				Yes		Don't Know		NO	
		n	%	n	%	n	%	n	%
Western Isles	1	1	100	1	100	0	0	0	0
Strathclyde	16	21	76	10	63	2	13	4	25
Lothian	5	15	33	3	60	1	20	1	20
Highlands	2	5	40	2	100	0	0	0	0
Grampian	7	28	25	5	71	1	14	1	14
Fife	1	1	100	1	100	0	0	0	0
Dumfries/Galloway	5	17	29	2	40	1	20	2	40
Central	8	13	62	3	38	3	38	2	25
Borders	1	6	17	1	100	0	0	0	0
All	**46**	**109**	**42**	**28**	**61**	**8**	**17**	**10**	**22**

was thir findins, mair nor ony ithers, at convinced me at – sadly – Máté was richt in his conclusion at it wasnae possible for tae frame a valid question, for the purposes o the Census, anent abeelity tae spick Scots.

Table 5 shaws at there a wheen geographical variations in the percentage giein the 'sometimes' repone. Grampian has a muckle 'yes' figger for spickin Scots, an a relatively sma figger for 'sometimes' yaisin Scots wirds. Maist o the 'sometimes' bodies says they spick Scots. In Central an Strathclyde, be contrar, a heich proportion walit 'sometimes' an they were less likely nor in Grampian tae say at they spoke Scots. We micht weel suspeck at 'sometimes' means different things in different regions. In Grampian, we wad be expeckin mair code-switching – whiles ye spick Scots, whiles ye spick Inglis – bit in Strathclyde mair style-driftin alang a continuum (in Aitken's 1979 terminology). Bit style-driftin is mebbies spreadin intae the mair tradeetional areas – Melchers (1999) recently reportit at this is becomin the pracktik amang young Shetlanders.

Ah hae cried Scots a leid sae faur, an Ah see nae pint in denying it that status noo that it's offeecially been conferrit be government wi the signin an ratification o the European Charter. It micht weel be, nanetheless, a deein language. If sae, Ah wad be aw the mair inclint tae deegnify its passin wi the name o language daith – raither nor dialectalisation (*pace* Görlach 2000) – if for nae ither reason, acause the academic gaberts or framework o language daith offers us a valuable research perspective on whit is happenin.

Ane aspeck o the decline o the leid is its replacement be a throughither language variety. This is evidently whit a large proportion o the fowk i the cognitive research thocht had awreadies happent. They were therefore correck, i their ain terms, tae say at they didnae spick 'Scots', gin be that they unnerstuid an ideal Scots typified be the sangs o Burns. Ma research in Glesca (Macafee, 1994)

Table 6:   Mean percentages of lexical items known and used in several studies (Macafee, forthcoming, *q.v.* for further discussion; updated from Macafee, 1997)

[Ed. note: *In each of the three tables below, each study has the same reference number between 1 and 10 for ease of comparison between the studies and the age-classes of informants.*]

No.	Study	Place	Source	n.
1	Graham (1979)	Shetland	Jakobsen 1890s	360
2	Wickens (1980)	Caithness	Earlier dialect glossary	461
3	Macaulay (1977)	Glasgow	old Scots words	10
4	Pollner (1985)	Livingston		23
5	Nässén (1989)	Shetland	Jakobsen1890s	323
6	Hettinga (1981)	Fife	old Fife words	21
7	Agutter and Cowan (1981)	Stirling-shire	LAS	33
8	Lawrie (1991)	Fife	LAS	20
9	Hendry (1997)	North-East	adults recalling childhood words	41
10	McGarrity (1998)	Aberdeen	old Doric words	96

No	Adults			Young Adults		
	n	%known	%used	n	%known	%used
1	1	29.1				
2	40	44.8	27.2			
3	16	78				
4	47	45				
5	35	c.20				
6	3	81	3	3	57.1	
7	10	77.3	52.1			
8	16	23.3	12.2			
9						
10	7	41	23	33	38	17

No	Teenagers			Children		
	n.	%known	%used	n	%known	%used
1	1	18.1				
2	34	26.1	13.5			
3	16	33				
4	9	26				
5						
6				3	7.1	
7				10	52.1	33.6
8				16	9.8	6.9
9				778	61*	
10	20	23	13			

wad suggest at this throughither variety is characterised be Scots grammar an wirdform, bit Inglis vocabulary. It's worth pintin oot at, for the auldest generation, the shift tae this throughither variety was a muckle cheynge tae their normal mainner o spickin, an they cried this 'spickin plain'. It was an effort at sud hae ensurt intelligibeelity tae non-Scots spickers. Sic non-Scots spickers, on the ither haun, hearin this throughither variety, thinks they are hearin braid Scots. Anither aspeck o the daith o the leid is the absolute erosion o its substance, an especially the lexicon. It is, naiterally, vera deeficult tae quantify this.

Table 6 shaws age-relatit means fae a nummer o studies, dune at deeferent times an in deeferent airts. Aw thir studies shaws a – whiles drastic –

decline in knowledge o Scots wirds ower time an, whaur applicable, be age. Some o the gradients o decline are steeper, some are mair shalla, bit there nae relationship atween time an the steepness o the gradient. Ma ain feelin is that it's doon tae methodological deeferences amang the studies an, abuin aw, the chyce o winds tae speir. The ae thing at thir data shaws, hooever, is the consistency o *decline*.

Discoorses aboot Scots

At weel, yon is the state o the leid, sae faur as we can ascertain it at this pint in time. We turn noo tae the discoorses aboot Scots at governs debate an research acteevity aroon the leid.

There is, first ava, **the minority leids discoorse**. This is focussed on the requirements at Scots hes tae meet tae be regairdit as a leid in its ain richt separate fae Inglis, an on the actions needit tae fulfil thae requirements. The requirements are maist aften discussed in terms of the strictures o Stewart (1968) an Kloss (1967, 1978, 1986). In Stewart's view, whit separates a 'dialect' fae a 'standard language' is precisely staunardisation, an this has been the dock-nail o Scots leid activism, at least sin the spellin reform acteevities o Wilson (1926). The ither formulation is that o Kloss wi his crucial distinction atween leids separate be virtue o development (*Ausbau*), an thaim separate, athoot further effort, be virtue o their genetic distance fae the dominant state leid (*Abstand*). In terms o this binary disteenction, Scots is clearly an *Ausbausprache*. As weel's staunardisation, he emphasises the requirement o a functional or non-leeterary prose. Again, this wes awreadies pairt o the agenda, wi Douglas Young ettlin at a prose in Scots as early as 1949 (appearinly unawaur o the 19th century tradeetion o serious journalism in Scots later brocht tae licht be Donaldson, 1986). There hae been mony valiant efforts sinsyne, bit their lack o impact is illustratit be the wey at ilk new generation feels the need tae invent academic prose in Scots aw ower again.

It is no ma intention here tae offer a critique o the minority leid discoorse or ony o the discoorses at Ah'm ettlin tae describe (bit see Macafee, 2000b). Hooever, ma shorthan for this ane is 'fur coat an nae knickers'. Ah believe at it hes divertit the energies o leid activists intae kempin wi Staunart Inglis in areas whaur there nae howp o success, leadin tae a negleck o the real areas o strinth – the folk tradeetion an - the *sine qua non* o leid maintenance – the spoken leid in communities. That means, o needcessity, support for speceefic *regional* dialecks. In this Ah am conscious o the analysis o Fishman (1991), an his views on leid revival.

Personally, Ah feel we maun be ware o vera 'in-your-face', purely symbolic an potentially inauthentic initiatives the likes o offeecial documents in Scots – at least as lang as we cannae even hear *authentic* Scots spoke on TV aless there an agricultural or fishin crisis i the North-East or Shetlan an local fowk are interviewed on the news.

The saicont discoorse, which could be criticeesed as **bleedin-hert leeberalism**, is the academic discoorse o sociolinguistics. It dominates the teachin o Scots in mony o the institutions o higher eddication an mair especially teacher trainin. It is responsible, Ah wad suggest, for the inabeelity o the leid plannin discoorse tae bear the gree. The central doctrine – at aw leids is equal – pits tae the horn ony possibeelity o spickin aboot 'guid Scots' – an that concep is central, o coorse, tae the leid plannin discoorse. The emphasis on variation gars us see the Scots-Inglis continuum as a normal situation, raither nor a process o language daith. The sociolinguistic discoorse encourages toleration o the leid bairns brings tae the schuil, seein this as a cless issue raither nor a historical or cultural ane, an emphasisin questions o social justice an access tae eddication – weel, ye cannae be bad tae that. It micht be questiont, hooever, whether the resultin lip-service tae wirkin-cless Scots achieves vera muckle o thir noble aims.

Ah hae hained for the last the discoorse athin which Ah place masel. This is the tradeetion o dialectology an lexicography gaein back tae Murray (1873). This is marginalised tae, be the sociolinguistic discoorse, bit hes had a heeze fae the Scottish Pairlament, which has biggit up the heritage aspeck o the leid.

Creetics micht see this as **a gless-case approach**. There obvious parellels atween dictionars an museums, an Ah wad claim at the Scottish National Dictionary Association (SNDA), lik modren museums, hes made a successfu transeetion fae a stoory curatorial role tae yin o ootreach an the biggin up o the culture. Like museums they hae had tae switch fae a rhetoric o curatin byganes tae projeckin – if no sellin – cultural heritage.

This conservation approach is a wee oot o kilter wi the discoorse o leid plannin an aw. The feerin for the SNDA's pleuch is whit Ah cry 'flexible staunardisation'. For instance, the SNDA continues tae include regional variants, no juist i the academic dictionars bit i the schuil anes. This openness tae the regional dialecks is a feature o *The Kist* anaw (the anthology o Scottish lecterature wi teachin materials, pitten oot be the SCCC). It is therefore, it seems tae me, awreadies pairt o the evolvin offeecial consensus, gin it maks ony sense tae spick o sic a thing. Ah think we are noo seein a maturity i the Scottish approach, efter three-quarters o a century – a readiness tae jouk the mair deeficult an divisive elements o the minority leid discoorse, an no gae peltin uphill, baldy-heidit, efter parity wi Inglis.

References

Abercrombie, David (1992) "Sociolinguistics and British dialects" in Claudia Blank *et al.* eds *Language and Civilisation. A Concerted Profusion of Essays and Studies in Honour of Otto Hietsch* Frankfurt: Peter Lang, 6-10.

Agutter, Alexandra and L. N. Cowan (1981) "Changes in the vocabulary of Lowland Scots dialects", *Scottish Literary Journal* Supplement 14, 49-62.

Aitken, A. J. (1979) "Scottish speech: a historical view with special reference to the Standard English of Scotland" in A. J. Aitken and Tom McArthur eds. *Languages of Scotland* Edinburgh: Chambers, 85-118.

Aitken, A. J. (1982) "Bad Scots: some superstitions about Scots speech", *Scottish Language* 1, 30-44.
Donaldson, William (1986) *Popular Literature in Victorian Scotland. Language, Fiction and the Press* Aberdeen University Press.
Fishman, Joshua (1991) *Reversing Language Shift* Clevedon: Multilingual Matters.
Görlach, Manfred (2000) "Ulster Scots: a language?" in John M. Kirk and Dónall P. Ó Baoill eds. *Language and Politics. Northern Ireland, the Republic of Ireland, and Scotland* Belfast: Queen's University, 13-31.
Graham, John (1979) *The Shetland Dictionary* Stornoway: Thule.
Hardie, Kim (1997) "Lowland Scots: Language Politics and Identity" unpublished University of Edinburgh PhD thesis.
Hendry, Ian (1997) "Doric - an Investigation into its Use amongst Primary School Children in the North East of Scotland", unpublished University of Aberdeen MLitt thesis.
Hettinga, J. (1981) "Standard and dialect in Anstruther and Cellardyke", *Scottish Literary Journal,* Supplement 14, 37-48.
Kloss, Heinz (1967) "'Abstand languages' and 'Ausbau languages'", *Anthropological Linguistics* 9: 7, 29-41.
Kloss, Heinz (1978) *Die Entwicklung neuer germanischer Kultursprachen seit 1800,* 2nd. edn., Dusseldorf: Schwann.
Kloss, Heinz (1986) "Interlingual communication: danger and chance for the smaller tongues" in Dietrich Strauss and Horst Drescher eds. *Scottish language and Literature, Medieval and Renaissance: Fourth International Conference, 1984, Proceedings* Frankfurt: Peter Lang, 73-77.
Lawrie, Susan (1991) "A linguistic survey of the use of Scottish dialect items in North-East Fife", *Scottish Language* 10, 18-29.
Löw, Danielle (1997) "The Doric in Pitmedden: Language Attitudes in a Scottish Village" unpublished dissertation, Ruprecht-Karls-Universität Heidelberg.
Löw, Danielle (2001) "Language attitudes in Pitmedden (Aberdeenshire): Some findings on instrumental and affective/integrative attitudes" in John M. Kirk and Dónall P. Ó Baoill eds. *Language Links: The Languages of Scotland and Ireland* Belfast: Queen's University, 133-148.
Macafee, Caroline (1994) *Traditional Dialect in the Modern World: A Glasgow Case Study* Frankfurt: Peter Lang.
Macafee, Caroline (1997) "Ongoing change in Modern Scots: the social dimension" in Charles Jones ed. *The Edinburgh History of the Scots Language* Edinburgh University Press, 514-550.
Macafee, Caroline (2000a) "The demography of Scots: the lessons of the Census campaign", *Scottish Language* 19, 1-44.
Macafee, Caroline (2000b) "Lea the leid alane", *Lallans* 57, 56-63.
Macafee, Caroline (forthcoming) "Studying Scots vocabulary" in John Corbett *et al.* eds. *The Edinburgh Student Companion to Scots* Edinburgh University Press.
Macafee, Caroline and McGarrity, Briege (1999) "Scots language attitudes and language maintenance" in *Leeds Studies in English* 30, 165-179.

Macaulay, Ronald K. S. with the assistance of G. D. Trevelyan (1977) *Language, Social Class and Education. A Glasgow Study* Edinburgh University Press.

McGarrity, Briege (1998) "A Sociolinguistic Study of Attitudes towards and Proficiency in the Doric Dialect in Aberdeen", unpublished University of Aberdeen MPhil thesis.

[Máté, Ian] (1996) *Scots Language GRO(S). A Report on the Scots Language Research carried out by the General Register Office For Scotland in 1996* Edinburgh: The General Register Office For Scotland.

Melchers, Gunnel (1999) "Patterns of variation in a bidialectal community: the case of Shetland", paper given to the 10th International Conference on Methods in Dialectology, Newfoundland, 1999.

Menzies, Janet (1991) "An investigation of attitudes to Scots and Glasgow dialect among secondary school pupils", *Scottish Language* 10, 30-46.

Middleton, Sheena (1999) *Doric: the Cock of the North: Points of View on a Linguistic Compass: Interviews with North East Folk* Elphinstone Institute, University of Aberdeen.

Murdoch, Steve (1995) *Language Politics in Scotland* Aberdeen: Aberdeen University Scots Leid Quorum.

Murdoch, Steve and Gordon, R. (1995) "The Language in Politics Data-base", Aberdeen: Aberdeen University Scots Leid Quorum.

Murray, James (1873) *The Dialect of the Southern Counties of Scotland* London: Philological Society.

Nässén, Greger (1989) "Norn. The Scandinavian element in Shetland dialect" Report 3 "Norn weather words. 323 meteorological terms in Jakobsen's dictionary and their extent in present-day Shetland dialect", Department of English, Stockholm University.

Pollner, Clausdirk (1985) "Old words in a young town", *Scottish Language* 4, 5-15.

Review of Scottish Culture Group (1998) "Scottish culture and the curriculum. A report to the Scottish Consultative Council on the Curriculum from the Review of Scottish Culture Group", leaked report.

Scotland in the Schools. A Report on the Scottish Content of our Education (1953) Edinburgh: The Saltire Society.

Stewart, William (1968) "A sociolinguistic typology for describing national multilingualism", in Joshua Fishman ed. *Readings in the Sociology of Language* The Hague: Mouton, 531-545.

Wickens, B. (1980, 1981) "Caithness speech", *Scottish Literary Journal* Supplement 12, 61-76; Supplement 14, 25-36.

Wilson, James (1926) *The Dialects of Central Scotland* London: Oxford University Press.

Young, Douglas (1949) *The Use of Scots for Prose* Greenock: John Galt Lecture for 1949.

Wha Ye Writin For?

Andy Eagle

Scots is nou an offeecial recogneezed langage.[1] Gin a bodie taks sic recogneetion tae be mair nor 'lip service', it wad implee the revival process tae be mair nor juist encouragin spoken Scots whither in the media or in the commonty. It implees that Scots can be uised as an ilka day ubiquitous alternative tae English. The European Chairter[2] (Pairt II Airticle 7 pynt d) itsel implees forderin in the uiss o written Scots, no juist for a puckle local ditties an couthie rhymes, but for aw kin kynd o writin, exposeetion, nairative an reportin an sae on. An nou that an element o Scots is tae be pairt o the schuil curriculum, schuil beuks in Scots wad be the logical oncome. Ower an ayont thon demaunds is bein made for public signage in Scots. Cultural tourism mebbes bein o interest here. For aw that it wad seem some kin o pan-dialect furm for formal writin is obligatory. Gin no, formal writin wad bide the privilege o English. The thocht bein that the mair veesible the uiss o written Scots for mair nor couthie rhymes an humourous stories the mair liken fowk micht be tae uise Scots in seetiations whaur thay nou tend tae gang ower intae English. O coorse, onie furm o formal written Scots, shoudna or winna hinder thaim that conceeders thairsels 'creative writers' daein as thay please. Tho e'en here some writers micht uise the formal written furm for the nairative an juist be 'creative' whan it comes tae dialog. The wiss tae pit ower the local soond an identity o the chairacter, compeart wi the neutralness o the formal written furm.

Altho langage plannin is for ordinar conceedert tae be reddin up some kin o normative grammar an an orthography for writers an speakers in a nane-homogenous speech-commonty. Haein a formal pan-dialect furm o written Scots wad juist hae adae wi raiglarizin orthographic practice, no langage staundartisation. The grammar differs atween the Scots dialects isna eneuch tae scomfish comprehension atween speakers. Onie gremmar wad an shoud be descreeptive oniewey. Fowk coud uise thair ain ilka day grammar athoot bein feart fae it bein 'wrang'. Maist o the pronunciation differs atween Scots dialects is aften pit ower as a raison hou a pan-dialect orthography isna possible. Monie o thir differs is predeectable, an it wad be nae surpreese gin siclike myths is pitten aboot for tae hinder haein a pan-dialect furm o written Scots – a thrait tae the staus quo?

Ae strynd o thinkin taks the view it wad be eneuch juist tae haud wi a 'lassez faire' approach whaur fowk juist writes hou thay perceive thair vyce tae soond. Sic like tends tae owerstress dialect differs. The kinch wi this is that it leads fowk tae identifee mair wi thair ain dialect as agin the concept o Scots as a naitional, or aiblins wi Ulster Scots a trans-naitional langage. The ootcome o

---

[1] European Charter for Regional or Minority Languages. For the U.K. in effect fae 01.07.01 http://conventions.coe.int/Treaty/EN/cadreprincipal.htm
[2] As pynt 1 abuin.

this can be linguistic localisation mairchin on isolationism an langage internal insularity. Acceptin a 'lassez faire' approach for offeecial an eddicational maiter wad implee haein a wheen versions o awthing sae as no tae affront onie parteeclar airt. This isna like tae gang doun weel wi a bawbee coontin admeenistration. Economies o scale wad demaund 'ae size fits aw'. It's no the cost o prentin anither copy that's the haud-back but the cost o haein tae redd a wheen different versions. Localised creative writin is guid an fine but gin the revivalist ettle is tae hae public signage an offeecial maiter etc. set furth in Scots, an bairns in schuils bein teached no juist hou tae read, but hou tae write Scots - no juist writin for a local audience but for a naitional ane an aw – wad aw implee haein a formal furm o written Scots that encourages fowk tae see thair ain leid as pairt a naitional langage an no juist as a hamelt byleid.

Ither fowk pits forrit that spellin conventions fae middle Scots shoud be inrowed an conventions that's unique tae English shoud be evitit. The threap bein that the orthography shoud pit ower the langage status o Scots bi bein heteromorphic tae English. Firstlins naebodie speaks middle Scots oniemair an maist fowk isna fameeliar wi the spellin conventions o middle Scots, aft representin pronunciations that dinna kythe onie mair. Ee'n middle Scots wis influenced bi English orthographic practice. Seicontlie the threap aboot gien the status o the leid a heeze is haivers. A heeze in whase een? Thaim that awreadies haes a guid conceit o Scots isna needin tae be persuadit an the nairae nebbit arna gaun tae chynge thair wey o thinkin juist acause written Scots leuks awfu fremmit.

Syne the union o baith Crouns an Pairlaments a state o diglossia haes kythed in lawland Scotland an Ulster forby. Whaur ae langage 'English' haes taen on the functions o the 'heich langage' bein uised bi state offeecials, eddication an for writin an sae on. The tither 'Scots' taen on the functions o the 'laich langage' for ordinar uised alanerlie in speech an informal circumstances. Scots bein sib til English, it haesna stuiden up sae weel agin English influence on it speech furms as Erse haes. An the day it canna honestly be threapit that onie furm o contemporar spoken Scots functions as an autonomous langage.

Sic like facts is chiels that winna ding an shoud be taen intae accoont whan reddin a formal furm o written Scots. The furm shoud be fameeliar tae thaim that speaks the langage. Monie Scots speakers is mair or less acquent wi post-union Scots as written bi Burns, Fergusson, Stevenson, Scott an ithers forby. Thair writin o coorse aft uised 'English' spellins, but at the time thae writers kent fou-weel that thair readership wadna pronounce it onie ither wey but Scots. Siclike disna haud true the day wi mass inlat tae the soond o spoken English, but aw the same monie o thair tradeetional conventions can be applee'd for tae evite onie perceived misunnerstaundins athoot makkin written Scots leuk fremmit.

The fact that Scots an English mixter-maxters awfu weel is a 'prima facie' case for haein a spellin seestem that allous fowk tae mixter-maxter Scots an 'English' athoot the 'perceived' Scots element staundin oot lik the proverbial sair thoum. Siclike gies written Scots, whither dense or no, a homogenous leuk. On the eddicational side siclike wad aft evite haein twa spellins for the ae wird altho thay're pronounced the same in baith Scots an English. Mair oot ower, fremmit fowk fae abreed that haes the English micht be willint tae ettle a bittie for tae acquire a ken o Scots gin it leuks sib til a tongue thay ken awreadies. Some wad threap that this approach is juist bouin doun tae Anglo-centric thocht-haunts plantit bi the 'Scots' eddication seestem. Weel its no, its alanerlie pragmatic. The mair eith readin an writin Scots can be learnt the mair likely thaim that speaks it will mak the effort necessar. Its no likely that thaim that haes owerance ower the nation's bawbees will pit a lot o siller tae learin Scots. Thair conceit o language is ane o economic utalitarianism. Tae thaim Scots disna hae onie economic utility, an till thay're persuadit ither, thay're no like tae chynge thair conceit.

Tae maist ordinar fowk deriviations fae the 'English' spellin seestem learnt at the schuil is aft confuisin, disturbin an no walcome. Speed o reception is reduced bi unfameeliar wird eemages, the message michtna be received or misread e'en whan it conforms tae thair ain pronunciation. The acceptit tradeetion in oor pairt o the warld is that the state caws cannie whan it comes tae cultural maiters an taks a back seat sae the state isna likely tae dictate whit Scots orthography shoud or shoudna be. Onie pan-dialect orthography wad hae tae tak tent tae the fact that whan it come tae siclike maist fowk is awfu conservative an is sweir tae tak tae that, that thay dinna ken.

Uta Frith[3] argied that fowk tends tae write bi lug an read bi ee – that is fowk flits fae the veesible letter-sequences tae the greein vocabular items hained in thair harns athoot phonic mediation. Frith did an experiment whaur fowk read sentences distortit in twa weys:

1. A robln hoppeb up to my windcw.
2. A robbin hoppt up to my winndo.

Frith fund that sieven year auld bairns an, surpreesin eneuch, growen-ups haed mair problems readin 2 nor 1. In 1 the leuk o the sentence is aye still thare tho some letters wis replaced bi veesually seemilar anes. In 2 the leuk o the sentence is mair thrawn, tho the phoneme/grapheme correspondence rules o English wad implee an undistortit pronunciation. Frith's experiment shaws that fowk is mair liken tae tak tae an orthography whaur the '*Schriftbild*' (wird-pictur) is fameeliar.

Altho Frith's experiment wis foondit on English, it dis shaw that monie fowk finds ower 'phonetic' writin haurd tae follae. Ae argiement pitten forrit for 'phonetic' furms is that learners wadna pronounce it richt. Is the pynt o written Scots tae gar nane-speakers wi a ken o the soond tae letter correspondences o staundart English come oot wi something akin tae Scots whan thay read it loud oot? Shuirlie the pynt o onie furm o written Scots is tae ser the needs o native speakers an no the learner. Haes onie ither language redd its orthography sae that monoglot English speakers micht pronounce it richt whan readin it lood oot? Monie dis ettle at some kin o 'perfit' written 'phonetic'

---

[3] Expoondit in Sampson, G. (1985) p. 208

representation o actual speech this is aye dingit doun bi the naitur o the sindrie strynds o Scots an the Roman ABC. Siclike maks e'en a tholable accurate 'phonetic representation' difficult tae win at an whit is wun at is mair lik some kin o code nor a leid native speakers wad recogneeze. Thay dinna identifee wi't an micht think thay dinna speak Scots – pittin aff the verra fowk langage-upsteerers is ettlin at inrowin.

Ower pedantic 'phonetic' orthographies pits aff fowk. Fowks that's pitten aff isna likely tae mak the effort nott tae learn siccan orthography. The preenciple ahint the orthography shoud be tae pit ower the information that the reader needs[4], nae mair an nae less. This shoud be foondit on the 'English' rules o readin that the reader kens sae that unnecessar information isna includit. Unnerwritten featurs micht coud pit ower the conceit that the langage an its speakers isna o muckle wirth - the langage isna awfu important. Ower written features micht be taen as a compliment tae the leid but aften comes ower as pedantic an e'en heich heidit. Sic like aft leads tae some fowk makin a gype o't, tho monie o thaim hauds Scots in distain oniewey sae it wad be pytnless bein fasht bi siclike. Thay wad aiblins tak a rise o onie furm o Scots. Langage-upsteerers shoud see the sibness atween written Scots an English as a strenth an no a weakness. Ye'll no can stop fowk mellin whit's perceived as 'English' intae Scots, but ye coud mell Scots intae English athoot it lowpin aff the blad acause o its fremmit leuk - Scotticisation bi stealth.

As mentiont abuin, monie Scots speakers is acquent wi the Scots orthographic tradeetions uised bi Burns etc. It is this tradeetional model that's maist weel-kent amang Scots speakin fowk an pragmatic logic wad dictate that this tradeetional model shoud be the foonds o a formal furm o written Scots. Monie o the tradeetional practices thairsels is diaphonemic, ithers is whiles morphological an etymological, servin the moniefauld predeectable pronunciation differs athort Scots dialects. This aiblins shaws hou siclike writers wis, an tae a certain extent, aye is sae popular amang Scots speakers nae maiter whit thair hamelt airt. Thay coud aw read an identifee wi't nae bother.

In maist aa leeterate kintras written formal furms o the language aye shaws less variation nor the spoken furms, written Scots o coorse disna necessar hae tae be sae strict. Thare's nae raison whit for it coudna thole sindrie variants that disna fit intae a diaphonemic orthography, formal Scots bein kin o poly-centric. The diaphonemic an morphological spellins actin as a coonter-wecht hinderin formal Scots fae gaun oot o ither intae a hatter o dialect strynds.

O coorse, monie fowk finds readin Scots difficult, e'en an orthography sib til that o English canna me maistert athoot a meenimal o lear whither in the schuil or fae beuks. The less lear necessar the better. It's o coorse in the schuil that the maist best chances lies for instillin the orthography on a upcomin generation o Scots speakers an writers. Thare's thaim that's set agin the teachin o onie furm o Scots, for ordinar threapin that its a haud-back tae the learnin o 'richt' English. It's for that verra raison, amang ithers, that langage-upsteerers shoud be threapin for mair proveeision for the teachin o Scots. Akis o whit's

---

[4] See Haugen, E (1980) in *Dialekt und Dialektologie* pp. 275-276

cried interference, Scots speakin fowk's English grammar is aft coloured bi Scots furms akis thay'v seendle been shawn the differ atween the twa. Lairin bairns the differs atween English an Scots bi compearin the linguistic seestems o baith tongues, an mebbe a puckle ither sib tongues forby, wad no juist better thair unnerstaundin o whit baith Scots an English is, but upbig thair abeelitie an skeel in learnin ither fremmit tongues. In thon wey, thaim that's fleetchin agin haein Scots teached in the schuils, winna juist be fleetchin agin learin Scots but agin giein bairns a guid commaund o English an aw. Mair oot ower thay'll be hinderin bairns haein a grundit inlat intae the learnin o ither fremmit tongues. Siclike argiements taks the wind oot the sails o thaim that wad want tae pit the upsteerers' gas at the peep.

Ayont the abuin, a mention maun be gien tae a puckle weys that wirds is whiles spelt that seems tae ser nae ither purpose nor tae produce a hyper-phonetic maximal differentiation fae English. An is tae aw effects nocht mair nor sair on the een 'ee-dialect' that aft maks readin Scots mair an exerceese in code-brakkin nor semple readin.

Firtlins[5] is thon cless o wirds that's aften written wi sae monie spellins as thare is pronunciations. Thir wird's pronunciations differs accordin tae 'emphasis'. For ordinar auxiliar verbs, personal an relative pronoons, a wheen conjunctions, a puckle adverbs an some lexemes. The pronunciation o thaim canna be predictit wi onie accuracy sae convention wad implee uisin the ae 'strang' spellin when writin sic 'weak' furms in formal Scots. The Roman ABC bi its naitur disna hae a grapheme for thir 'soonds' oniewey an it's weel seen that nane o the vouel graphemes we hae tae haund is mair better nor onie ither for pittin the soond ower. Native speakers wad gie thaim the richt stress oniewey. Ensaumples o thir is:

> *thair*: *thir, thur,*
> *thaim*: *thum, em,*
> *wis*: *wiz, wes, wus,*
> *for*: *fer, fir, fur,*
> *are*: *ir, ur,*
> *your / yer*: *yur, yir,* etc.

Seicontlie[6] comes writin that draps letters atween wirds acause o phonetic paitrens whaur wirds is pronounced different in connectit speech nor when thay're pronounced alane. Siclike is aft 'heard' when wirds rins thegither an consonant clusters kythes that canna be pronounced, thir is o coorse semplifee'd in speech.

For ensaumple /t/ an /d/ is aft drappit when thay kythe in the mids o consonant cluster, for ordinar when /t/ follaes a stop or fricative an /d/ follaes an approximant:

---

[5] Discussed in McClure, J.D. (1997) " in *Englishes around the World I* pp. 173-184.

[6] Expoondit in Hawkins, P. (1984) pp.162-192

Auld /ɑld/ auld man /ɑl man/
Daft /daft/ daft days /daf dez/
First /fʌrst/ first ten /fʌrs tɛn/
Juist /jɪst/ juist nou /jɪs nu/
Saft /saft/ saft pillae /saf pɪle/

An affcome o monie 'lay-fowk' observin siclike is spellins that's "jiss plain daf".

Thirdlie comes spellins uisin <z> whaur Scots tradeetionally aye haed <s>. e.g. diz for daes, giez for gie's, uz an iz for is, jalooze for jalouse, sez, sayz an saiz for says, wiz an wuz for wis etc. This is o coorse nocht mair nor 'ee-dialect'. Thair's phonological rules[7] ahint this that's maistert bi native speakers athoot haein tae think on it.

An finally the uiss o a medial <ei> whaur aw dialects haes /i/ maks written Scots seem fremmit tae monie fowk Obviously duin bi analogy wi the kenspeckle central Scots pronunciation o *breid, deid, deif* an *heid* etc. Tho some dialects further north haes /e/ in thae wirds. An, debatable it micht be, whan this is duin alang wi the uiss o final <ie> whaur fowk is mair acquent wi <y> - it can lead tae "incomprehensabeilitie".[8]

The abuin juist shaws a puckle writin practises that monie a native speaker finds sair o the een. Oniebodie that's interestit in writin Scots shoud aye ask thirsels "wha ye writin for?" A wee curn enthusiasts or Scots speakers as a hail?

References

Allan, Alasdair (1995) "Scots spellin - ettlin efter the quantum lowp", *English World-Wide* 16:1, 61-103.

Haugen, Einar (1980) "How Should A Dialect Be Written?" in *Dialekt und Dialektologie*: Ergebnisse d. Internationalen Symposions 'Zur Theorie des Dialekts', Marburg/Lahn, 5. - 10. Sept. 1977 / hrsg. von Joachim Göschel ... . - Wiesbaden: Steiner.

Hawkins, Peter (1984) *Introducing Phonology* London: Hutchinson.

Kavanagh, James F. and Venezky, Richard L. (eds) (1980) *Orthography, Reading and Dyslexia* Baltimore: University Park Press.

Lallans 56, (2000) 'Walit frae the Report o the Scots Spellin Comatee', 51-106.

Lallans 57 (2000), 'Sindrie views anent Report o the Scots Spellin Comatee', 48-73.

Luelsdorff, Philip A. (Ed.) (1987) *Orthography and Phonology*, Amsterdam: Benjamins.

---

[7] Expoondit in Hawkins, P. (1984) pp.127-128
[8] *Lallans,* Nummer 56 Voar 2000 p.94

McClure, J. Derrick (1981) "The spelling of Scots: a phoneme-based system", *Scottish Literary Journal* Supplement 12, 25-29.

McClure, J. Derrick (1985, 1995) "The debate on Scots orthography" in J. Derrick McClure *Scots and its Literature*, Amsterdam: Benjamins, 37-43. Originally published in Manfred Görlach ed. *Focus on: Scotland*, Amsterdam: Benjamins, 203-209.

McClure, J. Derrick (1997) "The spelling of Scots: a difficulty" in Edgar Schneider ed. *Englishes around the World I. General Studies, British Isles, North America. Studies in Honour of Manfred Görlach*, Amsterdam/Philadelphia: Benjamins (1997), 173-184. Price, Glanville (2000), *Languages in Britain and Ireland*, Oxford.

Purves, David (1979) "A Scots orthography", *Scottish Literary Journal* Supplement 9, 61-76.

Sampson, Geoffrey (1985) *Writing Systems*, London: Hutchinson.

Scragg, Donald G. (1974) *A History of English Spelling* Manchester: Univ. Pr. Barnes & Noble .

Ulster-Scots: Politicisation or Survival?

Ian Parsley

The forehannd pynt A wid be for makan in ma inpit tae this edeetion wid be at the
steerars o Ulster Scots haes a chyce – 'politicization or survival'. Sae this isna
juist a moral chyce o forderan the leid sae as aa can uise it (an no juist Protestants
or unionists), but it is a strecht chyce atween uisean the leid as a poleetical fitbaa
an watchan it die, or takan the leid awa frae politics an politics awa frae the leid,
sae giean it a chance o survival.
    A wis for giean ensamples frae screeds as haes been sat furth in 'Ullans'
no sae lang syne, but A am thinkan, ithergates in this edeetion, Dauvit Horsbroch
an Andy Eagle haes ay shawed whitwey monie sic texts gaes agin the tradeetions
o guid Scots writein on the baith sides o the Sheuch. Sae A am blythe juist uisean
this inlet tae mak a conclusion tae aa at wis said in their inpits an ithers anent the
qualitie (or want o it) o modern writein in Scots. Mairatowre, we hae haen the
inlet o heiran frae ithergates in Europe about the oncum o ither leids in seemilar
situations, an A cud aiblans mak comment about thaim anaa.
    Gif we stairt wi a wee keek at whit the Lord Laird allous in his inpit, we
sud tak tent o an tae the commeetment o the Ulster Scots Agentrie tae
'inclusiveness' an 'impartiality'. A cudna say but onie richt thinkan steerar at bes
wirkan for the guid o the Scots tongue aagates wid gree at the fen o the leid
lippens tae sicna commeetment. The oncum o the leid maun be daen for the guid
o ane an aa, no juist for an aefauld group. Deed, 'inclusiveness' an 'impartiality'
wid be the lane road foreairt.
    But we hae seen monie 'Ullans' screeds (comprehendan ane in ma ither
inpit tae this edeetion) daesna tak tent o thon commeetment, an the ar policies for
the oncum o the leid forby as canna be seen tae gae wi it. A guid Scots text, nae
maitter whilk byleid ye ar for writean it in, maun be recogneesable tae the fowk it
is made for (sae 'inclusive' an 'impartial') – thaim as taaks the tongue forordinar.
For this tae be sae, the makar maun gae wi a mixter maxter o the tradeetions o the
leid in its leeteratur an the wey fowk taaks the tongue thenou, aa in wi an aefauld
conseestant seistem. A gaes mair wi the 'mixter' o the tradeetions, an A wid allou
at the maist fek Scots taakars can unnerstannd near aa A writes forordinar. In his
ain writein, Fenton gaes mair wi the 'maxter' o the modren uiss o the tongue, an
the fowk he is for representan in his wark (the guidfowk in rural airts o the
Countie Antrim) wid hae nae problems unnerstanndan him. (For thaim no
acquent wi his wark, his wirdbeuk[1] haes brocht tears tae the een o monie fowk for
thay cud recogneese thair ain wey o taakin athin it, an his poetrie (on kisties lyke

---

[1] James Fenton, *The Hamely Tongue: A Personal Record of Ulster-Scots in
County Antrim.* Newtownards: Ulster-Scots Academic Press, 1995; Second
Edition, Belfast: The Ullans Press 2000.

Thonner an Thon[2]) gaes up wi the best in the Ulster Scots tradeetion – tho course he made it foremaist for fowks ears, no for thair een.)

The ar fowk wid aiblans allou thay hae nae need for gan wi the tradeetions o guid Scots writein for thay ar writean 'Ulster Scots', no 'Scots'. Sic taak canna gae wi nae comment.

- The laa taaks o Ulster Scots 'understood to be a variant of the Scots language spoken in parts of Northern Ireland and County Donegal';
- Scots haes the ae leeterar tradeetion – the *stannart habbie* verse form an sic spellins as 'mair' an 'nae' is pairt o a differ leeteratur tradeetion frae the Inglis, but the ar nae sic differ atween Orr or Porter in Ulster an Burns or Ramsay in Scotlann;
- Nae linguist cud allou the ar mair differ atween Ulster Scots an ither byleids o Scots bys the ar atween American Inglis an Britis Inglis;
- 'Unit we stannds, divid we faas': naebodie allous the ar nae differ ava atween Ulster Scots an ither byleids (for ensample, in Ulster A taak<u>s</u> Scots wi a habitual anaa, but in Scotlann thay speak it wi nae habitual!)

Sae the laa, the tradeetions o the tongue, the linguists an the practicalities aa gaes agin the notion we hae twa saiparit Scots leids – but naebodie wid gae agin fowk as bes for takan pride in thair ain dialect o Scots, sae bean thaim wi the pouer for sairan the Scots tongue taks tent at thir is aa dialects o the ae historical an tradeetional tongue. But thaim as gaes wi the fair notion o the ae saiparit leid can taak o a leid at haes a Bible translation[3], a weel kent leeteratur tradeetion (Burns), an influence tae the Inglis ('weird', 'eerie', 'daft' etc), an a linguistic influence tae the cultur o the warld (near aa the terms o gowf, for ensample). A bodie canna allou siclyke for Ulster Scots alane. Oniehou, wid it no be mair 'inclusive' an 'impartial' tae tak tent o whit bes a-dae in Scotlann sae as Scots can tak pairt? Ar we for bearan the gree for pittan Scots intae the seistem o lear in Airlann but no dae the lyke in Scotlann, wid it no be better wirkan thegither an bean 'inclusive'?

But the ar fowk yet as wid reject sic evidence an practicalitie, an gae on writean thair ain saiparit 'leid' for Ulster, unner the poleetical motivation sae as 'Ulster Scots' (or ein juist 'Ulster Protestants') haes thair ain leid (lyke the sae cried 'Irish' haes). An thay ar wunnert hou fowk allous it wid be juist a 'DIY language for Orangemen', but thay maun tak action tae shaw that isna the wey o it! The outcum o the attempt tae mak a differ atween 'Ullans' an 'Scots' bes aften juist haivers, a leid wi vague founs on the leeteratur o Scots but at bes nae mair nor a mixter maxter o Belfast Inglis dialect, Scots terms lang syne deid (aften uised wrang forby), an invention. Takan juist the first blad o an aefauld text, we hae differ spellins o the ae etymological souns, uiss o wirds an spellins frae

---

[2] James Fenton, *Thonner an Thon: An Ulster-Scots Collection*. Belfast: The Ullans Press, 2000.

[3] W.L. Lorimer, *The New Testament in Scots*. Edinburgh: Mercat Press, 1984

Elizabethan Inglis (sae muckle as Middle Scots), paraphrases as juist besna necessar, an basic mistaks in grammar (sae it souns mair Inglis nor Scots). An the makars o sic haivers haesna taen tent o the auld maxim 'the job o the translatear wid be translatean whit kythes in the text, no whit thay wid be for kythean thar!' The outcum canna richtlie cum unner the heidins o 'inclusiveness' or 'impartiality', gif ein the taakars haes nae notion o whit bes a-dae wi thair ain leid!

The fowk as cam up wi thon wey o writein (an a bodie cudna richtlie cry it a 'seistem') wis aiblans for giean 'Ullans' a nue register. Thay daen that aaricht! But it isna ane at ansuers the need for a formal register, mair ane at wid ansuer better the caa heirt at this confeerence for an airtificial langage at cud cum the warld leid! Mebbe, braid the Baa, siclyke wid 'apen the daeins for tae insense us aa intae ettlin til a roadin for the graithin o fowkgates an billiehoods' or ocht seemilar? A hae ma douts the lyke wid be conseedered 'inclusive' or 'impartial'!

Nae dout sic haivers is the outcum o anither kin poleetical motivation for tae shaw 'Ullans' is juist sae differ frae the Inglis bys the Earse (a poleetical motivation shawan nae dedication tae 'inclusiveness' or 'impartiality'). But, weel, it juist isna! A bodie canna get awa frae the common springheid o the baith leids, an tryan tae gae agin this pynt juist gies ammunition tae thaim as wid ding doun the claim o Scots tae status as a leid. Gan owre the score an settan haivers furth as confounds ein the tongues ain uisears daes skaith tae the leid on baith sides o the Sheuch – steerars mebbe haes the richt tae dae aa thay ar for daean in Airlann, but whan it aa haes an ill impact on Scotlann forby it is tyme tae say 'nae mair'!

But hou can A allou siclyke about a leid wantan a stannart written form? Ay, the ar nae 'richt' or 'wrang' wi the Scots tongue, but the ar 'authentic Scots' an 'no authentic Scots'. The haill pynt o leid status is at the ar sicna thing as 'Admeenistrative Scots' (at wis uised in the first Pairlament o Scotlann), sicna thing as 'Guid Scots' (for formal uiss), sicna thing as 'General Scots' (at cud comprehend echtie per cent o the owreaa vocabular frae last surveys frae the SNDA), an sicna thing as 'Gutter Scots'. A bodie canna ignore siclyke an allou thay ar writean 'richt' or 'authentic' Scots. Scots haes its ain lang written tradeetion, an wirkan furth o sic tradeetions juist shaws fowk contermit at the leid bes aucht thaim, an no its ain taakars. Fowk maun tak tent o thae tradeetions. Juist lyke onie ither leid, gif a bodie isna sicar about a term or a wird or a grammatical pynt, thay canna juist mak it up! Thay taks a keek in the dictionar or better yet, wi the want o prescriptive dictionars for the Scots tongue, thay speirs at a bodie at kens! That wey ye gets written screeds as bes 'inclusive' an 'impartial', for aabodie can unnerstannd thaim richtlie. For taakars knaws fine weel whitwey a bodie maks the differ atween makars as haes a feelin for the leid, an thaim as haesna.

The pynt wid be at Scots besna sae faur awa frae a written stannart. The 'niffer' o emails atween Scots taakars brocht on frae the oncum o the Wab (on sic listies as *lallans-l*, *lowlands-l* an *ullans-l*) haes gien fowk the inlet tae see the wey ither fowk writes the leid, an tak tent o 'best practice'. Naebodie haes onie problems unnerstanndan oniebodie else, an nou the ar, at maist, twathree differ options for an aefauld wird.

Nou, the ar nae appearant strategie a-dae wi the Ulster Scots muivement as a haill – taak o the 'forder' o the leid gies nae idea whit the exact tairgets wid be. This juist lats fowk be thinkan the tairget wid be poleetical. For tae be richtlie 'inclusive' an 'impartial', fowk is needan tae set an exact tairget at canna be seen tae be poleetical, an we hae heirt twa ensamples o siclyke in this edeetion. Frae Kevin McCafferty in Norroway we hae a warnin at onie 'stannart' written form canna be owre far frae the wey fowk knaws the tongue aareddies – sae no owre far frae the leeteratur. We maun caw cannie wi makan equeevalents, but, for the poleetical grunds for the oncum o *Nynorsk* wis, or sud be, differ frae the social grunds for the oncum o Ulster Scots. Frae Andeas Fischer (in this edeetion anaa), we haen an ensample o a gey strang leid, the Swiss German, at cam sae strang wi nae stannart written form ava. A dout we can learn frae that. At least afore tryan tae cum tae greeance anent a stannart, fowk is needan tae decide juist for why thay ar needan ane.

For aa that, onie deceesions anent the final 'authenteecitie' o the leid in writein an tairgets sat for it lies wi the taakars thaimsels. For ensample, in Omagh Juin 2000 Professor Michael Montgomery (President o the Ulster Scots Leid Associe) said 'the futur o the leid lippens tae its ain taakars'. Donall Ó Riagáin haes made the pynt at Ulster Scots is cum sae far in ten yeir as the maist fek minoritie leids in fiftie. An som wise bodie cried Ian Parsley gart fowk tak tent o the differ atween the steerars an the taakars baith in Airlann an Scotlann, twa saiparit groups. A wid be aa for writean nou at fowk taen tent o aa thae pynts, but unfortunatlik A canna. The poleetical side in Norlin Airlann, wi tryan tae shaw a saiparit leid frae the Scots o Scotlann an a leid sae differ frae the Inglis as possible, is takan owre an wirkan strecht agin the Ulster Scots Agentries ain heid values o 'inclusiveness' an 'impartiality'. The linguistic outcum is written screeds as haes nae real grunds in the tradeetions o the written leid an o nae uiss ava tae the modren taakars o the leid. No tae be ane o thae wid mebbe be unfortunat, but no tae be aither leuks lyke caurlessness!

A bodie cudna say but the Ulster Scots tongue is nou poleeticised – 'part of the problem, not part of the solution'. The wey fowk writes it aften shaws a tairget o a leid for Ulster Protestants – gif that isna the wey o it, hou wid fowk no tak tent o the tradeetions o the tongue an the inlets as wid cum frae wirkan thegither wi Scotlann? Hou wid thay tak nae tent ava o the wark o linguists an thaim as taaks the leid forordinar? Sic want o tent wid be a threat tae the Scots leid, no juist in Airlann but in Scotlann forby. The lane wey for survival wid be 'depoliticization', an the lane wey for 'depoliticization' wid be wirkan thegither wi thaim as kens the eesues a-dae wi sic complicate maitters in an 'inclusive' an 'impartial' wey. Deed, 'inclusiveness' an 'impartiality' is the lane wey foreairt for 'depoliticization', an sae 'survival'. We ar needan chynges sae as that cums the case, an Ulster Scots can ay be 'part of the solution, not part of the problem'.

Authenticity of Scots

Ian Parsley

We have heard a lot at this Conference, as we do at any conference of this nature, about the so-called 'process of standardisation'. There is no right answer to the problem. Caroline Macafee has made a strong case against any kind of 'standard' for Scots, and Andreas Fischer has shown that it is indeed possible for a minority language to thrive without one. Dauvit Horsbroch on the other hand argues with some justification that in fact a 'standard' is necessary if Scots is ever to be taken seriously, and experience from elsewhere in Europe shows that this is often the case. However, experience also shows that the process is fraught with difficulty – as Kevin McCafferty has shown us, carelessness can lead to two competing versions of the same national tongue. Indeed, even the recent experience with German shows that the 'best qualified' cannot carry out these processes alone.

Few would doubt that, in the medium term at least, any 'standard' for Scots would be much more restricted in use than one for English. I would suggest that a standard is indeed required, but only for use in educational materials and formal documents, one which would need to hold for some time (lest people become confused by constant changes, as seems to be the case with *Nynorsk*) but still be subject to review and periodic change (maybe every generation or so). It would be pointed out at every opportunity that the 'Standard' is only for use in those circumstances, and otherwise any form of 'authentic Scots' (which I discuss later) is acceptable. In fact, because of this, I actually prefer to refer to *Agreed Guidelines for Writing General Scots*; this smacks less of imposition and suggests, as would probably be necessary, a compromise among spoken dialects to reach an agreed written form.

How do we achieve this? Well, as the experience with German and many minority languages shows, not by forming exclusive 'spelling committees' or 'editorial boards'. The process does of course require the guidance of well-qualified linguists to ensure consistency at all times (it is this that stops us just adopting the headwords in the Concise Scots Dictionary), but ultimately the writers themselves will decide simply by writing Scots to each other, in books, poems, letters and emails. Gradually people will adopt forms that appear prevalent, and with some academic guidance you will not be far off having *Agreed Guidelines* for writing.

The fact is, we are not too far off such *Agreed Guidelines* already. Given a bit of 'mense' among writers, there is now no fear of incomprehension or unintelligibility on any of the many email lists or poetry volumes for Scots already in existence, involving writers from all 'airts an pairts' of the Scots-speaking world.

So although it is too early to talk about a single 'right' written form of Scots, you can still talk of 'acceptable Scots' or 'authentic Scots' versus 'unacceptable Scots' or 'inauthentic Scots'. It is possible for people, and above all native Scots-speakers, to tell whether a text is written by a Scots speaker or not, and whether it is representative of 'acceptable', 'authentic' Scots or not.

Research is required to identify with precision the markers that show a text to be 'acceptable' and 'authentic', but the texts below show the difference perfectly. The first 'Ullans edited original' version, and believe me there are many worse examples than this, is doubtless written by a well-meaning activist, but is clearly identifiable as 'unacceptable' or 'inauthentic' – if you like, it is simply not Scots! It appeared in the *News Letter*, Saturday 11 August 2001.

It must be said that the 'Ullans' version is probably victim of some typos. However, there is some evidence of misunderstanding the basics of 'acceptable', 'authentic' Scots in the texts below, a commentary on which follows.

Text 1: English

The 'Twa Charlies' along with Nattie Shaw of mid Antrim and others are carrying on a tradition which several decades ago was graced by such well known rhymers as John Clifford and Alex McAllister. They were associated with the 'Larne Folklore Society' which is still going. Charlie's tape includes five of Alex McAllister's poems.

This tape shows just how well this old county [sic] Antrim tradition is surviving and thriving into the twenty first century. Anyone wanting information can contact 'Loanen En Rhymes'.

Text 2: Ullans (edited original – see above)

Tha 'Twa Charlies' alang wi Nattie Shaw fae mids Antrim an ithers bis hauden on wi a tradeetion whit a wean o daiken syne wis mensit bi sic kenspeckle makers lik John Clifford an Alex McAllister. They waur claugh wi tha 'Larne Folklore Societie' whit bis gangin yit. Charlie's tapes haes fyve pomes o Alex McAllister includit.

This tape kythes jist hoo weel this auld Countie Antrim tradeetion bis tae tha fore an forderin intae tha neist hunner yeir. Oniebodie lukin mair wittens may awn 'Loanin En Rhymes'.

Text 3

The 'Twa Charlies', alang wi Nattie Shaw frae mid Antrim an ithers, wid be hauldin a tradeetion at wis graced a wheen decades syne frae sic weel kent rhymears lyke John Clifford an Alex McAllister. Thay war associate wi the 'Larne Folklore Society', at bes gaein on yet. Charlies kistie wid hae on it five o Alex McAllisters poems.

This kistie shaws juist the wey this auld tradeetion o the Countie Antrim is pittin owre an thrivein weel intae the twintie first centurie. Oniebodie for mair wittins can speir at 'Loanen En Rhymes'.

Text 4

The 'Twa Charlies', alang wi Nattie Shaw fae Mid Antrim an ithers, is hauldin the tradeition that a whein decades syne wes graced bi sic kenspekkil rhymers as John Clifford an Alex McAllister. Thay war associate wi the 'Larne Folklore Society', that's aye til the fore. Charlie's kistie taks in five o Alex McAllister's poems.

This kistie shaws juist whit braw this auld Countie Antrim tradeition is pittin ower an thrivin weill intil the twintie-first centurie. Oniebodie wantin wittins can get ahauld o 'Loanen En Rhymes'.

Text 5

The 'Twa Charlies' alang wi Nattie Shaw in mid Antrim an ithers is cairriein on the tradeition that wes graced bi sic weil kent makars as John Clifford an Alex McAllister a whein decade syne. Thay tuik tae dae wi the 'Larne Folklore Society' that's gauin yet. Charlie's kistie comprehends five o Alex McAllister's poyems.

This kistie fairlie shaws that this auld Coontie Antrim tradeition is hail an fere intae the twintie first centurie. Onie bodie that's efter infurmation can speir at 'Loanen En Rhymes'.

Text 6

The 'Twa Chairlies' alang wi Nattie Shaw fae mid Antrim, an ithers is cairyin on the tradeetion that a wheen decades syne held in sic weel-kent rhymers as John Clifford an Alex McAllister. Thay wis associate wi the 'Larne Folklore Society' that's aye tae the fore. Chairlie's tape haes five o Alex McAllister's poems inby.

This tape pits ower juist hou weel this auld Coontie Antrim tradeetion is tae the fore an daein guid intae the twinty first century. Onybody wantin wittins can speir at 'Loanin En Rhymes'.

The last four texts are the 'authentic' translations, combining generally accepted spelling alternatives, representation of modern speech and traditional writing, and accuracy of translation. The only spelling issues are:

- <ee> versus <ei> (*wheen* and *tradeetion* versus *whein* and *tradeition*)
- final *–ie* versus final *–y* (*twinty* and *cairy* versus *twintie* and *cairrie*)
- agent noun *–er* versus agent noun *–ar* (*rhymer* versus *rhymear*)
- other pairs: *wes* versus *wis*; *frae* versus *fae*; *gauin* versus *gaein*.

All these spellings are in common use in modern Scots writing, and the patterns (e.g. of using <ei> or <ee>) are well established – that is to say people either use *whein* and *tradeition* or *wheen* and *tradeetion*, they form part of a consistent system.

There are also minor grammatical differences: *Thay war* is a regularized representation of the (probably) more common *thay wis*. Each writer has chosen a quite different way of rendering *how well*. There is evidence of the more common use of the conditional in Ulster. However, all are acceptable and authentic Scots, perfectly recognizable and comprehensible to other speakers.

It should be noted that each translation is just that, a representation of the original English. Each displays a feeling for Scots and a feeling for language generally, where needless paraphrases are avoided but typically Scots terms are included.

All of this contrasts with the '*Ullans* edited original', which is no doubt well-meaning but displays all the usual evidence of a text written by an activist rather than by a speaker with a feeling for language:

- Anglicized semantics (vocabulary) – Scots equivalents of English words used inappropriately: *kythe* does indeed mean 'show', but usually only in the sense of '(physically) appear', not 'illustrate';
- Anglicized semantics (grammar) – inauthentic grammatical usage based on English rather than Scots: use of *whit* as a relative pronoun is more typical of non-standard colloquial English than most Scots dialects;
- Wrong words: *Wean* means 'child'; here *wheen/whein* is the equivalent word;
- Non-existent words: *Daiken* presumably is some attempt at respelling *decade* (we should possibly assume a typo here, too);
- Inappropriate grammatical forms: *bis* is used all over the place, where in actual fact it is a habitual term, occasionally also found in subordinate clauses traditionally;
- Untraditional spelling for no apparent reason: why is *waur* an improvement on *war* or even *were*?
- Determination to include *marker* words: *forder* appears in just about every *Ullans* text, even though it cannot possibly mean 'thrive' (as presumably is the aim here);
- False translation: the English says *the twenty-first century*, not *the next hundred years* (again this is probably done to include the unmarked plural grammatical form, just to get it into the text somewhere).

People make mistakes, of course, and the '*Ullans* edited original' was probably the victim of numerous typos. However, there are eight cast-iron examples of 'inauthenticity', which makes it clear to native speakers and qualified linguists alike that the text is not written by a speaker, and therefore cannot qualify as a genuine example of Scots writing (no matter which variety its author claims to represent).

So it is important to recognize, as we move further into the debate surrounding 'standardisation', that although there is no 'right' or 'wrong', there is 'acceptable' and 'unacceptable' and there is 'authentic' and 'inauthentic'. Within 'Authentic Scots' some variation is currently 'permissible', but this is not a licence for uncommon forms of words, lack of grammar, invented terms or semantic falsehoods. If nothing else, etiquette dictates that writers remain within the bounds of the general principles of Scots writing already well established in correspondence, on email lists, and in poetry. The truth is also that such principles may form the basis for *Agreed Guidelines* for use in specifically defined situations, and that those *Guidelines* really are not as far away as people might think.

A Hairst For A Bit Screive: Writin Historie In Scots

Dauvit Horsbroch

Whit Wey Historie: Haes It No Been Duin Afore?

In the hairst o 1994, a curn students - masel comprehendit - forgaithered tae speak anent settin up a bodie for the forderment o the Scots leid at the Univairsitie O Aiberdeen. Amang the subjecks that cam up wes the want o onie academic buiks wrutten in Scots, at least the want o onie modren anes. *Lallans* haes duin a bittie wark this gait, but it seemed til us Scots-speakin students that the feck o fowk war aye wrytin poyems an cuttie stories, but no monie fowk - gin ava - war wrytin academic prose. We war fair stervin an suin concludit that naebodie wad plenish the harns wi maet but wursels.

Maist fowk we kent, an ken yet, wes sweirt tae dae academic prose. Whit wad ither academics think? Ane meisur o the wey thay leuked on Scots wes the fact that guid academics that did contreibut til oor projeck didna gie onie references or buikleits tae stairt wi, yet wadna dream o leain an airticle in Inglis wantin the lyke. Bein historiens we concludit that we wad be maist at haim makkin a jurnal o historie, an it wadna seem sae orra tae maist fowk. For some reason historie an the Scots leid gang thegither weil, in a wey that a jurnal o medicine an Scots wad oxter ill thegither.

Anither consideration wes the bairns. Whit better wey tae bring academic Scots prose intae the scuils. Bairns an younkers in the scuils canna learn a guid conseistent Scots fae poyems alane whan we conseider that maist poyems belang aw the airts; thay maun hae academic prose tae, an a prose that's intressin tae thaim. We conseidered, in the hairst o 1994, that whit wes on offer cuid be bettered. We jaloused that teachers micht weil see a historie o Scotland as mair uissfae in clesses makin uiss o Scots nor say, Lorimer's Bible, braw as it is. An bodies mauna think A'm dingin doun ither fowk's wark, becis A'm no. Whit A am sayin is the reinge o subjecks an the registers that monie works in Scots is in, is ower narra, an ower couthie.

Anither conseideration in wrytin historie by wey o Scots is the wey we see oorsels. A think the historie o Scotland that is wrutten nouadays is, for the maist pairt, modren, economic, an becis o the modren romance wi awthin Celtic, ower gien til a Gaelic an Heilan view o the bygane. The average historien daesna affen gie the Lawlan or Scots-speakin braith. Sae whit we read is aether Inglified or born-again Celtic. It wes wi this in mynd that A wrate a lang airticle on the thrawn historie o Scotland's bygane, for the first edeition o *Cairn*, oor historie jurnal. A wadna be sae heich-bendit as tae claim A wes the first cheil tae wryte prose in Scots, or even the first historie prose wark in Scots, becis a bodie daes hae juist ane or twa ither ensamples gauin aboot in modren tymes. Houanever, a puckle o the anes on offer sae faur daesna mak the nick stick.

Tak the scrcid o buikies cryed　*A Scots Life*　bi *Argyll Publishing*　an editit bi Stuart McHardy. A hae a dooble o ane o thir buikies *Robert the Bruce*, bi Glenn Telfer.[1] The'r a whein problems wi this buikie. The batters proudlie intimate:

> *This is the first book on Bruce to be written in the Scots language since Barbour's Brus in 1376.*[2]

Weil, this is misleadin becis buiks o historie - comprehendin the raign o Robert the Bruce - war bein wrutten in Scots as late as the 17t centurie. An even efter this, aulder texts war bein prentit again richt doun til oor ain days. Gin a bodie leuks haurd at the text o this buikie it winna staun up til a scance. In ma ain opeinion it faws short o bein clessifeed as Scots at aw. Here a bit extrack tae shaw whit A mean:

> *Bruce's very presence maun hae been disconcerting at times. Wheneer the question o kingship arose, Bruce woud be sitting there representing an alternative - regardless o whit he sayd or felt. That he stuck wi the Scots' cause is the important fact. We woud scarcely hae a story o Scotland tae write o, neer mind Bruce himsel, if he steyed wi King Edward frae the beginning or returnt tae him eftir Falkirk. Imagine Bruce on the English side during aa this period and the haill south-west o Scotland an English fastness? Bruce's apparent lack o activity is, I believe, an illusion created bi oor lack o knawledge. Whit wes happening in Bruce's ain land and in the south-west in general was nae sideshow.*[3]

This - tae this bodie - is Suddron Scottified, an even the Scots is wersh. Even takin Inglis wurds sic as *would* an takin the *l* awa daesna mak it Scots. Whaur is the Scots *wad*, we maun speir? But the eidiom, as faur as the lenth o this bit screive, is Inglis. Tak sentences sic as: *The English wer jist too strang for the Scots tae risk anither battle wi them.* Patentlie, *ower strang* is wantin here. Thir weys o wrytin juist lowp up at Scots speakers.

Ane o the things wantin in buiks o Glenn Telfer's ilk is the proper names in Scots for fowk, kintras, an occurents in historie. Gey few fowk taks the tyme tae raik the buiks an register hooses tae airt-oot the richt names. In fact, a bodie daesna hae tae gae ower faur as the maist kenspeckle texts is aw in prent buik furm in librars the braid o Scotland. It is a queer norie, faurben wi fowk, that whitever a bodie happens tae be reared up speakin in Scotland can be coontit as Scots, an for some this is a bit daud o Scots in amang Inglis. Sae whit we affen get is the Inglis names for aw kin kyn o stuffrie; tak the maist recent *estuary* for firth. It's no haurd tae see the gait that Glenn Telfer an his ilk haes traivelled. Even buiks for scuils affen gang agley. A'm no ane for doun-pittin the wark o

---

[1] Glenn Telfer, *Robert the Bruce*, (Argyll, 1996).

[2] Ilk.

[3] Ilk, page 44.

scuil teachers forderin Scots - God kens thay haena muckle lift fae Govrenment - but here tae a bodie cuid neegur mair baws in the richt dale.

A can shaw whaur the confusion stairts. Tak the *Grammar Broonie* whaur on ane page the owthors speak aboot nummers in Scots. [4] Nummer *1* is gien as *ane*, *yin, wan* an *een*; whit wey shuid bairns be gien aw thir furms whan the spellin *ane* wes eneuch for monie hunner year? We affen think that bairns canna haunle the idea that thay spell the wurd ae wey but pronounce it the wey thay dae in thair ain airt. Tae spell ane wurd monie gaits can cause a fankle an juist uphauds the owerance o Inglis spellin an graimar on oor Scots. We wadna learn Inglis bairns *one* bi giein the spellins *wun, won,* an sae an on. Tak tent o the sentence (in the *Grammar Broonie*) "Which o these words is maist like the wey **you** say **5**". Again, this is naether fish or foul; patentlie *whit ane o thir* is wantit insteid o *which o these*.[5] This is whit wey A reckon it's important tae wryte academic prose in a furmal Scots register for tae haud up a conseistent model o Scots. Onless we dae this, we gie a lift tae the idea that Scots can never hae braider easins an maun aye be the infurmal crack o poyems an stories alane.

Anent Register An Vocabular

Whit is the richt register for wrutten academic Scots? Whit gait shuid we tak? Shuid academic Scots marra academic Inglis, aw for lang-nebbit Latinate wurds, an cauldrif tae the reader, or shuid it hae a style aw its lane? Is it in the tradeition o Scots tae be mair couthie, mair infurmal in style? Shuid academic Scots be the exack same Scots that a bodie wad hear oot on the gait or shuid it differ fae it? Thir questions haed tae be conseidered bi fowk in Aiberdeen whan thay first brocht *Cairn* thegither. An the answer; weil, the'r nae richt answer ava, ceptna get wrytin.

A'm sweirt tae uise the wurd *staunart* - tho A wad lyke tae feel free tae - in case fowk deek for thair guns an don steil bunnets. Insteid A'll say conseistent general Scots. Athoot this we canna howp tae set furth guid academic *or* admeinstrativ Scots. The'r aye some bodies in Scotland that hauds the braith that Scots alane, amang aw the leids o the warld, shuidna hae onie general staunart for heicher registers, becis this, thay claim, wad kill the leid aff.

The register an the vocabular shuid be foundit as muckle as possible on the leid o the gait; whither we lyke it or no the'r an onus on Scots tae be lyke this, else we'r open tae bein accused o forderin a wrutten leid that naebodie speaks. An Scots haes unfreins eneuch. Nou modren staunart leiterar Inglis is a register gey few fowk speaks, but fowk daesna quaistion it, becis it's sae weil estaiblisht, whyle Scots isna. Whit a bodie haes tae dae is balance the register atween whit is spoken on the gait, an whit is in the tradeition o Scots as fund in oor aulder buiks, an amang the speech o oor elders. Ane o ma first ploys wes tae airt-oot aulder histories wrutten in Scots, tae hae a guid scance o the style. For ensample, *The Diurnal of Remarkable Occurents* - or, in Inglis, 'the day book of noteworthy

---

[4] Rennie an Fitt, *Grammar Broonie* (Polygon, 2000).
[5] *Grammar Broonie*, p.25

events' - wes ane weil kent wark, wrutten in the 16xt an prentit in the 19t centurie. Here pairt o the text recountin the fecht at Pinkie Cleuch in 1547 whaur Ingland defait Scotland. The prose is fell braw:

> *The Inglismen begouth to gif bakkis, and to rouk and round,*
> *sayand, it wes ane greit matter to brek the Scottis; the Scottis*
> *persauenand this, incontinent fled, and the Inglismen followit, and*
> *chasit thame to Edinburgh ...*[6]

An sae it gangs on. Anither wark o this ilk is *The Historie And Life of King James The Sext*, wrutten in the 1590s, an cairried on aboot 1617.[7] The register an prose is muckle the same as the *Diurnal*. Tak, bi wey o ensample, the follaein waled fae oot a passage o the *Historie O King James The Sext* whan Jamie VI led an airmie furth o Stirlin in 1584:

> *Bot the king upon a suddan convocat an armie, and past directlie*
> *in battell aganis thayme, whareat thay war sa effrayit, that*
> *immediatlie thay fled in Ingland ...*[8]

or rare descriptions (in this case, o ceivil weir) sic as:

> *... it was nocht thocht expedient that the state ... sould be cassin*
> *lowse ...*[9]

It is fae sicna warks that A stairtit walin oot vocabular taewards a corpus o terms in historie for Scots. Tak for ensample, the leit that wes prentit in the saecon edeition o *Cairn*. An this wes juist a preliminar ane. But this can be a fair darg for ae bodie An we canna jouk the fact that the ae wey tae mak fowk mair at hame wi academic Scots is tae fleitch mair acdemics wryte it. Hou monie fowk forgaithered at the *Literary Scots 1975-2000* confeirance can say in aw honestie, that in twintie, thrittie year thay'v wrutten muckle prose ava in a leid thay threap on savin fae deith ? As lang as it is the ae bodie alane, than Scots wull be cawed orra.

---

[6] Bannatyne Club, *Duirnal of Rremarkable Occurents That Have Passed Within The Country Of Scotland Since The Death Of King James The Fourth Till The Year M.D.LXXV*, (Edinburgh, 1833), p. 45

[7] Bannatyne Club, *The Historie And Life Of King James The Sext: Being An Account Of The Affairs Of Scotland, From The Year 1566, To The Year 1596; With A Short Continuation To The Year 1617*, (Edinburgh, 1825).

[8] Ilk, p.203

[9] Ilk, p.19

A Breith On Spellin

This bodie is aye sweirt, atweil, feart, tae ingang the howf whaur the spellin lion ligs its teethie heid. This is a baest that haes etten the banes o the best. It is a maiter that fowk faws oot ower, an teir ane anither apairt ower. A'v seen freins no speak tae ane anither efter spellin differs. The'r monie spellins we maun gae hauf-gaits wi, A think, juist for tae get aheid o the gemm. For ensample, *ou* shuid be oor ordnar spellin but *oo* whaurever it cuid be confoundit wi the Suddron pronunciation. *Ei* for ordnar but *ee* whaurever a word is nou weil kent wi the spellin or whaurever *ei* wad juist leuk unco tae the een. It gaes athoot quaistion that apostraphes is tae be cryed doun whaurever a bodie fins thaim, ceptna wurds sic as the verb *dee'd* tae evyte confusion wi the noun *deed*, for ensample. Ae sign o a bodie that haesna taen pairt in onie debates aboot the leid is ane that uises apostraphes. It is dowie tae conseider, that maist local screivars uise apostraphes yet, an thay 'll no tak a tellin. Whit A hae tae say anent historie bi wey o furmal Scots prose daesna hae ower muckle dae dae wi the subjeck maiter that local screivars for ordnar concerns thairsels wi, but A dae howp tae be a model for thaim that wants tae ken.

The Pratticks

Cairn nummer ane an nummer twa cam oot in Mairch 1997 an Januar 1999. In Mairch 1997 Steve Murdoch an masel brocht thegither a puckle historie airticles bi wursels an ithers an set thaim furth as a historie jurnal cryed *Cairn*. This wes oor first ettle at historie throu Scots in an academic, furmal register. The first *Cairn* didna come aff hailscart an haes problems wi graimar, spellin, an eidiom, an A'm siccar A wad wryte ma ain airticle anither wey nou. A wad chynge a puckle spellins, leuk haurder at the graimar, an evyte Suddron eidiom whaurever A cuid.

On the hail, fowk haed guid comments tae mak aboot this ploy in historie.This is whit Ron Walker sayed in his scance o *Cairn* nummer ane for *Scottish Studies Newsletter*:

> *Yet the overall impression (at least for this Scottish reviewer) is that the use of Scots often gives a greater interest and accessibility to the topics treated here, as well as, perhaps more surprisingly, lending a greater weight and authority to some contentions, and this alone justifies the appearance of such a journal, presenting as it does, a counter argument to the one which says that Scots is pawky and English serious.*[10]

---

[10] Ron Walker, *Reviews, Scottish Studies Newsletter*, FASK, Johannes Gutenberg Universität, Mainz, simmer 1997.

An Billy Kay, in *The Aberdeen University Review* haed the follaein tae say:

> While some rejoice in Scots' lack of status and continue their death wish mentality towards it ... the Aiberdeen Scots Leid Quorum have confidently produced a major addition to the burgeoning wealth of material now being published in the language. They have also changed perception of what you can do in Scots, and who you can get to do it, with non-natives simply translated into a flexible Standard Scots prose.[11]

Sae whit did we learn fae this first ettle; daena listen tae the advyce o ower monie fowk whan wrytin as thay'll hae a bodie in a swither. Even fowk reared up wi Scots - as we ar - an no uised tae wrytin the leid doun in sic a furmal wey, wull affen gang agley. Daena be guidit wi ideologie, that is, makin the Scots leuk different fae Inglis tae mak as political pynt. We ken hou orra sic a ploy haes turnt oot in Ulster. Anither aspect tae conseider, as A say, is hou easy it is tae dae a bit screive an fin oot that it is fou o Suddron eidiom. Oor scuil Inglis, threapit bi braidcastin an Govrenment, haes a strang grip o oor wrytin an whyles it is a sair fecht tae lowse fae it. Nae maiter hou versant a speaker a bodie is, academic Inglis is aw aroun us an daes kythe in oor wrutten langage.

Efter the first *Cairn*, A taen on the editin o nummer twa masel an felt that A haed brocht thegither somethin mair skeilie in Scots. An this bodie suin cam tae appreciate that whit maks for guid academic wrytin in Scots is the uiss o Scots Latinate wurds cognate wi Inglis anes. An whither we lyke it or no, this means borraein fae a hunner, twa an even three hunner year syne tae lift the richt phrases an eidioms. This haes been a rare help tae this bodie's ain wrytin, an it haes tae be sayed, the vocabular daesna leuk oot o place.

David Purves' *A Scots Grammar* haes been a rare help tae, an A'm gled tae hae this tae haun.[12] He haes airtit oot pairts o speech that this bodie wad say, but haedna thocht aboot pittin doun on paper afore his graimmar cam oot. For ensample, the shortened *a* furm o *hae*. An this is richt; nouadays Scots speakers wad say *A wad a haen* whauras *A wad hae haen* souns no juist richt. It is pairts o speech lik this that shuid be set doun in academic wrytin tae balance atween the tradeitional an the ilka day speech o the kintra. A guid splairge o up-tae-date eidiom is aye guid, tae gie the Scots as authentic a soun as a bodie can; whyles this can mean takin the risk o uisin vocabular or expressions that maist speakers wad conseider slang. Shuid we say, for ensample, that king Alexander haed a *scance* or a *swatch* o the chairter? Shuid scance be uised in a gey furmal sense, an swatch in an infurmal? Wrytin Scots A reckon is affen a balancin act; a bodie canna makk furmal prose athoot uisin the tradeitonal leid, an as we aw ken, monie fowk haesna been reared up speakin this. Sae ye can be dilatit o wrytin

---

[11] Billy Kay, *Reviews, The Aberdeen University Review*, LVII, 4, Nu. 2000, hairst 1998.

[12] David Purves, *A Scots Grammar Scots Grammar and Usage*, (Edinburgh, 1997).

somethin auld farrant. On the ither haun tae gie thir tradeitions up wad be tae ding doun the verra identitie o the leid an a bodie wad be as weil juist wrytin his or her bit screive in Inglis.

The semantics is gey important; the'r a danger - weil seen in monie modren Scots wrytins - in ower usin parteiclar Scots vocabular for ower monie meanins an the sense o the wurd is tint awthegither.

Ae thing A wad say anent *Cairn* is that, awtho academics haes maistlie haen guid things tae say, juist aboot naebodie in academia haes gien it support bi wey o subscreives or biggin up contacks wi ither intressitit fowk. We aye hae the problem tae, that academics ootwi oor ain circle is sweirt tae sit an wryte airticles in Scots sae we aye hae a sair want o airticles fae oot o Aiberdeen. Ither fowk a bodie wad expeck tae gie it a shout daena; *Chapman* speirt us for a dooble tae scance, but never did. But, conseiderin the ettle ahin *Cairn*, anither jurnal o historie wad be mair richt lyke.

Ane anonymous screivar in the Dundee *Courier and Advertiser* brocht up anither maiter; the idea that ye hae tae be a Scot, speakin aboot Scots or Scotland alane, tae wryte in Scots. The screivar cryed doun the fact that ane contreibutor wes Swaddish an anither Roushien, regairdless o the fact that baith is qualifeed in Scots studies an can mak a guid fend at speakin the leid. The screivar wrate

> *I'm a bit concerned about some of them. Two actually ... Since I'd be*
> *willing to bet neither of them hails from Auchtermuchty, I wonder who*
> *does the translations.* [13]

The sel same bodie admittit that thay haedna, in maiter o fact, read *Cairn* but haed seen the adverteisment on a wabsteid wi the names o the contreibutors alane. Is this no an affa cheek on a bodie? But it shaws fyne an weil, that monie fowk wull discriminate juist becis it *is* wrutten in Scots, regairdless o the qualitie an register.

Ane Auld Sang: A Cuttie Historie O The Scots Naition

Haein tried oot Scots for a jurnal, the neist big ploy for this bodie is tae wryte a ane buik historie, an whit better nor the Scots naition itsel, a subjeck familiar eneuch tae maist fowk. A'v cryed this historie: *Ane Auld Sang: A Cuttie Historie o the Scots Naition.*

Ma ettle is tae pit thegither a ane buik historie o the naition plenished wi aw the proper Scots names for fowk, kintras an occurents, but afore A cuid get fair yokit tae the actual wrytin A haed tae awa an raik aw kin kyn o sources tae bigg up ma ain dictionar. In daein this, whit surprised me wes the bing o rich terms that Scots daes hae but naebodie maks muckle uiss o. An maist o this isna sae auld farrant as it wad a been kent tae fowk at the stairt o the 20t centurie. The ither thing that dings a bodie's harns is that aw oor concepts o tyme, an fowk, an

---

[13] 'The Mother Tongue as few of us ken it', in *The Courier and Advertiser*, 10 November 1997.

places, is gien expression throu Inglis; it stairts in the scuil an is cairried on throu the owerance o the meidia. Whit, for ensample, is the Scots marras o the Inglis *internal politics, Duchy, Prussia*, or a *skirmish*, tae name ane or twa? Weil, thay ar domestical politics, Ducherie, Sproushie, an a wee blatter. An the leit can gae on; the Inglis *Suit of armour* becomes staun o airmor in Scots, *Danish* becomes Dens, *occupation* - as in takin ower a kintra - becomes usurpation, the Antonine Wall, *Grimsdyke*, an sae an on. It suin becomes a hairst for a bit screive.

Forby raikin for ma vocabular - an this pairt pit us in mynd o Lorimer's chauve whan ingaitherin vocabular for his Bible - A haed tae pit thegither a plan o whit A wes awa tae wryte. Ower twa year A foutered an chynged this til A cam up wi a table o heids settin oot the periods o tyme alang wi the Scots names. Sae the nou A hae ma table o heids shawin whit gait the historie wull gang, an A hae a vocabular that A'm eikin tae yet. But this is for the oncome an A daena think fowk will see heid or hyde for a whein year yet.

Pirlicue

The parteiclar concerns o this bodie haes aye been wi biggin up the corpus raither nor fashin wi perjink maiters o spellin. Tho a canna jouk spellin awthegither. Sae monie fowk spen thair tyme fechtin ower the spellin but isna tentie tae the leid itsel, tae the graimar, the ediom, an abuin awthin, whit is in the tradeition o Scots. As A shawed, A eikit a whein wurds in *Cairn* nummer twa, but it micht be an idea tae set furth a sma dictionar o Scots terms for historie wrytin ance ma dictionar haes aw come thegither. We aweadie hae anes for Gaelic sae whit wey no for Scots?

Gauin bi the scances o *Cairn* wrutten in academic jurnals, academia wad judge in favour o sic a wark, but wad Jock an Jeanie leuk at it as anither Lorimer New Testament, bonnie eneuch an skeilie, but ower faur fae thair ain speech, an sae no warth a preen tae thaim? A think that we can get the balance richt sae lang as we comprehend Jock an Jeanie's speech. At the hinneren it *is* warth daein it tae shaw thaim that daesna ken, that Scots *can* be the medium o academic prose, nae bother at aw.

Encouragement and Facilitation:
A New Paradigm for Minority Language Education

Stephen Peover

Obstructive Beyond The Ways of Men: Images of the Civil Servant

The title of this section of my paper is a paraphrase of the title of an article by Aodán Mac Póilin,[1] in which Mac Póilin examines the diverse conceptions of the Gael, varying from hostile to sympathetic to highly idealised and sentimental, which have been employed by writers on Ireland and the Irish down the centuries. By contrast, I want today to examine *the* conception of the role of the civil service in relation to Irish medium education in Northern Ireland. I use the phrase 'the conception' advisedly since there is no diversity of view in the published material about that role, which is uniformly seen as hostile and obstructive. In my view, this is a gross oversimplification and, since it is seldom that civil servants like myself have the opportunity to progress from, to use Anthony Giddens' terms, the level of practical to discursive consciousness about our work or to defend it in public, I am grateful to Dónall Ó Baoill and John Kirk for the invitation to participate in this symposium.

One of my aims, therefore, will be to provide a perspective on developments during the 1980s and 1990s, though viewed, this time, from the 'other side of the fence', from the perspective of the Department of Education, which I joined in 1988, since most of the earlier published material reflects the rather different perspective of those who saw themselves as struggling against a reluctant and obstructive officialdom. I realise, of course, that, in speaking from my own perspective, I run the risk of false consciousness, and of being seen as engaged in a crude attempt at self-justification on behalf of the Department. This is a risk I am prepared to run on the basis that no one else seems to have attempted it, and that, as an exercise in what social anthropologists call 'indigenous exegesis', it may be interesting in its own right.

My underlying theme will be to use the example of developing official attitudes to the Irish language as an illustration of the view expressed by Joep Leersen:[2]

> *Within Irish society, those two cultural camps, native and English, while being implacably opposed to each other, did not exist in*

---

[1] Aodán Mac Póilin, "Spiritual Beyond the Ways of Men: Images of the Gael" in *Irish Review*, Autumn/Winter 1994, Queen's University Belfast: Institute of Irish Studies, pp. 1-22.

[2] Joep Leersen, *Mere Irish and Fíor-Ghael*. Cork: Cork University Press, 1996, p. 383.

*mutual isolation. There was always a hybrid middle ground where
the black and white contrast could become complicated or blurred.*

If I succeed in persuading some of you that such hybrid middle ground did and
does indeed exist, I will be very satisfied, but I will leave that to you to judge.

The Negative Image

Images of the role of the civil service in stifling the use of the Irish language and,
more recently, in hindering the growth of Irish-medium education abound in the
literature. In some cases, those images seem to be justified as, for example,
emerges from Liam Andrews' review of the material in the Public Record Office
from the early 1920s in relation to the teaching of Irish as a subject in elementary
schools in Northern Ireland.[3] Such careful analysis of the original source material
is not, however, always characteristic of other writers who seem to prefer slogans
to detail. For example, Pól Ó Muirí[4] argues that one of the reasons why Irish
frightens so many people is that the terms of the:

> *...cultural debate have been dominated by politicians and
> journalists for so long...Distinctions, contours, subtleties, are all
> lost in the rush to file copy and to get a scoop.*

No doubt this view is at least partly correct, but it is disappointing to find Ó Muirí
fall prey to the same tendency when he concludes from a mere six lines of
discussion of the *Glór na nGael* funding controversy that:

> *...The authorities are often abrasive in their dealings with the Irish-
> language movement..." and "...Their attitude towards the language
> fluctuates from being hostile to patronising to obstructive. Their
> policy seems to be to do as little as possible whenever possible and
> when backed into a corner to spend money on academic projects
> which, while worthwhile, do little to alleviate the daily struggle of so
> many other schemes.*

Still worse is his remark that:

---

[3] See Liam Andrews, "The very dogs in Belfast will bark in Irish" in Aodán Mac
Póilin (ed) *The Irish Language in Northern Ireland*. Belfast: The Ultach Trust,
1997, 49-94; also Liam Andrews, 'Historical Nationalists and the politics of the
Irish language: The Historical Background', in John M. Kirk and Dónall P. Ó
Baoill (eds.) *Language and Politics: Northern Ireland, the Republic of Ireland,
and Scotland*. Belfast: Cló Ollscoil na Banríona, pp. 45-63. Belfast Studies in
Language, Culture and Politics 1.

[4] Pól Ó Muirí , "Irish in Belfast", *Irish Review*, xx, 1993, pp. nn-nn.

> Naturally, *an administration as alienated from its populace as Stormont is from West Belfast, relies heavily on the Press for its information ...Policies or the lack of them are formulated according to this doleful colour scheme.* (Ó Muirí, 1993: 83).

The use of the word *naturally* to introduce an assertion is, of course, an indication that what follows is about to be asserted without adequate support, and certainly Ó Muirí adduces no evidence either about the sources of advice to government about the Irish language or about the background of any of the officials involved. Though not myself involved in the *Glór na nGael* controversy, I can assure you that government policy does not derive heavily from the media (though views expressed in the media are of course taken into account by any sensible administration), and that the understanding of the officials involved in providing advice to the government on the wide range of Irish language issues is rather deeper and more subtle than Pól Ó Muirí believes. Indeed some of those officials even come from Catholic and nationalist areas, and some in fact are Irish speakers.

Another example of such unsatisfactory elliptical argument is to be found in Camille O'Reilly's otherwise fascinating book *The Irish Language in Northern Ireland*,[5] in which she, too, shows herself not to be immune from over-generalisation. Thus she says:

> *Different government agencies and representatives, from the CCRU to DENI, and from civil servants to the Secretary of State, have had to engage with the revival movement and its representatives, particularly over areas of expenditure on the language. They have adopted aspects of cultural discourse to do this, exerting control by requiring conformity to a government ideology on the language which emphasizes cultural identity and delegitimates the use of Irish in a political context. (O'Reilly, 1999: 176)*

As regards my own Department (now DE rather than DENI), this is simply false. Whatever criticisms Irish-language groups have made of us (and they are many), they have never, to my knowledge, accused us of having sought to link the funding of Irish-medium education or the teaching of Irish as a subject to any ideology on the language, nor does Camille O'Reilly seek to substantiate her allegation in the text.

The Origins of this Image

I could quote other examples of such weak argumentation, but these two may suffice for present purposes as exemplars of their type. However, if much of the

---

[5] Camille O'Reilly, *The Irish Language in Northern Ireland: The Politics of Culture and Identity.* Basingstoke: Macmillan Press, 1999.

characterisation of the role and attitudes of civil servants is assumed rather than argued, why is it a *negative* image which is assumed? Where does this image of the civil servant as the hostile, anti-Irish bigot come from? As regards the Department of Education, some of it certainly derives from past disputes since, if the dates of 1690 and 1916 are of immense symbolic significance to the loyalist and republican communities here, then the year 1965 has an analogous significance for the Irish-language community in West Belfast. It was in that year that a group of Irish-speakers who wished to establish an Irish-medium school for their children was informed that such an education would not be regarded by the then Ministry of Education as "... efficient full-time education suitable to [the children's] age, ability and aptitude ...". The Ministry went on to say that it would serve a complaint on the proprietors of an independent school which sought to teach through the medium of Gaelic and this would have resulted in court proceedings. In those days, this proved sufficient to dissuade the parents concerned, who appear to have been remarkably law-abiding, and who did not return to their initiative until 1971, by which time the threat of such rather minor court proceedings must have seemed rather less persuasive, given the widespread civil disorder which had intervened.

The papers on our files from that era (which are open to the public now) make fascinating reading though the relative paucity of the papers, and the speed with which the policy decision was given, are rather surprising to me as a successor to those earlier officials. More importantly, the file indicates a sharp contrast between the approaches which were taken by some in the then Ministry, and those which were adopted less than a decade later and which remained broadly typical of our approach until 1998. In 1965, the question of the acceptability of Irish-medium education was approached at two separate levels. First, as an issue of educational principle – in effect, as a theoretical issue with discussion of whether education in a minority language would be inherently disadvantageous to the children involved both educationally and in their adult and working lives. In this context, advice was sought from the Senior Chief Inspector and his colleagues and, it may perhaps surprise those involved in proposing the creation of the independent school to know that the educational advice was that there was no evidence that education through the medium of Irish would be detrimental to the educational interests of the children involved.

This did not, however, prove to be the decisive consideration because the Senior Chief Inspector went on to suggest that, as a matter of policy, it would be wrong to allow the creation of even an independent school which did not teach through the medium of what he called the official language of the state. How far his colleagues agreed with him on this is not entirely clear from the file, but certainly there was sufficient concern for it to be recommended to the Permanent Secretary that his response should indicate that, should the proposed school be established, a complaint would be made against the proprietors. The file shows, however, that the officials concerned were not at all clear about what the outcome of such a complaint might have been and certainly did not exclude the possibility that a court might have ruled in the parents' favour! In the circumstances of such uncertainty, it is perhaps a pity that the parents did not proceed with their proposal since we might then have had clarification as early as 1965 or 1966 about the legal rights of parents to choose minority language education for their children.

It should be unnecessary for me to say that such approaches – and particularly an approach based on a concept of what was the official language of the state - would now be regarded as inappropriate, and we would be prepared to allow parents to establish any of a wide variety of forms of school (subject to certain minimum safeguards) and would reach a judgment on their suitability only when their actual operation had been evaluated. It is true, nevertheless, that, while doubts about the appropriateness of educating children from Irish-speaking homes through the medium of Irish have never really figured in official discussions of the policy, there remained concern amongst some in the Department during the 1970s about the wisdom of this form of education for children from non-Irish-speaking homes. The history of those events is chronicled in some detail by Gabrielle Maguire in her book *Our Own Language*[6] but, by the time the *Bunscoil Phobal Feirste* was finally registered as an independent school in 1979, even this was no longer a significant issue, though it did not disappear entirely from official discussions until some time later.

Policy Towards Irish-Medium Education 1979-1998

The decision to grant final registration as an independent school to Bunscoil Phobal Feirste in 1979 marked a significant development in policy but the Irish language movement (like the integrated schools movement subsequently) was to find that, while its schools were not actively opposed by the Department, nor were they in any sense encouraged and that first Irish-medium school had to operate as an independent school until 1984 when it finally achieved maintained or grant-aided status. It may be cold comfort now to those who bore the burden of fundraising for the school throughout the 1970s, but when the development proposal for the acquisition of maintained status was being considered in 1984, there was no theoretical discussion whatsoever of the appropriateness of the Irish language as a medium of instruction except in the rebuttal of an objection which had been lodged to the development proposal. Moreover, in the rebuttal of that objection, attention was drawn to the existence of Welsh and Scots Gaelic medium schools and units, to parental commitment to Irish and to the Government's recognition of what were described as "the two different cultures" which exist in Northern Ireland. This in itself was an indication of the broadening base of this whole area of policy and a first indication of a more considered approach.

However, the resolution of the problem with the funding of Bunscoil Phobal Feirste was not the end of the disputes between the Department and the Irish language community. Instead, the battleground moved to the establishment

---

[6] Gabrielle Maguire, *Our Own Language, Clevedon: Multilingual Matters,* 1991: 76-80

of more schools both in Belfast and elsewhere and the difficulty those other schools had in satisfying the required viability criteria.

In the late 1980s and through until the mid-1990s, there was a considerable degree of frustration in the Irish language community over what was seen as the inflexibility of the Department's approach, particularly to the application of the viability criteria for Irish medium schools. At the start of that period, the criteria for viability were set at potential long-term enrolments of:

Type of school	Enrolment
Urban primary	200
Rural primary:	100
Urban secondary:	600
Rural secondary	300

These were enormously difficult for new schools, supported financially only by parents and their wider local communities, to achieve but, despite our reputation for inflexibility, following an extended debate within the Department, it was agreed that the 'rural' criteria should be applied to Irish medium schools wherever they were located. The rationale for this was that the catchments of Irish medium schools are not like those of their English medium counterparts, but are rather more like the catchments of rural schools, drawing children from a broad area. This change of policy was welcomed by Irish language groups at the time, though it drew forth a demand for a parallel reduction in the criterion for rural Irish medium schools on the grounds that, if an urban school needed only 100 pupils, then the even more dispersed catchments of rural Irish medium schools should be reflected in a still lower enrolment threshold for them.

We did not regard this as a wholly unreasonable request, but we were reluctant to concede it on the grounds that a long-term enrolment of 100 was (and remains) the minimum which would sustain a 4-teacher primary school. Such a staffing complement enables a school to ensure that no teacher has more than 2 age-groups in any class and we took the view that, while this was desirable in all schools, it was virtually essential in the Irish medium sector where teachers might otherwise be faced with 3 or more separate age-groups of children at widely varying levels not only of ability generally but of competence in Irish. This view was not accepted by Irish language groups who pointed to small schools in the English medium sector here and in both the Irish and English medium sectors in the South, as well as to practice in Scotland. But this was, I would argue, a genuine difference of view about what was in the best interests of the children rather than an attempt by the Department to obstruct or thwart the growth of Irish medium education and represented a new, more satisfactory stage in the relationship between the government and the Irish language community here.

Another, earlier example of flexibility which is often ignored is to be found in the creation of the Irish-medium unit at Steelstown Primary School in Derry. That unit opened in September 1983 (and so became the first grant-aided Irish-medium provision in Northern Ireland – a full year ahead of Bunscoil Phobal Feirste) with some 23 pupils spread across 3 separate year groups and this was achieved without any financial burden on parents. Moreover, unlike the 13 year struggle for funding for the Bunscoil, the approval process for the Steelstown unit took only 6 months and of course that unit has now evolved into a fully-fledged separate school.

These progressive steps were somewhat undermined when the viability criteria were raised again in the mid-1990s from intakes of 15 to 25 for primary and from 60 to 80 for secondary. This applied to both the Irish-medium and integrated sectors and in fact derived more to the growing demand for capital resources resulting from the growth of the integrated sector than to any difficulty with the more limited growth of Irish-medium schools. However, the impact of this change was mitigated by the fact that additional resources became available under the European Union's Special Support Programme for Peace and Reconciliation which permitted both capital and recurrent funding for Irish-medium schools. This proved to be very significant though Camille O'Reilly's assertion that only "... Bunscoil and Droichead (sic), opened in 1996 with European funding ..."[7] is misleading in two separate respects. First, EU funding was applied not only to Bunscoil an Droichid, but also to Bunscoil an Iúir in Newry and to Gaelscoil Éadáin Mhóir and Meánscoil Dhoire in Derry. More importantly, it should be stressed that this funding was administered, not by the EU itself, which one might infer from the way Camille O'Reilly phrases her statement, but by the Department of Education which itself devised and applied the criteria for funding. As chair of the selection committee within the Department which handled all the applications for EU Peace Package funding, I am grateful for the opportunity to make it clear that we consciously and deliberately adopted a radically different approach to the funding of Irish-medium schools. That approach involved a willingness to support projects which fell far short of the normal viability criteria in the hope that, with the tangible encouragement of such interim funding, they would ultimately become self-sustaining.

I would suggest that the significance of this development has either not been noticed at all or has been underestimated. From a stance which was largely bureaucratic (or at least technocratic) insisting on the achievement of fixed numerical intake targets before funding would be granted, there was a move to a much more pragmatic approach which in effect accepted the argument of the Irish language community that experience had shown that there was a considerable unmet demand for Irish-medium education and that the risks involved in funding new projects were low. In this way, the contrast between a purely reactive approach and a proactive one became blurred, to use Leersen's term.

The New Paradigm: Encouragement and Facilitation

This change occurred in advance of the political developments which led to the Good Friday / Belfast Agreement (another example perhaps of the

---

[7] Gabrielle Maguire, *Our Own Language, Clevedon: Multilingual Matters,* 1991: 22.

Derry/Londonderry phenomenon) and meant that the Department was in fact well placed to respond to the paradigm shift which the Agreement entailed.

Amongst other matters, the Agreement committed the British government to:

- take resolute action to promote the [Irish] language
- facilitate and encourage the use of the language in speech and writing in public and private life where there is appropriate demand
- seek to remove, where possible, restrictions which would discourage or work against the maintenance or development of the language
- place a statutory duty on the Department of Education to encourage and facilitate Irish medium education in line with the current provision for integrated education; and so on ...

This last commitment was carried through in the *Education (NI) Order* 1998 which states:

Section 89
(1)   It shall be the duty of the Department to encourage and facilitate the development of Irish medium education.

(2)   The Department may, subject to such conditions as it thinks fit, pay grants to any body appearing to the Department to have as an objective the encouragement or promotion of Irish-medium education.

(3)   The approval of the Department to a proposal ... to establish a new Irish speaking school may be granted upon such terms and conditions as the Department may determine.

I have quoted these sections of the 1998 Order at some length because they provide the background to explain some of the Department's more recent actions in relation to the support for Irish medium schools.

I do not intend to rehearse these recent developments at length since they will be familiar to most people here but they include:

- the creation of *Comhairle na Gaelscolaíochta* as the promotional body for Irish-medium education, representative of the the two main voluntary sector bodies, *Gaeloiliúint* and *Altram*, as well as of the major education service organisations;
- the creation of *Iontaobhas na Gaelscolaíochta* as a trust fund to support innovative projects in Irish-medium education with an initial capital base of £1.75 million;

- the reduction in the viability criteria for primary schools and a proposal to reduce those for secondary schools which will be brought forward in September;
- the separation of the criteria for urban and rural primary schools with initial thresholds of only 12 for rural schools and 15 for urban but with a commitment also to look flexibly at the circumstances of every individual project;
- the granting of full recurrent funding on the achievement of those initial thresholds;
- the availability of capital funding from the *Iontaobhas* with such capital grants being subsequently repaid to the trust in appropriate circumstances when the target intake levels for capital grant (15/20: rural/urban) are attained;
- a lower standard of evidence for the achievement of the thresholds than was hitherto required.

These are significant developments but more significant still, in my view, is the improvement in the relationship between the Department and the Irish language movement. A constructive, pragmatic working relationship is being forged between the Department and *Comhairle na Gaelscolaíochta* and *Iontaobhas na Gaelscolaíochta*, which will hopefully lead to an agreed strategy for the development of the sector. In this context, I particularly want to stress the word 'agreed' in case there is any suspicion that we are seeking to 'domesticate' the sector and channel it into safe forms of development. This is emphatically not the case. We have no intention of seeking to impose a Departmentally-determined strategy on the Irish-medium sector (or its integrated education counterpart, for that matter): rather we take seriously our statutory duty to encourage and facilitate the development of Irish-medium education and accept that this can only be taken forward in proper partnership with the sector and with the other agencies such as the Education and Library Boards and the Council for Catholic Maintained Schools.

This does not of course mean that there will never again be differences of view about the needs of and best development path for the sector. For example, there is a debate beginning now about the need for additional second-level provision in Belfast. In that debate, there is room for a genuine difference of view about whether it is better to expand the existing *Meánscoil* to create a large 800-1,000 pupil school capable of providing a wide range of academic and vocational options for pupils or whether it would be better to create a second *Meánscoil* in another part of the city, perhaps operating in some sort of federated arrangement with the existing school to achieve the same end of a broad range of curricular provision for pupils. This is a real issue with a value for money dimension but it is primarily an educational not a political issue and it is a question of tactics not principle. Provided we can develop our discussions with the sector on that level and leave behind us the troubled history of the development of Irish-medium education here, then I believe we have a real opportunity to create a shared enterprise which will meet the needs of parents and young people and work to the long-term advantage of the Irish language as an integral part of the diverse culture of this part of the island.

From Cause to Quango?
The Peace Process and the Transformation of the Irish Language Movement in Northern Ireland

Gordon McCoy

In this paper I will consider the changing relationship of the Irish language movement with the authorities in Northern Ireland. This relationship was informed by the differing forms of government in the region, the attitudes of Irish speakers to these administrations, and the requirements of language activists as the revival of Irish developed.

Campaigners and community groups may, broadly speaking, adopt one of two approaches - conflictual or consensual. These are exemplified by the case of Friends of the Earth and Greenpeace. Friends of the Earth received government funding and ran 'Keep Britain Tidy' campaigns. According to some environmentalists, Friends of the Earth's fangs were drawn and the organisation was transformed into a quango, a quasi-autonomous non-governmental organisation, which implements Government policy by proxy (the term 'quango' is considered pejorative by officials, who prefer 'non-departmental public body'). Greenpeace refuse state funding, thus maintaining their independence, and continue to embarrass governments everywhere, but the organisation is sometimes dismissed as a group of cranks. The problem with radical groups is that unless these 'madmen at the door' have a large groundswell of support and powerful friends on the 'inside', especially opportunistic politicians, they will scream in the wilderness.

The consensual approach stresses lobbying, a professional image, and cultivating useful contacts with 'the powers that be'. Civil servants, ministers and councillors are wooed, and even invited to have a positive input into the campaign. This is the method employed by the Scottish Gaelic language movement. Without any natural sponsors - in the 1980s the Scottish National Party were not particularly influential or interested in Gaelic - the Scottish Gaelic movement set out 'to win friends and influence people', including councillors and Government ministers. Using right-wing economic arguments they secured 9 million pounds from Mrs Thatcher's Government for broadcasting in Gaelic. Positive statements by Government ministers about the regeneration of Gaeldom are reproduced in Gaelic promotional literature, together with smiling photographs of said ministers (e.g. Comunn na Gàidhlig 1994: 3)

But groups using this approach must be wary of being co-opted by Government policy and patronage. They are asked to prioritise, to consider budgets, to be pragmatic, to compromise, to consider present policies and to consider opponents of their views. In Scotland disaffected Gaelic activists accuse others of being deferential, of having a fear of 'What will the minister think?'

Other groups remain out of the system and refuse to compromise their values. Their demands may appear outrageous and their tactics aggressive, but they do not care; they will stick to their principles. Campaigners remain close to their 'grass roots', but lack influence beyond their immediate constituency, losing valuable networking and lobbying opportunities. They keep their 'street cred', but only on the street itself.

Welsh language activists adopted confrontational tactics, by defacing English-only road signs, occupying television stations, and pouring superglue into monolingual cash dispensers. Nevertheless, their campaigns were successful, and many members of the radical Welsh Language Society were later recruited by the Government-funded Welsh Language Board.

Irish language groups also varied in their approach to the authorities. I will consider the interaction of the language movement with the authorities in Northern Ireland in three chronological stages, roughly corresponding to the three administrations: unionist majority rule, direct rule from Westminster, and the devolved Assembly.

Unionist Majority Rule 1920-1972

From the 1920s until the 1970s the Irish language movement had little relationship with the unionist-dominated Government. There was no point in having one anyway, as Irish was effectively banned from public life; the authorities restricted the language to the private domain and Catholic schools. Unionist calls for a complete ban on Irish were resisted on the grounds that such an action would make the language more attractive to nationalists; in the words of Lord Charlemont, the Minister of Education, '...forbidding it under pressure will stimulate it to such an extent that the very dogs in Belfast - at any rate, the Falls Road dogs - will bark in Irish' (Andrews 1997: 81). While unionist officials regarded Irish speakers as seditious, lack of support for the language was justified on modernist or utilitarian grounds, which appeared to be less politically partisan. The Regional Director of the BBC refused to produce Irish language broadcasts, writing in 1940 '...there are no Gaelic speakers in Northern Ireland, by which I assume is meant Erse or Irish...' (Cathcart 1984: 111).

The Irish language represented an alternative to the public British ethos of the Northern Irish state. Irish speakers tended to have day jobs unrelated to the language, and to restrict their interest in Irish to their leisure time. No-one expected to gain financially from the language. The prevailing culture was one of self-sacrifice on behalf of others, for example, teaching Irish for free. Indeed, voluntary work on behalf of the language conferred a large amount of symbolic capital on the volunteer (O'Reilly 1999: 30).

Many Catholics had an ambivalent relationship with Irish. On the one hand it was part of Catholic symbolic ethnicity; Catholics believed that Irish was part of their identity, even if they did not speak the language. Thus the hostile attitude of the Government to Irish revealed its antipathy to the Catholic community; conversely issues involving the language could be used to test the commitment of individuals and groups within this community (Andrews 2000: 55). The ideology of the language movement was informed by Catholic communalism (Andrews 2000). However, in a strictly communicative sense, Irish was the pursuit of a relatively small interest group. Some Catholics, forced to learn Irish at school, were puzzled at those who pursued this topic outside the classroom.

In the late 1960s Irish speakers formed a small community in west Belfast. They established a primary school where Irish was the medium of instruction. They had the option of opting out of the state educational system. However, being outside the system exacted a heavy price, particularly in a poor community in west Belfast where affluent sponsors were non-existent. One past pupil at the school described to me his abiding memory of 'frozen knuckles'; of standing outside shops and pubs in the cold, collecting money for his school. The board of management began protracted negotiations, thirteen years in fact, for funding from the authorities.

Direct Rule 1972-1998

In 1972 the Stormont parliament was suspended and direct rule from Westminster was introduced, and ministers from Great Britain assumed responsibility for departments in Northern Ireland. There were various attempts to devolve power to local assemblies again, but these were abortive and short-lived before 1998. A slow process of adapting British policies of multi-culturalism to the Northern Irish situation began.

In the 1980s republican prisoners demonstrated that ordinary working-class people could learn Irish, and there was an enormous upsurge of interest in the language; previously Irish had represented a middle-class intellectual activity. Many republicans invested the language with republican ideology; indeed, Andrews suggests they ensured that Catholic communalism became the dominant ideology of the language movement (2000: 60). Nevertheless, the meaning of Irish was contested using cultural interpretations of the language which were used by non-republican Irish speakers. Indeed, many republicans perceived the language in a cultural sense themselves, so the relationship between language and politics was complex. As Camille O'Reilly (1999) attests, the meaning of Irish was discussed using three discourses: *decolonizing* discourse - speaking Irish became a form of resistance which complemented the armed struggle; *cultural discourse* - speaking Irish as a form of cultural heritage and identity, which became popular in Government circles; and *rights discourse*, which concentrated on the rights of Irish speakers, but could draw upon elements of the other two.

The language movement attempted to take Irish out of hobbyism and academia, and to create full-time employment through Irish. This entailed cultivating a relationship with the British Government, for few Irish language organisations are economically self-sustaining. This process was related to the rise in community action and self-help in nationalist areas, as many groups were founded in the early 1980s to negotiate for better funding and status for their districts.

The option of cultivating a relationship with the Irish Government was pointless for many years. Before 1985 the Government department with responsibility for the Irish language could not fund language groups outside its jurisdiction. After the Anglo-Irish Agreement of 1985 this became possible, but large-scale funding was not forthcoming, although from the mid 1990's the Irish Government exerted pressure on the British authorities to increase funding to the language movement in the North.

Few Irish speakers from the Republic were willing to travel North during the 'troubles'. Given the differing circumstances of the Irish revival in the South, few Northerners had reason to take a consuming interest in the Irish language infrastructure South of the border. North-South co-operation was at an informal and individual level.

For most of the 1980s and the early 1990s the Irish language movement used a mixture of consensual and oppositional tactics. The latter approach is a distinctive feature of these times. Civil servants with responsibilities for the Irish language were represented at best in the *Andersonstown News* as distant, dehumanised, and obstructive; 'grey suits' (18 March 1995) and 'Stormont mandarins' (18 May 1996), characterised by 'bureaucratic obtuseness' (18 March 1995). At worst they were portrayed as 'bigoted' (28 August 1993), a word which suggests sectarian attitudes; most senior civil servants at the time were Protestants. The British Government was regarded as hostile to Irish people and to the Irish language, if not Catholics per se.

According to strident language activists, officials needed to be pressurised and embarrassed into funding Irish language groups. Funding which was forthcoming was considered to be insufficient, hard-won, and not proportionate to demand. Articles in the *Andersonstown News* covering the Irish issue used the emotive language of conflict; examples include 'Irish language battleground' (December 4 1993), 'school battle hots up' (30 April 1994), 'Cultural *Krystallnacht*' (26 November 1994), 'virtual war of attrition' (18 March 1995), and 'City Centre Irish Invasion' (18 May 1996).

Irish speakers' approaches to the Government tended to draw upon the 'official' cultural discourse of the language. A common approach of the 1980s and early 1990s was the Celtic 'pro-rata' argument; that Scottish Gaelic and Welsh were given preferential treatment to the Irish language. This method had the advantage of drawing on existing Government practice to highlight the inconsistency of language policies in different parts of the United Kingdom.

The language movement also used the Government's own statistics in its campaigns. We live in the 'age of statistics'; statistical measurement is the basis for an objective science of society (Urla: 1993). The 1991 Northern Ireland Census report indicated that 142, 000 people had a knowledge of Irish. This was used to maximise the language movement, and conduct campaigns based upon 'objective' criteria. For example, one deputation to the Northern Ireland Office stated that there were just 60,000 Gaelic speakers in Scotland, compared to 142, 000 Irish speakers in Northern Ireland; despite the superior numbers of Irish speakers, the British Government funded Scots Gaelic television to the tune of eleven million pounds, yet provided nothing for Irish language broadcasting in Northern Ireland (*Andersonstown News* 23 August 1997).

The Government response to the 'Celtic pro-rata' argument indicates official doubts about the relative size of the Irish language movement. One senior civil servant with the responsibility for Irish, Tony Canavan, considered the census figures to be inflated, and urged Irish speakers to be more 'realistic' about the size of the Irish language community (*Irish News* 30 September 1995). He also stated that Irish in Northern Ireland, unlike Scottish Gaelic and Welsh had 'no geographical heartland with an unbroken tradition of daily use of the language'(*Irish News* 30 September 1995). This minimised the impact of the revival of Irish in English-speaking areas. Because Irish speakers in Northern Ireland were not native speakers living together in long-standing communities, they were not considered to require the same degree of funding as their Celtic counterparts.

Unionist critics considered the British Government's approach to Irish too pro-active, revealing Westminster's preparations for a united Ireland. They tended to minimise the number of fluent Irish speakers, occasionally in an 'objective' scientific manner. Roy Bradford, a unionist politician, wrote, 'Only 0.55 per cent of the population in this Province have full fluency in that language. Compared with 19 per cent of the people of Wales who have full fluency in their language' (*News Letter* 10 April 1989). He later attacked 'Government subservience to the all-Ireland and Gaelic culture lobby' (*Andersonstown News* 18 May 1996).

The Government attributed its caution to the fact that Irish was a sensitive political issue in Northern Ireland compared to the case of Scots Gaelic and Welsh. The debate about who 'politicised' the language was heated. According to the Irish language movement the Government 'politicised' the language by refusing to fund language projects, and by stigmatising Irish speakers.

Meetings between civil servants and Irish speakers were often tense. In one leaked memo a senior civil servant stated, 'the Minister... has been exposed to several meetings with the abrasive end of the Irish language spectrum' (Canavan 1998: 9). Funding was forthcoming, perhaps begrudgingly, but another product of the meetings was the dislike of certain civil servants and ministers for Irish speakers.

Positive noises made by officials and civil servants about the Irish language were ignored, rejected outright, or treated as ironic, given other policies which worked to the disadvantage of language groups. Many republicans in the Irish language movement felt that the Government would fund 'safe' academic projects, but would be reluctant to support groups involving themselves, thus introducing self-vetting to Irish language circles. For Irish-speaking republicans, this 'divide and conquer' policy maintained the conceptual relationship between the Government and Irish speakers as one of oppressor and oppressed. Less confrontational critics interpreted the Government's approach as ad-hoc and reactive, with some hostility and a few massive blunders along the way.

One of these critics was the ULTACH Trust, the organisation for which I work. ULTACH was partly funded by Government sources, and advocated a consensual approach to Government rather than a conflictual one. The Trust was accused by republican Irish speakers of being co-opted by the state, and even of being a branch of the Northern Ireland Office. The organisation was represented as a distant, politically servile and unaccountable quango, outside the language movement proper.

It may not be the case that officials would have been more receptive to a less confrontational approach. Many people, especially the middle-classes who staffed the civil service, were suspicious of Irish language activists. They stereotyped them as ultra-nationalists who were motivated by at best blind idealism or at worst a desire to destroy Northern Ireland. These attitudes may have conflicted with the duty of civil servants and service providers to be fair and impartial to all sections of the community. Yet some civil servants and funders felt they bent the rules and cut corners in order to fund Irish language groups, for example, by not asking funded groups to produce annual accounts or reports.

Overall, the British Government response to the Irish language movement was cautious and piecemeal. Official policy was reactive; in it's own words 'to respond positively, where practical, to soundly based requests for assistance' (letter to Nóirín Uí Chléirigh from Tony McCusker of the Central Community Relations Unit, 25 January 1993). Irish language groups were funded through the 'back door', on temporary employment schemes, but not on language schemes per se.

In 1992 the Secretary of State announced 'We have no plans for a bilingual society' (Mayhew 1992: 17). Government policy was to keep Irish at a community level, rather than an institutional one. This kept Irish away from the eyes and ears of suspicious unionists, but kept the status of the language low. However, there were some symbolic straws in the wind. For example, in 1993 Irish-speakers from Newry were surprised when they were greeted in Irish by the Minister for Education (*Sunday Life* March 28 1993).

Irish speakers adopted consensual tactics and worked the system when progress seemed possible. This was particularly the case in education; Irish-medium schools implemented the core curriculum and welcomed departmental inspections. The Department of Education facilitated the development of the curriculum and teaching in Irish, although disputes over funding criteria based upon enrolment were protracted and acrimonious.

Yet as events unfolded in the 1990s the Irish language activists discovered that they did not need to woo civil servants and ministers, even if that was possible. The language had a powerful political sponsor in the peace negotiations, Sinn Féin, and to lesser extent the SDLP and the Irish Government. Irish speakers, using the rhetoric of the peace process, claimed that 'parity of esteem' for Irish speakers was commensurate with the much vaunted 'parity of esteem' for nationalists in Northern Ireland.

This convergence of language and political issues is demonstrated by the case of Meánscoil Feirste, Belfast's Irish-medium secondary school. For some years, Meánscoil campaigners adopted a consensual approach, hoping that the Department of Education would reduce the enrolment criteria for grant aid. When the consensual approach failed, a more confrontational high-profile stance was adopted in 1993. This culminated a year later with Gerry Adams raising the issue at a meeting with President Bill Clinton's National security advisor, Tony Lake (*Andersonstown News* 10 December 1994). At the time, the American

Government was putting pressure on the British to undertake 'confidence-building measures' which would keep republicans in the peace process. Interim funding was made available a year later and the school was fully recognised and funded in 1996.

The Irish language flourished in tightly-knit working class Catholic communities. The close community bonds nourished the revival, but there were disadvantages. There was a lack of contact with 'outsiders' who could contribute to the revival. In particular, there was a shortage of professional skills in the Irish language movement; a scarcity of book-keepers and business managers, for example.

Three years ago I overheard an interesting conversation between a teacher in an Irish-medium primary school and the language officer from an education board. The teacher said she was looking for tiles to put in the school that would not hurt children if they fell on them. However, builders claimed they were very expensive. The officer told her to buy them in gardening centres and she even knew where to get tiles with a Celtic design. The teacher then mentioned that she did not know how big the playground should be considering the increase of pupil numbers. The officer told her of the Board's environmental expert, who would advise her on these issues. The conversation went on in a similar vein, demonstrating that there were useful contacts to be made outside the usual Irish language circles.

One side cannot be blamed for these problems, for it is certain that Irish speakers were cold-shouldered by civil servants and service providers in the past. Among the more memorable examples are the following. In 1995 campaigners for Irish language street signs were told by the Northern Ireland Housing Executive that their computers 'only accept the English language'(*Andersonstown News* 23 September 1995). In 1997 disability leaflets in Irish were withdrawn from the City Hospital after a complaint from a unionist member of the public. The chief executive of the health trust involved later apologised for any distress caused by the leaflets (*Andersonstown News* 13 September 1997). These incidents, highlighted in the Irish language media, reinforced the representation of Irish as a symbol of communal victimisation.

However, during the 1990s some institutions adopted bilingual policies to improve their relationship with Irish speakers in west Belfast. These include the Bank of Ireland, the Citizens' Advice Bureau, the Halifax Building Society, Northern Ireland Electricity and some shops and supermarkets. These policies usually amounted to bilingual signage and leaflets, if not Irish-speaking staff, although one supermarket provided an Irish-speaking checkout assistant.

The Agreement and Devolution 1998

In the 1998 Good Friday *Agreement* the British Government undertook to promote the Irish language for the first time (Northern Ireland Office 1998: 19). In fact, the Irish version of the *Agreement* is the first document produced by the British Government in that language in the modern era. Policy was informed by the belief that former combatants should be actively encouraged to participate at all levels of society in Northern Ireland. The New Northern Ireland Assembly, with 108 members, is a super-inclusive democracy, large enough to include fringe loyalist parties. This form of devolution was accepted by the vast majority of nationalists and Irish speakers in the North, and it heralded a new era for the Irish language in the region. For example, Bairbre de Brún, a senior member of Sinn Féin, is now the Minister for Health, and she regularly delivers speeches in Irish in the Assembly.

Partnership Boards were established to bring together the private sector, statutory bodies, community groups and politicians. These were to channel funds in district council areas, and politicians, including Sinn Féin members, were invited to serve on them according to their electoral strength. Thus the previous policy of excluding republicans from public bodies was ended. Government departments and these boards distributed European funding aimed at securing the peace by stimulating community development. Irish language groups benefited enormously from this European funding, particularly schools which did not meet Department of Education enrolment criteria. Furthermore, Irish language projects accrued extra sums from the International Fund for Ireland and the National Lottery.

Sinn Féin placed an emphasis on Irish language issues during the Stormont negotiations leading to the Agreement. In particular, they argued for the creation of a cross-border implementation body for the Irish language; this was to be one of six such bodies designed to give the Agreement an all-Ireland dimension. Unionist negotiators succeeded in their efforts to include the promotion of Ulster-Scots within the language body's remit. When eventually established, the Irish language agency of this body became known as Foras na Gaeilge. The board members were chosen by the political parties North and South, with the body being responsible to both Governments. I am a choice of the Ulster Unionist Party, for example.

Some Irish speakers have had their reservations about the cross-border body. Northern and Southern Irish language activists felt that the board members, as political appointees, were unrepresentative of the language movement (Ó Murchú 2000: 83-4); the usual problem with quangos. 'Grass roots' activists felt that this Dublin-based organisation would become another self-perpetuating bureaucracy. This was the stereotype many applied to the Republic's old language board, Bord na Gaeilge, which was transformed into Foras na Gaeilge. For their part, some Southerners hoped that the Northerners would shake up the bureaucracy of the old Bord. In Northern Ireland there was a fear of the language movement coming under Southern domination.

Some of the Northern fears have been allayed, and indeed, the cross-border body became a symbol of nationalist victimisation, as unionists were blamed for political manoeuvrings, including Assembly suspensions, that hindered the development of the organisation. The fear of Southern domination is offset by the fact that the board membership of Foras na Gaeilge is 50-50 Northerners and Southerners; 8 from the North and 8 from the South. This seems rather unrepresentative, as the Southern Irish language movement is much larger, yet the 50-50 arrangement was done at the insistence of the Northern negotiators, who did not want their representatives on the cross-border bodies to be outvoted by their Southern counterparts.

Furthermore, there has been some influence flowing in the North-South direction. All public bodies operating in Northern Ireland, including the cross-border bodies, must have an equality policy which ensures that they will not discriminate on the grounds of criteria such as gender or race. This is enforced by the Equality Commission in the North. Therefore legislation originally designed for the North will have an impact on the Dublin employees of *Foras na Gaeilge*. Also the Financial Memorandum related to the cross-border bodies is based on UK economic practice. In effect, this will tighten up the procedures for monitoring and evaluation of Irish language activities in the South.

Foras na Gaeilge, with its initial budget of eleven million pounds, gave Irish speakers in the North good reason to joke that an Irish language 'gravy-train' was on the way; indeed, the organisation's funding for Northern language projects has been substantial. The body is also having an important social impact on language circles in Northern Ireland; the organisation is increasing contacts between Northern and Southern Irish speakers, which were few and far between during the 'troubles'. The end of hostilities in Northern Ireland has resulted in more cross-border Irish language traffic. After the ceasefires more native speakers of Irish from Donegal sought employment in the Irish language movement in Northern Ireland, and groups North and South have begun co-operating at the organisational level.

Irish has undergone a rapid transformation from counterculture to officialdom. The British Government has ratified the *European Charter for Regional or Minority Languages* for Irish and the language will be mentioned in the forthcoming Human Rights Bill for Northern Ireland. The Department of Health produces all press statements in Irish and English and advertises for posts in both languages. The Department of Education has established Comhairle na Gaelscolaíochta, a council which has a remit of developing Irish-medium education. (Comhairle na Gaelscolaíochta is also discussed by Peover in this volume.)

The Linguistic Diversity Unit at the Department of Culture, Arts and Leisure has the responsibility to promote the Irish language. The unit is responsible for the implementation of the *European Charter for Regional or Minority Languages*, which introduces a level of officialdom; a fledging bureaucracy in Irish to Northern Ireland. The Unit commissioned research on the needs of the Irish language community and set up an inter-departmental working-group to develop an overall policy for Government and to implement the Charter.

Many public documents are being translated into Irish for the first time. This process entails more frantic Dublin-Belfast co-operation in terms of lexical expansion, as translation services in the South are well established. In the North, there has been difficulty in meeting the huge demand for translators; a lot of pressure is being put on a few skilled individuals. There is a pressing need for an agreed terminology to facilitate communication at the official level, as translators at meetings are sometimes unaware of neologisms. Translators North and South are working on a Dictionary of Terminology for the Assembly and the Dáil as part of the European Language Initiative, which produces dictionaries for public service.

The Department of Culture, Arts and Leisure commissioned the University of Ulster to prepare a report on services provided to the public in the Irish language (Dunn, Morgan, & Dawson 2001). The report was submitted in February 2001 and there are plans for its eventual publication, but I can reveal some of the findings here. The report found that Irish language activists were keen to have better services in Irish, but held opposing views about its promotion.

One view was that 'since everyone who spoke Irish also spoke English, to insist on doing everything through Irish - down to running meetings in Irish - gave an impression of small-mindedness. It also succeeded in excluding - if not antagonising - those who could not understand what was being said' (Dunn et al 2001: 33). An approach like this could give ammunition to those opposed to the language. According to this view Irish speakers should be pragmatic and realistic, and establish their priorities with the Government, building upon smaller gains over a period of time.

The second view was that the only way to ensure that the Irish language developed its full potential was to insist on giving it full recognition in all contexts, so that it could never be perceived as a special case or an exception. This could only be achieved by legislation, which would force those with power to live up to their responsibilities. Mere cosmetic changes would weaken the language and perpetuate its second-class status. By using Irish in all contexts the mind-sets of important actors, such as civil servants, would be changed. Compromise with opponents, who disparaged the language, would only play into their hands.

Opponents to services in Irish believed it was 'a political football exploited by republicans' (Dunn et al 2001: 30), or that the numbers of speakers were too small to have any real claim on the public purse. They also said resources were too limited and the provision of key services such as education, health, and transport were more urgent.

Officials were divided about Irish language policies. Some dismissed them as too expensive and said Irish-speaking staff were rare. Others felt that many measures would be relatively inexpensive, such as information leaflets and electronic services on the internet. Some felt there was no demand for services in Irish, whereas others felt the supply would increase the demand, as Irish-speakers had been deterred from asking for services in the past.

There was little antipathy in both Protestant and Catholic communities to Irish-medium education. Some Protestants feared their own children would be forced to learn Irish and they were very opposed to this. There was often 'general mystification' at people who voluntarily agree to have their children taught subjects such as maths and history through the medium of Irish (Dunn et al 2001: 42). The report also found that the two communities were very divided about the use of public signage in Irish; most Protestants, forty-three per cent of the total, believed that Irish language signs should never be provided in any circumstances, whereas fifty-four per cent of Catholics believed they should be provided where the majority of people would be in favour of them. Forty-four to fifty per cent of those interviewed were in favour of a number of Government services in Irish being made available on request, such as census forms, birth certificates, and voting cards; and between 47-48% of these were Protestants. Between seven and nine per cent of those interviewed thought that Irish language versions should be provided as a matter of right.

Many public bodies in Northern Ireland now produce information brochures in Irish and Ulster-Scots. Immigrant languages are catered for in the effort to introduce multi-lingualism, a context for Irish which does not disturb unionists. So a by-product of the peace process has been more leaflets in Chinese and Urdu! There are few bilingual brochures and documents, as in Canada. Dual language documents would draw accusations of linguistic favouritism from unionists; why not trilingual brochures, with Ulster-Scots being included? Instead, an opt-in approach is used; smaller print runs of Irish and Ulster-Scots brochures are produced and distributed to interested parties. Thus, unionists, many of whom consider Irish to be offensive, do not have to encounter the language every time an official document comes through the letter-box.

In this era of principled ambiguity, service providers invoke discourses of diversity in public, while some joke and moan in private about politically-correct language policies. They puzzle at job adverts in Irish only, marvel at Ulster-Scots neologisms, wonder why they provide simultaneous translation facilities for Irish speakers who know better English, and worry how they will cater for both the Irish and Ulster-Scots constituencies at every juncture. My favourite example of our linguistic zeitgeist is a card produced in 2001 for census enumerators, which they show to people who do not understand English. The card contains messages in immigrant languages such as Urdu, Chinese, and Arabic, as well as Irish and Ulster-Scots. This card is therefore a functional necessity, but also has a symbolic role with the addition of Irish and Ulster-Scots - speakers of both understand English perfectly well. In another act of muddled political correctness, the Northern Ireland Statistics and Research Agency provided on-line versions of the 2001 census form in Irish and Ulster-Scots, but insisted that only a completed English language version of the form would be accepted.

For the first time, a Government of Northern Ireland has a Department which takes an active role in promoting the Irish language. Indeed, in the 2001/2 financial year, the Department's budget for linguistic issues (£4m) was greater than the budget for sport (£3.4m). The concept of Government departments promoting the language is a novel one, and one that may require some acclimatisation on the part of the Irish language movement and the civil service. (A personal perspective on the Department of Culture, Arts and Leisure's language policy is presented in this volume by Edward Rooney.)

There are signs of a rapprochement, however. The Irish-speaking Under Secretary for the Department of Education, Stephen Peover, was invited in 1995 to defend the Department's policy in the Cultúrlann, an Irish language centre on the Falls Road. This would have been unthinkable before the IRA ceasefire; as a British civil servant he may have been in some danger from republican paramilitaries. In 1998 he was invited by an Irish language business company in west Belfast to present certificates to teenagers who had completed an internet training course in Irish. Thus his standing had improved in the eyes of the Irish language movement; he may even have become an honorary member of it. The conceptual opposition of Irish language activist to civil servant has broken down somewhat; the 'grey suit' has become more human.

The complement has been returned. Irish speakers have been invited to receptions at Government departments, and found themselves drinking wine and having nibbles with 'the great and the good'. There has been a reduction of hostility on both sides. As a civil servant described the change, 'These people used to come through the walls. At least they come through the doors now'.

Irish speakers are also changing their approach, not to mention dress code. Informality, de rigueur casual dress, self-sacrifice and dark, drafty rooms are being exchanged for suits, well-paid jobs, corporate logos, glossy brochures, 'chief executives' and showcase events in the Waterfront Hall or Europa Hotel. Some Irish speakers lament the old days when only 'true believers' were involved in the language movement; those who had nothing to gain from speaking Irish. They fear that overdependence on state subsidies may ultimately weaken independent language activism at the community level (cf. Lo Bianco 2001: 8). Others welcome the professional approach as a natural development, and believe Irish speakers deserve their place in the sun after years of penury.

Thus the peace process has had a profound impact on the interaction between the Irish language movement and the state, or indeed *states*. Many of the changes were evident at a conference organised in September 2000 by POBAL, an umbrella organisation for Irish language groups. Michael McGimpsey, the unionist Minister for Culture, opened the conference *in* the Irish language. The event was attended by civil servants and representatives from boards and trusts who were wondering what their own policies should be on the Irish language. The language was discussed in terms of recent legislation, international human rights, the 'diversity dividend' and 'cultural pluralism' (POBAL 2001). Notably absent from these future-oriented speeches were discussions of the language in terms of nationalist rights, or the use of emotive and conflictual language. The status and funding of Irish has become secure enough for campaigners to concentrate on rights for the Irish language community, rather than the nationalist community. Thus the chief discourse now employed by the Irish language movement is *rights discourse*; this can be interpreted as a metaphor for nationalist rights, or the discourse may express a conceptual distance from nationalism. By signing the Charter and implementing other measures, the British Government has used this discourse itself.

There are new ways of talking about the Irish language as well. Grants for language projects are no longer represented as 'victories' over reluctant Government departments. The rhetoric of resistance was discarded after the Agreement, and replaced by discourses of language rights, economic regeneration, and consumerism. The 1980s republican phrase which described every phrase in Irish as 'a bullet in a freedom struggle' (Ó Maolchraoibhe 1984: 4) seems rather anachronistic today; in fact, it is used only by unionist opponents of the language. We are more likely to read the following:

... the Irish language will become a key marketing tool for companies seeking to defend their share of the Irish-speaking consumer market into the millennium (Andersonstown News, 19 December 1998).

Despite the peace process, some Irish speakers experience a sense of *plus ça change, plus c'est la même chose.* Some long-standing animosities between constitutional nationalist and republican Irish speakers have not been resolved; rather they have taken a new form. Since 1998 there has been disquiet among some constitutional nationalist Irish speakers, who feel their own schemes will be neglected in the rush to empower their republican counterparts; they suggest that in the new order the republican 'poachers' have become the 'gamekeepers'. A possible countervailing trend is a relaxing of attitudes, or even interest in Irish among republicans, as the language of romantic revolution becomes one of red tape.

The predominant 'Catholic' or 'republican' image of Irish has not changed much since the early 1980s, despite a number of cross-community initiatives aimed at reducing Protestant hostility to the language. Most people in Northern Ireland only encounter the language in media reports of Assembly proceedings, during which Sinn Féin members deliver speeches in Irish or use it in opening addresses. It is not likely in the foreseeable future that the radical transformation of Government attitudes to the language will be replicated within the unionist community. For many unionists Irish remains a language of the 'other', to be tolerated occasionally and opposed often.

Conclusion

Irish speakers have moved from having no relationship with the state to a conflictual and eventually a more consensual one. Activists are moving beyond their bounded communal base to networking beyond their immediate constituency, with the attendant horse trading and lobbying opportunities this shift implies. There has been a degree of convergence between the style and presentation of the campaigner and the civil servant, even if their objectives differ. The peace process has resulted in an administration which has moved from a reactive to a pro-active role regarding the Irish language. While some particular issues regarding the language remain controversial, it appears that much can be done to raise the status of Irish in Northern Ireland with widespread cross-community approval. It remains to be seen if official mainstreaming and developments within the language movement will increase the appeal of Irish beyond its present working-class Catholic base.

References

Andrews, L. (1997) '*The very dogs in Belfast will bark in Irish*: The Unionist Government and the Irish language 1921-43'. In A Mac Póilin (ed) *The Irish Language in Northern Ireland*. Belfast: Iontaobhas ULTACH / ULTACH Trust. 49-94.

Andrews, L. (2000) 'Northern Nationalists and the Politics of the Irish Language: The Historical Background'. In J. M. Kirk and D. Ó Baoill (eds.) *Language and Politics: Northern Ireland, the Republic of Ireland, and Scotland*. Belfast: Cló Ollscoil na Banríona. 45-63.

Canavan, J. A. (1998) *European Charter for Regional or Minority Languages and Other Irish Language Issues* (unpublished).

Cathcart, R. (1984) *The Most Contrary Region: The BBC in Northern Ireland 1924-1984*. Belfast: Blackstaff.

Comunn na Gàidhlig (1994) *Comunn na Gàidhlig: ag obair dhuibhse*. Inverness: CNaG.

Dunn, S. Morgan, V. & Dawson, H. (2001) *Establishing the Demand for Services and Activities in the Irish Language in Northern Ireland. A Research Report for the Linguistic Diversity Branch Department of Culture, Arts and Leisure*. Unpublished.

Lo Bianco (2001) *Language and Literacy Policy in Scotland*. Stirling: Scottish CILT.

Mayhew, P. (1992) *Culture and Identity. Text of speech delivered today by the Secretary of State, Sir Patrick Mayhew, MP, at the Centre for the Study of Conflict, University of Ulster at Coleraine. Wednesday 16 December 1992*.

Northern Ireland Office (1998) *The Agreement: Agreement reached in the multi-party negotiations*. London: Stationery Office.

Ó Maolchraoibhe, P. (1984) 'The Importance of Learning Irish' in *Learning Irish: A Discussion and Information Booklet*. Belfast: Sinn Féin.

Ó Murchú, H. 'Language, Discrimination and the Good Friday Agreement: The Case of Irish.' In J. M. Kirk and D. Ó Baoill (eds.) *Language and Politics: Northern Ireland, the Republic of Ireland, and Scotland*. Belfast: Cló Ollscoil na Banríona. 81-88.

O'Reilly, C. (1999) *The Irish Language in Northern Ireland: The Politics of Culture and Identity*. Basingstoke: Macmillan.

POBAL (2001) *An Ghaeilge: Ag cothú na héagsúlachta, ag tógáil na sochaí úire. Tuairisc na Comhdhála 9 Meán Fómhair, Halla Cois Cladaigh, Béal Feirste. The Irish Language: Promoting diversity, building our new society. Conference Report. Saturday 9th September 2000, Waterfront Hall, Belfast*. Belfast: POBAL.

Urla, J. (1993) 'Cultural Politics in an Age of Statistics: Numbers, Nations, and the making of Basque Identity'. *American Ethnologist* 20 (4) 818-843.

An Ghaeilge: Reachtaíocht

Seán Ó Cofaigh

Mar a deirtear, BEATHA TEANGA Í A LABHAIRT. Ar an mbonn sin, is cúis áthais dom a bheith ag caint libh inniu faoi chúrsaí teanga trí mheán na Gaeilge. Buíochas don nua-theicneolaíocht agus don chóras chomhuaineach atá curtha ar fáil dúinn inniu ní bheidh aon fhadhb agaibh le *ciall* an mhéid atá le rá agam! Dár ndóigh tá difríocht an-mhór idir *ciall* agus *réasún* agus is ceist daoibh féin an mbaineann an dara ceann le mo chuid cainte inniu. Tá mé ag súil, ar a laghad, go mbeidh léargas níos fearr agaibh ar ball beag ar an stádas reachtúil mar a bhaineann sé le teanga na Gaeilge chomh maith le léargas níos fearr ar an treo ina bhfuilimid ag treabhadh linn sa Roinn Ealaíon, Oidhreachta, Gaeltachta agus Oileán.

Le linn mo chuid cainte, beidh mé ag díriú isteach go sonrach ar theanga na Gaeilge in Éirinn agus ar an reachtaíocht atá ar na bacáin ag an am seo. Is dóigh gurb í an bhuncheist atá le freagairt agam ná an bhfuil gá ann le haghaidh reachtaíochta chun an Ghaeilge a chur chun cinn? Agus an freagra, i mbeagán focal, ná, tá gá dá leithéid. Is fíor go bhfuil stádas bunreachtúil ag an nGaeilge ach níl aon reachtaíocht ann faoi láthair chun éifeacht agus fiacail a thabhairt don stádas sin. Cinnte tá tús áite tugtha don Ghaeilge faoi Airteagal 8 de Bhunreacht na hÉireann (1937), áit a leagtar síos *"Ós í an Ghaeilge an teanga náisiúnta is í an phríomhtheanga oifigiúil í"*, ach caithfear a adhmháil, faraor, nach bhfuil an stádas reatha ag teacht i gcomhréir leis an ardmhian seo. Ba chóir dom a luadh ag an bpointe seo go bhfuil aitheantas tugtha faoin airteagal céanna den Bhunreacht do theanga an Bhéarla mar *"theanga oifigiúil eile"*. Glactar leis, áfach, nach gá aon bheart a dhéanamh chun teanga an Bhéarla a shlánú os rud é nach bhfuil an teanga sin ag dul i léig nó i mbaol a bháis - a mhalairt ar fad atá ann agus, chun an fhírinne a rá, an scéal amhlaidh don teanga sin ar fud na cruinne.

Mar sin, taobh amuigh den Bhunreacht, níl aon reachtaíocht ann chun cearta lucht na Gaeilge a chinntiú. Mar gheall ar an easpa reachtaíochta seo, bíonn sé deacair ó am go chéile a chur ina luí ar eagrais Stáit go bhfuil cearta ag pobal na hÉireann maidir le seirbhís trí Ghaeilge a fháil. In ionad cothrom na féinne a thabhairt do lucht na Gaeilge, bídís ón nGaeltacht nó bídís lasmuigh di a roghnaíonn an Ghaeilge a úsáid mar a bpríomhtheanga labhartha, tá an meon ann seirbhísí a chur ar fáil trí Bhéarla amháin. Níl mórán amhrais faoi ach go bhfuil neamh-aird á tabhairt go forleathan ar na treoirlínte neamhreachtúla a réitigh Bord na Gaeilge (mar a bhí) i 1993 maidir le seirbhísí Stáit a chur ar fáil trí Ghaeilge.

Is léir nár éirigh agus nach n-éireoidh le tionscnamh deonach nó le treoirlínte deonacha gan aon phleanáil shonrach bheith taobh thiar dóibh bunaithe ar na riachtanais éagsúla. Sna cúinsí uile glactar leis anois go bhfuil gá le hathrú ó threoirlínte neamhreachtúla go dtí córas foirmiúil reachtúil. Gealladh a leithéid de reachtaíocht i gClár Oibre an Rialtais don Mhílaois nua agus arís i gClár Oibre Athbhreithnithe an Rialtais don Mhílaois nua agus beidh mé ag caint go sonrach faoin mBille atá ar na bacáin níos deireanaí. D'fhéadfá a rá go mbeadh a leithéid de reachtaíocht ag teastáil ar aon chuma chun teacht i gcomhréir leis an bhfealsúnacht atá taobh thiar den Tionscnamh Bainistíochta Straitéisí. Is é cuspóir foriomlán an Tionscnaimh Bainistíochta Straitéisí ar thug Státseirbhís na hÉireann faoi sa bhliain 1994 ná sármhaitheas a bhaint amach le linn seirbhís a sholáthair don phobal. Tagann an Plean Gníomhaíochta maidir le Seirbhís Ardchaighdeáin don Chustaiméir faoin scáth céanna agus beidh mé ag trácht ar an bplean sin níos deireanaí chomh maith.

Ag an bpointe seo ba chóir dom a mhíniú go bhfuil sé mar aidhm ag an Roinn Ealaíon, Oidhreachta, Gaeltachta agus Oileán an Ghaeilge a chur chun cinn agus a neartú ar fud na tíre agus déantar é seo trí dheontais agus scéimeanna éagsúla a chur ar fáil. Sa bhliain 2000 caitheadh níos mó ná IR£54m (€68m) ar na spriocanna seo, trí dheontais-i-gcabhair do na heagrais chuí agus trí scéimeanna na Roinne laistigh agus lasmuigh den Ghaeltacht, mar seo a leanas:-

Eagras/Scéim	Caiteachas 2000	
	IR£m	€m
Údaras na Gaeltachta	31.5	39.9
Scéimeanna Feabhsúcháin sa Ghaeltacht	9.7	12.3
Scéim Tithíochta sa Ghaeltacht	1.9	2.4
Scéimeanna Cultúrtha agus Sóisialta	3.7	4.7
Ciste na Gaeilge	1.2	1.5
Foras na Gaeilge	6.0	7.6

Anuas ar an gcaiteachas sin, caitheadh IR£4.6m (€5.9m) ar na hOileáin, idir Ghaeltacht agus Ghalltacht, agus caitheadh IR£14.9m (€18.9m) ar TG4.

Níl aon amhras ann mar sin ach go dtugann an Roinn Ealaíon, Oidhreachta, Gaeltachta agus Oileán tacaíocht mhór don Ghaeilge laistigh agus lasmuigh den Ghaeltacht ach tá níos mó ná airgeadas ag teastáil chun cothrom na féinne a chinntiú do lucht labhartha na Gaeilge.

Ag glacadh leis anois go bhfuil reachtaíocht de shaghas éigin riachtanach chun cearta lucht na Gaeilge a chosaint, an chéad cheist eile ná céard a bheas ins an reachtaíocht seo? Go bunúsach bheadh dhá rud inmholta ann. Ar an gcéad dul síos, ba chóir ráiteas soiléir a bheith ann maidir le cearta teanga an tsaoránaigh, is é sin, ag rá go soiléir go bhfuil an ceart ag an gcainteoir Gaeilge gnó a dhéanamh leis an Stát trí mheán na Gaeilge más mian leis nó léi sin a dhéanamh. Ansin, an dara rud, ba chóir dualgas reachtúil a chur ar Ranna Stáit agus ar Eagrais Stáit pleanáil chuí a dhéanamh maidir leis an nGaeilge ionas go mbeidh siad ábalta seirbhís ar chomhchaighdeán le seirbhís trí Bhéarla a chur ar fáil dá gcustaiméirí trí Ghaeilge.

Ach caithfear a bheith reádúil faoi na cuspóirí seo ionas nach dteipfidh ar an gcoincheap. Sa chomhthéacs seo, is cuí cuimhneamh ar an seanfhocal Gaeilge, "de réir a chéile a thógtar na caisleáin". Ní tharlóidh an t-athrú thar oíche agus, faraor, níl sé sin indéanta. Ach an rud is tábhachtaí ná tús a chur leis an bpróiseas agus pleanáil stráitéiseach a dhéanamh don todhchaí ionas go mbeidh seirbhísí den scoth ar fáil don chustaiméir de réir a rogha féin. Ní bheadh aon chiall ann spriocanna mí-réalaíocha a leagan síos nó córais do-oibrithe a chur ar bun. Beidh cothromaíocht, comhoibriú, comhthuiscint agus comhréiteach ag teastáil ón dá thaobh, an dream atá ag éileamh seirbhísí trí Ghaeilge agus an dream atá dá gcur ar fáil, chun an aidhm áirithe a bhaint amach. Séard a bheadh ag teastáil ag an tús ná córas céimiúil a bhunú agus béim ar leith a chur ar na heagrais Stáit atá ag cur seirbhísí ar fáil díreach chuig an pobal. Dár ndóigh ní Bille uileghabhálach a bheadh ann a rachadh isteach go mion i ngach gné den cheist (go háirithe gnéithe a bhaineann go sonrach le freagrachtaí Airí Rialtais eile) agus chaithfí a chur san áireamh nach bhféadfadh gach eagras seirbhís iomlán dátheangach a chur ar fáil i ngach réimse. Go hachomhair ní bheidh an reachtaíocht in ann freastal ar na mianta uile ón gcéad lá agus dá bhrí sin, ionas go mbeidh rath uirthi, beidh sí ag díriú ar na féidearthachtaí ag an tús agus ag tógáil orthu siúd de réir a chéile. Is léir chomh maith go mbeidh costais i gceist, go háirithe ag an tús, ach caithfear breathnú ar an gcostas seo mar infheistíocht náisiúnta, sa chaoi chéanna is a bhreathnófaí ar aon chóras seirbhísí a chuirfí ar fáil do shaoránaigh.

Ceist mhór eile ná an mbeidh sé ar chumas na státseirbhíse agus na n-eagras Stáit an reachtaíocht a chur i bhfeidhm? Chaithfeá a aithint go mbeidh impleachtaí móra ann don Státchóras, go háirithe sa chomhthéacs go bhfuil ganntanas foirne ann go ginearálta agus go bhfuil ceist faoin méid daoine atá ann cheana féin atá ábalta oibriú trí Ghaeilge. Chaithfeá a aithint chomh maith na deacrachtaí atá ann faoi láthair chun daoine a mhealladh isteach sa Státseirbhís. An méid sin ráite, ceaptar go mbeidh an Státchóras in ann an dúshlán seo a shárú trí phleanáil cheart a dhéanamh, trí úsáid níos fearr a bhaint as na hacmhainní atá ann faoi láthair, trí chomhoibriú agus araile. Dár ndóigh is minic a cuireadh dúshláin eile roimh an Státchóras, mar shampla, an tAcht um Shaoráil Faisnéise, an Tionscnamh Bainistíochta Straitéisí, an Plean Gníomhaíochta maidir le Seirbhís Ardchaighdeáin don Chustaiméir, agus tógadh ar bord iad.

Ag trácht ar an gclár deireanach seo, an Plean Gníomhaíochta maidir le Seirbhís Ardchaighdeáin don Chustaiméir, atá mar chuid den Tionscnamh Bainistíochta Straitéisí agus a thagann faoi chúram Roinn an Taoisigh, is fiú dom a chur in iúl anseo gur cuireadh 3 phrionsabal nua leis na naoi gcinn a bhí ann ón tús, is iad sin, 'Comhionannas', 'an Custaiméir Inmheánach' agus, ceangailte leis an ábhar atá faoi chaibidil agam inniu, 'Comhionannas Teangacha Oifigiúla'. Sonraítear faoin bprionsabal seo go ndéanfaidh an Státchóras seirbhísí ardchaighdeáin a shólathar i nGaeilge agus/nó go dátheangach agus a chur in iúl do chustaiméirí go bhfuil an ceart acu a roghnú go ndéileáilfear leo i gceann amháin de na teangacha oifigiúla. Ina theannta sin, is tráthúil cinneadh na Cúirte Uachtaraí le gairid i gcás *Shéamuis Uí Bheoláin* maidir leis an dualgas atá ar an Stát chun Achtanna Oireachtais a chur ar fáil i nGaeilge.

B'fhéidir gur fiú cúpla focal a rá faoin gcás cúirte seo dóibh siúd nach bhfuil ar eolas faoi. Go bunúsach forálann Airteagal 25 de Bhunreacht na hÉireann *inter alia,*

I gcás an tUachtarán do chur a láimhe le téacs Bille i dteanga de na teangacha oifigiúla agus sa teanga sin amháin, ní foláir tiontú oifigiúil a chur amach sa teanga oifigiúil eile.

Mar gheall ar chúiseanna áirithe, ganntanas foirne sa Rannóg Aistriúcháin i dTeach Laighin agus brú oibre na cúiseanna is mó, ní raibh sé seo dá dhéanamh go rialta le scór bliain anuas. Dúradh mar chosaint i gcás *Shéamuis Uí Bheoláin* i mí Aibreán seo caite go raibh sé i gceist ag an Stát tabhairt faoi na riaráistí seo sa thodhchaí. Ba é cinneadh na Cúirte Uachtaraí i gcás *Uí Bheoláin* go bhfuil dualgas bunreachtúil ar an Stát leagan Gaeilge de gach Acht Oireachtais a chur ar fáil ag an am céanna agus a shíníonn an tUachtarán iad. Ina bhreithiúnas luann an Breitheamh Hardiman *"neamart oifigiúil éifeachtach"*, *"cion i gcoinne mheon agus bhunbhrí na bhfocal sa Bhunreacht"*, agus déanann sé comparáid le cur chuige an Aontas Eorpaigh ag rá,

"Tá an dátheangachas, nó an t-ilteangachas i réim i dtíortha iomadúla agus ar ndóigh cuireann an tAontas Eorpach doiciméid choimpléascacha, ar doiciméid dhlíthiúla cuid mhór díobh, ar fáil gach lá sna teangacha oifigiúla go léir."

Bheadh an méid seo lárnach do reachtaíocht comhionannais teanga - ba chóir go mbeadh an leagan Gaeilge de dhoiciméid thábhachtacha ar fáil ag an am céanna is atál fáil ar an leagan Béarla díobh chun comhionannas a chinntiú. Go bunúsach cuireann cinneadh na Cúirte Uachtaraí sa chás seo dualgas ar gach Roinn Stáit tiontú oifigiúil a chur amach i nGaeilge i gcás aon reachtaíocht a dhéantar i mBéarla.

Ag filleadh go dtí an pointe a bhí agam ar ball beag - ní hé nach n-aithnítear na deacrachtaí a d'fhéadfadh a bheith agus na deacrachtaí a bheidh ann gan dabht ach meastar go mba chóir an bhéim a chur ar na féidearthachtaí in ionad na ndeacrachtaí. Tá dea-thoil don Ghaeilge le feiceáil go forleathan agus caithfear tógáil air seo sula mbeidh sé ró-dheireanach. Ní leor na seanráitis polasaí - tá gníomhaíocht agus gníomhaíocht dhearfach ag teastáil go géar. Is léir mar sin nach féidir cúrsaí teanga a fhágáil ar an méar fhada - ní leor "gan a bheith diúltach", caithfear a bheith dearfach chun teangacha a shlánú. Dár ndóigh tá comharthaí dóchais ann don Ghaeilge cheana féin - tá mé cinnte gur luadh nó go luafar fás na nGaelscoileanna, TG4, Raidió na Gaeltachta agus na meáin chumarsáide ag dul ó neart go neart - ach tá tuilleadh le déanamh. Glactar go forleathan nach mbeidh an stádas ceart ag an Gaeilge go dtí go bhfaigheann sí a háit cheart agus an t-aitheantas cuí sa Státchóras agus sa saol poiblí. Tá stráitéis ag teastáil agus creidtear anois gurb í an reachtaíocht an bealach ceart le brú ar aghaidh.

Ag tabhairt faoi reachtaíocht teanga chomh maith le rud ar bith eile, is fiú breathnú ar a mhacasamhail de fhorbairt i dtíortha agus i ndlínsí eile. Inár gcás féin, chuathas i dteagmháil leis na húdaráis chuí i gCeanada agus sa Bhreatain Bheag. Ba mhór an spreagadh dúinn agus ba mhór an chúis dóchais dúinn chomh maith an dul chun cinn leanúnach atá ar siúl sna tíortha sin. I gcás na Breataine Bige, mar shampla, faoina cuid reachtaíochta sa bhliain 1993 tá an Béarla agus an Bhreathnais curtha ar chomhchéim i saol poiblí na Breataine Bige. Go simplí cuireann an *Deddf yr Iaith Gymraeg* nó an *Welsh Language Act, 1993* dualgas ar an earnáil phoiblí déileáil leis an dá theanga ar bhonn chomhionannais agus iad ag cur seirbhísí ar fáil don phobal. Tugann sé ceart absalóideach do chainteoirí na Breathnaise an teanga sin a labhairt sna cúirteanna. Níos tábhachtaí fós, bunaíonn sé an *Bwrdd yr Iaith Gymraeg* nó an *Welsh Language Board* chun an tAcht a chur i bhfeidhm agus chomh maith leis sin, chun an teanga a chur chun cinn. Tá an Bord sin, a bhfuil 11 ball ann agus foireann de 30 acu, freagrach do, agus maoinithe ag, *y Cynulliad Cenedlaethol* nó an *National Assembly for Wales*. Faoin *Welsh Language Act* tá dualgas ar na heagrais phoiblí scéimeanna teanga a aontú leis an mBord. An cur chuige atá ag an mBord ná feidhmiú ar bhonn praiticiúil agus réasúnta agus, dá bhrí sin, cé nach bhfuil aon dualgas reachtúil ar eagrais taobh amuigh den earnáil phoiblí, tá cuid mhaith acu siúd tagtha ar bord go deonach, mar shampla, Abbey National, Tesco, Lloyds Bank, Cardiff Bus, Marks and Spencers, HSBC, agus Stena Line. Tá aonad ar leith curtha ar bun ag British Gas chun deileáil le custaiméirí atá ag iarraidh gnó a dhéanamh le BG trí Bhreathnais agus tá córas dátheangach do na billí curtha ar bun dá gcuid custaiméirí uile sa Bhreatain Bheag. Tuigeann na comhlachtaí seo an buntáiste tradála atá ann mar thoradh ar sheirbhís dhátheangach - tá siad ag feabhsú na seirbhíse dá gcuid custaiméirí, tá siad ag mealladh gnó agus custaiméirí nua, tá siad ag méadú dílseachta a gcuid custaiméirí, tá siad ag cruthú dea-thola ar chostas fíor-íseal, agus tá siad ag fáil buntáiste ar a gcuid iomaitheoirí agus ag cur lena gcaidrimh phoiblí.

Is léir ó na staitisticí go bhfuil ag éirí go maith leis an *Welsh Language Board* leis an gcur chuige seo - tá níos mó ná 210 scéim i bhfeidhm san earnáil phoiblí chomh maith le níos mó ná 65 scéim dheonach idir an earnáil phríobháideach agus an earnáil dheonach. Glactar leis anois gur féidir leis an mBreatain Bheag saol dátheangach a bhaint amach. Tharla an dul chun cinn seo mar thoradh ar bhrú an phobail, forbairtí sa chóras oideachais agus, dár ndóigh, an reachtaíocht i 1993. Rud an-suntasach a chuir an *Welsh Language Board* in iúl dúinn ná, nár éirigh leo thar oíche mar gheall ar an reachtaíocht <u>ach</u> ba é áfach, an tús-phointe riachtanach agus rinneadh dul chun cinn go réidh thar na blianta ina dhiaidh nach bhféadfaí a dhéanamh dá uireasa na reachtaíochta sin. Tugann an sampla seo an-mhisneach agus an-dóchas dúinn agus muid ag dul síos an bealach céanna in Éirinn.

Ba mhaith liom filleadh arís ar an mBille Comhionannais um Theangacha Oifigiúla atá á ullmhú ag an Roinn Ealaíon, Oidhreachta, Gaeltachta agus Oileán faoi láthair. Go bunúsach leagfaidh an Bille seo bonn reachtúil i dtaca leis na teangacha oifigiúla (Gaeilge agus Béarla) agus chomh maith leis sin cinnteoidh sé cearta teanga an tsaoránaigh ina c(h)aidreamh leis an Stát. Tharla an chéad chéim thábhachtach i mí Iúil 2000 nuair a ghlac an Rialtas i bprionsabal leis an mBille sin agus nuair a tugadh cead chun Scéim Ghinearálta nó na ceannteidil a dhréachtú. Tá mé sásta a chur in iúl go bhfuil céim thábhachtach eile bainte amach le deireanaí nuair a ghlac an Rialtas leis an Scéim Ghinearálta ar 12 Meitheamh 2001 agus nuair a tugadh cead an téacs a dhréachtú mar ábhar práinne. Is iad na bunaidhmeanna atá leis an mBille seo ná :

- Cearta teanga saoránach a shonrú i gcomhréir le stádas bunreachtúil na dteangacha oifigiúla;
- Dualgais Ranna Stáit agus na hEarnála Poiblí a shonrú maidir le seirbhísí a chur ar fáil do shaoránaigh sna teangacha oifigiúla ;
- Dualgas reachtúil a chur ar Ranna Stáit agus ar an Earnáil Phoiblí maidir le leibhéal aontaithe sheirbhísí Stáit a chur ar fáil trí Ghaeilge;
- Freagracht ghinearálta a chur ar an Aire Ealaíon, Oidhreachta, Gaeltachta agus Oileán maidir le seirbhísí Stáit a chur ar fáil trí Ghaeilge, agus
- Oifig Choimisinéir na dTeangacha Oifigiúla a bhunú chun maoirseacht agus monatóireacht a dhéanamh ar an Acht agus chun féachaint chuige go gcuirfear i bhfeidhm é.

Tuigfidh sibh nach féidir liom níos mó a rá faoin mBille nó a bhfuil ann go dtí go mbeidh sé foilsithe. Ag an bpointe seo táimid ag súil leis go bhfoilseofar é san Fhómhar agus táimid, in éindí le lucht labhartha na Gaeilge, ag tnúth go mór leis an ócáid stairiúil sin.

Críochnóidh mé leis sin. Go raibh maith agaibh as ucht bhur n-aire.

Abstract

This paper describes the preparation being made for the forthcoming language legislation in order to give effect to the Constitutional Status of the Irish language in the Republic of Ireland. This will help meet and give effect to the philosophy underlying the Government's (1994) Strategic Management Initiative: namely, achievement of excellence in the provision of service to the public. It is felt that mutual understanding and compromise will be required from both sides - those seeking services in Irish and the providers. The Bill will be an all-encompassing one, focusing initially on the feasibilities. It is now an urgent matter due to a recent Supreme Court decision. Goodwill for the language is widely evident and the Official Languages Equality Bill, to give it its official title, will ensure the language rights of all citizens in their dealings with the State.

Coimisiún na Gaeltachta agus an Ghaeltacht

Bertie Ó hAinmhire

I mí Aibreán anuraidh (2000), d'fhógair an Rialtas go raibh Coimisiún Gaeltachta bunaithe. Is i 1925 a bhí an Coimisiún deiridh ann. Cén fáth Coimisiún nua anois mar sin? Is dócha go gceapann an Rialtas go bhfuil an Ghaeilge fós ag cúlú sa Ghaeltacht in ainneoin iarrachtaí an Stáit agus iarrachtaí an phobail féin. Iarradh ar an gCoimisiún nua seo moltaí a dhéanamh maidir leis an nGaeilge a láidriú mar ghnáth-theanga phobal na Gaeltachta.

Bhí os cionn 3 mhilliún cainteoir dúchais Gaeilge in Éirinn roimh an nGorta mór. Faoi dheireadh an chéid sin bhí líon na gcainteoirí dúchais íslithe go dtí thart ar 700,000. Faoin am ar bunaíodh Coimisiún na Gaeltachta i mí Eanáir 1925 ní raibh de chainteoirí dúchais Gaeilge sa tír ach 250,000. Ba é Coimisiún na Gaeltachta 1925 a rinne an chéad iarracht sainmhíniú a thabhairt ar an téarma Gaeltacht. Is é cumas an phobail Gaeilge a labhairt a bhí á mheas ag an gCoimisiún sin seachas leibhéal úsáide na Gaeilge sa phobal.

Tá Téarmaí Tagartha leathana tugtha don Choimisiún nua. Is Coimisiún Rialtais é an Coimisiún rud a thugann stádás don obair atá ar siúl aige agus le cúnamh Dé don tuarascáil atá a ullmhú faoi láthair. Ar ndóigh, ós rud é gur Coimisiún Rialtais é caithfidh sé tuarascáil agus plean gníomhaíochta a chur faoi bhráid an Rialtais féin amach anseo. Sna Téarmaí Tagartha a tugadh don Choimisiún iarradh air anailís a dhéanamh ar éifeacht na n-eagraíochtaí Stáit atá ag plé go díreach le buanú agus caomhnú na Gaeilge sa Ghaeltacht. Táimid ag caint anseo faoi Údarás na Gaeltachta, An Roinn Ealaíon, Oidhreachta, Gaeltachta agus Oileán, Raidió na Gaeltachta agus TG4. Éifeacht na n-eagraíochtaí sin maidir le buanú agus caomhnú na Gaeilge atá i gceist. Ar ndoigh tá obair mhór i gceist anseo agus bhí ar an gCoimisiún comhairleoirí a fhostú chun cabhrú leo leis an gcúram seo.

Iarradh ar an gCoimisiún freisin anailís agus staidéar a dhéanamh ar na tionchair eile atá ar an teanga sa Ghaeltacht. Tá a fhios ag gach duine a thug cuairt ar an nGaeltacht go bhfuil fórsaí láidre ag cur an-bhrú ar an nGaeilge faoi láthair. Mar sin is dócha go mbeidh fórsaí tacaíochta níos láidre fós ag teastáil má tá an teanga le maireachtáil sna limistéir Ghaeltachta sa todhchaí. Ag úsáid foinsí eolais atá ar fáil cheana ar nós an Daonáirimh agus Scéim Labhairt na Gaeilge atá á riaradh ag an Roinn Ealaíon, Oidhreachta, Gaeltachta & Oileán, beidh an Coimisiún ag déanamh anailíse ar a mhéid atá an Ghaeilge in úsáid mar gnáth-theanga sa Ghaeltacht inniu. Tá cúrsaí pleanála thar a bheith tábhachtach sa Ghaeltacht freisin agus tá forálacha san Acht Um Phleanáil agus Forbairt 2000 a bhaineann le teanga agus cultúr na Gaeltachta. Tá moltaí curtha ar aghaidh ag an gCoimisiún cheana chuig an Aire Comhshaoil agus Rialtais Áitiúil maidir le cur i bhfeidhm na bhforálacha seo. Tá roinnt mhaith rudaí eile iarrtha ar an gCoimisiún sna Téarmaí Tagartha agus tá sonraí ar fáil ar an suíomh idirlín atá ag Coimisiún na Gaeltachta ag www.coimnagael.ie

Rinne an Coimisiún cinneadh ag an tús go mbeadh ról lárnach ag an bpobal féin in obair an Choimisiúin agus go mbeadh sé an-tábhachtach tuairimí an phobail a fháil i scríbhinn agus ó bhéal. Cuireadh fógraí sna nuachtaín ar an raidió &rl ag lorg aighneachtaí i scríbhinn agus fuair an Coimisiún suas le 150 aighneacht ó eagraíochtaí agus ó dhaoine aonair. Ach go deimhin ní bhíonn fonn ar gach duine dul i mbun pinn agus chinn an Coimisiún go gcaithfí cruinnithe poiblí a eagrú chun tuairimí an phobail a fháil ó bhéal. Eagraíodh 28 cruinniú poiblí taobh istigh agus taobh amuigh den Ghaeltacht. Rinneadh freastal maith ar na cruinnithe sin go háirithe taobh istigh den Ghaeltacht agus bhí mé féin mar Rúnaí an Choimisiúin i láthair ag gach uile cheann acu. Rinne suas le 1,500 duine freastal ar na cruinnithe poiblí, ionadaithe na bpobal éagsúil ar nós Comharchumainn, Coistí Forbartha, Coistí Tuismitheoirí Scoile &rl. Ní hamháin gur thug na cruinnithe sin deis do na pobail a dtuairimí a chur i láthair an Rialtais ach freisin chuir siad ceist thodhchaí na Gaeilge sa Ghaeltacht ag snámh in intinn an phobail. Ba iontach an bealach inar léirigh na gnáthdhaoine a dtuairimí agus moltaí go soiléir agus go beacht agus an tuiscint agus an meas atá acu ar a dteanga.

Rinneadh go leor cláracha faoi obair an Choimisiúin ag an am sin - ar Raidió na Gaeltachta, ar na staisiúin Raidió Áitiúla ar TG4, RTÉ agus ar staisiúin eile. Ba é an rud is suimiúla faoi na cruinnithe seo domsa ná an chosúlacht a bhí idir na tuairimí agus na moltaí a tháinig aníos sna ceantair éagsúla. Bhí sé seo go háirithe fíor i gcás na gceantar a bhfuil an Ghaeilge láidir iontu. I gceantair eile bhí íontas ar na pobail féin gur tháinig an oiread sin daoine amach chuig cruinniú faoi thodhchaí na Gaeltachta agus i gcásanna áirithe chabhraigh cruinnithe an Choimisiúin le feachtais áitiúila eile m.sh., meánscoil ar Inis Meáin i gCo na Gaillimhe. D'éirigh go maith i mo thuairim leis an sprioc a bhí ag an gCoimisiún plé poiblí oscailte a thosú faoi cheist na Gaeilge sa Ghaeltacht.

Céard é an chéad chéim eile? Táimid ag scríobh faoi láthair agus tá súil againn go mbeidh Tuarascáil agus moltaí ar fáil roimh dheireadh na bliana. Níl aon amhras ach go bhfuil pobal na Gaeltachta ag súil le hathruithe móra ó thaobh an Stáit. Is léir go gceapann siad go bhfuil a lán cur i géill ann faoi lathair agus éilíonn siad seirbhísí comhionanna trí Ghaeilge don Ghaeltacht.

Braitheann go leor freisin ar phobal na Gaeltachta féin. Tá sé riachtanach go mbeadh pobal na Gaeltachta sásta agus muiníneach an teanga a thabhairt go dtí an chéad glún eile. Muna bhfeiceann óige na Gaeltachta gurbh fhiú dóibh agus gur féidir leo a dteanga a úsáid agus gan aon mhíbhuntaiste a bheith ag baint léi leanfaidh an claonadh atá ann faoi láthair. Ar an lámh eile má thugtar an t-aitheantas agus an stádas don teanga atá ag dul di, ar a laghad beidh údar dóchais againn.

Abstract

This paper outlines in very broad terms the setting up of Coimisiún na Gaeltachta *and its Terms of Reference. The Coimisiún's brief is to draw up an extensive action plan for immediate implementation in order to stabilise language usage and the transmission of Irish within Gaeltacht areas. Extensive consultation took place. Written submissions were requested and received. Further studies and analyses were subcontracted to various language advisors and researchers to report in particular on the impact of State Bodies on language usage and maintenance within the Gaeltacht. The use of language within other domains was also examined. The Coimisiún must now draw up its plan of action and the people of the Gaeltachtaí are expecting radical and far-reaching measures and proposals to provide equality of service and status to the Irish language on a par with English.*

An Struchtúr tacaíochta atá le bunú faoi Alt 31 den Acht Oideachais 1998: An Chomhairle um Oideachas Gaeltachta agus lánGhaeilge

Breandán Mac Cormaic

Is éard ba mhaith liom a dhéanamh ar maidin ná cúlra an struchtúir a mhiniú daoibh agus cén caoi ar baineadh amach é, na riachtanais oideachais a lua, an struchtúr féin a mhíniú agus cúlpa focal maidir leis an ngaol idir an struchtúr agus an eagraíocht "Gaelscoileanna" a lua chomh maith. Críochnóidh mé le roinnt pointí maidir leis an nGaeilge agus an todhchai.

Cúlra

Is sna caogaidi agus na seascaidi a tháinig meath, ar fháthanna éagsúla, ar lion na scoileanna a bhíodh ag múineadh tri Ghaeilge, agus is dá bharr seo gur bhunaigh tuismitheoiri cúpla bunscoil lánGhaeilge i mBaile Átha Cliath sna seascaidi. Ach is ó 1975/6 i leith a thosaigh an borradh nua sa scolaiocht lánGhaeilge, borradh atá fós faoi lántseol sa lá atá inniu ann.

Is i 1973 a bunaíodh an eagraíocht "**Gaelscoileanna**" mar áis tacaíochta do thuismitheoirí ar theastaigh uathu oideachas IánGhaeilge a fháil dá bpáisti, agus mar áis tacaíochta do na scoileanna a bhunaigh na tuismitheoiri seo, mar is iad na tuismitheoirí agus ní hé an Stát a bhunaigh iad.

Láidrigh **Gaelscoileanna** de réir a chéile go háirithe ó fuair sé deontas bliantiúl ó Bhord na Gaeilge ó 1979 i leith. Leagadh síos ceithre bhunchloch do **Ghaelscoileanna** sna hochtaidi:

- go ndéanfaí obair na heagraíochta go proifisiúnta,
- gur eagras bainistíochta é (ag plé leis na Boird Bhainistíochta amháin sna scoileanna),
- gur comhpháirtíocht idir tuismitheoiri agus múinteoirí a bheadh ann, agus
- gur eagras oideachais é (seachas eagras Gaeilge).

Bhí agus tá an ceathrú bunchloch an-tábhachtach mar gur chuir sé **Gaescoileanna** i lár na páirce leis na heagrais oideachais eile: na ceardchumainn, na hEaglaisí, agus eagraíochtaí na dtuismitheoiri. Agus is de bharr an seasamh sin gur bhain **Gaelscoileanna** áit amach mar Phairtnéir Oideachais. Is é an toradh concréideach a bhí air seo ná go bhfuil ionadaíocht ag **Gaelscoileanna** ar na coimisiúin éagsúla a bhuníonn an Rialtas ó am go chéile ar nós an Coimisiún um Chóiríocht Scoileanna. Ach bhí toradh eile air - gur thug sé stádas don eagríocht a bhí an-tábhachtach agus muid i mbun feachtais (le grúpai eile) chun struchtúr tacaíochta a bhaint amach.

Mar sin féin bhí agus tá **Gaelscoileanna** lasmuigh den chóras oideachais sa Stát; is brúghrúpa é ar son na gaelscolaíochta agus níl sé ar chumas nó níl sé mar chúram ag **Gaelscoileanna** na riachtanais a bhaineann leis an gcóras gaelscolaíochta a sholáthar.

Go deimhin is córas eile oideachais é an córas gaelscolaíochta a fheidhmíonn comhtreomhar leis an ngnáthchóras, a d'fhás go tapaidh le tríocha bliain anuas agus nach bhfuil freastal á dhéanamh ag an ngnáthchóras ar a shainriachtanais. Lena chur go gonta: ní fhéadfadh an Roinn Oideachais, a fheidhmíonn trí Bhéarla leis an 95% de na scoileanna a mhúintear tri Bhéarla freastal cuí a dhéanamh ar an 5% a fheidhmíonn tri Ghaeilge.

Thuig **Gaelscoileanna** mar sin gur gá struchtúr tacaíochta stáit a bhunú agus ghlac an eagraíocht páirt ghníomhach sna diospóireachtaí a bhí ar siúl maidir le cúrsaí oideachais a spreag an tAire Oideachais, Niamh Bhreathnach, ag an am.

Lorg **Gaelscoileanna** struchtúr tacaíochta ar leith san aighneacht a chuir an eagraíocht chuig an Chomhdháil Náisiúnta Oideachais i 1995, agus nuair a bheartaigh an tAire Boird Reigiúnda Oideachais a bhunú tháinig trí eagras le chéile le feachtas a chur ar bun le Bord Oideachais Gaeltachta agus lánGhaeilge a bhaint amach; **Gaelscoileanna, Eagraíocht Scoileanna Gaeltachta agus Comhdháil Náisiúnta na Gaeilge.** Ní raibh an tAire sásta géilleadh faoina leithéid, ach pé scéal é thit an Rialtas agus thainig Fianna Fáil agus an Páirtí Daonlathach chun cumhachta. Ní raibh an Rialtas nua i bhfábhar na mBord Oideachais ach lean an grúpa "comhghuallaíochta" ar aghaidh leis an bhfeachtas le Bord nó struchtúr ar leith a fháil agus mar thoradh ar an bhfeachtas sin cuireadh a leithéid isteach sa Bhille Oideachais a d'fhoilsigh an tAire Oideachais nua Mícheál Martin i Mí na Nollag 1997

Idir foilsiú an Bhille Oideachais agus teacht i bhfeidhm an Achta Oideachais i Mí Eanáir 1999, tharla athrú amháin ar Alt 31: de bharr brú ó Bhord na Gaeilge agus an INTO cuireadh cúram maidir le múineadh na Gaeilge isteach in Alt 31 in éindí le múineadh trí mheán na Gaeilge. Athrú bunúsach é sin a d'fhéadfadh fócas an struchtúir a scrios. Os rud é go bhfuil 95% de scoileanna na tíre ag múineadh trí Bhéarla tá seans maith ann go gcuirfí brú amach anseo le go gcuirfí an chuid is mó d'airgead an struchtúir ar fáil do mhúineadh na Gaeilge sna scoileanna Béarla seachas do scolaíocht trí Ghaeilge agus Gaeltachta.

Botún mór polaitíochta ba é freisin, i mo thuairimse, mar go mbaineann sé cúram mhúineadh na Gaeilge sna gnáthscoileanna den Roinn Oideachais agus cuireann anuas é ar struchtúr a bunaíodh chun aidhm eile a bhaint amach - freastal ar scolaiocht trí Ghaeilge.

An Chomhairle

Maidir le bunú na Comhairle féin theastaigh uainn:

1. go mbeadh an comhdhéanamh daonlathach agus ionadaíoch do na scoileanna Gaeltachta agus IánGhaeilge
2. go gclú dódh na téarmaí tagartha na riachtanais chuí, agus
3. go mbeadh sí ina hinstitiúid fheidhmeach seachas ina hinstitiúid chomhairleach amháin.

Ó thaobh an daonlachais de d'éirigh linn. Beidh 21 ball ar an gComhairle comhdhéanta mar seo a leanas:

Title	No.
Ionadaithe Ghaelscoleanna	3
Ionadaithe Eagraíocht Scoileanna Gaeltachta	3
Roghnaithe ag na Scoileanna IánGhaeilge	3
Roghnaithe ag na Scoileanna Gaeltachta	3
Foras na Gaeilge	1
Comhdháil Náisiúnta na Gaeilge	1
INTO (ceardchumann)	2
TUI (ceardchumann)	1
ASTI (ceardchumann)	1
Ainmnithe ag an Aire Oideachais	2
An Cathaoirleach	2
Total	21

Is ionadaithe ó na Páirtnéiri Oideachais ag leibhéal na scoileanna atá i gceist le ionadaíocht na scoileanna i.e. múinteoir amháin, tuismitheoir amháin agus ionadaí na bPátrún roghnaithe ag na baill chuí ar na Boird Bhainistíochta.

Ó thaobh na riachtanas de, tá ceithre cinn ann go príomha - taighde, oiliúint múinteoirí, seirbhísí tacaíochta agus achmhainní teagaisc. Clúdaítear na riachtanais sin in Alt 31 agus tá cúram freisin ann comhairle a chur ar an Aire maidir le polasaithe ó thaobh soláthar oideachais trí Ghaeilge sa Ghalltacht agus sa Ghaeltacht agus comhairle a chur ar an gComhairle Náisiúnta Curaclaim agus Measúnaithe. Tá soláthar ann freisin go bhféadfadh an tAire a chuid feidhmeannas i leith aon ceann de na cúraimí thuasluaite a tharmligean chuig an struchtúr nua.

Gaelscoileanna agus an Struchtúr Nua

Tá difríocht an-soiléir idir an ról a bheas ag **GAELSCOILEANNA** agus feidhmeanna an structúir nua. Leanfaidh **Gaelscoileanna** mar bhrú-eagras agus mar eagras deonach: ag cuidiú le tuismitheoiri scoileanna a bhunú, ag déanamh ionadaiochta ar son scoileanna leis an Roinn Oideachais maidir le foireann, foirginti agus mar sin de.

Leanfaidh sé freisin mar Pháirtnéir Oideachais ag déanamh ionadaiochta ar son na nGaelscoileanna ar na Coimisiúin éagsúla.

Níl fáth ar bith nach lorgódh **Gaelscoileanna** conradh ón struchtúr nua cuid de na seirbhísí do na scoileanna lánGhaeilge a sholáthar; cúrsaí oiliúna do bhaill na mBord Bainistíochta cur i gcás, mar déanann Gaelscoileanna a leithéid a chur ar fáil cheana féin.

Go deimhin d'fhéadfadh sé tarlúint nach n-aontódh lucht na gaelscolaiochta le polasaithe nó le feidhmiú an struchtúir nua amach anseo; nó go ndéanfadh an Rialtas comhdhéanamh an struchtúir a athrú agus ionadaíocht óna scoileanna

LánGhaeilge agus Gaeltachta a laghdú. Dá dtarlódh a leithéid bheadh sé rí-thábhachtach go mbéadh eagras láidir neamhspleách fós ann chun freasúra éifeachtach a chruthú agus a chur ar fáil.

Cúrsaí go dtí seo

Tá an coiste náisiúnta nach mór curtha le chéile, ach níl ainm oifigiúil an struchtúir aontaithe fós. Níl buiséad na chéad bhliana socraithe agus níl socrú déanta fós maidir le Príomhfheidhmeannach a cheapadh. Níl ionad na hArdoifige socraithe ach an oiread.

Ba mhaith liomsa go gceapfaí Príomhfheidhmeannach ar dtús agus ansin go ndéanfaí plean stráitéiseach a chur le chéile - rud a thógfaidh roinnt míonna ar a laghad. Feictear dom go dtógfaidh sé roinnt blianta an struchtúr a thógáil i gceart, neart a chur isteach ann agus líon na ngníomhaíochtai a fhorbairt mar creidim nach bhfuil morán machnaimh déanta ag an Státchóras ar an gceist agus nach dtuigeann ach dornán beag d'oifigigh na Roinne Oideachais - ach atá ag an leibheal is airde - an mianach atá sa struchtúr seo.

Pointí Ginearálta

Is féidir coimre a dhéanamh ar an méid atá ráite agam mar a leanas:
1. Bunaíodh an struchtúr seo de bharr brú ón mbun, agus ní de bharr cinneadh polasaí neamhspléach ag aon Rialtas.
2. Is féidir le grúpaí beaga, le dúthracht, diongbháilteacht, foighne agus sáreagrúchán, torthaí suntasacha a bhaint amach.
3. Tá muintir na scolaiochta IánGhaeilge ag feidhmniú i bhfolús polasaí teanga.

Mar sin is gá ceist na Gaeilge ina hiomláine a ardú - Todhchaí na Gaeilge sa Ghaeltacht - An Ghaeilge lasmuigh den Ghaeltacht - Na struchtúir atá ag teastáil - Caighdeán na Gaeilge/Saibhreas na teanga inniu – Líon na gcainteoiri dúchais lasmuigh den Ghaeltacht a mhéadú - Ról an Stáit i gcomhthéacs nach bhfuil agus nach mbeidh polasaí cuimsitheach ag an Stát féin. Is léir go bhfuil fealsúnacht nua teanga de dhíth go crua.

Abstract

This paper gives a succinct account of the background to the proposals made in Section 31 of the Education Act, which came into effect in the Republic in January 1999. The co-ordinating efforts of Gaelscoileanna, Eagraíocht na Scoileanna Gaeltachta and Comhdháil Náisiúnta na Gaeilge were instrumental in achieving a separate structure for all-Irish education, which will deal with the particular needs of that sector under four headings: research, teacher training, support services and teaching materials. The structure of this new Body is under consideration at present. a new Chief Executive is to be appointed soon. It is hoped that all-Irish education will at last begin to achieve its objectives under a well-documented and applied language policy. The implications are immense – the recommendations of Coimisiún na Gaeltachta are also likely to add further weight to the necessity of having definite and workable language policies and supporting planning structures. A new sociolinguistic philosophy, encompassing language planning and maintenance in a bilingual society, is needed and should be informed by clear and constructive debate.

Minority Language Rights Regimes: An Analytical Framework, Scotland, and Emerging European Norms

Robert Dunbar

I have chosen to address three topics in this paper. In the first section, I will consider the different approaches to minority linguistic regimes that may be taken by national, regional and local governments and will briefly explore some of the substantive content of different linguistic regimes. In the second section, I will consider the present situation in Scotland, with particular reference to Gaelic. I will conclude in the third section with some thoughts about the practical value of language rights and their role in broader linguistic revival initiatives. While the linkages between these three topics may not seem immediately obvious, I hope that some coherence will emerge.

1.   An Analytical Framework for Minority Language Rights Regimes

No two language rights regimes are the same, and the content of each will be affected by numerous factors. One crucial issue is the determination of which linguistic minorities should be covered. There may be many types of linguistic minorities in any particular State. For example, there may be speakers of minority languages which are indigenous to the State – "autochthonous" language communities, to use the language of the *European Charter for Regional or Minority Languages* (the "Charter"),[1] – which in a Scottish context would include Gaelic speakers and Scots speakers. There may be speakers of languages which have come to the State by virtue of more recent immigration – "immigrant languages", "heritage languages"[2], or "community languages" as they are known in the UK – which in a Scottish context would include Urdu, Punjabi, Cantonese and other languages. There are also minorities composed of persons with special linguistic needs, such as users of sign languages. In devising a minority language policy, States must determine the extent to which these different groups of language users should be treated differently.

A second crucial issue is the determination of the policy objective underlying a minority language regime. In many States, the dominant minority linguistic policy in respect of all groups of minority language users has been one of **assimilation**; that is, the stated or unstated goal of State language policy has been to ensure that speakers of minority languages become unilingual speakers of the majority language of the State. Sometimes the motive for such policies is linguistic nationalism, with language being used as a means of forging a new nation or creating a unity where previously there was none. Sometimes, the motive is a fear of separatism or irredentism. Sometimes, the motive is more enlightened, at least in conception, if not in effect: classic liberals such as John

---

[1] Strasbourg: Council of Europe, Publishing and Documentation Service, 1993.
[2] The term which is used in Canada, for example.

Stuart Mill argued that the creation of a common language was a necessary pre-condition to full participation in a democratic polity.[3] It was, for example, in revolutionary France that we see an early effort at the creation of a common citizenship based on a common language: French was to be the medium through which subjects became citizens.[4] Certainly, one of the key moments in the decline of Gaelic in Scotland was the passage of the 1872 *Education Act*, which for the first time created universal public education; there was, however, no provision in this act for instruction through the medium of Gaelic, and with the creation of the new school system, a lively system of local Gaelic-medium education was brought to an end. The goal of the 1872 Act was not, of course, to preserve a Gaelic-speaking community in Scotland, but to create a modern English-speaking population which could participate in an English-speaking British polity and, perhaps more importantly, an English-speaking British imperial administrative state and labour market.[5]

A somewhat different approach to linguistic (and other) minorities is a **policy of integration**, under which the State not only tolerates but celebrates diversity, while at the same time ensuring that members of linguistic and other minorities are entitled to participate fully in the life of the society. Under a policy of integration, however, the State does not necessarily commit itself to taking positive measures to preserve such diversity; indeed, the prevailing view tends to be that linguistic and other aspects of minority identity are essentially a private matter, which should be respected and be left unmolested by State interference.

What are the contours of a linguistic rights regime based on a policy of integration or tolerance? Such a regime would include the right to use the minority language in private domains: in the home, in the street, in private associations such as churches and social clubs, and in private sector economic transactions. It would also permit the use of minority languages in privately run schools, and in privately-owned communications media such as newspaper, book and journal publishing, private radio and private television. It is likely that the right to use a minority language in all of these domains is already guaranteed by basic civil and political rights such as the right to freedom of expression, the right to freedom of assembly and association, and the right to respect for private and family life, under instruments such as the *European Convention on Human Rights* (the "ECHR")[6]. In particular, the right to freedom of expression has been recognised by courts in countries such as Canada[7] and by the United Nations

---

[3] For a discussion of Mill's views, see, for example, Stephen May, *Language and Minority Rights: Ethnicity, Nationalism and the Politics of Language*, (Harlow: Pearson Education Limited, 2001), at pp. 20-23.
[4] See, for example, May, *ibid*, at pp. 156-163.
[5] See Kenneth J. MacKinnon, *Gaelic: A Past and Future Prospect*, (Edinburgh: Saltire Society, 1991), at p. 75 *et seq* for a discussion of the 1872 Education Act.
[6] See Articles 10, 11 and 8 of the ECHR, respectively.
[7] See, for example, *Ford v. Que.*,[1988] 2 S.C.R. 712.

Human Rights Committee[8] to include the freedom of expression in a particular language, and to cover freedom of commercial expression.

Two other key elements of a policy of integration or tolerance are the principle of non-discrimination and what could be described as the principle of protection. The principle of non-discrimination provides that it is impermissible to discriminate, either directly or indirectly, on the basis of, among other things, language.[9] The principle of protection is given expression through legislation which protects minorities, including linguistic minorities, from acts of violence and abuse.

Under a regime of integration or tolerance, speakers of minority languages often have the right to use their language in certain interactions with public institutions. Most notable here is the right to use the minority language in proceedings before the criminal courts and the right to be promptly informed in the minority language, when charged with a criminal offence, of the nature of the charges.[10] If, however, the person speaks and understands the majority language, he or she may not entitled to expect the use of his or her language.[11]

While generally not mandated by instruments such as the ECHR, it is increasingly common for government departments and other public bodies to provide information and certain communication services through the medium of certain minority languages, especially so-called "immigrant" languages, where speakers of such languages do not speak or understand the language of the State. Like the use of minority languages in the criminal justice system, the provision of such minority language services by governments is not meant to preserve and promote the use of such languages – as noted, use of the minority language is generally limited to cases where the majority language is not spoken – but to ensure that monolingual speakers of minority languages enjoy the same procedural fairness, administrative fairness and access to important public services as other members of society. In most cases, any such provision is not statutorily mandated, but results from the exercise of administrative discretion. "Majority language as second language" programmes in schools are commonplace in many jurisdictions, and are meant to promote fluency in the majority language amongst immigrant children and children of non-majority language speaking parents. Again, the aim is fairness – to ensure that such children enjoy full and equal access to educational and employment opportunities in the majority language.

In some jurisdictions, limited steps are taken to recognise linguistic and cultural diversity through publicly-funded "heritage language" or "community language" classes. Usually run outside of class hours, and for only a limited

---

[8] See, for example, *Ballantyne, Davidson and McIntyre v. Canada*, (1993), CCPR/C/47/D/359/1989 and 385/1989.

[9] See, for example, Article 14 of the ECHR.

[10] See Article 6, paragraphs 3 (e) and (a) of the ECHR, respectively.

[11] See, for example, Alpha Connelly, "The European Convention on Human Rights and the Protection of Linguistic Minorities", (1993) I.J.E.L. 277 at pp. 281-283 for a discussion of the relevant case law.

amount of time each week, these classes are meant to promote some awareness of minority languages and cultures to children who are members of minority communities. Such classes are generally not the creature of any special minority linguistic regime, however, and it is not clear that they are very useful in, for example, promoting fluency in languages in which children are not already fluent.

For many minority language communities, a regime of integration or tolerance is insufficient. For such communities, the essential problem is not one of toleration by or integration into the wider community, but the **maintenance of their minority linguistic group identity**, the preservation of their distinctive language community. For such communities, the desired policy is one of **support**, and in some cases **strong support**, for the minority language, primarily through legislation but also through executive, or administrative, initiatives.

Policies of **support for the maintenance of minority linguistic group identity** typically focus on the provision of a range of public services through the medium of the minority language, and tend to be mandated through the creation of rights to such services. Such linguistic rights regimes can be enacted in a constitution, a bill of rights, or in legislation such as a language act. One of the cornerstones of these policies is the provision of education through the medium of the minority language. Generally, the right to such education is limited to primary and secondary education (though it need not be so limited), and the exercise of the right is made contingent on sufficient demand for such minority language education services. The reason for such limitations is typically the cost and administrative inconvenience of offering an alternative form of education. While such concerns may be understandable, they can also be used as an excuse for not providing minority language medium education.

Typically, policies of support of minority group linguistic identity also make provision for the use of the minority language in accessing certain other public services, such as health care, social welfare, and other services provided through local councils, and for the use of the language in correspondence with and from public bodies, including legislative and executive branches of government. Once again, the availability and extent of minority language services is often made contingent on sufficiency of demand. In some cases, users of minority languages will be given a statutory right to such services; in other cases, public bodies are merely required to make and implement language plans under which policies for the provision of minority language services are developed, implemented and, as appropriate, extended. This latter approach is the one taken in the *Welsh Language Act 1993*, for example, and although some critics of this approach argue that language plans are a less certain means of ensuring the provision of minority language services than enforceable statutory rights, language plans can nonetheless be effective mechanisms, if their development by public bodies is assisted and/or directed by a language board staffed with experts in minority language development, and if the implementation of such plans is overseen and enforced in some way, perhaps by a language commissioner or other public body charged with that task.

Policies of support of minority linguistic group identity also often provide for the right to use the minority language for certain "official" purposes, such as the right to use minority language versions of personal, organisation and business names, the right to execute contracts, wills and other such legal documents in the minority language, and so forth. Such policies also often provide for a right to use the minority language before courts (both criminal and civil), tribunals and administrative bodies, even in cases where the person exercising such a right speaks the majority or official language. The extent of this right often varies: in some cases, it is limited to the use of the minority language in the giving of oral evidence by parties and witnesses; in other cases, it includes the right to present a case and adduce other evidence in the minority language; and in some cases, it requires that the judge or decision-maker is able to speak and understand the minority language, thereby potentially dispensing of the need for translators. Finally, such policies sometimes provide for the right to use the language in political institutions—for example, the right to use the language in national and/or regional parliaments and in local councils and their committees—and for the use of the language in the official record of debates and committee proceedings, as well as in the signage and media of such institutions.

Policies of support of minority linguistic group identity often provide for broadcasting on public media or publicly-regulated media through the medium of the minority language. Such provision may be in the form of a separate public or publicly-supported radio and/or television station which broadcasts through the medium of the minority language for some or all of the broadcast day, or in the form of provision for a certain number of hours of minority language broadcasting on existing majority language public broadcasting outlets or publicly-funded broadcasting outlets, or in the form of a statutory requirement on private sector broadcasting outlets to provide a certain number of hours of programming through the medium of the minority language.

The final category of language policies could be described as those of **strong support for the maintenance of minority linguistic group identity**. Such policies tend to go beyond those of support for the maintenance of minority linguistic group identity in at least two ways: first, they can involve an element of compulsion in respect of the use of the minority language in the provision of at least some of the public services described above; and second, they often attempt to regulate language use not only in the public but also in the private and voluntary sectors. Such policies have been tried in Quebec[12] and, less rigorously, in Catalonia[13], for example. With regard to the use of the minority language in the provision of public services, policies of support can, as we have just seen, give users of minority language the right or opportunity to obtain public services, such as education, health care, and so forth, through the medium of the minority language, but do no require them to do so, and such policies certainly do not require non-speakers of the minority language to make use of minority language

---

[12] See Bill 101 (1977), as amended.
[13] See the 1983 Linguistic Normalization Law and the 1998 Linguistic Policy Law, and Sara Gore and John MacInnes, *The Politics of Language in Catalunya*, (Edinburgh: Edinburgh Working Papers in Sociology, Department of Sociology, University of Edinburgh, 1998), for a discussion.

services—to do so would tend to force non-speakers of the minority language to become speakers of such languages, at least for some purposes. Policies of strong support can include this element of compulsion. For example, they may provide that, at least in certain geographical areas, children must be educated through the medium of the minority language, even when the children come from households in which the minority language is not spoken. Under such policies, provision may be made that certain public business will be conducted only through the medium of the minority language—for example, the minority language could be made the only working language of regional or local parliaments and other public bodies.

Policies of strong support also often attempt to regulate language behaviour outside the public sector. For example, businesses and voluntary groups may be required to use the minority language in both their dealings with the public (for example, through advertising and in-shop service) and in their internal operations (for, by example, requiring that the minority language be the language of the workplace, the language through which contract negotiations take place, and so forth).

If the goal of linguistic policy is to maintain the existence of a minority language through increasing its status and use, or to revive a minority language which has been in decline, policies of strong support for the maintenance of minority linguistic group identity have some appeal, as they radically alter the prestige and status of the minority language and ensure that not only its speakers but non-speakers develop at least some competence—willingly or otherwise—in the language. Such policies tend, however, to be politically controversial, precisely because they do involve an element of compulsion, and also tend to raise broader human rights issues. Indeed, one often hears discussion of the potential clash between group rights, such as a group right to preserve group identity, and individual rights, such as the right to freedom of expression (through whatever language one chooses), freedom of association (through whatever language one chooses), and so on. Space does not permit a fuller discussion of this important issue. But the clash between group rights and individual rights tends to be more likely under policies of strong support for the minority language, precisely because of this element of compulsion; weaker measures of support tend to facilitate minority language use for certain purposes, without placing burdens with respect to linguistic choices on individuals, and should therefore excite much less controversy. In a Scottish context—and in a Northern Irish context as well—it is unlikely that policies of strong support for Gaelic, Scots, Irish and Ulster Scots will be contemplated, and that any regime will likely be limited to weaker (though still important) measures of support.

2. Language Rights in Scotland (and within a Council of Europe Framework)

State policy in the UK towards minorities is, in general, one of integration, and has been since at least 1966, when the then Home Secretary, Roy Jenkins, in stating government support for such a policy, defined integration "not as a flattening process of assimilation but as one of equal opportunity, coupled with cultural diversity, in an atmosphere of mutual tolerance."[14] However, evidence of a clearly articulated and coherent *minority language* policy, either at the UK level or in Scotland, is scarce.

Public pronouncements of minority linguistic policy by government ministers have generally been banal. The treatment of two submissions by Scotland's leading Gaelic development agency, Comunn na Gàidhlig (CNAG), in which specific legislative measures of support for the language were recommended[15], is illustrative. When the first submission, entitled "Secure Status for Gaelic", was delivered in December, 1997 to Brian Wilson, the then Westminster minister with responsibility for Gaelic, Mr. Wilson thanked CNAG for the report, but said little more. The next minister with responsibility for Gaelic, Calum MacDonald, instructed officials to begin consultations with CNAG on the Secure Status proposals, but took no substantive steps towards implementing them. Things have not improved with the new devolved Scottish government. Alasdair Morrison, until 28 November 2001, the Deputy Minister in the new Scottish Executive with responsibility for Gaelic, described Gaelic in the following terms during the first-ever debate through the medium of Gaelic in the Scottish Parliament, which took place early in 2000:

> *Gaelic is a precious jewel in the heart and soul of Scotland. It is not constrained within strict boundaries or herded into tight corners. Gaelic is national, European and international. It is fundamental to Scotland; it is not on the periphery or on the fringes. It must be normalised and its rights must be secured.*[16]

He has, however, been opaque as to what all of this goodwill and rhetoric means in terms of actual government policies. Mr. Morrison has repeatedly said that his party, the Scottish Labour Party, and his government would continue to "work towards secure status" for Gaelic, but has not made any commitments to a legislative timetable, nor to any of the particular details of CNAG's recommendations. At various times, he has said that legislation on Gaelic may not be necessary, although a Gaelic Language Act is at the heart of the CNAG Secure Status proposals. Significantly, neither the Westminster government nor the Scottish Executive has ever even bothered to formally respond to the CNAG proposals.

---

[14] Quoted in Sebastian Poulter, *Ethnicity, Law and Human Rights: The English Experience*, (Clarendon: Oxford, 1998), at p. 16.

[15] CNAG has called their package of proposals "Secure Status for Gaelic": *Inbhe Thèarainte dhan Ghàidhlig / Secure Status for Gaelic*, (Inverness: CNAG, 1997), and *Inbhe Thèarainte dhan Ghàidhlig - Dreach Iùl airson Achd na Gàidhlig / Secure Status for Gaelic - Draft Brief for a Gaelic Language Act*, (Inverness: CNAG, 1999).

[16] Scottish Parliament Official Report, Session 1 (2000), Vol. 05, No. 04, 2 March, 2000, Col. 382 at Col. 388.

Government policy on minority languages, and government policy in respect of Gaelic in particular, can therefore only be inferred by reference to measures which governments, both Westminster and Scottish, have taken. General government policy at both levels appears to be one of integration or tolerance, with only minimal evidence of a coherent policy directed at the maintenance of group linguistic identity.

The principle of integration or tolerance towards linguistic minorities is, like that policy in respect of other minorities, quite strong in the UK and in Scotland. The principle of non-discrimination is given expression in Article 14 of the ECHR, which provides that the various rights and freedoms set out under the ECHR shall be secured "without discrimination on any ground such as . . . *language*, [and] . . . *association with a national minority*", among other grounds. As a result of the *Human Rights Act 1998*, Article 14, like other provisions of the ECHR, have become part of UK domestic law. The principle of non-discrimination is also given expression in the *Race Relations Act 1976*, which makes discrimination, both direct and indirect, on "racial grounds" unlawful in employment, education, training and related matters, in the provision of goods, facilities, services and premises, and in the disposal of premises. "Racial grounds" is defined to mean colour, race, nationality or ethnic or national origins,[17] and because no direct reference is made to language, it is not immediately clear that discrimination based on language alone would necessarily be prohibited. In the leading case of *Mandla v. Dowell Lee*[18], Lord Fraser, in enunciating the tests for what constituted an "ethnic group", made clear that a common language was a relevant factor in constituting such a group, but was not determinative, and as a result of the decision in *Gwynedd County Council v.Jones*[19], in which the Employment Appeal Tribunal concluded that Welsh-speaking Welsh people were not a separate ethnic group from English-speaking Welsh people, the status of autochthonous linguistic minorities such as Scottish or Irish Gaels under the *Race Relations Act 1976* is not altogether clear.[20]

The principle of protection has been given expression in the UK in legislation such as the *Public Order Act 1986*, which creates the offence of inciting racial hatred, and essentially uses the concept of "racial group", described above, in order to determine the identity of those who are to be protected. Under the *Crime and Disorder Act 1998*, a new offence of racially-aggravated harassment was created.[21]

---

[17] *Race Relations Act 1976*, subsection 3(1).

[18] [1983] 2 AC 548.

[19] [1986] ICR 833.

[20] It should be noted that in the recent decision of the Inner House of the Court of Session in *BBC Scotland v. Souster*, 2001 SLT 265. Lord Cameron of Lochbroom, in *obiter*, seemed to recognise that Gaels could constitute an "ethnic group".

[21] Section 33 of this act creates this new offence in Scotland by way of a consequent amendment to the *Criminal Law (Consolidation) (Scotland) Act 1995*.

Persons who do not speak English are entitled to translators when they appear before Scottish courts, although the case of *Taylor v. Haughney*[22] made clear that Gaelic-speakers had no right to use Gaelic and obtain the use of a translator where they were capable of speaking and understanding English. As there are no monolingual Gaelic-speakers left in Scotland, Gaels will therefore not benefit from this aspect of the policy of integration or tolerance, although members of other linguistic minorities can be expected to do so.

In respect of a policy of maintenance of group linguistic identity, however, neither the Scottish Executive nor the Westminster government seems to have considered any linguistic group other than Scottish Gaels as the potential beneficiary of such a policy, and even in respect of the Gaels, neither government appears to have considered this issue with any great attention. Gaels would be the most obvious candidates for such a policy. At the 1991 census, for example, there were some 65,978 people (or 1.35% of the total population) in Scotland who reported themselves as being able to speak Gaelic.[23] Most estimate that the number of Gaelic-speakers has declined significantly since then, and that the 2001 census will show something in the region of 50,000 to 55,000 Gaelic-speakers.[24] It is difficult to know with any certainty how many speakers of other languages there are in Scotland, because governments have omitted to solicit this information in censuses; indeed, the Scottish Executive refused a request to include a question on the 2001 census form with respect to the Scots language. The 1991 census for Scotland did show that there were 21,200 Pakistanis, 10,476 Chinese and 10,500 Indians then living in Scotland, and this may give some very rough idea of the numbers of people in Scotland who potentially speak such languages as Urdu, Hindi, Punjabi and Cantonese, although such extrapolations are unreliable.[25]

Thus far, any governmental initiative in Scotland in furtherance of a policy of maintenance of group linguistic identity has been directed only at the Gaelic language community, and it is unlikely that this policy will change. The European Charter is of some relevance here. I have been critical of the Charter, and many of my concerns have been borne out by the approach to the Charter that the UK government seems to be taking, at least in respect of Scottish Gaelic.[26] I am, however, of the view that the Charter at least has the potential to impose some coherence on government policy — both at the Scottish and the

---

[22] 1982 S.C.C.R. 360 (16 June, 1982).

[23] General Register Office Scotland / Àrd Oifis Clàraidh Alba, *1991* Census / *Cunntas-sluaigh 1991, Gaelic Language / A' Ghàidhlig, Scotland / Alba*, (Dùn Èideann: HMSO, 1994), 24, 39.

[24] See, for example, Comunn na Gàidhlig, *Gàidhlig plc: Plana Leasachaidh Cànain / A Development Plan for Gaelic*, (Inverness: CNAG, 1999), 43.

[25] See Viv Edwards, "Community Languages", in Glanville Price, ed., *Languages in Britain and Ireland*, (Oxford: Blackwell, 2000), 213

[26] See, for example, Robert Dunbar, "Implications of the European Charter for Regional or Minority Languages for British Linguistic Minorities", (2000) 25 E.L.Rev. Human Rights Survey 46.

Westminster level – and I am also hopeful that the State reporting system, a type of treaty enforcement mechanism which has been much maligned by international lawyers,[27] may yet prove useful to minority language communities such as the Scottish Gaels.

The Charter is useful, despite its many limitations, in two key respects. First, it answers fairly clearly the question of which minority language groups should benefit from a policy of maintenance of group linguistic identity. Second, it expresses fairly clearly what should be the general principles underlying such a policy. With regard to the beneficiaries of such a policy, the Charter creates State obligations in respect of "regional or minority languages", defined in Article 1, paragraph a to include languages that are traditionally used within a given territory of a State by nationals who form a group numerically smaller than the rest of the State's population and is a language different from the official language(s) of the State. The definition goes on to specifically exclude the languages of migrants. The explanatory report makes clear that the Charter is directed at autochthonous languages. The Charter makes clear, then, that in the Scottish context, a policy of maintenance of group linguistic identity should be directed at Scottish Gaelic and Scots, and not at languages such as Urdu, Punjabi, Hindi and Cantonese. The UK government has indicated in its instrument of ratification, deposited with the Council of Europe, that it considers both Scottish Gaelic and Scots to be regional or minority languages within the meaning of the Charter and to benefit from its protection. Gaelic will benefit from the more detailed provisions of Part III as well as the more general provisions of Part II of the Charter, which Scots will benefit from Part II alone.

With regard to the general contours of a policy of maintenance of group linguistic identity, the Charter is also fairly clear. First, it clearly expresses the positive value attached to the maintenance of group linguistic identity; in the preamble, for example, it is recognised that "the protection of the historical regional or minority languages of Europe . . . contributes to the maintenance and development of Europe's cultural wealth and traditions" and that "the protection and promotion of regional or minority languages in the different countries and regions of Europe represent an important contribution to the building of a Europe based on the principles of democracy and cultural diversity." Article 7, in Part II of the Charter, which applies in respect of both Scottish Gaelic and Scots, is of particular importance, because it sets out the general objectives and principles upon which States party to the Charter "shall base their policies, legislation and practice". Under Article 7, the Westminster government and Scottish Executive will be required to recognise Scottish Gaelic and Scots as expressions of cultural wealth, and the need for resolute action to promote them in order to safeguard them. Under Article 7 the UK is further required to facilitate and/or encourage

---

[27] See, for example, Donna Gomien, "The Rights of Minorities under the European Convention on Human Rights and the European Charter on Regional and Minority Languages", in J. Cator and J. Niessen, eds., *The Use of International Conventions to Protect the Rights of Migrants and Ethnic Minorities*, (Strasbourg: Council of Europe, 1994), at 49.

the use of Scottish Gaelic and Scots in speech and writing, in public and private life. These provisions are of considerable importance because they will presumably provide the context within which the performance of the Westminster government and the Scottish Executive in respect of the more detailed Part III obligations undertaken in respect of Gaelic will be interpreted and scrutinised.

With respect to actual measures in furtherance of a policy of maintenance of minority linguistic group identity, I will concentrate on Scottish Gaelic, mainly because only Gaelic has benefited from such measures. Indeed, Scots has been largely neglected, both in terms of legislative and administrative support, at both the national and local level in Scotland, and just how the Scottish Executive will implement its obligations under Article 7 of the Charter in respect of Scots is unclear. As a result of UK ratification of the Charter, though, governments will for the first time have to consider what the policy with respect to Scots should be. In speaking of existing government measures of support, I will make reference to the UK's obligations under the Charter, and to the CNAG Secure Status proposals,[28] both of which will provide useful yardsticks by which present government policy can be assessed. All of this must, however, be set against the demographic reality facing Gaelic, which is, by any standards, grim. As noted earlier, it is likely that the 2001 census will show a continued rapid decline in numbers of Gaelic speakers in Scotland. CNAG and others, including our foremost sociolinguist, Dr. Kenneth MacKinnon, note that there must be something like a five fold expansion in the numbers of children in Gaelic-medium education merely in order to maintain present numbers of speakers.[29] Reseach by Dr. MacKinnon has indicated that Scotland's Gaelic speaking population is concentrated more heavily in older age groups, and that intergenerational transmission of Gaelic is weak, particularly where only one parent is a Gaelic speaker. He has also shown that the breakdown of intergenerational transmission of Gaelic is particularly serious in the remaining Gaelic "heartlands" of the Western Isles.[30] Therefore, if the Scottish Executive does accept a policy of support of minority linguistic group identity, and if it also accepts, as it is required to do under the Charter, that government policy should be directed by the protection and promotion of autochthonous minority languages in order to maintain and preserve them, then there is a need for particularly resolute action in respect of Scottish Gaelic. The question is, can existing governmental measures be remotely described as "resolute" action; can the existing measures of support come remotely close to achieving the objective of maintaining and preserving the Gaelic language in Scotland?

I will concentrate on five areas of particular importance: education, the use of Gaelic in administrative settings; the use of Gaelic in Scottish courts; the

---

[28] *Supra*, note 15; further references to the CNAG proposals will be to these two documents.

[29] See, for example, *Gàidhlig plc*, *supra*, note 24.

[30] See, for example, Kenneth MacKinnon, "Neighbours in Persistence: Prospects for Gaelic Maintenance in a Globalising English World", delivered at the *Aithne na nGael / Gaelic Identities* Conference, Belfast, March 27-28, 1998.

use of Gaelic by and within the Scottish Parliament and the Scottish Executive; and Gaelic broadcasting.

The use of Gaelic in education

Nowhere is the confusion at the heart of present government policy towards Gaelic more clear than in the fundamentally important area of education. In 2000/2001, there were 1,862 primary school pupils receiving Gaelic-medium education ("GME") at 59 units within English-speaking schools in various parts of Scotland and at one Gaelic school in Glasgow. There were 326 secondary school pupils receiving some, though certainly not all, of their education through the medium of Gaelic at 14 secondary schools in various parts of the country. There were also 3,209 secondary school pupils studying Gaelic as a subject at 40 secondary schools.[31] A small number of post-secondary students receive their education through the medium of Gaelic at the Sabhal Mòr Ostaig, the Gaelic college in Skye, and at the Lews Castle College in Stornoway, both of which are part of the University of the Highlands and Islands project.

Virtually all of this provision has no real statutory basis, and is dependent to a very great extent on the voluntary support of local education authorities – essentially, committees of local councils. Until the passage of the *Standards in Scotland's Schools (etc) Act 2000* (the "2000 Schools Act"), for example, the only statutory reference to Gaelic in respect of education was in section 1 of the *Education (Scotland) Act 1980*, which placed an obligation on local education authorities to provide for "the teaching of Gaelic in Gaelic-speaking areas". The precise meaning of these terms, and consequently the extent of the obligation imposed on local authorities, has never been clear and has never been tested in Scottish courts, but it is clear that all of the development to date has not been pursuant to this provision. If section 1 does create a right to GME, which is questionable, it is a limited right, as it is geographically circumscribed.

The expansion of GME has been facilitated by a system of grants to local authorities, now administered by the Scottish Executive under authority of the *Grants for Gaelic Language Education (Scotland) Regulations 1986.*[32] Under these grants, local education authorities receive three pounds of Scottish Executive funding for every pound invested by the local education authority in a Gaelic-medium education project, and in 2000/2001, total funding for these "Gaelic-specific grants" was £2.634 million. The grants are obviously a useful tool, but hardly form the basis of a coherent and sustained policy, and cannot be confused with a statutory right to GME.

Subsection 5(2) of the 2000 Schools Act introduced a requirement that local education authorities must, as part of their annual statement of education improvement objectives, provide an account of the ways in which or the circumstances in which they will provide GME and, where they do provide GME,

---

[31] These figures were kindly provided by Ms Margaret MacIver, Education Officer, Comunn na Gàidhlig.

[32] Regulations made under Section 73, the *Education (Scotland) Act 1980*.

to provide an account of the ways in which they will seek to develop their provision of such education. Furthermore, paragraph 5(4)(a) of the 2000 Schools Act also imposed an obligation on local education authorities to set education improvement objectives in respect of "national priorities in education", as defined by the Scottish Executive, and subsection 5(6) imposed a requirement on local education authorities to report as to their success in meeting these objectives. Amongst the national priorities defined by the Scottish Executive is "to . . . help every pupil benefit from education, with particular regard paid to . . . Gaelic and other lesser used languages".[33] By making reference to "Gaelic" rather than GME, and by grouping Gaelic with "other lesser used languages", it is not clear whether the promotion of GME, as opposed to merely the offering of classes in the Gaelic language, is even a national priority. In any case, neither of these new requirements creates significant statutory duties in respect of GME nor, significantly, do they create anything approaching a right to GME. Local education authorities are free to set modest targets, and it is not clear that failure to meet them would result in any significant consequences.

If the 2000 Schools Act provisions on Gaelic have an air of minimalism and "ad hoc-ery" about them, there is good reason for this. In the first draft of the Bill which became the 2000 Schools Act, there was no mention of Gaelic whatsoever. It was only after strong representations by Gaelic groups, particularly *Comunn nam Parant* (*Naiseanta*), the body which represents parents of children enrolled in GME, that there should be a statutory right to GME along the lines of the CNAG Secure Status recommendations that the Scottish Executive included even these relatively weak measures. Surprisingly, given its stated policy of "working towards secure status for Gaelic", the Scottish Executive refused to create a statutory right of the sort recommended by CNAG in its secure status proposals, and urged the Parliament to reject an amendment tabled by Michael Russell of the SNP and John Farquhar Munro of the Scottish Liberal Democrats that was based on the CNAG proposals. The Executive's excuse was that the amendment was "well intentioned" but suffered from fatal "drafting problems".[34] Of course, the executive had several months to include their own presumably "well-drafted" provision creating a statutory right along the lines recommended by CNAG, had they truly wished to do so; their failure to do so, given their nominal commitment to Secure Status, speaks for itself. At a time when GME must be expanded significantly and rapidly, it would in my view be impossible to describe the legislative provision in the 2000 Schools Act as "resolute action to promote" Gaelic.

As a result, parents still have no statutory right to ensure that their children receive GME. While the transmission of minority languages appears to be more effective in stand-alone schools than through units in schools in which the majority language is used, there is, as noted, only one such school in

---

[33] Subsection 3(3), Scottish Statutory Instrument 2000 No. 443, *The Education (National Priorities) (Scotland) Order 2000.*
[34] Peter Peacock, Scottish Parliament Official Report, Session 1 (2000), Vol. 07, No. 01, 7 June, 2000, Col. 21.

Scotland, and there is no right to such schooling nor any articulated policy, either at the national or local level, for the development of such schooling. As GME is primarily developed by local education authorities, there is no consistent approach to its provision, and no clear basis for the development of a national strategy or national targets; even if such targets were developed, it is not clear how local education authorities could be required to meet such targets. Thus, while, as noted, most experts in Scotland are agreed that there must be a rapid expansion in GME, it is not clear how, given existing structures, the Scottish Executive can ensure that such an increase takes place. As parents have no clear right to GME, parental demand alone will not ensure that such an expansion takes place.

The UK has committed itself to 10 paragraphs in respect of Education under Article 8 of the Charter: paragraphs 1a (i), 1b (i), 1c (i), 1d (iv), 1e (iii), 1f (iii), 1g, 1h, 1i, and 2 (see Ó Riagáin in this volume for the text). In every case but one, that being in respect of Gaelic in the courts, to which I shall return shortly, the UK government's designation of obligations under Part III has been based wholly on what is presently being offered; the UK has made clear that it does not regard ratification as imposing any additional burdens or the need for any new initiatives. That the UK is able, based on a wholly inadequate status quo in respect of GME, to sign up to 10 paragraphs under Article 8 of the Charter is not a heartening indication of the likely impact of the Charter on the Gaelic language community in Scotland. But this is perhaps being too precipitate. The UK's compliance with its obligations under the Charter, including those which it has assumed in respect of Gaelic, will be scrutinised by the committee of experts within one year of the Charter's coming into force for the UK – this will mean the submission by the UK of a state report on or before 1 July, 2002. The UK's performance in respect of these Article 8 obligations in relation to Gaelic will be scrutinised by reference, presumably, to the general objectives and principles set out in Article 7. The committee of experts will then be able to report on whether the existing provision and legislative framework amounts to "resolute action to promote" Gaelic.

CNAG has been quite clear as to what it wants in respect of GME; namely, the right to GME wherever in Scotland there is "reasonable demand", defined as demand on behalf of 5 or more pupils. CNAG has made a number of other recommendations, both within its Secure Status documents and other documents relative to education, and space does not permit a fuller coverage; CNAG is mindful, however, of the need to ensure that the quality of such education is at least equal to that of English medium education, and this will have implications for matters such as teacher training, provision of teaching materials, support services, and so on. Suffice it to say that CNAG feels that a rights-based approach to GME is an essential starting point. Such an approach would ensure that GME is provided where demand exists. It would give parents and activists an effective tool for expanding the numbers of children in GME. The creation of a statutory right would also, by implication, impose a statutory duty on local education authorities and this would effectively force both these bodies and the

Scottish Executive to seriously gauge levels of demand for GME and to take measures to plan how such demand will be met in a satisfactory way.

The use of Gaelic in administrative settings

With regard to the use of Gaelic in administrative settings—for example, in the provision of services by public sector organisations, local governments, and so on—and the use of Gaelic within public sector organisations, there is no statutory provision at all, nor is there even any clear government policy on such matters. The local council in the Western Isles, *Comhairle nan Eilean Siar*, has had a Gaelic policy since the 1970s, does conduct some meetings in Gaelic, does have some Gaelic-speaking staff, and does make available some documents in Gaelic. However, the application of the bilingual policy has been haphazard, and has been adversely affected by a lack of suitably-trained bilingual staff. It is difficult to imagine conducting much business through the medium of Gaelic. A few public sector and voluntary sector organisations, particularly those active in the traditional Gaelic "heartlands", including the Highland Council, have a Gaelic policy, but once again, provision is haphazard, uncoordinated, and entirely discretionary.

The UK has committed itself to 8 paragraphs in respect of Administrative authorities and public services under Article 10 of the Charter: paragraphs 1c, 2a, 2b, 2d, 2e, 2f, 2g, and 5 (see Ó Riagáin in this volume for the text), and, as was the case with education, the UK government's designation of obligations under Part III has been based wholly on what is presently being offered. I might add that the obligations which the UK has assumed under Article 10 are not, themselves, the most onerous of those available under that article. Once again, this is not a heartening indication of the likely impact of the Charter on the Gaelic language community in Scotland. But, again, performance in respect of these commitments will be scrutinised, and the Charter's committee of experts may be expected to ask hard questions, particularly about the extent to which these obligations are really being met and, more generally, whether the existing provision and legislative framework amounts to "resolute action to promote" Gaelic.

Once again, CNAG has been quite clear as to what it wants in this area. In the Secure Status proposals, CNAG has recommended that all public bodies in Scotland be placed under an obligation to prepare Gaelic policies, which would specify what measures the public bodies will take with regard to the use of Gaelic in communication with the public, the use of Gaelic on public signage, the use of Gaelic in the provision of services, and so on. In areas where there are significant concentrations of Gaelic speakers—according to CNAG's proposals, where Gaelic speakers make up at least 30% of the population – the public body must treat Gaelic and English on the basis of equality, and in preparing their Gaelic policies, the public body must be guided by the principle of full bilingual provision. In areas where there are lesser but still significant concentrations—for example, in the mainland Highlands, in Argyll and Bute, and in Glasgow and Edinburgh—there should be higher levels of Gaelic provision, in some cases approaching full bilingualism in key areas such as education services, healthcare, and so on. In other areas, levels of Gaelic provision would be more limited.

The use of Gaelic in Scottish courts

With regard to the use of Gaelic in the Courts and in administrative tribunals, the picture is perhaps even more bleak, and in no area is the Scottish Executive's minimalist, tokenistic and ad hoc approach to the principle of maintenance of linguistic group identity more apparent. At present, legal proceedings are generally conducted exclusively through English. Since both the Scottish Land Court and the Crofters' Commission are statutorily required to have one member who speaks Gaelic[35], this may imply a right to use Gaelic before both of these bodies[36], although such a right is not anywhere statutorily expressed. With respect to the courts of general jurisdiction, the 1982 case of *Taylor v. Haughney*[37] made clear that a litigant cannot present a case or testify in Gaelic unless he or she had insufficient command of English. As there are no unilingual Gaelic speakers left in Scotland, this means that there is essentially no right to use Gaelic in the Scottish legal system outside of crofting matters coming before the Land Court or the Crofters' Commission.

This state of affairs presented the Westminster government and the Scottish Executive with a problem. The Charter requires that States which designate a language under Part III must sign up to at least 35 paragraphs in that Part, including at least one paragraph from Article 9, Judicial authorities, and both governments recognised that Britain would not be able to meet any of the provisions of Article 9 based on the present provision. This forced the Scottish Executive to make the only change that ratification of the Charter has thus far necessitated. Paragraph 1b(iii) of Article 9 of the Charter (see Ó Riagáin in this volume for the text) provides that States undertake, in respect of those judicial districts in which the number of residents using the regional or minority languages justifies the measures, in civil proceedings to allow documents and evidence to be produced in the regional or minority languages, if necessary by the use of interpreters and translators. On 11 June, 2001, by an Act of Court, the Sheriff Principal of Grampian, Highland and Islands ordered that litigants could address sheriff courts in the sheriff court districts of Portree, Lochmaddy and Stornoway in Gaelic, and that any party to any such litigation in such courts could give oral evidence in Gaelic. The author has been told by Mr. Peter Beaton of the Scottish Courts Service that Gaelic may be used in appeals arising from cases heard in the sheriff court in which Gaelic was used. The sheriff courts covered by this order are located in Skye and the Western Isles, the Gaelic "heartlands".

---

[35] See the *Scottish Land Court Act 1993*, 1993 c. 45, subsection 1(5), and the *Crofters (Scotland) Act 1993*, 1993 c. 44, subsection 3(3), respectively.
[36] See A.C. Evans, "The Use of Gaelic in Court Proceedings", *1982 Scots Law Times*, 286-7, at 286.
[37] 1982 S.C.C.R. 360.

However, only a minority of Gaelic speakers live in the areas affected by this order, with the result that Gaelic-speakers in these areas have greater rights with respect to their language than those in other areas of the country. Furthermore, the right to use Gaelic is limited to civil proceedings. This is peculiar, because it is difficult to see why litigants in criminal proceedings should not have the same right, particularly when criminal matters can potentially have much more serious consequences, such as the loss of personal liberty. Also, the right is far from unconditional. A person wishing to use Gaelic must lodge a written application at least 14 days before the date on which the address or evidence is to be given, although the sheriff has the discretion to shorten or waive this notice period. This is an exceptionally long notice period, and it would be surprising, given the often frenzied manner in which much litigation takes place, if many litigants or parties appearing in court would be likely to make such an application. The order provides that the sheriff or sheriff principal may refuse an application to use Gaelic "where he considers that to grant the application would hamper the proper administration of justice". It is not clear what principles a sheriff would use to come to this conclusion, or whether such a decision could be appealed. Finally, the order provides that where an application to use Gaelic is granted, the sheriff clerk will arrange for an interpreter to be made available to the court, but the order does not make clear who will bear the costs of the interpreter, the parties or the court. In sum, it is difficult to disagree with the views expressed by my colleague Wilson McLeod in respect of this change. Noting, correctly in my view, that "the UK government has taken a disappointingly narrow approach to ratification" of the Charter, he argues that

> *[t]his is a derisory, tokenistic change and will not lead to any meaningful improvement in the position of the Gaelic in the legal system. If it complies with the letter of the Charter—and there is some doubt whether it does so, as a legal matter—it certainly goes against its spirit.*[38]

CNAG has recommended that there be a general statutory right for all persons appearing before all courts of general jurisdiction in Scotland, both criminal and civil, administrative tribunals and all other judicial and quasi-judicial bodies to present cases and give evidence through the medium of Gaelic. The person would have to give some reasonable notice of his or her intention to both the judicial body and other parties, and the Scottish court authorities would both locate and pay for translators. Present provision clearly falls well short of these proposals.

---

[38] Letter to the Editor, *The West Highland Free Press*, Friday, 20 July, 2001, p. 11.

The use of Gaelic by and within the Scottish Parliament and the Scottish Executive

With regard to the use of Gaelic in the Scottish Parliament and by the Scottish Executive, there was no provision for Gaelic at all in the act which created these institutions, the *Scotland Act 1998*. The Standing Orders for the parliament—essentially, its rules of procedure – provide that members of the parliament may speak in Scots Gaelic[39] and that members and others appearing before committees and subcommittees may also do so[40], in both cases subject to the discretion of the Presiding Officer—essentially, the Speaker. Thus, there is no absolute right to use Gaelic, even for these purposes. In practice, the Presiding Officer has allowed the use of Gaelic when prior notice is given. CNAG has argued in its Secure Status proposals for an absolute right to use Gaelic, and while they accept that some notice period is appropriate, in order to allow for a translator to be found, the period should be a relatively short one, perhaps four hours. Significantly, though, Gaelic is *not* permitted to be used for many types of important parliamentary business: the Standing Orders provide that motions[41], petitions[42], and, most significantly, questions to the Scottish Executive[43] must all be in English. There is no provision for the language in which legislation and statutory instruments must be made, but none has appeared in Gaelic. Taken together, the Standing Orders will ensure that the use of Gaelic will tend to be reserved largely for symbolic set-pieces, such as the first Gaelic debate, and for appearances by Gaelic bodies and Gaelic-speakers before committees. Aside from the Standing Orders, there is no other statutory or quasi-statutory provision made for the use of Gaelic in either the parliament or by the executive. However, some of the public signage at both the Parliament and the Executive is bilingual. Where Gaelic is used in debate, the Gaelic original plus an English translation appears in the official record. The Parliament has hired a Gaelic officer, uses Gaelic on its website and, with the Scottish Executive, has published a dictionary of procedural terms which will unquestionably be of considerable use to the parliament and executive, other public bodies and Gaelic-language journalists who cover these institutions. The Scottish Executive also follows a policy of responding in Gaelic to correspondence in Gaelic, and has also published either full Gaelic versions or Gaelic summaries of certain important public documents.

Thus, both the Parliament and the Executive have taken steps to increase both the profile and the actual use of Gaelic. However, none of these endeavours have been put on a firm statutory basis, and there has not yet emerged a clearly-stated policy with respect to the use of Gaelic nor a clearly-stated strategy for the use of Gaelic in either institution. In spite of CNAG's recommendations, there has not yet been established a full-time translation service. The Scottish

---

[39] Rule 7.1.1 and 7.1.2.
[40] Rule 7.8.1.
[41] Rules 8.2.2(a) and 8.5.2(a).
[42] Rule 15.4.3.
[43] Rule 13.3.3(c).

Executive has not yet acted on the recommendations of the MacPherson Task Force of September, 2000,[44] to ensure Gaelic representation at a senior level within the Scottish Executive—a small Gaelic-speaking Department of the Gaidhealtachd—to advise Ministers on Gaelic policy, and to establish a Gaelic Development Agency responsible to the Executive and Parliament to, among other things, produce an overarching strategy for Gaelic, although it has established the transitional Ministerial Advisory Group on Gaelic ("MAGOG") recommended by the Task Force.[45] MAGOG is not expected to report until December 2002, and the executive appears unwilling to take any substantive action on Gaelic in the meantime. Given the significant passage of time – by the time MAGOG reports, it will have been over four years since CNAG delivered its Secure Status proposals and over two years since the MacPherson Task Force was set up – and the demographic crisis facing the Gaelic language community, the Scottish Executive's handling of the Gaelic issue cannot reasonably be characterised as "resolute action to promote" Gaelic, the basic approach mandated by Article 7 of the Charter. Indeed, the relative inaction of the Scottish Executive may now be contributing to the further decline of Gaelic, rather than its promotion.

The use of Gaelic in broadcasting

Finally, I would like to briefly consider the case of Gaelic broadcasting. Pursuant to the *Broadcasting Act 1990*, as amended by the *Broadcasting Act 1996*, a Gaelic Broadcasting Committee – the *Comataidh Craolaidh GBidhlig*, or CCG – was created to, among other things, fund the production of Gaelic television and radio programmes. The CCG currently receives annual funding of £8.5 million from the Scottish Executive.[46] Through the work of the CCG, Gaelic television output has been considerably expanded. However, the present structure of Gaelic broadcasting has a number of serious shortcomings, which were

---

[44] *Gaelic: Revitalising Gaelic, a National Asset*, (Scottish Executive, 2000). The task force was appointed by the Scottish Executive in December, 1999 to "examine the arrangements and structures for the public support of the Gaelic organisations in Scotland, to advise Scottish Ministers on future arrangements, taking account of the Scottish Executive's policy of support for Gaelic as set out in the Programme for Government, and to report by 30th April, 2000. Subsequently, the reporting date was extended, because of "the complexity of the task and the amount of evidence to be considered."

[45] MAGOG's four members are Prof. Donald Meek, the Chairperson and Professor of Celtic at the University of Aberdeen, Dr. Kenneth MacKinnon, Jo MacDonald of BBC Scotland, and Donald MacLeod.

[46] In October 2001, the former Deputy Minister with responsibility for Gaelic, Alasdair Morrison, announced a £450,000 increase to the fund.

thoroughly reviewed in two reports, one by Neil Fraser[47], and one by a task force chaired by Alasdair Milne, former Director-General of the BBC (the "Milne Task Force").[48] The most fundamental problem is that the CCG can only fund the development of Gaelic programmes, but cannot commission or schedule them; this power continues to lie solely with the broadcasters, principally the independent Scottish Television, and BBC Scotland. As a result, scheduling of Gaelic programming is, in the words of Neil Fraser, "sporadic across all hours of the day and night and seasons of the year. . . . The concept of a Gaelic *service* remains elusive; the extended provision has become just a larger collection of programmes randomly scheduled across several channels with no overall control of the range and quality of programmes on offer".[49] Furthermore, unlike that of the predominantly Welsh-language S4C, the funding of the CCG was never based on a non-discretionary statutory formula, with the result that the value of the CCG's fund has since 1992 fallen in real terms by some 24%.[50] As a result, a fund which was designed to facilitate the creation of about 200 hours of new Gaelic television output per year is now only sufficient to fund about 160 hours.[51]

The Milne Task Force has recommended the creation of a stand-alone Gaelic Broadcasting Authority which would, among other things, have overall responsibility for the scheduling and broadcasting of Gaelic-medium output. The authority would be funded by a statutory formula designed to produce an annual amount of £44 million, adjusted for inflation. The Milne Task Force estimates that this would ensure about 3 hours of Gaelic television output per day, which is far in excess of existing output, and would increase employment in Gaelic broadcasting from the present level of about 316 full-time equivalent positions to about 802. These proposals are now before the Westminster government, which under the *Scotland Act 1998* retains authority over broadcasting, and many in the Gaelic community are hopeful that the proposals will be acted upon in a broadcasting bill which is expected to be put before Parliament in 2002.

The UK has committed itself to 8 paragraphs in respect of Media under Article 11 of the Charter: paragraphs 1a (ii), 1b (ii), 1c (ii), 1d, 1e (ii), 1f (ii), 1g, and 2 (see Ó Riagáin in this volume for the text). Once again, the UK government's designation of obligations under Part III has been based wholly on what is presently being offered. However, paragraph 1a (ii) does commit the UK to encouraging and/or facilitating the creation of at least one Gaelic-medium radio station and one Gaelic-medium television channel. The creation of a stand-alone, securely funded Gaelic broadcasting service was recommended by CNAG in its Secure Status proposals, and CNAG have warmly welcomed the Milne Task

---

[47] "A Review of Aspects of Gaelic Broadcasting", May 1999, prepared for the Scottish Office, Education and Industry Department, Arts and Cultural Heritage Division.
[48] Gaelic Broadcasting Task Force Report, *Gaelic Television: A Dedicated Channel*, (The Stationery Office, 2000), prepared for the Scottish Executive.
[49] Fraser, *supra*, at 4.
[50] Fraser, *ibid*, at 6-7.
[51] Fraser, *ibid*.

Force report's recommendations. If implemented, this would be a significant measure of support by the Westminster government.

Yet the creation of such a Gaelic Broadcasting Authority would raise some significant issues. One of the most fundamental is the impact that it would have on the Gaelic labour market. The assumption is that the significant expansion in jobs in Gaelic broadcasting that the new service would occasion would encourage young Gaels to maintain and improve their language skills, encourage more parents to put children in GME for the purposes of winning good, well-paid jobs in the media industry, and encourage young people to learn Gaelic. However, there are already serious shortages of suitably trained Gaelic speakers for jobs, particularly in GME—indeed, shortages of teachers qualified to teach through the medium of Gaelic is one of the major obstacles at present to the expansion of GME. It is not clear what impact a significant expansion in media-related jobs would have on the recruitment of skilled Gaelic-speakers for teacher training and other areas, but given the relatively small numbers of young Gaelic speakers, the consequences could be serious. At the very least, this is an issue which will require very careful consideration and planning, but there has thus far been no acknowledgement by the Scottish Executive or many in the Gaelic community itself of a potential problem.

More fundamentally, in terms of revitalising small and declining languages like Gaelic, leading sociolinguists such as Joshua Fishman recognise that broadcasting can play an important role, but argue that it is not necessarily the top priority in the process of revitalisation, and the pursuit of a rapid expansion in broadcasting can, in many circumstances, be dangerous. In particular, a broadcasting service must be conceived of and operated as a means of reversing language shift, where the yardstick of effectiveness is not necessarily the quality of programming, but the extent to which the service can contribute to the transmission of the minority language within the home, in the workplace and at the community level. It is not at all clear that a Gaelic Broadcasting Authority will be set up in such a way as to promote such principles. At very least, the work of such an authority should be integrated with broader language planning initiatives, and this presents at least two fundamental problems in a Scottish context. The first is that legislative responsibility for broadcasting lies with Westminster, and for most other aspects of Gaelic language development with the Scottish Parliament and Executive in Holyrood. It is unclear how, given this separation of competencies, such integration can be achieved. More to the point, the Scottish Executive has, as should be clear from the foregoing discussion, done relatively little in terms of putting in place a solid base for reversing language shift away from Gaelic, and there is not much evidence of any coherent language planning or policy-making taking place at all. A new Gaelic Broadcasting Authority would be an extremely powerful institution, comparatively speaking, and would be operating in a virtual vacuum. It would be difficult to conceive of a strategy for minority language maintenance that is more bizarre than this. The concept of a broadcasting-led language revival is certainly untested, and existing linguistic theory suggests that it would be a very, very expensive strategy with relatively little prospect of success.[52]   A huge investment in television broadcasting, in particular, at a time when so little else is being developed on a secure and sensible basis, would likely be an extremely poor use of public funds.

As far as **strong measures for the maintenance of group linguistic identity**, these are non-existent in Scotland with respect to Gaelic. Governments have chosen not to take coercive measures such as enforced GME, and not to regulate the use of Gaelic in the private and non-profit sectors, although arguably they do seek to support "the Gaelic economy" through the provision of grants and subsidies, both directly and through the economic development agencies such as the Highland and Island Enterprise network, to private and voluntary sector bodies which produce "Gaelic" goods. From the perspective of theoretical approaches to reversing language shift, the whole concept of the "Gaelic economy" in Scotland is a very suspect one, because the focus is generally on products which have some Gaelic component, for example, recordings of Gaelic song. But this tells us little, if anything, about the more important issue of the use of Gaelic in the places in which such "Gaelic" products are produced, bought and sold or consumed. Generally, subsidies to promote the "Gaelic economy" are not, for example, made conditional on the use of Gaelic in the enterprises receiving such subsidies.[53]   The development of meaningful Gaelic language plans by economic development agencies such as Highlands and Islands Enterprise, which would be required under CNAG's Secure Status proposals, would create the possibility of developing policies which focus more effectively on strategies aimed at reversing language shift.

3.   Making Language Rights Effective: Enforcement, and the Relationship between Rights and Language Planning

In this final section, I would like to consider three issues which are of fundamental importance in any language rights regime that is aimed at maintenance of linguistic group identity. The first is enforcement, and the second is planning, and the third is "active offer".

Often, the issue of how a language rights regime is to be **enforced** is not considered in sufficient detail. The assumption is that once the rights are created in the appropriate statutes, all will be well. What happens, however, when a public body which is obliged to provide minority language services fails to do so? We know that this can happen, and there may be any number of reasons as to why: outright opposition, either amongst politicians, or civil servants, or both; an unwillingness to consider issues relating to the minority language seriously, or at least as a serious priority; shortages of funding; shortages of human resources

---

[52] See Joshua A. Fishman, *Reversing Language Shift*, (Clevedon: Multilingual Matters, 1991), chapter 14, especially pp. 403-404, and pp. 374-375.

[53] For an excellent discussion of the concept of the "Gaelic economy" and its limitations from the point of view of linguistic maintenance, see Wilson McLeod (Sabhal Mòr Ostaig, Isle of Skye), "Language Planning as Regional Development? The Growth of the Gaelic Economy" (in *Scottish Affairs*, 2002, forthcoming).

which cannot be overcome quickly due, for example, to lack of materials in the minority language or to a lack of suitably trained staff who are fluent in the minority language; and so on. What is to be done in such circumstances?

The beneficiaries of minority language rights may be able to take the public body to court, using any generally available legal remedies, such as judicial review.[54] However, such remedies are not always terribly effective. They can be costly. They require people who have the financial resources and, as importantly, the courage to confront a public body in a courtroom setting. The outcome is not always certain, and the process can be risky, not only for the litigants themselves, but also for other rights beneficiaries, who may be adversely affected by a court decision which goes against the users of the minority language services and thereby effectively circumscribes the real extent of the minority language "right".

It is for these reasons that supplementary or alternative means of enforcement should be considered. The minority language legislation may, for example, create special remedies for beneficiaries of the rights which are different from general legal remedies such as judicial review. This may alleviate some of the problems which are generally associated with the use of general remedies, but it does not respond to issues such as cost, uncertainty and so on. An alternative would be the creation of a special public office or body – perhaps an Office of the Language Ombudsperson or Language Commissioner – which would have powers to investigate complaints about infringements of language rights and to order public bodies to discharge their obligations properly. The public bodies affected may be entitled to challenge such orders in the courts, but this would mean that the special enforcement body, and not individuals, would be engaged in the litigation.

There are problems associated with this approach as well. The enforcement body may be inadequately funded. It may be staffed by persons hand-picked by a government for their malleability. If all enforcement powers are turned over to such a body, it could mean loss of effective control by the beneficiaries of the rights. On balance, though, there is much to recommend the creation of such a body, particularly if it is given investigatory powers that do not rely solely on individual complaints. It could pursue a more co-ordinated strategy for the enforcement of the language rights regime. It could help to ensure that the provision of minority language services is not so much of a lottery, dependent on highly changeable variables such as the willingness of different groups of users in different areas to pursue their language rights through the courts, the level of intransigence of differing public bodies in differing areas, and so on.

To be effective, such a body must have sufficient independence from governments so that it is able to perform its role as a watch-dog. It must be

---

[54] Judicial review is a means by which failures by public bodies to fulfil duties imposed upon them by statute can be challenged in the courts, and the courts may require such public bodies to discharge the duty: see, generally, A.W. Bradley and K.D. Ewing, *Constitutional and Administrative Law*, (London: Longman, 1997), 12th. Ed., ch. 29 at pp. 781-782, and ch. 30.

adequately funded, and must be able to make staffing decisions wholly on merit. Nonetheless, the enforcement body would be a public body, and would have to be accountable to the legislature which created it in the first place. Annual reports of such bodies, appearances by its officials before Parliamentary committees, and so on can, by themselves, perform the useful function of educating the politicians and the wider public on minority language issues.

The second issue that is often inadequately considered is that of **language planning**. The creation of a minority language rights regime without the creation of a language planning body can be problemmatic. The reason is that there are a myriad of technical issues about which a language rights regime cannot speak. In the provision of educational services, for example, local authorities cannot be expected to train minority language-medium teachers, or to create minority language-medium teaching materials, to develop appropriate minority language terminology, and so on. Even if local authorities were able to do all of these things, this would mean duplication of efforts, insufficient co-ordination, varying standards, and so forth. Many of these tasks should be centrally planned and co-ordinated. When it comes to the preparation by public bodies of language plans, some central planning and co-ordination is once again essential. Drawing up an appropriate language plan for a public body can be a complicated matter. Language planning is becoming an increasingly sophisticated specialisation. It must be done in a professional manner. Only through the creation of a language planning body can local efforts be co-ordinated and the quality of local output be maximised.

Again, though, there are a number of structural issues which must be considered. What, for example, will be the relationship between the body and the legislature which has created it? What will be its relationship to the language community, the ultimate beneficiary of its work? What will be its relationship to the Language Commissioner or Language Ombudsperson?

I would like to conclude with a word about the extremely important concept of "**active offer**". The creation of a solid minority language rights regime would be compromised if potential users of minority language services, the beneficiaries of the language rights, did not know what their rights were or how to use them, or were reluctant to do so because of lack of confidence in their linguistic ability, inbuilt assumptions about the inferiority of their language for a range of uses outside the traditional ones, and so on. For this reason, it is important to build into the regime an obligation on public bodies to inform the public of their rights and even encourage the use of the minority language. This is the concept of "active offer". Language Commissioners or Ombudspersons, and Language planning bodies also have an important role to play in encouraging the use of minority language services, the exercise of minority language rights, and the development of linguistic competencies and confidence of speakers of the minority language.

Fàs no Bàs (*Prosper or Perish*):
Prospects of Survival for Scottish Gaelic

Kenneth MacKinnon

Introduction

In December 1999 the Scottish Executive set up a task force chaired by John Alick Macpherson to examine arrangements for the public support of Gaelic organisations, and to advise on future policy. Its report was published in September 2000. In December 2000, a Ministerial Advisory Group on Gaelic (MAGOG), chaired by Professor Donald Meek, was established to progress the Macpherson Task Force Report. It specified language planning and development as one of its four areas of concern, and was asked what is the objective of maintaining and promoting the language.

As the group member appointed with this remit, I have suggested that Gaelic is uniquely significant to Scotland in the continuing story of the Scottish people from their earliest origins; the key to most of Scotland's cultural heritage, placenames and personal names; and powerful symbol of identity in a globalising and anglicising world.

Above all I would put forward, the concept of normality and normalisation in this context. Throughout history Gaelic has always been a normal and continuing aspect of Scottish life and culture. Although displaced as the language of government and the majority, Gaelic is nevertheless an essential constituent of Scottish life and culture. Most of its speakers and fellow-citizens wish it to continue to be so in the future. The language is a national resource and asset to be maintained and developed. It has a defining contribution to make to Scotland as a whole, and our image abroad.

Gaelic Language in Society

In the past, those in power ceased to treat Gaelic as normal in everyday life and administration, and its speakers often came to accept this situation as legitimate. Today this is questioned, as these attitudes have reduced the extent to which the language is used and spoken. Normality implies passing on the language to future generations, and in regaining its rightful place in public life: media, administration, education, arts, and commerce - both visibly and audibly.

The present position of Gaelic in Scottish society has become highly precarious. At the time of the 1991 census only one Gaelic speaker in three lived in a local area where Gaelic was the majority language. Only one Gaelic speaker in three lived in a family in which all of whose members spoke Gaelic. Over 40% of all Gaelic speakers lived outwith the Highlands and Islands in Lowland Scotland, and only 37% in the Gaelic majority areas: Western Isles, Skye and Tiree.

Gaelic is not only precarious geographically, there is a demographic deficit with only one Gaelic speaker in five (20.5%) in the under-25 age-group (where one in three is the working minimum for speech-community viability.) Between 1981 and 1991 the national net loss of speakers was around 1,300 annually. During this period the incidence of Gaelic amongst 3-15 year-olds in the Western Isles fell from 67% to 49%.

Surveys over the past thirty years have clearly indicated that English has been displacing Gaelic between the generations in family life. The language has considerably weakened in the workplace, church and community life. There are residual strengths in crofting and potential strengths in education. In this last domain, there have been very considerable gains in Gaelic-medium education since its inception in 1985. In 2000/01 there were 34 Gaelic-medium nursery schools providing for 413 children and about 120 voluntary groups providing for about 2,000 children. In the primary sector 60 Gaelic-medium units were educating 1,862 pupils through the medium of Gaelic, and in the secondary sector there were 14 secondary schools educating 326 children in Gaelic-medium streams. In the Western Isles however, only 25.7% of primary pupils were in Gaelic-medium units, compared with 30.7% in Skye and 52.4% in Tiree. The Gaelic-medium primary sector would thus need to be increased some five times merely to keep pace with net language loss as experienced between 1981-91. At present only the preschool sector is operating at this level, and the numbers do not translate into primary one intakes. The secondary sector fails to provide Gaelic-language continuity: 249 P7 Gaelic-medium pupils in 1999/2000 were represented by only 144 S1 Gaelic-stream pupils in 200/01. However, 32 schools were returning a total of 270 fluent Gaidhlig pupils in S1 in this school year.

The pace of Gaelic-English language-shift

Recent research studies of the Gaelic community illustrate the speed of decline in family transmission in Scotland as a whole, and in the Western Isles in particular. The weakness of Gaelic family transmission compared with Welsh in 1991 means that a *single* Welsh-speaking parent was better at passing on the language than were *two* Gaelic-speaking parents, although this process differed in various areas of Scotland. Despite the small size of its Gaelic community, the most effective area for family maintenance of Gaelic was Skye & Lochalsh. The extent of marriage and family formation between Gaelic and non-Gaelic speakers means that effective transmission of the language must be supported outwith the home. This has long been the case in Wales. Without effective Gaelic-medium education, and modern cultural infrastructure, there are no realistic prospects of maintenance of the language-group.

The extent of use of Gaelic in everyday life has changed rapidly and considerably. Respondents in a mid-90s survey reported how public uses of Gaelic had declined since they were young. Gaelic was maintained best in exchanges outwith the home in the street, etc. Use of Gaelic in shopping declined further, and in church life even more, and at social events, clubs, etc. even further still.

There is considerable loss of Gaelic speakers through death, and this is only partially offset with gains through family transmission and Gaelic-medium education. The only sector which has operated at a comparable level to match net language-loss over recent years has been the pre-school sector. To secure the future prospects for Gaelic this level would need to be matched in the primary and secondary sectors.

Death is not the only source of loss. Migration is also important. There is substantial migration from majority Gaelic areas to the rest of Scotland, and beyond. When this happens many originally Gaelic-speakers seem no longer to regard themselves as such after they have not used the language for a long time. This seemed to be the case in 1991 for Gaelic speakers who had been long resident in Lowland Scotland. The people were still substantially there ten years on from 1981 – but many no longer regarded themselves as Gaelic speakers.

Securing Gaelic for the future

Following extensive public consultations, the Gaelic development agency Comunn na Gaidhlig (CNAG) published its proposals for legislation and 'secure status' for Gaelic, and a strategy report 'Gaidhlig PLC – a development plan for Gaelic'. Misunderstandings about *Secure Status for Gaelic* (e.g. over bilingual motorway signs in Ayrshire, court proceedings in West Lothian in Gaelic on demand, etc.) can be put into perspective by the recognition given to Romansch, with a similar number of speakers to Gaelic, in Switzerland, a society very comparable in size to Scotland. In over fifty years none of these fears has been realised, and without national recognition the prospects for Romansch would today be bleak to say the least. Status in itself would cost nothing, and might not by itself do a great deal for Gaelic. It would however be the necessary condition for a lot else. For example, BT enables telephone users in Scotland to use Welsh 'because it is an official language' (which it isn't) – and denies similar facilities for Gaelic. Fears and questions about Gaelic are still based on outmoded 19th century models of language in society, and failed examples of language-policy elsewhere. Secure Status proposes specific provisions for Gaelic in its heartland, in the rest of its historic area, and in the rest of Scotland.

Much money is today committed to Gaelic which would have seemed 'millenial' twenty or thirty years ago. It is however currently only about £200 per year per Gaelic speaker, and very small change indeed compared with what is spent per head on English language initiatives. It has sometimes been regarded as intended by itself 'to do the trick' and reverse the steep decline in Gaelic speakers by this year's census. This decline is the result of powerful social and economic forces which unplanned largesse will not by itself overcome. Research is needed into both the macro causes in society as a whole, and into the micro causes at the level of the family, community and the individual. A sound research basis is essential to effective language planning and policies for support of the language. Unco-ordinated ad hoc measures and impulse funding, however generous, needs to be targeted and strategised in a coherent pattern according to an overall scheme. Without Secure Status, appropriate research, and results feeding in to a national strategy, the Gaelic decline will become irreversible, and the living community will vanish as it has done for Manx and Cornish – where today strenuous efforts are being made for their revival.

For Gaelic to be maintained, there will need to be fresh policy initiatives. Education will need to be developed, and integrated, at all levels – with swift response to parental demand. Priorities for infrastructure will need to be forthcoming for Gaelic within the family and the community. This infrastructure needs to be available not only in 'heartlands' but for Gaels elsewhere in Scotland and beyond. Gaelic communities cannot flourish without economic stability. The language needs to be enhanced and normalised in everyday life. There are already strengths to build upon. Demographic growth can be demonstrated for some age groups and areas between recent censuses – although masked by overall losses. Family transmission has stood up better in some areas than others. Build on these facts. Research the reasons.

This then is the challenge facing the Gaelic community today: not merely the resolve to maintain itself, but the means to understand the social and economic processes which are making this difficult. The advisory group (MAGOG) is remitted to recommend a means of strategising the revitalisation of Gaelic. It will need considerable governmental goodwill and co-operation in order to do this. Any continuing body remitted to undertake language planning and normalisation will need a firm resource and research base from which to develop its work. If Gaelic is to be maintained as a living community language in Scotland, there will need to be commitment and political resolve on the part of the Scottish Executive. These are the issues confronting Gaelic and its speakers today. There is nothing inevitable about any social or human processes, given the will. So, at its 11th hour and 59th minute we can still ensure a continuing future for Gaelic. We do have the will and we can mobilise the power - let us use them!

References

Comunn na Gaidhlig (1999) *Inbhe Thearainte dhan Ghadhlig: Secure Status for Gaelic*, Draft Brief for a Gaelic language act, Inverness: CNAG
Comunn na Gaidhlig (no date) *Gaidhlig plc: a development plan for Gaelic.* Inverness: CNAG
Euromosaic Project (1995) Gaelic Language Use Survey, Bangor: Research Centre Wales. www.uoc.es/euromosaic/web/document/gaelic/an/e1/e1.html
Macpherson, J.A. (2000) *Revitalising Gaelic: A National Asset* (The Macpherson Task Force Report), Edinburgh: Scottish Executive ISBN 1-84268-025-0